PRAISE FOR THE

Best Food Writing

SERIES

"Longtime editor Hughes once again compiles a tasty collection of culinary essays for those who love to eat, cook and read about food . . . A literary trek across the culinary landscape pairing bountiful delights with plenty of substantive tidbits." —*Kirkus Reviews*

"What is so great about this annual series is that editor Holly Hughes curates articles that likely never crossed your desk, even if you're an avid reader of food content. Nearly every piece selected is worth your time." —**The Huffington Post**

"This latest annual anthology of short writings reveals a nation sorely conflicted about food's nutritional benefits versus the sheer sensual pleasures of the table." —*Booklist*

"The essays are thought-provoking and moving . . . This is an absolutely terrific and engaging book . . . There is enough variety, like a box of chocolates, that one can poke around the book looking for the one with caramel and find it." —*New York Journal of Books*

"A top-notch collection, Hughes brings together a wonderful mix that is sure to please the foodie in all of us." —*San Francisco Book Review*

"This collection will leave you both chuckling and pondering, and perhaps a little wiser about the American food scene." —*Taste for Life*

"Not just for foodies! This will delight anyone who enjoys the pleasures of a good read and a good meal. Highly recommended." —*Library Journal*

"There's a mess of vital, provocative, funny and tender stuff . . . in these pages." —*USA Today*

"An exceptional collection worth revisiting, this will be a surefire hit with epicureans and cooks." —*Publishers Weekly*, **starred review**

"If you're looking to find new authors and voices about food, there's an abundance to chew on here." —*Tampa Tribune*

"Fascinating to read now, this book will also be interesting to pick up a year from now, or ten years from now." —**Popmatters.com**

"Some of these stories can make you burn with a need to taste what they're writing about." —*Los Angeles Times*

"This is a book worth devouring." —*Sacramento Bee*

"The cream of the crop of food writing compilations." —*Milwaukee Journal Sentinel*

"The book captures the gastronomic zeitgeist in a broad range of essays." —*San Jose Mercury News*

"There are a few recipes among the stories, but mostly it's just delicious tales about eating out, cooking at home and even the politics surrounding the food on our plates." —*Spokesman-Review*

"The next best thing to eating there is." —*New York Metro*

"Stories for connoisseurs, celebrations of the specialized, the odd, or simply the excellent."—*Entertainment Weekly*

"Spans the globe and palate."—*Houston Chronicle*

"The perfect gift for the literate food lover." —*Pittsburgh Post-Gazette*

best
Food
WRITING
2014

best Food WRITING

2014

Edited by

HOLLY HUGHES

Da Capo
LIFE
LONG

A Member of
the Perseus Books Group

Set in 10 point Bembo BQ by the Perseus Books Group

Cataloging-in-Publication data for this book is available from the Library of Congress.

First Da Capo Press edition 2014
ISBN: 978-0-7382-1791-8 (paperback)
ISBN: 978-0-7382-1792-5 (e-book)

Published by Da Capo Press
A Member of the Perseus Books Group
www.dacapopress.com

Note: The information in this book is true and complete to the best of our knowledge. This book is intended only as an informative guide for those wishing to know more about health issues. In no way is this book intended to replace, countermand, or conflict with the advice given to you by your own physician. The ultimate decision concerning care should be made between you and your doctor. We strongly recommend you follow his or her advice. Information in this book is general and is offered with no guarantees on the part of the authors or Da Capo Press. The authors and publisher disclaim all liability in connection with the use of this book.

Da Capo Press books are available at special discounts for bulk purchases in the U.S. by corporations, institutions, and other organizations. For more information, please contact the Special Markets Department at the Perseus Books Group, 2300 Chestnut Street, Suite 200, Philadelphia, PA, 19103, or call (800) 810-4145, ext. 5000, or e-mail special.markets@perseusbooks.com.

10 9 8 7 6 5 4 3 2 1

CONTENTS

BACK TO BASICS

HOME COOKING

Personal Tastes

Extreme Eating

INTRODUCTION

Sugar. Vanilla. Chocolate. Sure, we all know they taste good. But what was even more important last winter was how good they smelled.

It was one of the hospice volunteers' main duties: To bake a non-stop supply of chocolate chip cookies—not only for the patients, but also for the heart-sore family and friends at their bedsides. So what if the volunteers were scooping premade industrial batter out of plastic tubs bought in bulk from Costco? These weren't artisanal chocolate chip cookies, not gourmet confections, and they didn't need to be. They were literally "to die for" (a term I'll never again use lightly).

After weeks in the Lysol-bedpan aroma of hospitals and nursing homes, that sugar-vanilla scent helped make the hospice a haven of peace for my nieces, my sister, and me. No more beeping machines and intercoms, no more rattling carts, no more nutritionists and phys-ical therapists trying to strong-arm my brother into "getting better." The freshly baked chocolate-chip cookies were the final touch, the stroke of genius that made it all feel homey and natural and honest.

Granted, it wasn't just the cookies that made us (okay, mostly me) pack on a collective 15 pounds that month. We couldn't even walk outdoors, not with snow banked up to the windowsills by a relentless series of blizzards, so in those agonizing weeks of waiting, hoping, denying, the necessity of eating provided our only escape. We des-perately snatched opportunities to run out into the snow for take-out food—first dashing to the hospital's sad fast-food court, later grabbing pallid heat-and-eats from a Stop & Shop near the nursing home. At last, it seemed like we'd hit a gustatory jackpot when we discovered near the hospice a Whole Foods, a Panera café, AND a Bertucci's. (Whoo-hoo!) What relief it was when one of the sons-in-law burst back indoors, cheeks red from the cold, loaded down with plastic bags of dinner. We craved the caloric buzz of starches and fats—until we craved salads even more. (With chocolate-chip cookies for des-sert, of course.) Comfort food, indeed.

The weekday afternoon shifts were mine. I sat at my brother's bedside as he dozed, working my way through stacks of magazines and books, looking for this year's *Best Food Writing* contenders. My brother was always a loyal *BFW* fan, buying multiple copies as presents for everyone he knew, and often slipping into bookstores (yes, brick and mortar bookstores—remember those?) to make sure they kept the book in stock. Now, drifting in and out of consciousness—pain meds wearing off, not yet ready for the next dose—he would ask what I was reading, hoping to distract himself from the pain.

Maybe it was those circumstances that gave me less patience than ever for fluffy food writing or glossy promotional hype—though admittedly, in the 15 years I've been editing this collection, I've never much liked the slick stuff, always focusing rather on more thoughtful, meaty pieces. But this year it particularly struck me how much food writing has matured lately, giving me a wealth of incisive, witty, in-depth, and provocative material to sift through.

How pleased I was to discover clear-eyed writers who define This Year in Food without succumbing to fads and buzz. Our opening section, "The Way We Eat Now," is full of balanced views on 2014's food trends, from $4 toast (John Gravois's "A Toast Story," page 11) to hot-'n'-spicy everything (Kate Krader, "Are Big Flavors Destroying America's Palate?," page 7) to bacon-mania (David Sax, "Baconomics 101," page 26). At the other end, we close with writers covering food phenomena so out-there, they may never even turn into trends: a chef trying to put invasive species on the menu (Rowan Jacobsen, page 306), an underground of insect-eating gourmets (Daniella Martin, page 317), or a foraging chef's mind-blowing inventiveness (Amy Gentry, page 326). Lest we get too caught up in the latest fashions, other writers put our gourmet preoccupations into historical context—Jay Rayner's memory of his first American foods (page 2), Tom Carson's memory of tuna fish sandwiches (page 277), Ann Hood's ode to Laurie Colwin's tomato pie recipe (page 296).

I also hit a mother lode of wonderful pieces questioning the equal rights of America's food conversation—a topic that felt especially important to me, sharing my brother's concern for social justice (as a Methodist minister, that was always a given for him). These meditations on culinary minorities come together in a new section titled A

Table for Everyone (starts on page 41). It must also have been my non-foodie brother's joy in honest real food (at least until chemo killed his appetite) that gave me special appreciation for the writers featured in another new section, Back to Basics—a hunter simply cooking his day's kill (Steve Hoffman, page 93), a coffee obsessive's epiphany on how little new-fangled gear matters (Oliver Strand, page 97), or an anti-gourmet foray into Asian street food (Matt Goulding, page 112).

Being with my brother—a consummate people person—helped remind me that it always comes back to people stories. Of course those have played a prominent part in *Best Food Writing* ever since the first edition in 2000, especially with the chef profiles that populate the section Someone's in the Kitchen (starts on page 219). A far cry from celebrity-chef puff pieces, these are snapshots of restaurant cooks from all over the country, at all stages of their careers, from Alex Halberstadt's portrait of the hip King of Cronuts™ (page 220) to John Kessler's bittersweet portrait of a young chef facing mortality (page 252) to Dave Mondy's look at an artisanal pizzamaker taking a step he never thought he'd take (page 264). And as the locavore movement has expanded the food stage, more artisans, farmers and suppliers are given their rightful place alongside chefs as essential players. In this year's Stocking the Pantry section (starts on page 179), you'll find a gallery of colorful individuals who make the ingredients we cook with. On top of that, I found a bumper crop of writers bringing their family stories into their cooking (Elissa Altman, page 80; Adam Sachs, page 124; Erin Byers Murray, page 128; Adam Gopnik, page 138; Sarah Bir, page 172; Josh Ozersky, page 292).

More than anything else, in those hospital-haunted days we needed to laugh. I've always tried to include a healthy dose of humor in each year's *Best Food Writing,* and this year is no exception. There's Irvin Lin's tongue-in-cheek "How to Boil Water" (page 108), Molly Watson's exasperated "How to Cook a Turkey" (page 119) or Albert Burneko's ranting "How to Cook Chicken Cutlets" (page 166)—a trio of how-tos that are anything but Betty Crocker-esque. Humor keeps us all honest, as Michael Procopio ("The Cheese Toast Incident," page 281) and David Leite ("Because I Can," page 286) prove yet again.

As I read bits of these stories out loud to distract my brother, I think we both knew he'd never see this year's edition. In fact, he died in March, his suffering finally over. But as I went on reading throughout the spring, I kept judging everything with him in mind. He was my Ideal Reader in many ways—not a fussy cook or a food snob, but fascinated by the interplay between the way we eat and our personal relationships, our sense of self, and even our role as stewards of this planet.

And somehow, that perspective felt just right to me. For at its best, isn't food writing just another lens through which to view the human condition? In a season of grief and eventual acceptance, pondering about food—and pondering it deeply—offered its own path of healing and comfort.

And if there's a chocolate-chip cookie (or two or three) involved, even better.

The Way We Eat Now

AGE OF INNOCENCE

By Jay Rayner

From Saveur

British dining critic (*The Observer*) and BBC food
personality (*MasterChefs, Kitchen Cabinet*) Jay Rayner is
known for his demanding palate. But he wasn't always
that way. In this essay, he wistfully longs for the days
when a Big Mac or Chicago pizza tasted blissful to him—
and wonders if modern foodies are really better off.

Growing up in a northwest London Jewish family, I was haunted
by a thought: that if my great-grandfather, Josef Burochowiz,
had just been blessed with a little more stamina and had stayed on
the boat a few days longer, I wouldn't have grown up in northwest
London at all but instead in New York. I would have happily been
one of those American Jews, living in the land of pastrami and bagels, where the buildings were taller, the skies bigger, and everybody
was from somewhere else. I liked my foreignness but wanted everyone else to be foreign too. Then, one Saturday lunchtime in 1977, a
little bit of America came to me.

My mother, a well-known health columnist, had been invited to a
Saturday event at the American embassy. I have no idea why; it was
just the sort of thing that happened to her. All I do recall was that it
was odd because Saturday mornings were when my parents did the
family food shop, so what were we to eat for lunch?

And yet, for the American embassy, Mom would make an exception. Lunchtime came and she was back and carrying with her a
shallow cardboard box containing a couple dozen soft, round packages wrapped in thin, glossy, greaseproof paper, endowed with the

mammarian curve of golden M's. She had brought us hamburgers.
A lot of them.

With hindsight, this could be viewed as a blatant act of cultural
imperialism. The first branch of McDonald's had opened in Wool-
wich, southeast London, in 1974, though it had yet to impact me. I
hadn't been there. Now here was the US Embassy—the US government itself, on UK soil—handing out McDonald's hamburgers to a
woman who, as a high-profile journalist, could influence opinion.
Perhaps there was a CIA briefing document somewhere outlining
how the American version of freedom could be spread about the
world by the judicious distribution of free McDonald's hamburgers
to tastemakers.

The truth of our hamburger windfall was probably a little more
prosaic: The embassy had got McDonald's to cater the event, and seeing a number left over and being appalled by the waste, my mother
had offered to take them home, thereby dealing with the lunch issue.
Whatever the cause, I was delighted.

I had never eaten hamburgers like them. Even cold, there was the
intense sweetness of the bun and the juicy meat of the patty and the
punch of the pickles. This was what America meant to me: food with
a certain shamelessness, lunch with its knickers around its ankles.
And, thankfully, I soon found more options from across the pond
to try out. Around this time, an American expatriate called Gabriel
Gutman launched the Dayvilles chain of ice cream parlors in Britain,
based on America's popular Baskin-Robbins.

"There is superb cream in England and excellent chocolate," he
told the *New York Times.* "Nobody ever married the two together. It's
been driving me crazy for years." The actress Lee Remick, who had
just starred in *The Omen* and was living in London, was more savage.
"They don't know from ice cream in this country," she said, as if
identifying the very heart of Britain's famed malaise. Remick had a
point. Until Dayvilles arrived you could have any flavor you liked in
Britain—as long as it was strawberry, chocolate, or vanilla. Plus the ice
cream itself wasn't creamy; it was hard and icy. British ice cream was
a beautiful promise, broken.

And now here, praise the gods of greed, was Dayvilles, which,
like its role model, proclaimed 32 flavors but seemed to offer many
more. There was banana split and bubble gum flavored ice cream,

toffee nut crunch, and something called peppermint fudge ripple, which, to a fat boy yet to navigate the hormonal rapids of puberty, sounded seriously naughty and indulgent. This was what America meant to me: It was a place where you could get 32 flavors of ice cream, and one of them was called peppermint fudge ripple.

It didn't end there. In 1977 another American expat called Bob Payton opened the Chicago Pizza Pie Factory off St. James's, and then a handful of Rib Shacks. Music blared, everything came slathered in a sticky vinegary barbecue sauce, and cutlery was optional. We overprivileged kids would go to these restaurants without our parents when we were 13 or 14 and play at being grown-up, while really we were just getting a big sugary, salty hit, eating with our hands, throwing away all of the breeding of our London childhoods. For an hour or two, we were American, and we'd become American through food. It tasted far better than eating British did.

Food in 1970s Britain was not, for most people, hugely encouraging. The generation that had lived through the Second World War still held sway and, as a result, gastronomic indulgence was frowned upon. There were a few restaurants of note, but in your average British home vegetables were still boiled until they could be eaten without the aid of teeth, and exotica rarely went beyond a rudimentary *coq au vin*.

In our house, fortunately, things were a little different. We were restless in matters of the plate and had what were regarded then as sophisticated tastes for the cuisines of countries like India and China, places we had no expectation of ever visiting. My mother may not have had much time for trends in décor or couture, but when it came to the kitchen, she cared greatly. She made fragrant chicken curries with Bombay duck, a pungent salted and dried fish from India. She bought packs of snails imported from France and laboriously stuffed the canned snail meat into shells filled with garlic butter. Robert Carrier's *Great Dishes of the World*, first published in 1963 and reprinted in updated editions for years after, gave recipes from the farthest reaches of the planet. The publication in 1961 of Julia Child's *Mastering the Art of French Cooking* seemed to have turned every aspirational American cook into the budding chef of his or her very own little Left Bank bistro.

She, cooking these international meals, and I, dreaming of hamburgers and fudge-flavored ice cream, were on trend. Back then, on both sides of the Atlantic for those who could afford it, the right way for the fashionable to eat depended upon exotica.

Today, though, the whirligig has turned; we're meant to be dismissive of imports, to be locavores. In Britain, if we dream of American hamburgers, they are no longer from McDonald's. Rather, they are supposed to be made from rare breeds of British beef, raised on local farms. We have come to understand that this is the truly sustainable way to eat; that, with the global population rising to 9 billion by 2050, to do otherwise is to play fast and loose with the planet's ecosystem merely to satisfy our appetites. Hence, we eat local food. Of course each way of eating—21st-century local and mid-century exotic—makes its own emotional kind of sense. We nurture each other through food and show our love through it. We celebrate and we commiserate through it. Localism, with its sweet wash of neighborliness and community, has a logic. To be honest, though, it's nowhere near as much fun as the kind of juvenile thrills I once got from cooling McDonald's hamburgers or flavors of ice cream with triple-barreled names involving the word fudge.

Indeed, as a result of research for a new book on food security in the 21st century, my adult self has come to understand that eating like a locavore is *not* the most sustainable option. In the late '90s when the term "food miles" was first coined by the British academic Tim Lang, professor of food policy at City University in London, it was simple and easily understandable: The farther your food traveled from field to fork, the worse for the environment it was by dint of the amount of fuel that journey took. It gave environmentally minded consumers a simple way to judge whether they should buy a product. Had it come from as close by as possible? If yes, then into the basket it went.

The problem is it's too simple. Just as eating chicken curry in 1970s Britain didn't make you sophisticated, so eating locally doesn't actually make you an ethical eater. The petrochemicals used in farming and in fertilizers, the energy to build tractors as well as to run them and to erect farm buildings and fences—all of that (and so much more) has to be measured against yield. When you do that, you discover the proportion of your food's carbon footprint caused by its transport is somewhere between just 2 and 4 percent. What matters is not where your food was grown but how it was grown.

Take the McDonald's hamburgers I so adored as a kid. It can take up to 20 pounds of grain to produce one pound of beef. So even if the cow that gave its life for my lunch lived in my garden, one could argue that what would really matter is the volume of carbon inputs that produced the soya it ate. Or to put it another way, a grass-fed animal raised a thousand miles from me would have a much smaller carbon footprint than a grain-fed one raised out back.

What would the fat-cheeked boy I once was, craving the caloric hit of Dayvilles ice cream and McDonald's hamburgers, have made of all this? What would my late mother, with her snails and menus culled from the pages of Robert Carrier, have thought? I think she would have been baffled. Back then we knew nothing about the way a debate around the environment and concerns about industrial agriculture would eventually come to dominate the conversation about how and what we ate. We had other worries. In the 1970s we had the Arab-Israeli wars, Vietnam, the oil crisis, and so much more. All of that was discussed around my family's dinner table—there was a lot of politics in our house when I was a kid. But dinner, the food actually on that table? We never considered it a part of it. Dinner was just dinner.

And sometimes when I think back to a time before the wars over localism and Big Ag, to those days when it was still possible to be thrilled by the first taste of a new kind of hamburger without any of the worry of how it became a hamburger, of how it arrived in its perfectly wrapped packaging and into my hand, I can't deny a certain wistfulness.

ARE BIG FLAVORS DESTROYING THE AMERICAN PALATE?

By Kate Krader

From Food & Wine

⌾⌾⌾

Food & Wine restaurant editor Kate Krader eats out,
by her own count, a minimum of five nights a week.
(Occupational hazard.) She's in the business of spotting
food trends before the rest of us. So when she sees a
flavor falling out of favor, it's a good bet we'll all grow
tired of it in the very near future.

I have a crystal-clear memory of one of the most perfect dishes I've ever eaten. It was a little potato gratin, served in a polished copper dish. The crispy mahogany-brown potato rounds on top glistened with duck fat; inside, the gratin was mashed-potato-tender. It was the late '80s, and I was at La Caravelle, an elegant, old-school French restaurant in midtown Manhattan that's now long gone.

Today, it isn't hard to find an exceptional potato gratin. Considering the heirloom potatoes that are out there now and the reverence for butter, lard and all those other fats, we are probably in the golden age of potato gratins. The problem is that I'm no longer so interested. When a dish isn't laced with chiles or some kind of fermented paste or doused with vinegary sauce, I can pass it by. I've accepted the fact that I crave a hit of fire, acid or funk in my food. The question I'm working through: Is this an evolution or a devolution?

A colleague at F&W has dubbed this predicament my culinary arms race—my quest for bigger and bigger flavors. It's not just me, though. The brick-red hot sauce Sriracha was one of the nation's most talked-about ingredients last year: A rumored shortage freaked everyone out. Then there's the pickling and fermenting obsession. Now every ingredient at the farmers' market gets pickled or half-pickled or, best of all, loaded with spice and pickled. The hot-and-tangy trend extends to cocktails, too. Chile-spiked drinks are hugely popular; so are pickleback shots (whiskey with a pickle-juice chaser). Sour beers are trending, as are extra-tart wines like Riesling (which happens to pair well with all the super-tangy food I eat).

When the excellent chef Andrew Carmellini opened his brasserie Lafayette in Manhattan last year, I marched over to get my hands on the signature rotisserie chicken—and then didn't eat much of it. The bird tasted boring. "What's up?" I asked Carmellini, who serves a super-flavorful roast chicken at Locanda Verde, his Italian place. Turns out, he wasn't satisfied with the Lafayette dish either. "I don't know what to do with it," he lamented. "Slather it in Sriracha? This is a French place. At Locanda, there's a lot more spice on that chicken than people realize: crushed red pepper, herbs, a ton of black pepper. It's high-end Wish-Bone Italian chicken." For the record, he has since made the Lafayette bird better; now he braises the legs with sherry vinegar. Still, I eat any leftovers with one of the hot sauces in my fridge.

"People are looking for a bigger blast when it comes to flavor," says Vinny Dotolo, chef and co-owner of Animal restaurant in Los Angeles, which specializes in over-the-top cooking. He thinks small plates and shared dishes have contributed to this evolution: When you only have one bite of something, it has to make a big impression. A best seller at Animal is the hamachi tostada, which sounds tame until you realize that the raw fish is topped with an especially pungent, tangy cabbage slaw. "We almost overdress that slaw with fish sauce and lemon juice so it can flavor the hamachi, too," he notes. Dotolo also credits the sous-chefs from Latin America and Asia who add flavor to the kitchens they work in. "Back in the day, 20 years ago, the head chef made the food; that was it. Now, kitchens are like a band: Someone will say, 'Hey, try this note,' or bring in a chile sauce he got from his cousin in Laos."

Bay Area chef James Syhabout has a unique perspective on the culinary shift. Born in Thailand, he was raised in Oakland; his family had a restaurant outside the city. "American Thai food used to always be so sweet," says Syhabout. He would ask his mother why they couldn't serve the spicy, intense dishes his family ate at staff meals, like crudités with chile paste and burnt garlic. "My mom would say, 'It's not the way Americans eat.'" At that time, pad Thai was a discovery for most Americans. Now, after years of watching adventurous TV chefs and culinary travelers like Tony Bourdain explore the globe, as well as making their own trips to foreign spots that serve potent specialties, people want whatever funky dishes the cooks are eating at the corner table. "My customers go for intense flavors like shrimp paste and miso," says Syhabout, who specializes in robust Southeast Asian food at one of his restaurants, Hawker Fare. "I'm really into this unfiltered fish sauce called *pla raa.* It's like a dirtier version of fish sauce; it's mixed into our beef tartare, and it makes the papaya salad more interesting. When I was growing up, we were afraid to use fish sauce. Now we can go crazy with the extra-funky kind."

As I debate whether my obsession with in-your-face flavors is a good thing or not, I consider the downside. Does everything I eat now taste to some degree like Sriracha? Have I lost the ability to appreciate the nuances in an elegant dish of sole in nasturtium broth? If a new Chinese restaurant isn't using a lot of Sichuan peppercorns and shrimp paste, will I dismiss the cooking as boring? I think I can still appreciate delicate flavors, but there's the strong possibility that I'll try the nasturtium broth once and never again.

Still, I'm a positive person, so I prefer to consider the upside, which is this: Nowadays, no matter where I am, I can almost always find the strong flavors I love, invariably prepared by a very talented cook. When I was at Syhabout's Hawker Fare, I loaded up on the chile-paste-tossed fried chicken, which had the word spicy next to it on the menu in capital letters. Plus, there were two kinds of hot sauce on the table, including authentic Sriracha from Thailand.

Across the Bay, at the outstanding San Francisco restaurant State Bird Provisions, my in-your-face food choices were more limited. Chef Stuart Brioza employs some fermented and spicy ingredients in his American-style dim sum, but not a lot; his food is layered with subtle flavors. And I discovered a new favorite dish. It's just-fried, doughnut-like garlic bread, topped with fresh burrata, rosemary salt and a sprinkling of pepper. The creamy, slightly chewy cheese covers the crispy, fatty pastry, melting just a little. Maybe, I thought, I'm becoming addicted to food with incredible texture. My evolution continues.

A Toast Story

By John Gravois

From Pacific Standard

As deputy editor of *Pacific Standard*—a magazine
devoted to West Coast culture—Berkeley-based writer
John Gravois spotted a phenomenon potentially ripe
for satire. His article could have made "$4 toast" a
symbol of foodie-ism gone berserk, but he dug deeper
and discovered so much more behind it.

All the guy was doing was slicing inch-thick pieces of bread,
putting them in a toaster, and spreading stuff on them. But
what made me stare—blinking to attention in the middle of a work-
day morning as I waited in line at an unfamiliar café—was the way he
did it. He had the solemn intensity of a Ping-Pong player who keeps
his game very close to the table: knees slightly bent, wrist flicking
the butter knife back and forth, eyes suggesting a kind of flow state.

The coffee shop, called the Red Door, was a spare little operation
tucked into the corner of a chic industrial-style art gallery and event
space (clients include Facebook, Microsoft, Evernote, Google) in
downtown San Francisco. There were just three employees working
behind the counter: one making coffee, one taking orders, and the
soulful guy making toast. In front of him, laid out in a neat row, were
a few long Pullman loaves—the boxy Wonder Bread shape, like a
train car, but recognizably handmade and freshly baked. And on the
brief menu, toast was a standalone item—at $3 per slice.

It took me just a few seconds to digest what this meant: that toast,
like the cupcake and the dill pickle before it, had been elevated to

the artisanal plane. So I ordered some. It was pretty good. It tasted just like toast, but better.

A couple of weeks later I was at a place called Acre Coffee in Petaluma, a smallish town about an hour north of San Francisco on Highway 101. Half of the shop's food menu fell under the heading "Toast Bar." Not long after that I was with my wife and daughter on Divisadero Street in San Francisco, and we went to The Mill, a big light-filled cafe and bakery with exposed rafters and polished concrete floors, like a rustic Apple Store. There, between the two iPads that served as cash registers, was a small chalkboard that listed the day's toast menu. Everywhere the offerings were more or less the same: thick slices of good bread, square-shaped, topped with things like small-batch almond butter or apricot marmalade or sea salt.

Back at the Red Door one day, I asked the manager what was going on. Why all the toast? "Tip of the hipster spear," he said.

I had two reactions to this: First, of course, I rolled my eyes. How silly; how twee; how perfectly *San Francisco*, this toast. And second, despite myself, I felt a little thrill of discovery. How many weeks would it be, I wondered, before artisanal toast made it to Brooklyn, or Chicago, or Los Angeles? How long before an article appears in Slate telling people all across America that they're making toast all wrong? How long before the backlash sets in?

For whatever reason, I felt compelled to go looking for the origins of the fancy toast trend. How does such a thing get started? What determines how far it goes? I wanted to know. Maybe I thought it would help me understand the rise of all the seemingly trivial, evanescent things that start in San Francisco and then go supernova across the country—the kinds of products I am usually late to discover and slow to figure out. I'm not sure what kind of answer I expected to turn up. Certainly nothing too impressive or emotionally affecting. But what I found was more surprising and sublime than I could have possibly imagined.

If the discovery of artisanal toast had made me roll my eyes, it soon made other people in San Francisco downright indignant. I spent the early part of my search following the footsteps of a very low-stakes mob. "$4 Toast: Why the Tech Industry Is Ruining San Francisco" ran the headline of an August article on a local technology news site called VentureBeat.

"Flaunting your wealth has been elevated to new lows," wrote the author, Jolie O'Dell. "We don't go to the opera; we overspend on the simplest facets of life." For a few weeks $4 toast became a rallying cry in the city's media—an instant parable and parody of the shallow, expensive new San Francisco—inspiring thousands of shares on Facebook, several follow-up articles, and a petition to the mayor's office demanding relief from the city's high costs of living.

The butt of all this criticism appeared to be The Mill, the rustic-modern place on Divisadero Street. The Mill was also, I learned, the bakery that supplies the Red Door with its bread. So I assumed I had found the cradle of the toast phenomenon.

I was wrong. When I called Josey Baker, the—yes—baker behind The Mill's toast, he was a little mystified by the dustup over his product while also a bit taken aback at how popular it had become. "On a busy Saturday or Sunday we'll make 350 to 400 pieces of toast," he told me. "It's ridiculous, isn't it?"

But Baker assured me that he was not the Chuck Berry of fancy toast. He was its Elvis: he had merely caught the trend on its upswing. The place I was looking for, he and others told me, was a coffee shop in the city's Outer Sunset neighborhood—a little spot called Trouble.

The Trouble Coffee & Coconut Club (its full name) is a tiny storefront next door to a Spanish-immersion preschool, about three blocks from the Pacific Ocean in one of the city's windiest, foggiest, farthest-flung areas. As places of business go, I would call Trouble impressively odd.

Instead of a standard café patio, Trouble's outdoor seating area is dominated by a substantial section of a tree trunk, stripped of its bark, lying on its side. Around the perimeter are benches and steps and railings made of salvaged wood, but no tables and chairs. On my first visit on a chilly September afternoon, people were lounging on the trunk drinking their coffee and eating slices of toast, looking like lions draped over tree limbs in the Serengeti.

The shop itself is about the size of a single-car garage, with an L-shaped bar made of heavily varnished driftwood. One wall is decorated with a mishmash of artifacts—a walkie-talkie collection, a mannequin torso, some hand tools. A set of old speakers in the back blares a steady stream of punk and noise rock. And a glass refrigerator case beneath the cash register prominently displays a bunch of coconuts and grapefruit. Next to the cash register is a single steel toaster. Trouble's specialty is a thick slice of locally made white toast, generously covered with butter, cinnamon, and sugar: a variation on the cinnamon toast that everyone's mom, including mine, seemed to make when I was a kid in the 1980s. It is, for that nostalgic association, the first toast in San Francisco that really made sense to me.

Trouble's owner, and the apparent originator of San Francisco's toast craze, is a slight, blue-eyed, 34-year-old woman with freckles tattooed on her cheeks named Giulietta Carrelli. She has a good toast story: She grew up in a rough neighborhood of Cleveland in the '80s and '90s in a big immigrant family, her father a tailor from Italy, her mother an ex-nun. The family didn't eat much standard American food. But cinnamon toast, made in a pinch, was the exception. "We never had pie," Carrelli says. "Our American comfort food was cinnamon toast."

The other main players on Trouble's menu are coffee, young Thai coconuts served with a straw and a spoon for digging out the meat, and shots of fresh-squeezed grapefruit juice called "Yoko." It's a strange lineup, but each item has specific meaning to Carrelli. Toast, she says, represents comfort. Coffee represents speed and communication. And coconuts represent survival—because it's possible, Carrelli says, to survive on coconuts provided you also have a source of vitamin C. Hence the Yoko. (Carrelli tested this theory by living mainly on coconuts and grapefruit juice for three years, "unless someone took me out to dinner.")

The menu also features a go-for-broke option called "Build Your Own Damn House," which consists of a coffee, a coconut, and a piece of cinnamon toast. Hanging in the door is a manifesto that covers a green chalkboard. "We are local people with useful skills in tangible situations," it says, among other things. "Drink a cup of Trouble. Eat a coconut. And learn to build your own damn house. We will help. We are building a network."

If Trouble's toast itself made instant sense to me, it was less clear how a willfully obscure coffee shop with barely any indoor seating in a cold, inconvenient neighborhood could have been such a successful launch pad for a food trend. In some ways, the shop seemed to make itself downright difficult to like: It serves no decaf, no non-fat milk, no large drinks, and no espressos to go. On Yelp, several reviewers report having been scolded by baristas for trying to take pictures inside the shop with their phones. ("I better not see that up on Instagram!" one reportedly shouted.)

Nevertheless, most people really seem to love Trouble. On my second visit to the shop, there was a steady line of customers out the door. After receiving their orders, they clustered outside to drink their coffees and eat their toast. With no tables and chairs to allow them to pair off, they looked more like neighbors at a block party than customers at a café. And perhaps most remarkably for San Francisco, none of them had their phones out.

Trouble has been so successful, in fact, that Carrelli recently opened a second, even tinier location in the city's Bayview neighborhood. I met her there one sunny afternoon. She warned me that she probably wouldn't have much time to talk. But we chatted for nearly three hours.

In public, Carrelli wears a remarkably consistent uniform: a crop top with ripped black jeans and brown leather lace-up boots, with her blond hair wrapped in Jack Sparrowish scarves and headbands. At her waist is a huge silver screaming-eagle belt buckle, and her torso is covered with tattoos of hand tools and designs taken from 18th-century wallpaper patterns. Animated and lucid—her blue eyes bright above a pair of strikingly ruddy cheeks—Carrelli interrupted our long conversation periodically to banter with pretty much every person who visited the shop.

At first, Carrelli explained Trouble as a kind of sociological experiment in engineering spontaneous communication between strangers. She even conducted field research, she says, before opening the shop. "I did a study in New York and San Francisco, standing on the street holding a sandwich, saying hello to people. No one would talk to me. But if I stayed at that same street corner and I was holding a coconut? People would engage," she said. "I wrote down exactly how many people talked to me."

The smallness of her cafés is another device to stoke interaction, on the theory that it's simply hard to avoid talking to people standing nine inches away from you. And cinnamon toast is a kind of all-purpose mollifier: something Carrelli offers her customers whenever Trouble is abrasive, or loud, or crowded, or refuses to give them what they want. "No one can be mad at toast," she said.

Carrelli's explanations made a delightfully weird, fleeting kind of sense as I heard them. But then she told me something that made Trouble snap into focus. More than a café, the shop is a carpentered-together, ingenious mechanism—a specialized tool—designed to keep Carrelli tethered to herself.

Ever since she was in high school, Carrelli says, she has had something called schizoaffective disorder, a condition that combines symptoms of schizophrenia and bipolarity. People who have it are susceptible to both psychotic episodes and bouts of either mania or depression.

Carrelli tends toward the vivid, manic end of the mood spectrum, she says, but the onset of a psychotic episode can shut her down with little warning for hours, days, or, in the worst instances, months. Even on good days, she struggles to maintain a sense of self; for years her main means of achieving this was to write furiously in notebooks, trying to get the essentials down on paper. When an episode comes on, she describes the experience as a kind of death: Sometimes she gets stuck hallucinating, hearing voices, unable to move or see clearly; other times she has wandered the city aimlessly. "Sometimes I don't recognize myself," she says. "I get so much disorganized brain activity, I would get lost for 12 hours."

Carrelli's early years with her illness were, she says, a blind struggle. Undiagnosed, she worked her way through college—three different colleges, in different corners of the country—by booking shows for underground bands and doing stints at record stores and coffee shops. But her episodes were a kind of time bomb that occasionally leveled any structure in her life. Roommates always ended up kicking her out. Landlords evicted her. Relationships fell apart. Employers either fired her or quietly stopped scheduling her for shifts. After a while, she began anticipating the pattern and taking steps to pre-empt the inevitable. "I moved when people started catching on," she says. By the time she hit 30, she had lived in nine different cities.

Like a lot of people with mental illness, Carrelli self-medicated with drugs, in her case opiates, and alcohol. And sometimes things got very bad indeed. Throughout her 20s, she was in and out of hospitals and periods of homelessness.

One day in 1999, when Carrelli was living in San Francisco and going to school at the University of California-Berkeley, she took a long walk through the city and ended up on China Beach, a small cove west of the Golden Gate. She describes the scene to me in stark detail: The sun was flickering in and out of intermittent fog. A group of Russian men in Speedos were stepping out of the frigid ocean. And an elderly man was sitting in a deck chair, sunbathing in weather that suggested anything but. Carrelli struck up a conversation with the man, whose name was Glen. In a German accent, he told her that people congregated regularly at China Beach to swim in the ocean. He had done so himself when he was younger, he said, but now he just came to the beach to sunbathe every day.

Carrelli left San Francisco shortly thereafter. ("Everything fell apart," she says.) But her encounter with the old man made such a profound impression that five years later, in 2004—after burning through stints in South Carolina, Georgia, and New York—she drove back across the country and headed for China Beach. When she arrived, she found Glen sitting in the same spot where she had left him in 1999. That day, as they parted ways, he said, "See you tomorrow." For the next three years, he said the same words to her pretty much every day. "He became this structure," Carrelli says, "a constant."

It was perhaps the safe distance between them—an elderly man and a young woman sitting on a public beach—that made Glen relatively impervious to the detonations that had wiped out every other home she'd ever had. "He couldn't kick me out," Carrelli says. She sat with her notebooks, and Glen asked her questions about her experiments with strangers and coconuts. Gradually, she began to find other constants. She started joining the swimmers every day, plunging into the Pacific with no wetsuit, even in winter. Her drinking began to taper off. She landed a job at a coffee shop called Farley's that she managed to keep for three years. And she began assiduously cultivating a network of friends she could count on for help when she was in trouble—a word she uses frequently to refer to her psychotic episodes—while being careful not to overtax any individual's generosity.

Carrelli also found safety in simply being well-known—in attracting as many acquaintances as possible. That's why, she tells me, she had always worked in coffee shops. When she is feeling well, Carrelli is a swashbuckling presence, charismatic and disarmingly curious about people. "She will always make a friend wherever she is," says Noelle Olivo, a San Francisco escrow and title agent who was a regular customer at Farley's and later gave Carrelli a place to stay for a couple of months. "People are taken aback by her, but she reaches out."

This gregariousness was in part a survival mechanism, as were her tattoos and her daily uniform of headscarves, torn jeans, and crop tops. The trick was to be identifiable: The more people who recognized her, the more she stood a chance of being able to recognize herself.

But Carrelli's grip on stability was still fragile. Between apartments and evictions, she slept in her truck, in parks, at China Beach, on friends' couches. Then one day in 2006, Carrelli's boss at Farley's Coffee discovered her sleeping in the shop, and he told her it was probably time she opened up her own space. "He almost gave me permission to do something I knew I should do," she recalls. It was clear by then that Carrelli couldn't really work for anyone else—Farley's had been unusually forgiving. But she didn't know how to chart a course forward. At China Beach, she took to her notebooks, filling them with grandiose manifestoes about living with guts and honor and commitment—about, she wrote, building her own damn house.

"Giulietta, you don't have enough money to eat tonight," Glen said, bringing her down to Earth. Then he asked her a question that has since appeared in her writing again and again: "What is your useful skill in a tangible situation?"

The answer was easy: she was good at making coffee and good with people. So Glen told her it was time she opened a checking account. He told her to go to city hall and ask if they had information on starting a small business. And she followed his instructions.

With $1,000 borrowed from friends, Carrelli opened Trouble in 2007 in a smelly, cramped, former dog grooming business, on a bleak commercial stretch. She renovated the space pretty much entirely with found materials, and with labor and advice that was bartered for, cajoled, and requested from her community of acquaintances.

She called the shop Trouble, she says, in honor of all the people who helped her when she was in trouble. She called her drip coffee "guts" and her espresso "honor." She put coconuts on the menu because of the years she had spent relying on them for easy sustenance, and because they truly did help her strike up conversations with strangers. She put toast on the menu because it reminded her of home: "I had lived so long with no comfort," she says. And she put "Build Your Own Damn House" on the menu because she felt, with Trouble, that she had finally done so.

Glen—whose full name was Gunther Neustadt, and who had escaped Germany as a young Jewish boy with his twin sister during World War II—lived to see Trouble open. But he died later that year. In 2008, Carrelli became pregnant and had twins, and she named one of them after her friend from China Beach.

That same year, after having lived in her shop for months, Carrelli got a real apartment. She went completely clean and sober, and has stayed that way. She started to hire staff she could rely on; she worked out a sustainable custody arrangement with her children's father. And Trouble started to get written up in the press. Customers began to flock there from all over town for toast and coffee and coconuts.

The demands of running the shop, caring for two children, and swimming every day allowed Carrelli to feel increasingly grounded, but her psychotic episodes hardly went away; when they came on, she just kept working somehow. "I have no idea how I ran Trouble," she says. "I kept piling through." In 2012, after a five-month episode, Carrelli was hospitalized and, for the first time, given the diagnosis of schizoaffective disorder. Under her current treatment regimen, episodes come far less frequently. But still they come.

At bottom, Carrelli says, Trouble is a tool for keeping her alive. "I'm trying to stay connected to the self," she says. Like one of her old notebooks, the shop has become an externalized set of reference points, an index of Carrelli's identity. It is her greatest source of dependable routine and her most powerful means of expanding her network of friends and acquaintances, which extends now to the shop's entire clientele. These days, during a walking episode, Carrelli says, a hello from a casual acquaintance in some unfamiliar part of the city might make the difference between whether she makes it home that night or not. "I'm wearing the same outfit every day," she says. "I take the same routes every day. I own Trouble Coffee so that people recognize my face—so they can help me."

After having struggled as an employee in so many coffee shops, she now employs 14 people. In an almost unheard of practice for the café business, she offers them profit-sharing and dental coverage. And she plans on expanding the business even further, maybe opening up to four or five locations. With the proceeds, she hopes to one day open a halfway house for people who have psychotic episodes—a safe place where they can go when they are in trouble.

When I told friends back East about the craze for fancy toast that was sweeping across the Bay Area, they laughed and laughed. (How silly; how twee; how *San Francisco*.) But my bet is that artisanal toast is going national. I've already heard reports of sightings in the West Village.

If the spread of toast is a social contagion, then Carrelli was its perfect vector. Most of us dedicate the bulk of our attention to a handful of relationships: with a significant other, children, parents, a few close friends. Social scientists call these "strong ties." But Carrelli can't rely on such a small set of intimates. Strong ties have a history of failing her, of buckling under the weight of her illness. So she has adapted by forming as many relationships—as many weak ties—as she possibly can. And webs of weak ties are what allow ideas to spread.

In a city whose economy is increasingly built on digital social networks—but where simple eye contact is at a premium—Giulietta Carrelli's latticework of small connections is old-fashioned and analog. It is built not for self-presentation, but for self-preservation. And the spread of toast is only one of the things that has arisen from it.

A few weeks ago, I went back to Trouble because I hadn't yet built my own damn house. When my coconut came, the next guy at the bar shot me a sideways glance. Sitting there with a slice of toast and a large tropical fruit, I felt momentarily self-conscious. Then the guy said to the barista, "Hey, can I get a coconut too?" and the two of us struck up a conversation.

Five Things I Will Not Eat

By Barry Estabrook

From CivilEats.com

Investigative food journalist Barry Estabrook has
written for *The Atlantic*, *Gastronomica*, the late great
Gourmet magazine, and his blog PoliticsOf ThePlate.
com. His 2011 book *Tomatoland* made readers think
differently about supermarket tomatoes; here are a few
more eye-openers he's discovered.

My partner eyed me sternly when I announced that my next
book was going to be an investigative look at pork production. "Does this mean that I'll have to give up eating bacon?" she
asked.

Deadly outbreaks of E. coli and *Salmonella* in spinach and can-
taloupes, antibiotic-resistant "superbugs" connected to pork and
chicken production, potent drugs that are banned in the United States
in imported shrimp and catfish: Nothing has the potential to destroy
your appetite quite as thoroughly as writing about industrial food
production or living with someone who does. Somehow, I have remained omnivorous, more or less. But there are only five things that
I absolutely refuse to eat.

1. Supermarket Ground Beef

I lost my appetite for prepared ground beef in the late 1980s, when
a friend's three-year-old daughter died after eating a hamburger
tainted with *E. coli* O157:H7, which lives in the intestines of healthy
cattle and other animals, but can be found in water, food, soil, or on
surfaces that have been contaminated with animal or human feces.

She endured a painful, lingering death, beginning with a tummy ache, and over two weeks progressing to bloody diarrhea, convulsions, and seizures as the *E. coli* bacteria destroyed her kidneys.

It's true that *E. coli* dies when hamburger is cooked to at least 160 degrees, by which point it is well-done. But even if you like dry, gray patties (I don't), why take the risk? Every time you buy a package of supermarket ground beef, you're playing culinary Russian roulette. *E. coli* comes from meat that has been contaminated with manure. A few *E. coli* cells can multiply into millions in a short time. Slaughterhouse scraps that go into ground beef come from the outside and undersides of carcasses, the areas most likely to come in contact with the hide and most prone to fecal contamination. Those parts can travel from several slaughterhouses to one facility to be ground and packaged.

In his Pulitzer Prize–winning article describing how a Minnesota woman was left paralyzed after eating *E. coli*–tainted hamburger, *New York Times'* Michael Moss reported that the meat in the single prepared, frozen patty she ate had been shipped to a Wisconsin processor from facilities in Nebraska, Texas, South Dakota, and Uruguay.

The easiest way to avoid supermarket hamburger is to buy a whole cut like a chuck steak or sirloin and grind it yourself. A few pulses from a food processor does the trick nicely, if you don't own a meat grinder. Or have a butcher grind it for you while you wait. You can also buy from a small producer. When I went to pick up my beef order last fall, the owner of the custom slaughterhouse was standing beside a stainless steel table holding a mountain of ground beef waiting for her to pack it into one-pound bags. "I can tell you exactly how many animals this hamburger came from," she said. "One."

2. Salad Greens in Plastic Bags or Clam-Shell Boxes

For starters, salad fixings bought whole and chopped in your kitchen are more nutritious than those from containers. Bagged and boxed greens are in for the long haul, and can stay "fresh" for as long as 17 days. But vegetables begin losing nutrients the second they are picked. Within eight hours, 10 percent of Vitamin C and between three and four percent of beta-carotene are gone. Chopping and shredding increase oxidation, driving out more nutrients. Even short stretches of time at room temperatures further lower nutrient levels.

Packaged greens are also vulnerable to bacterial contamination.

In packing houses, crops from many fields are washed in the same water, which allows bacteria from one field to spread to greens from clean fields. *E. coli* and other bacteria can hide in cut edges, safe from wash water. Allowed to become warm for even a short time, the containers become perfect incubators for bacteria. The result is that bagged greens have sickened or killed consumers in dozens of out-breaks over the last several years.

In a 2010 investigation, Consumer Reports found that bags and containers of greens contained levels of coliform bacteria (which doesn't make you sick, but is a sign of unsanitary handling) that were 39 percent higher than what is considered acceptable.

Avoiding packaged greens is simple: Buy whole heads or bunches and chop them yourself. While working on an article for the *New York Times Magazine* in 2011, I bought a head of romaine lettuce, rinsed the leaves individually, and chopped them. It took me two minutes and 53 seconds. As a bonus, I saved myself 80 cents.

3. Bluefin Tuna

Atlantic, Pacific, and Indian Ocean populations of Bluefin tuna are severely overfished. In the Atlantic, the species hovers on the brink of extinction. Some scientists say that it may have already passed the point of no return. In the Pacific, the population has been decimated by 96 percent. I liken eating bluefins to eating Bengal tigers. Both are beautiful, sleek predators. Bluefins can swim 60 miles per hour, dive to 4,000 feet, and migrate across oceans. Someone alive today could be the person who eats the last bluefin. I don't want it to be me.

International organizations that are charged with setting catch limits for bluefins regularly set quotas far above what their own sci-entists recommend. And there has been a thriving market in illegally caught fish. If that's not enough to put you off Bluefin, be warned, their flesh is extremely high in mercury.

4. Out-of-Season Tomatoes

The first question is, why would you want to eat an out-of-season tomato? Most of the hard, pale orbs are pithy and tasteless, at best. Compared to their local, in-season cousins, they are bereft of nu-trients. And varieties that do have a glimmer of tomato flavor are outrageously expensive.

But the real problem with winter tomatoes is the abuses suffered by the farmworkers who harvest them. These men and women in the tomato fields are underpaid, ill-housed, and often sprayed with toxic pesticides. Abject slavery is not uncommon. (I care so much about this topic that I wrote a book about it.)

In recent years, working conditions in Florida, the source of most American-grown winter tomatoes, have improved dramatically. New varieties have been developed that actually taste tomato-y, and most Florida growers have signed onto a Fair Food Program that guarantees workers some basic labor rights and provides them with a one-penny-a-pound raise (it doesn't sound like much but it's the difference between $50 and $80 a day).

However that's only if—and it's a big if—the end buyer of the to-matoes signs onto the program as well and agrees to pay that extra penny directly to the workers. So far, most fast-food and food-ser-vice companies have come aboard. But aside from Trader Joe's and Whole Foods Market, not a single supermarket chain has signed on. Until they do, they won't get my business.

5. Farmed Salmon

A salmon farm, even a so-called organic one in Scottish waters, is nothing short of a floating feedlot. Excrement, uneaten food, and dead fish fall into the ocean, along with a witch's brew of drugs and disease organisms that can kill wild salmon unlucky enough to swim in the vicinity of a farm's net pens. Farmed salmon are susceptible to infectious salmon anaemia, aquaculture's answer to highly con-tagious hoof-and-mouth disease. The "cure" is to eradicate entire farmed Stocks consisting of millions of fish. Captive salmon also spread sea lice to wild fish. The parasites feed on the mucous, blood, and skin and can kill young salmon.

Farmed salmon is also potentially harmful to humans who eat it. Studies have shown that farmed salmon contains significantly higher levels of chemicals known to cause everything from neurological damage to cancer than wild salmon.

As a way to produce protein, farming salmon is illogical. Although feed formulas have improved over the years, salmon still have to eat more pounds of fishmeal and oil than they put on as meat. That meal they are fed comes from stocks of small sardine-like fish that are already caught at maximum sustainable levels. It's far better to raise fish like tilapia that can be fed a vegetarian diet. But that's not where the money is.

Fortunately, there is a good alternative to farmed salmon. Wild salmon from Alaska is sustainable and its taste will remind you why you wanted to eat salmon in the first place.

So what about my partner? Will she feel obligated to forsake bacon? My pork research is still in the early stages, so I don't have a final answer. But at very least, it's looking like we're going to want to become very selective about what goes in our frying pan.

BACONOMICS 101

By David Sax

From The Tastemakers

In his 2009 book *Save the Deli*, Canadian journalist
David Sax rhapsodized about great Jewish delicatessens.
His new book *The Tastemakers* digs deep into the
nature of food fads, as Sax lays bare the sneaky cultural
forces that make us crave certain dishes (remember
cupcakes?) for a season.

W hen my taxi pulled up to the University of Illinois at Chicago Forum on the cold Saturday morning I flew in from DC, a crowd of several dozen people were already milling about outside, cradling coffees in their hands as they formed the start of a line. From a nearby tent the deli meat company Eckrich was handing out slices of five different delicatessen meats that had been infused with bacon. A banner proclaimed this "The Best Idea Ever," and they were scarcely able to open the packages quick enough for the hungry crowd that rushed to devour them. Inside the doors of the building several dozen volunteers were lined up behind long registration tables, ready to process the thousands who would soon arrive, ravenous and ramped up for greasy delights at the sold-out event called Baconfest.

The sprawling twenty-two-thousand–square foot floor of the Forum's event hall was abuzz with activity. Six long tables, each stretching the length of the room, had been taken over by eighty-two local restaurants and bars, beer and liquor companies, and other vendors. Another eighty waiters and bartenders, working for the catering company Sodexo, wandered like lost children in black shirts while chefs, cooks, bakers, and owners scrambled to get ready. Pallets of beer kegs were being pushed around to all corners of the room, as James Brown played over the sound system. Along the back wall a giant screen was flashing the Baconfest logo: Chicago's sky blue–and–white flag with red stars, rendered to look like a strip of bacon. Everywhere I looked people were carrying in trays, casseroles, Tupperware containers, and pulling huge hand carts piled with mountains of cooked bacon. Michael Griggs, one of the founders and organizers of Baconfest, now in its fifth year, was busy running around with a walkie-talkie, trying to corral the activity into some semblance of order.

"Hey," said one of the chefs from the restaurant Belly-Q, who literally stepped in front of Griggs's path to get his attention, "we have a fryer going. Can we leave the hot oil in or take it with us?"

"Take it with you," said Griggs over his shoulder as he blew past the chef and kept moving on to the next issue.

One by one the restaurants turned on their portable griddles and ovens, reheating their bacon creations, which ranged from simple candied strips of bacon to concoctions like bacon-spiked bloody Marys, bacon peanut butter macarons, bacon cupcakes, bacon pineapple donuts, bacon pizzas, bacon biscotti, chicken-fried bacon, bacon meatballs, and bacon cotton candy, to name just a few. Puffs of bacon vapor were visibly rising into the air, settling down a few minutes later as a fine mist of aerosolized bacon grease that clung to every possible surface. In the corner of the hall a chef from one of the restaurants walked up to a table run by Jones Dairy Farm, one of the few dedicated bacon producers attending Baconfest. They had hung a whole slab of bacon, several feet long, from a rack next to their table, while a glistening warm pork belly rested on a carving board, lit up by a heat lamp like a Broadway diva. "Look at how beautiful this is," said the chef, who was tapping his fingertips together rhythmically like Mr. Burns plotting something diabolical. "I'm like a moth to a flame. Or a fat guy to a slab of bacon."

At 11:30 the doors opened to 150 advance guests. These VIPs had paid $200 each for tickets that allowed them to enter an hour earlier than the rest of the 1,500 Baconfest attendees (whose general admission tickets still cost $100 each). All of the event's three thousand–odd tickets, for both the lunch session and the dinner session (identical format, but with different restaurants) had sold out months before, in just forty-one minutes, and others had paid even more for scalpers' tickets. The VIPs quickly fanned out with their Baconfest program guides in hand, heading to the tables that most interested them. There were families in newly purchased Baconfest T-shirts (including one portraying the Blues Brothers as flying pigs), wealthy well-dressed couples, hardcore foodies with expensive DSLR cameras, and a lot of burly men in Chicago Blackhawks jerseys. I walked outside and looked at the general admission line, which now stretched all the way around the corner and down two full blocks. Inside Griggs gave the signal over his radio to unlock the doors, and when they were flung open a cheer went up from the line. One man shouted "BACON!" at the top of his lungs like a general leading the cavalry charge.

"Oh my god," a woman said as she came into the hall and saw its sheer scope.

"Where's the bacon?" asked another man in a panic, making a beeline to the nearest restaurant's table, where he encountered the Signature Room's smoked bacon bread pudding, with pork tenderloin stuffed with chorizo and wrapped in bacon and topped in bacon-braised red cabbage and a bacon ancho sauce. He ate it in a single bite, then packed away another.

Some people entered the room and bolted to a particular booth, while others just froze for a minute, drunk with excitement at the overwhelming sight of so much bacon. Two men stood at the entrance and slow clapped. Nearby a police officer turned to his partner and said, "If this crowd gets out of hand, we may have to use bacon spray instead of pepper spray."

Walking around the festival during the lunch session I got a firsthand taste of how the cultural momentum of the bacon trend translated into economic opportunity.

At the Jones Dairy Farm table I spoke with Doug McDonald, the sales manager in charge of the company's foodservice accounts. "Bacon is our fastest-growing category. The past five years we've seen double-digit growth in food service sales. What you see now is bacon going from retail and pancake houses to mainstream bar and grills serving bacon during happy hour," he said. "There's a restaurant in

Arizona called Fifty/Fifty that we sell to. They take our thick-cut bacon, cook it, and put it on the bar in brandy glasses like peanuts."

At the other end of the hall Bob Nueske, the second-generation owner of Wisconsin's Nueske's, one of the largest independent bacon smokehouses in the country, looked out at the wild, ravenous crowd with wonder. "I always have a fear that trends are like hula hoops," Nueske, who is broad and tall, with a mobster's wall of coiffed hair, told me as strips of the company's applewood smoked bacon slowly sizzled on an electric griddle. "This bacon thing is beyond a trend. Thirty years ago I couldn't imagine kids making bacon like they are now."

Dave Miller, the owner of Bang Bang! Pie Shop, a Chicago bakery, was handing out bacon cherry rugelach, a traditional Jewish cookie rendered as unkosher as possible. "I see bacon as outdated," admitted Miller, "but it's a money maker and we do it because the economics demand it. It creates a cult following." The bakery sold strips of candied bacon at a dollar a piece, and these acted as a sort of honey trap for bacon lovers, who came to Bang Bang! for the bacon but invariably bought a loaf of bread or some other item.

Bacon's economic power was a shock even to those who built businesses around it. Sven Lindén was the founder of Black Rock Spirits, which made Bakon Vodka, a bacon-infused vodka that debuted in 2007 as a joke. It now does over $1 million in wholesale sales each year. "We knew there was a novelty component," Lindén told me as we stood by his booth, where they were handing out bacon bloody Marys, "but even in states where we've been around for five years they'll have a small bar do seven thousand bacon Bloody Marys a year." One of the few vendors not selling food but doing brisk business was Rebecca Wood, who owned the gift boutique Enjoy: An Urban Novelty Store, which had an entire bacon section filled with over a hundred novelty products. When she opened the store in 2005 her top-selling item quickly became bacon strip bandages, and today it remained in the top spot, followed by bacon socks, and I Love You More Than Bacon signs, which sold like gangbusters online.

Surrounded by bacon maniacs downing shots of bacon black bean stew, bacon cotton candy, and bacon root beer floats, it was impossible not to get caught up in the infectious exuberance of Baconfest. There were people like Jeaneed Kalakr and her grandson Parker, who wore matching, homemade T-shirts printed with a poem written for the occasion: "From one porker to the next / Don't give me no fat / I squeal for bacon / One good snort deserves another / I am a bacon lover . . . undercover." The miraculously petite sisters Christina and Danielle Wade were dressed in matching bacon earrings, socks, and T-shirts made for their 2011 Bacon Takedown Tour. "It's not a trend for me," the enthusiastic Danielle said. "It's a way of life." There were dudes wearing muscle shirts that said, "Bacon Gives Me a Lardon" and "Drink First. Pork Later"; babies in little pig outfits; a man wearing a homemade matching hat and shirt that displayed a peace sign made up of strips of bacon he'd ironed on; and my favorite, a T-shirt of a cat surfing a strip of bacon in outer space. "That's the coolest T-shirt here!" I told the owner and then immediately regretted it, as I saw someone with a T-shirt that had two bacon-surfing space cats. Yes, the bacon trend was about food, but it was also a money-making meme, like a live version of an online joke that just gets spun round and round and round until you wonder where it will end.

"Before the bacon bubble came into being it was very niche," said Aaron Samuels, who had bought VIP tickets with his wife, Charlotte, as an anniversary gift. The two of them were decked out for battle, with pink headbands, backpacks, and a studied knowledge of what was on offer. Samuels, who had a giant beard and was decidedly zaftig, wore a T-shirt that proclaimed "Man Boobs Are Sexy," while Charlotte's shirt featured an angel pig with wings and a halo floating above a plate of bacon, with the caption "It's what I would have wanted ." "If the bacon bubble bursts, we'll still be fans of bacon," Samuels said. "Most people at Baconfest are the O.G.s of bacon"—meaning its original gangsters, bacon's most hard-core fans.

Nearby I overheard a man ask a group of strangers in full-on bacon regalia whether they were baconheads. "No," said one of them, hoisting a bacon bourbon cocktail, "we're Chicagoans. Other cities do marathons. We do Baconfest."

THE RIGHT TO EAT

By JT Torres

From Alimentum

⟳

Fiction writer JT Torres grew up in Florida and now
teaches writing at the University of Alaska at Anchorage
(how's that for a geographic leap?). Growing up in a
Cuban-American family, he learned to finely parse
what is and what is not "American"—including our
addiction to junk food.

D r. Pepper or her gall bladder, one of them had to go. Her doctor
explained the option of eliminating soda and other acidic, fatty,
greasy foods and adopting a diet of cucumbers and broccoli—foods
that strengthen the stomach's lining and the digestive tract. "Your
gall bladder is currently operating at about 20%," he said, and then
went on to stress that a reversal of biliary dyskinesia and complete
relief of epigrastric pain could not be guaranteed without surgery.
My sister, Dezy, faced a decision that compromised her identity at its
core, both physiologically and metaphysically. She had been taught,
by our CPA father, that life is about costs and fluctuating supplies
based on demand. Now, Dezy had to decide whether she would pay
the new cost of enjoying her favorite beverage. Having a favorite,
mind you, is a big deal in my family. Dezy saw it as her right as an
American, echoing our father's famous saying, "He who has a sur-
plus has the benefit of favorites."

The panic that settled in Dezy's already unstable mind came not
from the pain she had been feeling the past couple months but from
the prospect of giving up the sweet, syrupy goodness, the pungent
aromas of peppermint pouring out of a single can of Dr. Pepper.

As a child, the substance was as verboten as dope, classified by our parents as a Schedule 1 drug with no medicinal benefits. Dezy didn't understand why her parents would criminalize something that lined supermarket aisles, sparkled on TV commercials, and tasted like the gods' ambrosia. Why should she be denied what is publicly available? Therefore, she made a pact with her soul that when she had her own house her refrigerator would be stocked from drawer to shelf with shiny, sweating burgundy cans of the liquid she wouldn't live without.

She learned to trust the marketplace over her family, for only in the marketplace can any desire be fulfilled, at a price.

And so she considered the price, as explained by her doctor. "Remove the gall bladder, undergo a brief period of recovery in which you will have to remain on a strict diet, and then reintroduce more volatile foods, such as soda. I can guarantee, in this scenario, that the functionality of your gall bladder will not be a factor, since, of course, you will no longer have a gall bladder." The doctor laughed, but then swallowed his smile at Dezy's failure to appreciate his joke.

"So the problem," Dezy asked, her legs going numb from the firm chair, "is the gall bladder itself?"

The sterile paper covering the chair crinkled under her shifting weight. Dezy, though bone skinny, felt heavy with the weight of a bowling ball pressing against her intestines.

"Indeed," her doctor answered.

"Then remove it," she said. And in that instant she felt a sudden release. Not from the pain twisting her stomach, but from the burden of having a very essential freedom taken away from her. She could survive an operation; in fact, she had already resolved herself to doing so. Hell, she had had her wisdom teeth pulled when she was fourteen. One operation is like any other. She could survive without auxiliary parts of her body. What she couldn't do: renounce her sovereignty and not eat and drink what she damned well wanted to.

My sister the proud American: She votes Conservative in every election. She listens to Toby Keith and cries every time he mentions the word "soldiers." She watches football every Sunday. The Star-Spangled Banner hangs from a post over her garage. Her kids are in gifted programs. Her husband is a manager. She is in the PTA. She supports the troops. Her last name is Blanco. Her last name before that was Torres. Her mother is Cuban, her father Columbian. She refuses learning Spanish on principle.

She buys the 24-pack of Dr. Pepper in sets of two, a habit she picked up from our father, who would buy cartons of cigarettes and stash them around the house. I remember being three years old and finding a carton tucked behind my Ninja Turtle toy box. Another time I found one under the matt in Thumper's crate. Thumper was our Yorkie. My father used to say he felt more relaxed knowing he had so many caches than he did when he actually smoked a cigarette. When he had to quit, following a hernia surgery, he still bought cartons and hid them. Although he never returned to smoking, he couldn't stand the thought of being denied possession. And so Dezy stocks her pantry and fridge with Dr. Pepper while her two kids have to come to my mother's house to find chicken or juice.

My mother raised the issue with her once. Only once.

Two months before the surgery, during the incipient stages of Dezy's growing discomfort, her mother said to her, "my house isn't a restaurant." This had been after a day of babysitting both my niece and nephew. "The kids told me they don't have any food at your house." Dezy, her face flushed as it had been the past week or so, sat at the table and gasped for air with one hand pinching the side of her stomach. At the time, she did not know that there was anything wrong with her. What she blamed on a cramp from a long day stocking shelves at Team Disney, a store that sold sports-themed apparel for the Dizzy Donalds, the Maestro Mickeys, and the Goaltending Goofys, was actually golfball-sized gallstones that blocked her bile ducts and threatened to rupture her gallbladder. What she blamed on a long day's work in one of Orlando's happiest kitsch shops was actually an activation of pancreatic enzymes that inflamed the area around her intestines and caused intra-abdominal hypertension.

She took in a deep breath and felt a razor-sharp string tighten around her gut.

"I already look after them all day while you're at work," my mother continued, as oblivious to Dezy's discomfort as was Dezy. "Can't you, I don't know, pack their lunches? I have to go shopping now in order to make dinner."

My mother collected my nephew's homework and stuffed it in

his backpack. Then she picked up my niece's clothes, festooned on the back of the couch. Without once looking at Dezy—my mother always felt a shameful guilt after scolding one of her children—she walked to the patio door, opened it, and called her grandkids out of the pool.

After they dried themselves and came inside, Dezy, who hadn't moved from the dining room chair, yelled at them for "playing the victim."

"From now on you wait until you get home to eat," she said.

"I like Nanny's food," my niece said.

Dezy stood up and the small patches of pink that had lingered in the fleshiest part of her cheeks vanished. She turned hospital-white all over. She grabbed an arm from each child and stormed out of the house.

Later on that night my mother called me and expressed her concern for my sister. "She's been getting mad so easily," she said.

"Next time you should ground her."

I didn't think anything was seriously wrong with my sister. It had always seemed to me that she lived a life without consequence. She dropped out of college to work for Disney because that's "always been my dream." Despite making less as a guest services representative than the hungover high school student in charge of the emergency break button on Space Mountain, she and her husband managed to buy a townhouse close to my parents' house. She went on to have two children and then bought a pedigree beagle, all on an hourly salary and periodical help from my mother. It had always seemed as long as she did what she wanted, life would never catch up.

I called my sister once before the surgery. Because I had just recently jumped on the organic bandwagon that swept the nation like yellow Livestrong wristbands, I suggested that she change her diet instead of having the procedure. I recommended she read articles proclaiming the benefits of a diet sans processed foods. I also tried echoing some of T. Colin Campbell's arguments that chronic illnesses can be linked to our eating habits. She firmly responded that she would not live her life in fear, as if she were giving in by not having surgery. "I'm not going to be one of those people that watches the news then hides under my covers," she said. "First Muslim terrorists, then socialist college professors, and now processed foods?"

I could hear the uncertainty in her voice. Her tone made a faint call for me to argue with her, prove her wrong. Tell her that she should be afraid. Before I could, however, she apparently detected the same tone betraying her words and said, "Besides, according to my doctor our bodies don't even need a gall bladder."

When the gall bladder is working correctly: The liver manufactures bile, which is used to help in the digestion of fatty foods. The bile is secreted from the liver cells into small bile ducts, which join together to form the common hepatic duct. The bile then goes into the gallbladder where it is stored and concentrated for later use. When you eat a meal with high fat content, say, condensed milk straight from the can (one of my sister's favorites), a hormone called cholecystokinin is secreted. It causes the gallbladder to contract and also causes relaxation of a small valve at the end of the common bile duct. This allows bile to flow into the duodenum and mix with food for digestion. After the cholecystokinin effect wears off, the valve closes, the gallbladder relaxes, and the cycle is repeated. The gallbladder stores the bile to be deposited into the small intestine to help break down fat. It also acts as a reservoir that uptakes excess bile when there is pressure in the bile ducts.

After her doctor provided the ultimatum—Dr. Pepper or gall bladder—Dezy found solace in the company of strong-willed friends. Anne and Claire, both of them neighbors and mothers of children who attended the same school as Dezy's children, came over to her townhouse. Each held a shoulder as Dezy cried onto wilted hands. Life, for her at that moment, became a steady process of losing certain parts of her body. At age fourteen went the wisdom teeth. At age twenty-one went the tonsils. At age twenty-seven went the ACL in her right knee. The gradual loss of her self sent her into an existential confusion, since her identity relied so much on the individual liberty and ownership promised by the movies, songs, and magazines of the 1980s to the 1990s. She had every song with the lyrics "I want (Insert: Candy, Money, to Be a Cowboy)" memorized. What did she know of songs of loss?

Anne, a freckled-face woman with the proud jaw of Southern gentries, told Dezy she'd feel better once she started talking. Claire hummed. Her voice, soft as the evening breeze, lifted a few strands of Dezy's long, frizzy hair.

Dezy felt surrounded by love. She told them the news.

"Honey," Anne said. "That's nothing. Neither of us have our gall bladders."

"Neither does my husband," Claire said. Even when she spoke she carried a melody.

"It hasn't changed a thing about our lives."

"What about the recovery period?" Dezy wanted to know. She lifted her swollen eyes and waited for any excuse to restore hope. Anything would have done.

"Honey," Anne started and squeezed Dezy's shoulders. "I ate a bag of Doritos the night after the surgery."

"You don't have any regrets?" Dezy asked. "I mean, that's an organ you never get back. What if I need it at some later point in my life?"

"Life's about sacrifices. You sacrifice aspects of your life that prevent you from getting what you want. This is the new millennium. You have every right to have what you want." The tone of Anne's voice changed somehow, as if inadvertently weighed by the careless intrusion of anger.

Claire hummed. The sweet sound caromed off the tile floors and onto the beige walls decorated with photos of Dezy's family. Photos of the beach. Photos of the townhouse on the day they moved in. Photos of her children rummaging under a Christmas tree. Photos of a life worth living, a life worth wanting.

"Get the surgery. When it's over, Claire and I will take you out for pizza and margaritas. We'll call Ruth and Evelyn. They both had their gall bladders out last year. On the same weekend, I think. Maybe there was a special going on. They said the doctor was drop-dead-gorgeous. How's yours in the looks department?"

"You promise it's a safe procedure?" Dezy trembled. She wanted Anne to continue holding her until her husband returned home from work.

She tried thinking about layers of cheese on a Chicago thick crust and the acidic kick of a José Cuervo–mixed margarita. "Either way,"

Claire said, "we're going out. Are you willing to watch us enjoy the foods we enjoy and not do a thing?" Dezy suddenly felt pressured, cornered in. The consolation she sought turned into a threat. However, she couldn't let her friends down. She couldn't let herself down. She shook her head.

Both Anne and Claire smiled and wrapped their arms around Dezy's pale, trembling body.

"Now, as for your doctor," Anne said in a much lighter tone, as if she were talking to a child, "is he handsome or not?"

Six years later, my niece had a similar choice: increase her dietary intake of fibers or remove her appendix. The way her doctor explained it to Dezy: the pain your daughter feels is a corollary of bowels blocked in her intestines. If her appendix were to rupture from the pressure, the damage could be detrimental. The quickest way to alleviate her of the pain is by performing surgery. It isn't quite appendicitis. We could try to treat it with antibiotics, but she would have to drastically change her diet in order to stand even the slightest chance of avoiding a laparoscopic appendectomy. On the other hand, if you do go through with the procedure, she will be back on her feet eating what she pleases in no longer than a month.

This doctor was handsome.

On the way home, Dezy talked it over with Kerstyn. The hot Florida sun pushed through the CR-V's tinted windows and pressed both mother and daughter against their seats. Even with the A/C on full blast, both felt a blanket of sweat, the loss of oxygen.

"Should I have Nanny make broccoli for dinner?" Dezy asked. She took one hand off the steering wheel and held it over her side, over the scar left by the choice she had made for fearless freedom.

"I don't like broccoli," Kerstyn said. Her obstinate voice felt far too familiar to Dezy. An echo from a recent past. A vague memory of a proud history. "I'm not eating broccoli." Kerstyn was determined as hell to beat her condition, to conquer her body, weakness by weakness.

"The doctor said you don't have to have surgery," Dezy offered in a tone that suggested not even she believed what she was saying.

"I want my appendix out. I'm tired of it hurting. I can't dance. I can't laugh. I can't do anything. I want it out." Kerstyn was twelve and already knew what she wanted in life. Tears welled behind the pale blue of her eyes. Her cheeks turned as red as her cherry-stem lips. She kept her arms crossed over her sweat-soaked stomach.

Dezy slowed down and pulled onto the right-hand lane. She needed time to negotiate. If she arrived at our mother's house before coming to a settlement with her daughter, she knew she would lose. Perhaps because she realized her own inconsistencies but wouldn't acknowledge them, perhaps because she feared making those inconsistencies public, but Dezy could not confront her children in front of our mother.

"You can't live off fried chicken fingers and chocolate."

This was precisely what Kerstyn lived off.

"You need to eat greens."

"You never eat greens."

Dezy came to a stop at a yellow light. The car behind her honked his horn.

"We're talking about your diet."

"You had surgery. We can put my appendix in a jar with your gall bladder and send the jar out to sea."

"Even if you get the surgery, you're going to have to start eating greens."

"I don't like vegetables. They taste like garbage. What's the point of eating if I can't eat what I like?"

When the light turned green, Dezy felt the sudden urge to floor it, to end the drive as quickly as possible and return to the typical relationship she shared with her daughter—best friends. They never fought. They rarely disagreed. The tension nauseated Dezy and confused Kerstyn. Throughout the CR-V, the churning air from the A/C swallowed the settling silence.

By the time they reached my mother's house, the only other time they spoke was when Kerstyn asked her mother to keep Nanny in the dark about the diagnosis. Eager to finally be on her daughter's side, Dezy agreed.

For dinner, they had fried chicken and pasta. For dessert, they had Oreos crumbled over chocolate ice cream.

My mother didn't find out about Kerstyn's condition until a week before the surgery. I had come down from Georgia to support my niece. It was the first time she was going to receive anesthesia. We ate fettuccini at my sister's townhouse for dinner to "celebrate." Surgery had become a festivity to the people in my family—the disburdening of vital organs a modern parallel to ancient purgative rituals.

Only once did my mother challenge my sister's reasoning.

"Why didn't you encourage a healthier diet?" she asked.

Only once.

"I didn't want to force her to do something she didn't want to do."

I felt angered by my sister's response. My mother had, after all, raised us on spinach, carrots, fish, asparagus, etc. We were only allowed junk food once a week. At times during my childhood, I remember calling my mother a diet-dictator, citing America's claim that we were in a "free country."

Why couldn't my sister realize what my parents tried to teach us, that freedom still requires self-restraint, that freedom and austerity aren't inherently opposed but, actually, co-dependent?

I went into the kitchen to refill my glass of water and when I opened the fridge the sheen of immaculate maroon cans, each deliciously reflecting the stale white refrigerated light, caught my attention. I stared at each can—the smooth aluminum curving with the grace of a midnight gibbous. Every shelf on the door stocked full of Dr. Pepper reminded me that my sister's refrigerator was, at the cost of all else, including personal health, a cache of the American dream.

A Table for Everyone

AMERICA, YOUR FOOD IS SO GAY

By John Birdsall

From Lucky Peach

Once a chef, always a chef, though Chow.com senior
editor John Birdsall has since drifted into food writing,
including the Bay Area's *SF Weekly* and *East Bay Express*.
But there were lessons learned in the kitchen—and
before that—that raised a nagging question. At last, he
has the courage to address the elephant in the room.

I was ten in 1970, a shy kid growing up in a scrub-oak suburb south
of San Francisco. Our house was pitched on stilts sunk in a steep
hillside, looking out onto a little arroyo and into the house of two
men I loved like uncles (and more deeply than some of the uncles
whose DNA I shared).

But besides me and my older brother, Walter, my mom, and my
dad, everybody on our street despised Pat and Lou. At a time when
it was still a crime in California for one man to give another man a
blowjob, the neighbors hated them because they shared the same
enormous bed, draped in a regal turquoise coverlet. Hated them because Lou stayed home like moms did, trolling Safeway for steaks
and stuffed potatoes to fix for Pat when he got home from the office.

(Why didn't my parents share the general loathing for Pat and
Lou, a disgust expressed through passive avoidance, active shunning,
and the occasional high-pitched catcall? I discovered later that my
mom, bless her, is a total fag hag. And my dad always hated bullies—it
trumped his ambivalence about the gay thing.)

Pat and Lou did cocktail hour nightly from a pair of velour bucket
chairs, in their beam-ceilinged, ranch-style canyon house overlook-

ing masses of scarlet and purple irises under the oaks. They put on matching poplin jumpsuits and corduroy house moccasins to sip Gibsons, tossing nuts to Kurt, their sleek miniature schnauzer, from fingers studded with big-jeweled cocktail rings. On nights when my parents would go to the Iron Gate restaurant for shrimp scampi and saltimbocca, they dropped us boys off at Pat and Lou's for babysitting.

On those nights, Lou would cook us crazy shit our mom never fixed, food so rich no adult should ever serve it to a ten-year-old. There were casseroles that used Monterey Jack as a suspension medium for olives, ground veal, and button mushrooms from a can. And there were Lou's famous burgers, so rich and salty, so crusted with a mixture of caramelized onions, Roquefort crumbles, and Grey Poupon—a thick impasto gilded beneath the electric broiler element—I could only ever eat half before feeling sick. I loved every bite.

Looking back, I recognize in Lou's burgers my first taste of food that didn't give a fuck about nutrition or the drab strictures of home economics. They were calibrated for adult pleasure, acutely expressive of a formalized richness—exactly the type of thing James Beard taught Americans to eat (for all I know, Lou's recipe was straight out of Beard). I see them now, those burgers, as unflinchingly, unapologetically, magnificently queer.

By 1970, America's interest in food had finally progressed from the stale international haute cuisine of the 1950s—we were more curious about the world, and were willing to spend more on food and travel than ever before. Three gay guys—Beard, Richard Olney, and Craig Claiborne—would become architects of modern food in America. You find their influence in the cooking of Thomas Keller and Daniel Patterson, and in the food Alice Waters has overseen in four decades of menus at Chez Panisse. It's food that takes pleasure seriously, as an end in itself, an assertion of politics or a human birthright, the product of culture—this is the legacy of gay food writers who shaped modern American food.

I admit, it's tricky pinning something as sprawling and amorphous as modern American cooking to anything as poorly defined as a queer point of view, and an exclusively male one at that. I first struggled with that task in the late '80s, when I was writing about food for the *Sentinel*, a now-defunct gay weekly in San Francisco. My editor, the late Eric Hellman, would always ask, "Is there a gay sensibility? Can you see it in a work of art?"

As I was falling in love with Lou's Roquefort burgers, a gay activist in New Mexico named Harry Hay was launching a movement called the Radical Faeries—they'd go off for days-long Faerie Circles in the wilderness, like all-male mini Burning Mans, only with psilocybin-fueled circle jerks. Hay was a founder of the early gay rights group the Mattachine Society. By 1970, he'd come to the conclusion that gay men were spiritually different from straight ones—homosexuals had always been shamans and prophets, jeered, beaten dead or barely tolerated, living on the margins. (Hay, who died in 2002, was anti-assimilationist, meaning he would have been horrified to see the current struggle for gay people to achieve hetero marriage.) Gay guys were artists, form-givers, shapers of the broader culture that hated them.

I don't totally buy Hay's theory of queer exceptionalism, but my editor's question—is there a gay sensibility?—became a kind of koan as I struggled to navigate life in the kitchens where I worked (I was a food writer part-time; my main gig was cooking in restaurants). Even in San Francisco, gayest city in America, homophobic dicks got all the prime line positions in the places I worked. In one kitchen, it was a running joke that the salad station was reserved for women and "effeminates," meaning gay boys like me. On the outside, I laughed along with everybody. On the inside, I told myself, *I'm fucking better than all of you.*

If there was a gay sensibility, you could find it on the cold line when I was cooking, where every plate I put up had a fierce edge born of imposed isolation. The fish stews coming off José's sauté station might have been technically perfect, but they were also mechanical. My *salades composées* were thickets of yearning, drifts of leaves and flowers, sprigs of herbs and tiny carrots that looked like they had been blown there by some mighty force of nature. I was fueled by sublimated rage, the outsider with something to prove, taking the ingredients I was handed and making sure they transcended their limits.

I recognize that same conviction in Olney. He grew up in Marathon, Iowa, and expatriated to Paris to become a painter, a decade or two after great gay expats like James Baldwin famously escaped America's racism and prudery. Olney turned out to be a so-so painter, but in a way, his art played out in the details of daily life. He bought a broken-down farmhouse in Solliès-Toucas, fifty miles east of Marseille, and slowly scrabbled the life back into it. He carved a wine cellar out of limestone, gathered *serpolet* (wild thyme) on its hillsides in summer for drying, made vinegars and jams. And from the reminiscences of plumbers and stonemasons who showed up to work on his property, he collected details on the rough-edged regional daubes, terrines, and matelotes that even in 1960s France were teetering on the edge of extinction.

Just as Walt Whitman's *Leaves of Grass* isn't so much a single book as it is a living body of poetic theory, Olney's *Simple French Food* (1974) has a heart that beats. Julia's *Mastering the Art* reads like a technical manual you prop open when obliged to cook for your husband's boss; *Simple French Food* is a manifesto for living. In 1974, you couldn't just drive to the A&P and buy a bunch of ingredients to start cooking like Olney. You had to begin by changing your life.

Olney mentored Jeremiah Tower, the first formal chef at Chez Panisse, and Olney's lover for a time. Waters made pilgrimages to Solliès-Toucas, and the soul of it, the imperative to stand outside of a spiritless system, the immersive quality of the food, and the yearning for a personal cooking that begins with sourcing—they remain the model for every serious cook working in America today. Olney was the queer little quiet kid on the salad station who ended up making everybody want that spot.

Claiborne was American food's establishment figure, in blazers and tasseled loafers and an open table at Lutèce. Though he was officially closeted until 1982, the date of his rather strange, gimlet-soaked autobiography, *A Feast Made for Laughter*, Claiborne lived the life of the gay professional in mid-twentieth-century America: officially a "bachelor," sexlessly flaunting his taste and discernment, the Mr. Belvedere of food. In 1957, he became food editor of the *New York Times*—a position without much cachet in the '50s, when the *Times'* food section was as dull and service-oriented as the ones in every daily in America. But Claiborne elevated food to the level of cinema or the ballet and made food writing matter, setting the foundation for a far better writer-critic like Jonathan Gold to have a platform as an observer of American culture.

I remember poring over my mom's copy of Claiborne's the *New York Times Cookbook* when I was a kid, stopping on a black-and-white photo of what the caption called a "typical brunch": glasses of fresh-squeezed orange juice sunk into bigger glasses of crushed ice, near a silver basket of shiny, bump-topped brioches. I wanted that life: waking up in a sunny apartment to face the day, the taste of butter and orange sweetness on my tongue like a meditation. Claiborne gave us permission to respect pleasure in eating—even small plea-sures—not as something guilty, but as the received wisdom of culture. *Bitch, we're eating brioche.*

Beard did something similar, though with a particularly American slant. In an era when McDonald's Ray Kroc was shrinking the ham-burger into something you could squeeze with your weak hand into a golf ball–sized lump of grease and starch, Beard convinced us that American food is something ineluctably large, hewn from ingredi-ents as pristine as virgin forest.

In the 1930s, Beard was booted from Reed College in Oregon af-ter someone busted him for making out with another man. Beard's cookbooks have the whiff of sublimated desire: the open-air fanta-sies, stout flavors, abundant fats, and tons and tons of gorgeous meat. Beard's public persona was the bow-tied bachelor gourmand with an unquenchable appetite, and he remade American food in his own triple-XL image. Even before McDonald's mass-produced them, burgers had always been cheap lunch-counter food. Beard made them seem as monumental as an Abercrombie model's torso: three-inch dripping slabs of sirloin you'd ground yourself, grilled over charcoal, and hoisted onto thickly buttered homemade buns—they're the burg-ers on menus of serious restaurants across America. Beard convinced us that burgers had always been that way, a reinvention that made the pursuit of pleasure seem like some timeless American virtue.

Beard made it okay for Americans to be hedonists at the table. Even in his paid endorsements for brands like Birds Eye and Omaha Steaks, Beard convinced us there was no shame in aspiring to be gourmets, the way most of us aspired to drive Cadillacs. *James Beard's American Cookery* (1972) was quietly subversive, a revisionist theory of American food traditions that argued we had always been a nation that embraced the pleasures implicit in scrapple, Boston baked beans, and cheeseburgers.

Beard was called the "dean of American cookery," as if this new doctrine of pleasure had the weight of scholarship behind it. He occupied a curious persona that combined decorum with total self-indulgence. On one of his regular trips to San Francisco in the 1980s, Beard ate at a restaurant where I worked, though on a night I was off. One of the bussers working that night was a young gay guy with boyish American looks. He mentioned to Beard that he wanted to be a baker, and the great man invited him to stop by his hotel the next morning to talk pastry. When the busser arrived, the dean of American food was seated in a chair in the hotel suite's bedroom, wearing a silk robe; Beard's assistant left the room. The aspiring baker told me he looked away at some point in the conversation, and when he looked back Beard, still talking pies and layer cakes, had opened his robe—underneath he was naked. The flustered kid looked away, kept his eyes averted. When he looked back, Beard had closed his robe again, still talking, like nothing had happened. That was the essence of Beard's food: draped in a respectable Sulka robe that was always threatening to drop to expose unashamed hedonism.

That embrace of pleasure—it set the stage for the luxury that defined American restaurant food in the 1980s and '90s, when ahi tuna and caviar and foie gras, crème fraîche and mascarpone showed up on menus in even midpriced restaurants. I think it helped America embrace Slow Food, a movement that values taste over corporate expediency, and argues that the pursuit of pleasure at the table is a political act. But as for gays breaking out in American restaurant kitchens, expressing a queer point of view in their cooking—well, apart from a few mavericks like Elizabeth Falkner, that hasn't really happened. Pastry—like the cold line I was relegated to back in my day—remains a safe space for gays in the kitchen. In a lot of ways we're still on the fringes, even if queer food writers fundamentally changed the way we think about food in this country.

I don't recall the last time Lou made a Roquefort burger for me, but it couldn't have been long after 1970. When I was in junior high, Pat suffered a heart attack and died—his mother and sisters came out from St. Louis and took the body back with them; Lou was not invited to the funeral. Pat's mother and sisters took everything with them: the clothes, the cocktail rings. The irises under the oaks got patchy. Lou drank a lot. He found another boyfriend, a short Canadian who drove a purple AMC Gremlin and who nobody liked, not even my mom (she thought he was "too gay"). I lost track of Lou when I went away to college—my mom said he sold the house and was living in a mobile-home park near the ocean. She hardly ever went to visit.

After college, I moved to San Francisco and got my own boyfriend. He continued my food education. We read passages from Olney's *Simple French Food* out loud, and cooked, and studied each other's pleasure like scholars.

DEBTS OF PLEASURE

By John T. Edge

From the Oxford American

John T. Edge wears a lot of hats—director of the
Southern Foodways Alliance, food columnist for the
New York Times, *Garden & Gun*, and the *Oxford American*,
and all-around promoter of Southern food. Which
sometimes means reminding us who really cooked that
food. . . .

On a summer day in 1949, ballerina Tanaquil Le Clercq, novelist
Donald Windham, painter Buffie Johnson, playwright Tennes-
see Williams, and writer-provocateur Gore Vidal gathered at Café
Nicholson, a bohemian supper club set in the back courtyard of an
antique store on New York City's Upper East Side. It was a heady
moment. Williams had won a Pulitzer Prize the year before. Vidal
had just published *The City and the Pillar*. Beneath the shade trees
in proprietor Johnny Nicholson's garden, they ate and drank. They
smoked and gossiped. They posed and preened, fully aware that photographer Karl Bissinger was there to capture their idyll for posterity.

In those postwar days, the café, decorated in what Nicholson described as a "fin de siècle Caribbean of Cuba style," served as a can-
teen for the creative class and a backdrop for fashion shoots. (Before
it finally closed in 2000, the café also served as an occasional movie
set; Woody Allen filmed scenes from *Bullets Over Broadway* there.)
Paul Robeson was a regular. So was Truman Capote, who sometimes
came bursting into the kitchen looking for biscuits.

Nicholson was the Barnum of their social set, presiding with a
parrot named Lolita on his shoulder. Bissinger, who served the cafe

as an early business partner and a sometimes gardener and host, made a living curating social tableaus for magazines like *Vogue* and *Harper's Bazaar.* During the postwar years he captured everyone from a languorous Henry Miller, lighting a cigarette, to a faunal Capote, reclining in a wicker chaise. But the photograph he shot that afternoon at Café Nicholson has proved his most famous. In a *New York Times* obituary of Bissinger, William Grimes called the scene a "class picture of the young and the talented in the American arts, more than ready for their close-ups."

I first glimpsed the image on a postcard I bought at a Memphis bookstore. In that rendition, the black woman in the background was left unnamed. Because I knew a bit about the history of Café Nicholson and the role that Edna Lewis, the African-American cookery writer and chef, played there, and because my eyesight isn't so great, I wondered, perversely, whether the black woman ferrying what appears to be a pot of tea to the table was Lewis.

Edna Lewis was the most respected African-American cookery writer of the twentieth century. Over the course of a long and varied career, she set type for the *Daily Worker* and labored as a dressmaker for clients like Marilyn Monroe. After working with Johnny Nicholson, she began to write and publish the cookbooks that earned her recognition as the grande doyenne of Southern cookery. Foremost was *The Taste of Country Cooking.* Published in 1976 and re-released in 2006, it was an homage to the land and larder of Freetown, the Virginia community where she grew up. In the foreword to that thirtieth anniversary edition, Alice Waters wrote that Lewis, the granddaughter of freed slaves, was an "inspiration to all of us who are striving to protect both biodiversity and cultural diversity by cooking real food in season and honoring our heritage through the ritual of the table."

If Lewis could go unnamed in a picture that foretold the promise of America in the postwar era, I figured that image might serve as a metaphor for the lesser role Americans have long ascribed to African-American contributions to the culinary arts. Telling that story might be a way for me to pay down the debts of pleasure, both culinary and other, that a privileged white son of the South like me has accrued over a lifetime. This spring, I attended a conference on food and immigrant life at the New School in New York City. Speakers from as close as NYU and as far away as UC Irvine talked about "gastronomic cosmopolitanism," defined "neophilia" and "neophobia," argued for the recovery of the "fragile orality of recipe exchange," and predicted that, for those of us who study food, "epistemological implosions" are on the horizon. (I'm still not sure what that last one meant.) But what really walloped me was a speech by Saru Jayaraman, director of the UC Berkeley Food Labor Research Center and author of *Behind the Kitchen Door: What Every Diner Should Know About the People Who Feed Us.*

The people who put food on our tables, Jayaraman argued, often can't afford to put food on their own. Primary among the contemporary culprits she identified was the National Restaurant Association, which she called the "other N.R.A." Jayaraman said that when Herman Cain, the Republican presidential candidate and former chief executive of Godfather's Pizza, was running the organization in the 1990s, he brokered a deal that has since kept the federal minimum wage for tipped workers like waiters and bartenders artificially deflated at $2.13 per hour.

Wages for non-tipped workers like line cooks have risen, she said, but not at the pace of other professions, nor have they earned benefits enjoyed by other workers, like paid sick days. Workers of color suffer the most. A four-dollar hourly gap separates them from white workers, she reported, citing two primary reasons. Within a single restaurant, workers of color are more likely to be hired for back-of-the-house positions that pay less, like busser and runner, and they rarely get promoted from those positions. Within the industry as a whole, workers of color are more likely to get jobs in fast food, which generally pay less than fine-dining jobs. She was speaking, for the most part, about new immigrants. But listening to her talk on that early spring evening in New York City, I heard what sounded like an old Southern story of the black housekeepers I knew in my Georgia youth, who suffered under the burden of coercive social pressures while scraping by on substandard wages and hand-me-downs, retold in this modern American moment.

Jayaraman's tales gave me a new reason to dig into the story behind Bissinger's photo and the circumstances surrounding Edna Lewis's tenure at Café Nicholson. Reading contemporary reviews of the restaurant, I learned that Lewis rose to fame there while serving simple and elegant dishes like roast chicken, which Clementine Paddleford, the reigning national critic of the day, described as "brown as a chestnut, fresh from the burr." She also favored Lewis's chocolate soufflé, which was "light as a dandelion seed in a wind." In the *New York Times* archives, I discovered that the 1948 partnership offer from Nicholson was timely for Lewis, who grew up on a farm near Freetown, Virginia, but had no other demonstrable experience in the industry. At the time they began working together, Nicholson told a reporter, "Edna was about to take a job as a domestic."

Café Nicholson employed a conceit that presaged the reigning white-tablecloth aesthetic of today. "We'll serve only one thing a day," Nicholson said to Lewis, as they schemed their first menus. "Buy the best quality and I don't see how we can go wrong." Long before farm-to-table was a marketing concept, Lewis was challenging chefs to learn "from those who worked hard, loved the land, and relished the fruits of their labors." Her approach, like her cooking, was straightforward. In a 1989 interview, she told the *New York Times,* "As a child in Virginia, I thought all food tasted delicious. After growing up, I didn't think food tasted the same, so it has been my lifelong effort to try and recapture those good flavors of the past."

The archives at NYU, where Nicholson deposited his papers, yielded a cache of Bissinger photographs that made clear the afternoon he captured in that iconic image was not singular. More important, I discovered that I was not the only one who saw metaphorical possibilities in that 1949 black and white. In October 2007, *Smithsonian* magazine published Gore Vidal's gauzy recollection of that moment at table on Johnny Nicholson's patio. "For me, Karl Bissinger's picture is literally historic, so evocative of a golden moment," he wrote, with the mixture of brio, ego, and privilege that was his signature. "I don't know what effect the picture has on those who now look at it, but I think it perfectly evokes an optimistic time in our history that we are not apt to see again soon."

With that dispatch, Vidal, who wrote the introduction to *The Luminous Years: Portraits at Mid-Century,* a collection of Bissinger's photographs, was finished. But *Smithsonian* wasn't. Two months after Vidal's recollection ran, the magazine published a letter to the editor by Edward Weintraut of Macon, Georgia. "I am troubled that his text does not make the slightest reference to the black waitress," wrote Weintraut, a professor at Mercer University. "I found myself wondering whether she shared Vidal's view about this time being so optimistic, whether she would welcome a revival of the society and culture in which this scene is embedded, whether she enjoyed a similar golden moment as the author and his friends did during lunches at Café Nicholson."

Over the years, I've taken a number of swipes at the "good food" movement. Because I think too many of its members are surfing trends and indulging passions that will prove dalliances, instead of forging a true path toward a better-fed future, I've referred to overzealous twenty-somethings trying to effect change in our broken food system as agriposeurs. After hearing Jayaraman speak, and after tracing the reception of the Bissinger photo, I recognize that my real complaint is that too much of the attention now focused on food skews toward natural resources instead of human resources—and that imbalance has proved more egregious when it comes to people of color.

Recent victories, won by groups like the Coalition of Immokalee Workers, which fights for the rights of tomato pickers in Florida, watermelon harvesters in Georgia, and others, have begun to right the wrongs in the fields. But precious little work has been done to address the plight of restaurant workers. The "meal that arrives at your table when you eat out is not just a product of raw ingredients," Jayaraman wrote in *Behind the Kitchen Door.* "It's a product of the hands that chop, cook, and plate it and the people to whom those hands belong."

It's a product too, of the men and women who serve that meal. Base wages for waiters and waitresses have not risen in more than twenty years. The notion that servers should be ill-paid conjures too easily a time when a permanent American underclass was defined by skin color. Today, the restaurant industry remains one of the last bulwarks of a system in which nameless workers of color labor out of sight, and often out of mind.

Readers with better eyesight than mine probably recognized on first glance that the woman in that photograph was not the same woman who appeared on the cover of *The Taste of Country Cooking,* wearing a lilac dress, picking tomatoes in a summer field bordered with sunflowers. Virginia Reed served the crowd that day. She wasn't a metaphor. She was bone and flesh. Scott Peacock, who co-wrote Lewis's fourth book, *The Gift of Southern Cooking,* published in 2003, and is now finishing a solo book about their relationship, told me that Nicholson and Lewis both called Reed a "character," which I take to mean that she was a woman with a quick wit and a bawdy humor. She was also the cook with a clock in her head, who had an uncanny ability to divine the exact moment when the Café Nicholson chocolate soufflé was ready to pull from the oven. Not much else is known about her life, which was often the case with the black workers who ran Southern restaurants in the twentieth century, and is now often the case with the twenty-first-century immigrants who have replaced them on the cooking line, at the dish bin, and on the dining room floor.

I'm pretty sure that Bissinger did not intend that his photograph be read as a metaphor for the exclusion of black labor from conversations about excellence in the culinary arts. Along the path of my argument, Bissinger was a fellow traveler, which is to say that he, like Lewis, had once been a member of the Communist Party, focused on workers' rights, the sort of thinker who would have owned up to a sin of omission. But I'm the petite bourgeois fellow who forced this issue. To do good work in the world of Southern food, I've come to believe, we have to start by paying down the debts of pleasure we owe to the men and women who sustain our society. For me, that means acknowledging Virginia Reed, the woman with the glowing smile and the clock in her head who brought that pot of tea to the table in 1949. For restaurateurs of today, that means renouncing the lobbying work of the other NRA, paying employees a working wage, and as Jayaraman puts it, taking the high road to profitability.

THE DIGNITY OF CHOCOLATE

By Eagranie Yuh

From Edible Vancouver

Eagranie Yuh is definitely a chocolate expert—a pastry
chef with a master's degree in chemistry who teaches
chocolate-making classes, as well as being a copywriter,
blogger, and freelancer for *Northwest Palate* and *Edible
Vancouver*. Chocolate may be a luxury indulgence to
most of us, but here she discover another side.

This was supposed to be a story about chocolate—specifically, an
unlikely chocolate shop in the Downtown Eastside. It was supposed to be about where chocolate comes from (it grows on trees),
how it is made from cacao beans (through many complex steps requiring chemistry, physics, and a bit of alchemy), and how it becomes
confections and truffles.

I soon learned that this story has everything and nothing to do
with chocolate.

I first met Shelley Bolton in the fall of 2012. Shelley's the director of
social enterprise for the Portland Hotel Society (PHS), which runs
several single-resident-occupancy hotels in the Downtown Eastside.
Shelley's job is to start businesses—more precisely, social enterprises.
PHS operates a few, including a thrift shop called Community, and
an art and sewing shop called The Window. These social enterprises
provide training and work for people with barriers to employment.

Over coffees at Nelson the Seagull, Shelley shared her plan to
open a chocolate shop and coffee roastery next door at 319 Carrall
Street. And not just any chocolate shop: one that would source its

own beans and turn them into chocolate, often called bean-to-bar chocolate. The shop would use the chocolate in confections and drinks.

Shelley and I met through a mutual friend—one Nat Bletter, co-founder of Madre Chocolate in Hawaii. Madre Chocolate is one of the companies that comprise the bean-to-bar chocolate movement in the United States. Since 2008, I've been connecting with these small-scale chocolate makers to help share their stories. The more I've learned about their work, the more I've realized that it's a labour of love, and often of heartbreak. I've learned that making chocolate is expensive and risky, and that it's hard to make good chocolate.

What I hadn't yet learned is that where Shelley goes, magic follows.

Leading up to the shop's opening in April 2013, Shelley hired eight women, collectively called "the ladies." Since East Van Roasters is on the ground level of the Rainier Hotel, it's fitting that the ladies, at least initially, were residents of the Rainier.

Shelley also recruited Merri Schwartz—former pastry chef at C and Quattro, and founder of Growing Chefs!—to teach the ladies how to make bars and bonbons. Merri was skeptical. Could culinary novices really create fine, polished products? But the class went well, one thing led to another, and Merri agreed to be the shop's head chocolatier.

East Van Roasters gets its cacao beans directly from farmers. The beans, which arrive astringent and ghostly in enormous burlap sacks, are coaxed into their burnished, full-flavoured selves when roasted. From there they are destined to be ground into a paste, mixed with sugar, and refined into smooth, luxurious dark chocolate. There's just one problem: the cacao beans are trapped inside a papery husk, which must be removed in a process called winnowing. Larger chocolate makers have winnowing machines; East Van Roasters has the ladies.

So on a bright, brisk day this past January, I join two of the ladies in the shop's back room. One of them, Sheree, agrees to be in this story. Her nails painted like fire engines, she shows me how to gently press each bean between my fingers. The husk falls away to reveal a perfectly shiny bean, which she deposits in a small bowl.

Over the rattle of beans and husks, we talk. Sheree lives on the third floor of the Rainier Hotel with Charlie, her three-legged cat. She describes herself as happy, healthy, and healthy-minded. She likes to write, and one of her stories—about robbing a bank twenty-ish years ago, only to get caught jaywalking afterwards—was published in an anthology.

Back then she was using heroin. She's been homeless, including a stint living in Stanley Park, and has been hospitalized a number of times. "I was really not taking care of myself properly . . . I'm bipolar . . . I was completely delusional and using street drugs, and not able to make good choices for myself." She looks at me, her bright eyes framed by a touch of mascara.

"Shelley's got great vision. [When] she told me she was going to open a chocolate shop, I couldn't vision it down here . . . Sure enough, here we are."

And here Sheree is. "There's three different types [of beans] we do—Peru, Dominican Republic, and Madagascar," she says. The Madagascar, which we've been winnowing, is the easiest. She grabs a few beans (she calls them nuts) from a bucket behind her. "Here's a Dominican nut. You need to cut it along the seam, along the side," she says, demonstrating with her bird's-beak paring knife. "You can see it's a lot more work, right?"

I mimic her technique as best as I can, then pop the liberated bean into my mouth. It tastes of freshly pressed olive oil and a grassy field on a spring day. Sheree inspects the bowl of Madagascan beans in front of us, picking one in particular and placing it in my palm. I taste it. It's bright, fruity, citrusy. "See the difference? Tasty, right." When she says "right," it's half question, half statement.

Sheree has come a long way since moving into the Rainier five years ago. "I have my family back in my life, and that's not something I thought would be possible again . . . Now that I've gotten older I can see how painful it must have been to see someone who's so hell-bent on destroying themselves, whether it's deliberate or not."

I ask what East Van Roasters means to her. "It's great to have some income coming in, and I leave here and I feel good about myself . . . I feel like a productive person. And even though what we're doing [winnowing] . . . you could look at this as menial, but it's the most important part of it, right. Without the nuts, there's no chocolate."

We keep on winnowing. "It was my birthday yesterday," she says. "I turned 45 yesterday."

Winnowing is one of the biggest jobs at East Van Roasters, but it's not the only one. As we work, one of the ladies runs the front cash. At Christmas, Sheree wrapped the finished chocolate bars in gold foil. "It's like origami from hell when you first start, right."

Raven, another one of the ladies, started working one day a week, and now works five. "I like the cleanup at the end of the day," she says over the hum of the dishwasher. "It's not my dream career by any means, but it keeps my mind stable."

It's not just the ladies who are finding their way. After working for more than a decade in kitchens where tough love rules, Merri has found joy in a new way to work. "The restaurant industry is just so harsh," she says as she lines heart-shaped molds with chocolate. "I'd come to believe that was the way to get best results, the way to train people. I had to retrain myself to approach problems with a whole different attitude, a different level of compassion."

Meanwhile, Shelley is nursing a batch of chocolate. Today she's making chocolate, but we've both learned that her job is much more than that. She's part counsellor, part wellness advisor, part negotiator. And while she may be the boss, she doesn't rule with power.

"If people don't feel respected and aren't given the ability to heal themselves, no matter what you try to teach them, they won't trust themselves to do the work," she says. "They need to feel that they are needed and a part of something bigger than themselves, and I think that's what we give people here."

All this time, a question has been tickling the edges of my brain. It finally crystallizes: of all the businesses to start, why this one? The answer is remarkably practical, yet philosophical. Because it's so labour-intensive, making bean-to-bar chocolate means more jobs. But more than that, says Shelley, "there's beauty in taking a raw product and creating something that's really refined and considered high quality."

For a moment, I have to remind myself that we're talking about chocolate.

The Indulgence of Pickled Baloney

By Silas House

From Gravy

∽⦿∾

Novelist/playwright/music journalist Silas House is
the chair of Appalachian Studies at Berea College in his
native Kentucky. His books (*Clay's Quilt, Parchment of
Leaves, Same Sun Here*) illuminate the rural Southern
experience through finely observed details of daily
life—like a jar of pickled baloney.

Dot's Grocery, owned by my aunt, was the community center
of tiny Fariston, Kentucky: a therapist's office, sometimes a
church, and—always—a storytelling school. Everyone gathered there
to gossip and to seek the sage kitchen wisdom of Dot. She kept a
Virginia Slim permanently perched in her fuchsia-lipsticked mouth
and latched her steely blue-eyed gaze on her customers while they
spilled their guts and sought her advice. A few times I witnessed
prayer services there. The epicenter of a largely Holiness community
was hard-pressed to escape that, after all. There were always the big
tales, swirling around like the twisting smoke of the regulars' cigarettes (in my memory, all of them smoked, everyone).

Looking back, the stories are what matter the most. But when I
was a child in the 1980s my favorite things were the cakes-and-candy
rack, the old-timey Coke cooler with the silver sliding doors on top,
and the huge jar of pickled baloney that sat on the counter next to
the cash register. Beside it were a loose roll of paper towels, a box
of wax paper, a sleeve or two of Premium saltines, and a large Old
Hickory–brand knife.

Cutting pickled baloney was a rite of passage, usually reserved for children who were past the age of ten. That may sound young to wield a butcher knife, but we were country children who had attended hog killings, watched the dressing of squirrels, cleaned our own fish, and stood in chairs by the stove so we could learn to cook.

The pickled baloney, submerged in vinegar, was one corkscrew of delicious processed meat. I did not know then, and wouldn't have cared, that baloney is usually made up of the afterthoughts of pork or beef: organs, trimmings, and the like. All I knew was that it was scrumptious paired with an ice-cold Dr Pepper and a handful of saltines. Dot indulged me with treats when I came to the store, and I usually asked if, instead of getting a free banana Moon Pie or a Bit-O-Honey, I could opt for pickled baloney. "Why sure," Dot always answered, expelling two wisps of blue smoke with her words.

Besides the taste, which my Uncle Dave said was "so good you had to pat your foot to eat it," there was the added bonus of brandishing the knife and sawing off my own piece, proving I was not a little boy anymore. I was an eleven-year-old eater of pickled baloney.

Pickled baloney was a delicacy in the rural stores of Appalachia, showcased right on the counter, where no one could miss it. Most people headed straight for that jar when they were sitting for a spell at Dot's. Others eyed the jar with desire, knowing they couldn't afford to add it to their bill. Dot's thrived in that last period of the jottemdown store, a small community grocery where local folks could buy on credit. The name referred to the fact that such stores kept a spiral-bound notebook on the counter to "jot down" purchases. Each customer had their own page and each month Dot totaled up what they owed. They came in on payday and paid off their debts. Dot seldom turned anyone down for more credit, even if they owed her for months on end. After all, she had opened the store as a single mother supporting her two daughters.

Many people I know now scoff at the very idea of eating baloney, much less *pickled* baloney. They do not understand that the purchase of such a thing was an extravagance, an indulgence. This was a different time. A different world. I knew no one who went to the movies or shopped on a whim. These luxuries required a long period of saving. They had to be planned far in advance.

We were the progeny of people who had been very, very poor.

And although I've painted the hamlet of Fariston as a romantic, bucolic place where people had the live-long day to gather around a woodstove in a little store to tell stories, the truth is much more complex than that. This was a place where poverty existed alongside great wealth.

A few yards from Dot's Grocery was a sprawling trailer park occupied by people who worked minimum-wage jobs in fast-food restaurants or at the Dollar General. Dogs meandered about the dirt yards, and children played on the porches while their fathers slept after working third shift or their mothers hung out lines of clothes that flapped in the wind.

Just past the trailer park loomed the mansion owned by a coal baron, built to resemble Southfork from TV's *Dallas*. Its opulence proclaimed, "We made it. You did not." The house was a few miles from the massive strip mine that destroyed that part of the county. The riches pulled from that mine by my people built the manor, but no matter: The baron had a three-car garage. And twelve-foot pillars flanked the front porch.

I am sure that the people in the South Fork mansion didn't serve pickled baloney hors d'oeuvres at their parties. But for people raised like my parents, pickled baloney was a symbol of attainment.

When she bought one of the gallon jars, my mother would return from the grocery with giddy excitement. As children, she and my father had never been allowed such indulgences. Both grew up in the sort of poverty people always associate with Appalachia. Still, they were quick to tell you they had never been hungry. Country people were good at providing food for themselves, whether by growing it, bartering for it, or making it stretch. Snacks were rare and sniffed of affluence.

By the time I was a child my parents had worked so long and so hard they had firmly rooted us in the middle class. We did not have a house that looked like J.R. and Sue Ellen's, but we had recently left the trailer park and moved into a small five-room house with a grassy yard dotted by pink-blossomed dogwood trees. Buying pickled baloney, which might be considered the lowest of foods, meant something to my family and our community.

Every once in a while, I still get a terrific craving for pickled baloney. I eat it with a strange mixture of guilt, because I know what's in it, and delicious nostalgia for a place and time that is gone forever. Food is more than merely taste or nourishment. In Appalachia, food is memory and heritage.

Today, when I cut a hunk of meat off that corkscrew, when I draw in the sharp fragrance of vinegar as I peel off the casing and take a bite, I remember the customers in Dot's Grocery. Their joys and sorrows, always on full display. I recall afternoons spent with my father after he woke up, before he left to work the third shift. I remember my Aunt Dot, gone now, and the way she cared for the whole community, provided a place for them, jotted down their purchases, and sometimes wadded up a whole sheet of debt when she realized a family was doing all they could to support themselves. That way of life is gone now, and I miss it so badly, in all of its awfulness and beauty.

AUSTERITY MEASURES

By Anna Roth

From SF Weekly

As lead food critic for this alternative weekly, Seattle
native Anna Roth—author of the guidebook *West
Coast Road Eats*—homes in on one of America's most
intriguing food cities. Somehow, amid all the artisanal
breads and trendy pop-ups, she found time to consider
food from a different, less privileged angle.

The marshmallow was the best thing I'd eaten in days, a soft,
white, silky hit of pure sugar that went straight to all the pleasure centers in my brain. Four days earlier, I wouldn't have believed
that a puff of corn syrup could bring me so much happiness.

I was participating in the Hunger Challenge, an initiative put on
by the San Francisco and Marin Food Bank to raise awareness about
poverty and food insecurity in the Bay Area. For five days, 150 participants and I—chefs, journalists, and regular people who signed up
on the Food Bank's website—were to live on a $4.50-per-day food
allowance, about the amount provided by SNAP (the government's
Supplemental Nutrition Assistance Program, formerly known as
food stamps). The meager budget was supplemented by pantry supplies from the Food Bank, a weekly allotment of produce, protein,
and dry goods that more than 150,000 individuals in San Francisco
and Marin counties depend on to survive.

Going in, I was aware that this was an imperfect simulation.
Choosing to live on a limited food budget for five days is nothing like
doing it out of necessity, and in my more uncomfortable moments I
wondered if I were any better than the people who take tours of the

Mumbai slums and then return to their luxury hotels, congratulating themselves on having a character-building experience. I knew that if I forgot my lunch or got stranded somewhere, a sandwich was just a swipe of my debit card away. And I knew that at the end of the week I would return to a life of overabundance. Which maybe made it that much more important: I thought about food all day, but I didn't think about what it meant to live without it.

I woke up Monday morning and ate a multigrain English muffin with peanut butter (both purchased on sale at Safeway the day before) before heading to the Food Bank on Potrero Hill for a tour and pantry-supply pickup. Executive Director Paul Ash walked us through the warehouse, stacked to the ceiling with pallets of canned beans, fruit juice, tomato sauce, cereal, applesauce, and other goods that the Food Bank provides to families, schools, and charitable organizations. After the tour, we lined up to get our pantry allotment. My two bags of groceries included a pound of rice, a half-dozen eggs, a small watermelon, a cantaloupe, two baskets of strawberries, three large carrots, two tomatoes, four potatoes, two onions, two oranges, two pears, and four plums. This isn't going to be so bad, I thought.

Two hours later, facing another English muffin with peanut butter, I gave in and went to McDonald's for a McChicken sandwich from the dollar menu. It was warm, tasted good, and filled me up with very little expended effort. I realized that if I were living on this budget permanently, McDonald's—a chain I hadn't patronized for years out of principle—would probably play a regular role in my diet.

The next few days were a blur of cranky, lightheaded hours punctuated by poorly cooked meals of beans, rice, potatoes, and eggs. A year of living off restaurant food had made me rusty in the kitchen, and when the chickpeas never softened and I over-peppered the black beans, I had to eat them anyway. Food usually doubles as entertainment in my life, but all these meals did was fill my stomach. Later in the week, I discovered that chefs participating in the challenge were facing the same thing. "Honestly, it's been tough trying to come up with food that is tasty, satisfying, and healthy on a SNAP budget," wrote Lincoln Carson, corporate pastry chef for Michael Mina, on Instagram. The sentiment was echoed by Central Kitchen's Ryan Pollnow, who says he wasn't thinking of it as the "Hunger

Challenge" as much as the "Food Enjoyment Challenge." None of us were starving, but we were far from satisfied.

On Wednesday, I went to St. Anthony's for a free lunch. The Tenderloin nonprofit gives out about 3,000 meals a day to anyone who shows up, and about half of its annual 2 million pounds of food comes from the Food Bank. The dining room was organized chaos. An emergency medical situation was partially obscured by a sheet in the corner. Lunch was a cafeteria tray of macaroni and cheese, a starchy salad, a banana, a slice of multigrain bread, a cup of juice, and four marshmallows. I ate with glee, grateful for the calories, grateful for a meal I didn't have to plan and prepare myself, grateful for the marshmallows I saved in a St. Anthony's-provided baggie and would savor slowly at my desk over the next few days.

Later that day, I caught up with Paul Ash of the Food Bank to talk about the bigger picture of hunger in San Francisco. One of the main causes, he says, is the high cost of living in the city. Because the qualifying amount for SNAP benefits is the same across the country, a person might make more dollars per hour here than someone in rural Pennsylvania, but have less buying power with that dollar.

I brought up my feelings of dilettantism; my trip to St. Anthony's had reminded me how far removed I was from poverty, even when I was pretending not to be. "If all we did is experience this and go back to our regular lives and didn't do anything differently, that would be kind of self-satisfying," he says. He brought up the bill currently in the House of Representatives to cut the SNAP budget by $40 billion, and how he's hoping this challenge will encourage people to speak out. "Active citizenry approaches issues from a base of knowledge, a base of understanding. It's easy to see data, but this is about showing people how it feels, and how you act differently [when you're living with food insecurity]."

And the Hunger Challenge was definitely having an impact on my life. I felt isolated and alone. A visit to the supermarket was just a reminder of all the things I couldn't buy. An invitation from my friends was just a reminder of all the bars and restaurants I couldn't afford. I didn't have much time to go out, anyway, with all the planning and cooking I had to do just to make enough food to get me through the day. On Wednesday night I was feeling so low, physically and psychologically, that I knew I had to make a good dinner. I spent half of my remaining budget on six chicken legs, a head of kale, and a lemon. That night I made the best meal I ate all week, with enough leftovers to last a few days. It was a kind of victory.

On Friday, I went back to the Food Bank and had lunch with the staff, who were all participating in the challenge together. The sense of camaraderie was palpable as they cooked their lunches in the kitchen, swapping recipe ideas and the names of stores where they'd found the best deals. We talked about our separate experiences and I was gratified to hear how similar theirs had been to mine. Those who'd been most successful on the challenge were the ones who'd had time—to comparison-shop or prepare food—or kitchen know-how, and had livened up their week with homemade potato chips, pickled watermelon rind, and pizza. "It's not just about the food, it's about knowing what to do with it and having the time to do those things," says Teri Olle, associate director of policy and advocacy.

You also need community, a lesson brought home by a phone conversation with Glenda Robinzine, a 65-year-old San Francisco resident who depends on the Food Bank every week. She said she'd just taken a pound cake out of the oven, made from butter and cake mix she'd received, and was planning to use her supplies to make peanut brittle, banana bread, pecan pralines, and other goodies for a Food Bank fundraiser she was holding at her church the next weekend. I asked if it was hard to plan ahead, not knowing what she'd receive every week. "I like to be surprised," she says, adding that she usually calls a friend in Bayview, who receives her Food Bank delivery a day before, to find out what might be coming.

Robinzine now lives in an assisted living facility; before she moved there, before she was homeless, before she was diagnosed with cancer, she volunteered at her church, giving out food to people who needed it. "Now I'm the one who needs it. Now I'm the one who's dependent on it," she says. "I never thought I would be, but I am."

The day after the Hunger Challenge ended, I went to Bi-Rite for groceries. I didn't know if I'd feel Veblenesque outrage at the Bay Area foodie lifestyle, but instead all I saw was community. Bi-Rite supports family farms and small local businesses, and it donates or sells food at low cost to charitable organizations like St. Anthony's. My week on the Challenge had made me feel stressed and alienated, but it also made me aware of all the ways, large and small, that we're all taking care of each other instead of behaving as though we live in different worlds.

With that in mind, it was as hard to adjust to abundance as it had been to austerity. My first meal after it ended was a rich bowl of tonkotsu ramen at a hip Mission spot that cost more than half of my food budget for the week. I threw it up.

WAITING FOR THE 8TH

By Eli Saslow

From the Washington Post

❦

In a year-long series that won him a 2014 Pulitzer Prize, *Washington Post** staff reporter Eli Saslow examined in depth the struggling lives of Americans in the food stamp system. Here's one poignant chapter in that big-picture story.

S
he believed you could be poor without appearing poor, so Raphael Richmond, 41, attached her eyelash extensions, straightened her auburn wig and sprayed her neck with perfume as she reached for another cigarette. "For my nerves," she explained, even though doctors already had written eight prescriptions to help her combat the wears of stress. She blew smoke into the living room and waited until her eldest daughter, Tiara, 22, descended the stairs in new sneakers and a flat-brimmed baseball cap.

"I look okay?" Tiara asked.

"Fresh and proper," Raphael said, and then they left to stand in line for boxes of donated food and day-old bread.

It was Thursday, which meant giveaways at a place called Bread for the City. Fridays were free medical care at the clinic in Southeast Washington. Saturdays were the food pantry at Ambassador Baptist

---

Church. The 1st of each month was a disability check, the 2nd was government cash assistance and the 8th was food stamps. "November FREEBIES," read a flier attached to their fridge, a listing of daily handouts that looked the same as October's freebies, and September's freebies, and the schedule of dependency that had helped sustain Raphael's family for three generations and counting.

Except this month had introduced a historic shift. The nation's food stamp program had just undergone its biggest cut in 50 years, the beginning of an attempt by Congress to dramatically shrink the government's fastest-growing entitlement program, which had tripled in cost during the past decade to almost $80 billion each year. Starting in November, more than 47 million Americans had experienced decreases in their monthly benefit, averaging about 7 percent. For the Richmonds, it was more. Not far across the Anacostia River from their house, Congress was already busy debating the size and ramifications of the next cut, likely to be included in the farm bill early next year.

It was a debate not only about financial reform but also about cultural transformation. In a country where 7 million people had been receiving food assistance for a decade or longer, the challenge for some in government was how to wean the next generation from a cycle of long-term dependency.

Raphael's challenge was both more pressing and more basic: Her monthly allotment of $290 in food assistance had been reduced to $246. She already had spent the entire balance on two carts of groceries at Save a Lot. There were 22 days left until the 8th.

"Mama's version of the hunger games," was how she sometimes explained the predicament to her six children, five of whom still lived with her, ranging in age from 11 to 22.

Feeding a family on zero income always had required ingenuity; she took the lights out of their refrigerator to save money on the electric bill and locked snack foods in a plastic tub in her bedroom to ration them throughout the month. In September, when she first heard rumors of an impending cut, she had taken Tiara to sign up for a food stamp card of her own, thereby increasing the family's take. Here was one surprising result of a government reduction: one new recipient added to the rolls. "A daughter looking out for her mother," was how Raphael had explained it, bragging to friends, but Tiara was less enthused. She chose not to carry the Electronic Benefit Transfer (EBT) card in her wallet, believing from personal experience that people who entered into the system tended to rely on it forever. "I'm not wanting to sign over my independence for good," she said.

Now, as they walked together up Good Hope Road toward the food bank, they took turns using a cellphone and passed a cigarette back and forth. "I used to apply for jobs at all these places," Tiara said, pointing out the convenience stores and check-cashing shops that lined the road. She also had tried to improve her job prospects by attending a health-care training program ("medical school," she called it) and a seminar on Microsoft Word ("a computer diploma"), and yet her last paid work had come five months earlier for a temp agency that had yet to pay her the $170 she was owed.

"I'm grown, and I don't own nothing," Tiara said, flicking away the cigarette. "It's pathetic."

"Pathetic?" Raphael said, rolling the word out of her mouth, considering it. "How you figure that?"

"Us going around, getting things, relying on people who treat us like nothing. I mean, I'm having to ask you for money we don't have."

"You ain't stealing. You ain't begging. We're just surviving, best we can."

Tiara flipped up the hood of her sweatshirt and walked ahead.

"Sur-viv-ing. You hear me?" Raphael called after her. "We're getting it while we can."

They walked into Bread for the City, where 40 people were crowded into the waiting room, and where the food line was a steady procession toward disappointment. "No more deer meat," read one sign. "Pick a holiday bag OR a regular bag. You cannot receive both," read the next. "Only one visit per month," read another. "Food is intended to last for three days," read the last notice, right by the counter, where Raphael handed over her number to a volunteer and waited for her bag of food.

"Thank you," she said when the bag came back three minutes later, filled with turkey, applesauce, yams and five cans of greens. Raphael turned away from the counter, doing the math in her head.

"So that's three days," she said to Tiara on their way out the door. "What are we supposed to do about the rest?"

"Lady Can Cook"

For all of her life, Raphael had been counting down to the 8th. It was her most reliable event, a monthly promise that she would have enough to eat when her parents spent their cash on heroin, or when asbestos and carbon monoxide forced her family to move houses three times in a year, or when a series of five "gone again" men fathered her six children and provided a total of $20 in monthly child support. Her life had been a swinging pendulum of uncertainty-of bad health, eviction and the sudden deaths of loved ones. But the 8th had always come, and the federal money had always been deposited on time into her account. "The golden date," she called it.

Only once, when she was in her early 30s, had she lived without government assistance. She had moved her children into a two-bedroom apartment near the Southwest waterfront and signed a lease for $925, working as a home health aide during the day and as a prep cook at RFK Stadium at night. "Climbing the ladder," she said, but then came the reality of what that meant. The increase in her income disqualified her from food stamps, and buying food with cash left nothing to pay the gas bill, and cutting off the heat made the winter seem endless, and the combination of the cold house and the 60-hour workweeks aggravated her arthritis, damaged her heart and compelled her to quit work and apply for disability.

After nine months, she packed three duffel bags and took a bus to the homeless shelter. Her family spent two months in the shelter and two years in transitional housing and then received a voucher for a four-bedroom house in Anacostia with a leaky ceiling and a front-porch view of a highway underpass. The subsidized rent was $139 a month. She covered the shag carpeting with plastic mats and decorated the living-room walls with Japanese characters for peace, tranquility and good health.

"I feel like I'm having a heart attack," she said now, sitting in that living room, 17 days before the 8th arrived again.

"A real one or a stress one?" Tiara asked, her eyes still glued to a rap video on the cellphone. In the past two years, she had taken her mother to the emergency room for stress, panic attacks, leg numbness and anxiety.

"Maybe I'm just depressed," Raphael said. "If I could just have a good day. One day with no stresses."

"Why don't you cook?" Tiara suggested.

It was the activity that made Raphael happiest. Her grandmother had worked as a cook for President Jimmy Carter in the White House, and her mother had used most of her monthly food stamps to make Sunday dinners for her 14 children. One of Raphael's most vivid memories was of her only trip to a sushi restaurant, in downtown Washington, where the colors of the fish seemed "more like art than food." Now she opened her freezer and grabbed a 32-pack of quarter-pound hamburgers, bought at Save a Lot for $7.99.

Raphael obsessed over the future of the food stamp program in part because she herself had become a neighborhood safety net, regularly feeding a group of castoffs who called her "mom." There were her own children at home: ages 11, 13, 15, 17 and 22, plus a 25-year-old living in Maryland. Then there were the twin 2-year-olds whose mother—Raphael's sister—disappeared for such long stretches Raphael had started potty training; and one of her children's friends who was always avoiding her foster parents; and the cousin who stayed a week in the living room in exchange for the last $27 on her EBT card. "No judgment, just love," was Raphael's motto. She believed people who had the least were also the most likely to give. "We know what it's like to suffer," she said. "That's the problem with this craziness going on right now. How many of those people cutting stamps are using stamps to eat? They're trying to make their budget, and I'm trying to make mine, but I'm the one who has to keep stretching noodles and apologizing to my family."

She watched the burgers sizzle on the electric stove. The smell of meat filled the house. She put on an apron as Tiara turned up some music.

"Hey, Ma, let me take a video of you cooking," Tiara said, taking out the cellphone, hitting record.

"We're eating good," Raphael said, dicing an onion and tossing it in with the burgers.

"Mm-hmmm. Lady can cook," Tiara said.

"You know it, baby," Raphael said, smiling at the camera. "We're in the fat part of the month."

Options

A week later, all 32 burgers gone, Tiara grabbed a package of instant noodles to make as her lunch for the third consecutive day. "I'm so bored of this," she said, mixing in vinegar, butter and black pepper. She sat down to eat and opened a newspaper to the job listings, compelled more by habit than ambition.

The ads made it sound so easy to get a job in the budding economic recovery of 2013—"Hiring now!" one read; "Start tomorrow!" promised another—but recent experience made Tiara believe she had better odds "playing lotto," she said. The unemployment rate in Ward 8 was 24 percent, triple the national average, and there were an estimated 13 job seekers for every open position. She had been offered a security job, but first the company wanted $500 to train her. Marriott had openings at a new hotel, but the application required her to submit a background check online. So she had gone to the police station and paid $9 for a form showing that she had no criminal record. And then enrolled with a nonprofit group that gave out free computers and scanners, since the ones at the nearby library always seemed to be broken. And then learned that she could only pick up the computer in Rockville, four bus transfers and a Metro ride away.

The latest advice from a caseworker assigned to help with her job search was to "make a list of options" and "stay prayerful," but lately Tiara sounded more like resigned in the songs she wrote under the rap moniker Madame T. "This is the life I was dealt with," she wrote in one.

"I'm sick of these job counselors," she said, pushing aside the classifieds. "What do they know? They have a job. They go home. They go on vacation."

"When God is ready for you to have certain things, you are going to have it," Raphael said.

"I bet it was better in the days of Martin Luther King, for real," Tiara said. "At least back then people were angry. They were doing something. How do they expect us to live? We got no jobs, no opportunities, and now they're cutting our benefits? What's Obama doing, for real? How can you be a good president when half of your own city is like this? Yo, Mr. President! We're here, right under your nose, living, struggling, going nowhere."

For 22 years, Tiara had successfully avoided what she referred to as the "ghetto woman traps." She had arrived at adulthood single and childless, a talented musician with a high school diploma and a clean record—"a miracle," Raphael called her. And yet none of those successes had earned her anything like stability, and she had little in her life that qualified as support. Her mother, fearing the next trip to the emergency room, had made her the default guardian for four younger siblings. Her absentee father, a Puerto Rican, had given her nothing but smooth brown skin, soft dreadlocks and, with some reluctance a few years earlier, a phone number where he could be reached in case of emergencies. Believing her life consisted of one long emergency, Tiara had called him the next day, only to learn the number was fake.

At the moment, the only "options" she could list for her case-worker were the new EBT card with her name on it and a food training class hosted by DC Central Kitchen. The class was free, but it was also three months of training that didn't guarantee a job. The class flier had been sitting on the kitchen table for weeks. "Must be able to lift 50 pounds," it read. Must stand for hours. Must work in a noisy environment.

"You remember your cousin Anthony?" Raphael asked one day. "He took that class, couldn't fry an egg, and he came out making $13 an hour cooking for the embassies."

"Who cares about embassies?" Tiara said.

"Thirteen an hour. You care about that?"

"No matter how many certificates I get, nobody's hiring. What's the point? I'm tired of trying for these things."

"You can stop trying if you want," Raphael said. "But that won't make things any easier."

Waiting

The alarm sounded one morning in the last week of November at 5:15, and Raphael stumbled throughout the dark and stepped over three relatives sharing an air mattress in the living room. She opened the door to the basement, where her children were sleeping, and yelled down the stairs. "Let's go, y'all!" she called. "It's time to get in line." Nobody answered, so she shouted again. "Come on! I need this!" A third time. "Get up and execute the damn game!"

Of all the stereotypes about urban poverty, the one Raphael re-sented most was the notion that a dependent life is a lazy life. Their food supply was down to four boxes of mac-and-cheese, three loaves of white bread, juice, rice and a few dozen canned goods. "Lazy would be getting in a car, turning on the heat, going to the grocery store and picking out some bacon," she said. Instead, she headed outside in 25-degree weather to walk a mile with three of her children in hooded sweatshirts and windbreakers, some of the best winter clothing they owned, so they could wait as long as it took for whatever food they were given.

"You know that real people are still sleeping now, right?" said her son Tiere, 17, who had come to help his mother carry home her grocery bags. "This is too damn early."

They turned a corner toward the church and saw that, in fact, they had come too late. The pantry wouldn't open for another hour, but already the line stretched two blocks, a collection of 250 people who had brought their own grocery carts, shopping bags and lawn chairs. Single mothers held their babies and paced to stay warm. A disabled man inched forward in his motorized scooter. Off in the distance, closer to the church, Tiara could see another line, just as long as hers. "What's that?" she asked the man standing in front of her, and he explained that because the pantry was especially busy before the holidays it had decided to divide the wait between two lines. Theirs was only for tickets, which would then earn them placement in the next line for food.

"This is crazy," Tiara said, leaning against a nearby car. "We should be leaving."

"It is what it is, T," Raphael said. "At least we're here. We're doing it. We're trying."

They inched forward for the next few hours, taking turns warming up in a nearby convenience store. Tiere lost sensation in his toes, so he went home to bed and his youngest brother, Anthony, 15, replaced him in line. Tiara's fingers trembled, so she tried to warm them by holding her mother's lit cigarette. They traded tips with people nearby about other food giveaways later in the day, the economy of Southeast Washington at the end of a month: D.C. Council member Marion Barry was handing out turkeys at 1 p.m. and Grace Memorial had vegetables at 3. One elderly woman stepped out of line to ask a pantry supervisor if she could use the church bathroom. "I'm sorry," the supervisor said, explaining that the bathrooms were off-limits because someone had vandalized them the week before. "All I can ask is please don't come here to wait at 4 or 5 in the morning," the supervisor said. "That's too many hours to be standing in line outside. It's getting cold. It's dangerous."

But even as she spoke, the people who had arrived at 4 or 5 began walking out of the pantry with full grocery carts of cakes, bread, Coke, cereal, hot dogs and collard greens. "High-end product," Raphael said, whistling as they passed. She wrapped her arm around Tiara to keep warm and tucked her chin under the collar of her coat.

An hour later, as Raphael neared the front of the line, a pantry volunteer made an announcement. "Plenty of bread, onions and sweet potatoes," he said, before explaining they had only 17 packages of nonperishable food left to give. Tiara counted the people in line. "We're 26th," she said, kicking the curb. "Count again," Raphael said. "Twenty-sixth," Tiara said again. "Been waiting out here for nothing."

Tiara walked after the pantry volunteer and gently tugged at his coat. "Can we go to the front if my mom's on disability?" she asked.

"Sorry," he said.

"If she's a regular?"

"Sorry," he said again.

A middle-age man cut in front of Anthony in line, and Raphael stamped her foot. "No. Hell no!" she shouted. "That's a baby, and you a grown-ass man." The man held up his hand to apologize and stepped back to his original spot. "What you need to do is get yourself a job," Raphael said, still fuming as she reached the front of the line and a volunteer ushered her into the emptying pantry.

The first table had only hot-dog buns. "Don't pout," Raphael told her children. "Be grateful for what God gives you."

The second was covered with onions. "Some countries got nothing," Raphael said. "They drink dirty water."

The third table was covered with a mound of sweet potatoes, and Raphael filled a 20-pound bag with the biggest ones she could find. A volunteer recognized her and brought out six pastries, frosted bear claws from a secret stash inside the church. "Sorry we don't have more," the volunteer said.

"That's okay," Raphael said. "This is more than we had before."

They walked back down Good Hope Road, passing a check-cashing store, a memorial for a gunshot victim and a mural with a quote from Frederick Douglass. "If there is no struggle, there is no progress," the quote read. It was the kind of walk that made them feel progressively better about the 20 pounds of sweet potatoes in their bag. "Mash 'em, boil 'em, fry 'em, pie 'em," Raphael said, imagining the dishes she could prepare.

A few blocks from their house, they walked through a park where seven people were sleeping on benches. One of them, a woman wrapped in a blanket, stretched out her hand. "Please," she said. "Can you help?"

"We all hurting," Tiara said. But she stopped and reached into their bag from the pantry. "Here," she said, and she handed over one of the pastries.

"The Golden Date"

One week left until the 8th, and now each scrounge through their emptied refrigerator was a reminder of what they didn't have and all the reasons they didn't have it. They weren't so much hungry as bored, anxious, tired, depressed. Tiere, normally a reliable student who talked about wanting to attend college, skipped school the Monday after Thanksgiving and stayed in the basement, dodging the truancy officer. Raphael turned off every light in the house to save money. Then, when her children kept turning them back on, she unscrewed the light bulbs. She skipped breakfasts and subsisted on coffee. Her blood sugar spiked, her feet went numb and she started walking around the house with a cane. Her temper flared. Her generosity wore thin.

"All you people got to go. Now," Raphael said, with six days left until the 8th, kicking out most of her relatives except for her children.

"I need to get out of this place before I flip, for real," Tiara said, with five days left. "Atlanta, Chicago, Charlotte—I'm talking about fleeing, anywhere."

"What are we going to do?" said Raphael, with four days left.

"I'm getting serious about signing up for that cooking class," Tiara said, with three days.

"I can't live like this," Raphael said, with two days.

"I feel like a damn failure," Tiara said, on the last day.

"Thank you, Jesus!" Raphael said on the morning of the 8th, back in the aisles of Save a Lot to purchase her family's groceries for the month, pushing two carts that creaked under the weight of 40 pounds of meat, 12 boxes of cereal, 11 packages of cheese and 75 bottles of juice. She set her items on the conveyer belt and handed the cashier her EBT card. "Take the whole balance off there," she said. And then, a minute later, she also handed over Tiara's card. "Take the whole balance, too," she said.

"Okay. You're cashed out," the cashier said, handing back both cards as the total hit $420. Raphael stared at the 35 items still on the conveyer belt, the ones she would have been able to afford before the government cuts. Ground beef. Tilapia. Snickers. Yogurt. "I guess just put these back," she told the cashier, and then, as she bagged up her items, she had an idea.

Her own food stamps no longer seemed like enough for the family, and neither did Tiara's, but there was another option. Her eldest son had yet to enroll in the food stamp program. He had no income. She was sure he would qualify. His likely benefit would be about $160 each month.

"I'm taking him to get signed up first thing tomorrow morning," Raphael said, already imagining what she would be able to buy with the extra EBT card when the 8th came again.

Congress could come up with its solutions, but so could she.

"With three, we should be good," she said as she carried her food into the house.

Back to Basics

A SORT OF CHICKEN THAT WE CALL FISH

By Elissa Altman

From PoorMansFeast.com

◈

Award-winning blogger, editor, and author of the
memoir *Poor Man's Feast*, Elissa Altman can wield
some wicked humor when the situation calls for it.
When it comes to navigating families and their holiday
traditions, sometimes all you can do is laugh.

Ten years ago, a few months after my dad died, Susan and I
cooked our first holiday dinner for my family, at my cousin's
house in Virginia. It involved a twenty-two pound artisanal turkey
that we drove south from Connecticut in the back of my Subaru;
it rode in a massive, two-ply food-grade storage bag stretched to its
limits like a water balloon, nestled in an ice-packed Coleman cooler
the size of a small casket.

The turkey traveled in its brine, which was composed of a misguided melange of water, salt, Grade B maple syrup, short-run
Bourbon, and late-harvest Tuscan rosemary clipped from our herb
garden. Susan and I made stuffing from slow-rise homemade bread—
one kind with fennel pork sausage, one kind with turkey; one with
chestnuts, one without (for the nut-intolerants)—and stoneground
cornbread dressing for anyone who didn't approve of the stuffed-
inside-the-bird variety. We made two kinds of crackers from
scratch—black pepper Parmigiana Reggiano, and garlic thyme—and
three kinds of pies. We roasted and pureed poblano peppers for
Smoky Butternut Squash Soup and garnished it with fried purple
heirloom sage leaves; we decided it would be a lovely and surprising
way to start the meal.

My family was surprised all right, especially my hot pepper–loathing aunt, who prefers her food simple and her flavors bland.

Susan and I sniped and snarked at each other that holiday; she was in my way, I was in hers, we were in a kitchen that wasn't ours, nobody much liked anything we made, and if they did, they didn't say so. The next day, as if to punctuate the weirdness of the occasion, twelve of us went out for dinner to a small Italian trattoria and arrived five minutes after the chef cut his hand off with a meat saw.

The holiday, start to finish, was an unmitigated disaster.

Susan and I had done everything we could to make a dinner we were sure everyone would love, and that would go down in the annals of family holiday history as one of *the best, ever.* We demanded, yearned, *ached* for everyone's approval. But in truth, we weren't cooking for them. We were cooking for *us,* and that was something that we just never took into account.

For one thing, nobody much wanted roasted poblanos in their butternut squash soup; they didn't want butternut squash soup *at all.* They wanted my aunt's traditional mushroom and barley soup, preferably made by my aunt, who had been serving it at Thanksgiving for half a century. Nobody wanted homemade crackers—*who the hell makes homemade crackers?*—and no one particularly cared whether or not the bird was of fine pedigree and had schlepped south from New England in the back of my Forester or had come with its own plastic pop-up thermometer, straight from the local Safeway. No one commented on the fancy French chestnuts in the heritage cornbread dressing, and the only words muttered during the flamingly-spicy soup course came from my father's sister, who said, as she coughed and dolefully dabbed at her running mascara, *I can't eat this.*

*Thank **God***—everyone gasped, taking their cue from the family matriarch and dropping their spoons. There was the simultaneous clatter of soup-silver-against-family-china: Susan and I got up and carried a stack of overflowing, gold-rimmed Lenox bowls dripping with thin, incendiary mush into the kitchen, where they were deposited in the sink, washed, and dried before the salad was tossed and the turkey carved.

This was the first year that things were different—my father was gone, his longtime girlfriend decided to celebrate with her own children, my aunt was no longer making the holiday meal on Long Island

and ringing her tiny kitchen cowbell to call her passel of buckaroos to the table—and so Susan and I went over the top to prepare a meal that I was certain would jettison us into position as the new keepers of the family culinary flame. This meal, we believed, would just be a lure, to let everyone know what they could all expect in the future: we were *certain* that it would be *our* table everyone would come to for the next forty years. We would make our own traditions, like my aunt and her cowbells had. And so that first holiday after my father died, we were determined to feed everyone a family dinner that was unforgettable and extraordinary.

And it was. Just not in a good way.

In my family, women make the leap over the transom from *child to adult* with the creation and serving of their first big holiday dinner. Likewise, the first time we get up to help the other adult women in the family clear the dishes—I was fifteen and no one asked me or gave me a signal; it was just my time and I knew it—is a little bit like hitting puberty: you're on your way to becoming a full-fledged member of the tribe, and everyone around you knows it. So cooking for my father's family for the first time just two months after his death was fraught with need and hunger and expectation: I wanted him back, to hear his laughter at the table, to feel his delight at seeing me finally as the adult woman that cooking for twenty heralds. I wanted him to look down from the heavens, and to be bursting with pride at the fact that I, the youngest of my generation, was providing sustenance for the people he loved. He would have thrilled at the fact that I'd made his family's most important meal and the one that always brought us together around the table every holiday season.

Cooking this meal was my way of keeping him alive. The only problem was, he wasn't.

When the shape of a family begins to shift and tilt—when there are fewer older people left and the younger ones begin to jockey into position to make their culinary mark on things—it's very easy to get caught in a scrum of desire, assumption, and emotional desperation; the presumption is that *you* will pick up the historical cooking mantle like a baton passed from one generation to the next. You'll get mired in making plans to wow and thrill, and you'll never quite realize that these people you're so set on wowing and thrilling may actually have *other* plans. They may not want change at all; odds are, they probably don't. They likely just want what they know and what they love. Oh, and that baton? It may never actually have been handed off to you after all. You and your raging kitchen ego just assumed it was.

Years ago, in an attempt to get her very young son to eat fish for the first time, one of my beloved cousins tried to pass it off as chicken, which she knew he liked. As he folded his arms, pursed his lips, stamped his feet and shook his head NO, his mother turned to the powers of logic.

This, she said, *is a sort of chicken that we call fish.*

Her child was unmoved; he knew better. He wanted what he wanted, not what she wanted to give him, regardless of how many times she told him it was the same thing. A chicken is not a fish; the only thing that's the same about them is that they both can be dinner. Smoky poblano butternut squash soup is not your family's favorite mushroom and barley soup; the only thing that's the same about them is that they're both eaten with a spoon.

Things may appear to be the same, but really, they're not.

Ten years ago, with my father's place at the table empty, I made my first holiday dinner for my family, certain that it would render me an adult in their eyes, and certain that it would bring my father back. Susan and I cooked a meal laden with overwrought dishes that had no place on their holiday table; desperate for my family's approval and acknowledgement as *head chef,* I received neither. It wasn't my time or my place.

When the holiday was over, Susan and I drove the seven hours home, took our coats off, and cooked what would soothe our souls: custardy scrambled eggs made in a double boiler, toast, and well-done bacon, just the way my father liked it.

We ate breakfast-as-dinner in the quiet of our home, and began to plan for Christmas.

Forget the Clock, Remember Your Food

By Joe Yonan

From Eat Your Vegetables: Bold Recipes for the Single Cook

Cooking for one—even on a vegetarian diet—doesn't have to be a chore, insists *Washington Post* food and travel editor Joe Yonan. To prove it, he's given us this common-sense cookbook, full of unfussy yet delicious recipes, plus bonus essays—thoughtful conversations about what really matters in the kitchen.

If we were taught to cook as we are taught to walk, encouraged first to feel for pebbles with our toes, then to wobble forward and fall, then had our hands firmly tugged on so we would try again, we would learn that being good at it relies on something deeply rooted, akin to walking, to get good at which we need only guidance, senses, and a little faith.

—Tamar Adler, *An Everlasting Meal*, 2011

Things were not going smoothly, not from the host's perspective anyway. It was a summertime dinner party; several of us were sitting on the back deck near the gas grill, and she was scrambling around trying to make sure everybody had a glass of wine or a cocktail or a beer while she also tried to get the food on the table. Judging from the look on her face as she rushed out onto the deck carrying a platter of cut-up chicken, opened the preheated grill, plopped the pieces onto the grates, shut the lid, and set the timer, I realized that she was in the state restaurant cooks refer to as "in the weeds."

She looked around to see who might help her check this item off her punch list. I was just about to offer when she looked at me, perhaps sensing my sympathy, and asked: "Could you turn these over when the timer goes off?"

"I'd be glad to take over the chicken, sure thing," I said.

That wasn't what she meant. She sighed. "This is a *Cook's Illustrated* recipe," she said with a little irritation in her voice. "And they say to turn them after 12 minutes, so when the timer goes off, would you just turn them?"

My mother raised me to be polite, so I wasn't about to argue with her—not out loud, anyway. In my head, I was running through all sorts of smart-alecky replies, such as, "I seriously doubt the *Cook's* recipe said that boneless chicken breasts, bone-in leg/thigh combinations, and little wings would all be done at the same time, and I doubt it said that the chicken breasts should be cut in such different-sized pieces, and I doubt it didn't give you any ways to tell the chicken would be ready to turn other than the timing." Or, "I know Chris Kimball, and, madam, you're no Chris Kimball."

Instead, I said, "Of course, no problem," and then as soon as she was back in the house, I turned off the timer. Sure enough, some of the smaller pieces were ready for flipping in just a few minutes, some of the bigger ones took a little longer, and still others—those leg-and-thigh combos—took the longest. I listened for their sizzle, I looked at the color, I felt them for firmness, I checked the juices, and I switched them around to parts of the grill that were cooler and hotter, depending on what I thought they needed. I took them off as they were ready, and kept them warm under a loose tent of foil. The host was too busy with other duties to notice my rebellion.

The venerable author and cooking teacher Anne Willan, who has been writing recipes for fifty years, tells a similar tale. "My recent trainees and even my current assistant cannot understand that timing, especially on baking, is approximate and you must keep in communication all the time with what you are cooking," she wrote me in an email when I reached out to her on the subject. "It drives me crackers!" Later, when we talked by phone, she elaborated. Her assistants "do this thing of putting on the timer, going away, looking at their computer or making phone calls. And then I say, 'That's going to be nearly done, I think.' I've developed an instinct for some things that it's nearly there. 'Oh, no,' they'll say. 'The timer hasn't gone, it's still

5 more minutes.' They think anything written down has got to be followed exactly, and it's quite difficult to get across that every time is a little bit different."

I've never really been like that in the kitchen, and I think it comes from having learned to cook my first dishes not from a cookbook but from my mother and stepfather when I was a kid. When my mom taught me how to whip cream using her stand mixer, for instance, she would caution me to keep stopping and checking the thickness— and to be careful not to whip it so long it would turn to butter. I had my own ideas, at age eight, of what thick whipped cream should be like—like Cool Whip, of course!—so I was confident in pushing past the point where she would have stopped. Similarly, in my stepdad's lesson on making chicken-fried steak, he showed me how to tell from the color of the crust when to turn each piece, and how it wouldn't be done in the middle if the juices were running red.

Hang out with any good home cook or professional chef, and you'll see less clock-watching and more poking and prodding, sniffing and tasting, and even listening, as they evaluate the food as it progresses and guide it along the way. (Sous vide cooking, which uses vacuum packs, is one exception, which is one reason I've resisted it.) I remember shadowing baker Renee McLeod at her Petsi Pies café in Cambridge, Massachusetts, one morning many years ago, and there was no timer in sight. Instead, right in the middle of answering one of my questions, her nose went into the air and she sniffed, then whirled around to her convection oven and pulled out a tray of coconut cupcakes, which were perfectly done—by a matter of mere seconds. She doesn't have to be in such close proximity, either. She told me, "I'll be sitting in the office and suddenly I'll call out to my people, 'Cookies are done!'"

Some people's senses seem born stronger than others', of course, but there's no doubt that much of this kind of skill comes from experience. McLeod adapted some of her cupcake recipes from her grandmother's instructions for larger cakes, which means that the first time she made them she would have had no idea how long they would take. She had to watch, sniff, and learn. In a professional setting like McLeod's, where recipes are standardized as they are made over and over again using the same equipment, and the equipment is professionally calibrated, the variability lessens and timing can become more consistent. But ovens can rarely be calibrated to within 25 degrees, and most home ovens are far more inaccurate than that. Moreover, when you're following someone else's instructions—someone who was using different ingredients and equipment—it's folly to depend solely on the clock rather than learning to evaluate your food and make adjustments as you go.

Take the simple sautéed onion. It's all too common for recipe writers to tell readers how long it will take to get it tender, along with that garlic or carrot or celery that might also be in the skillet. But an onion is not an onion is not an onion. Even if a "large" onion is called for and used, the actual size will vary; and it could be younger or older than it was last time, meaning juicier or tougher. And even if you call for a medium or large skillet, one person's medium is another person's large, and a heavy cast-iron one is not the same as a thin aluminum one, especially when the onion actually starts cooking. Sure, a writer can try to specify as many of those variables as possible—the number of cups the chopped onion should be, the exact size of the pan, even its materials—but who knows the age of an onion, unless you grow it yourself? All those factors will affect the cooking time, and yet too many writers, even as we acknowledge the variables, act like the timing is the one thing we can specify with some certainty.

Onions, as it happens, were the subject of some scorn heaped on recipe writers last spring, when Tom Scocca wrote a piece in *Slate* about the woefully short time so many recipes say it takes to caramelize an onion, something that, when done properly, can occupy the better part of an hour—or more. But as Chow.com editor John Birdsall wrote in response, "The thing that went mostly unnoticed in the scramble to accuse or save face was Scocca's larger indictment, which is that professional recipe writers' work can seem as far removed from actual cooking as a cognitive study in the testing lab with subjects wired to electrodes is from actual thinking. Recipe writing occurs under unnatural conditions, conducted by professionals with laptops and clipboards. They pretend they're doing stuff that ordinary home cooks might do, but they're not ordinary home cooks, and many are definitely not cooking at home, under ordinary conditions."

It was not always thus. In her fascinating book *The Cookbook Library*, Willan says that it wasn't until the twentieth century that writers started regularly listing precise timing, mostly because until then most cooks had wood stoves with no consistency of temperature whatsoever. Cooks would test the heat of wood stoves using their hands, or they would put in some newspaper and see how long it took the paper to scorch: thirty seconds was very hot and good for baking pastries, for instance, then as the temperature came down it was appropriate for bread, then roasts, then stews. "In Catholic countries, they would time it by saying a rosary," Willan says. "And of course if the paper didn't brown or scorch at all, then the oven wasn't hot enough for anything." Even when she went to Le Cordon Bleu in Paris in the 1960s, the equipment was so antiquated as to make timing estimates pointless. "The ovens had top heat, bottom heat or both together, and we controlled the heat by putting a wooden spoon in the door, propping it open," she said.

Exceptions to Willan's twentieth-century observation abound, naturally. Fannie Farmer's *The Boston Cooking School Cook-Book* of 1895 is largely credited with introducing specific measurements, times, and temperatures to recipe writing. When I scoured through some other antiquarian book, I noticed that *The Improved Housewife* of 1846 would include timing in one recipe and not in the next. For parsnips and carrots, you just "boil till tender," but for beets that same instruction is followed by "in summer one hour, in winter three." Don Lindgren, co-owner of Rabelais Books in Biddeford, Maine, says that even Mary Randolph included some timing in her influential 1825 book, *The Virginia House-Wife*. But the most entertaining outlier I saw was an excerpt from *The Nonpareil Cook Book*, an 1894 collection by the Ladies' Lend-A-Hand Society of the Baptist Church of Worcester, New York, that Lindgren sent me. The book includes a chart for vegetable boiling times that by today's standards are comical, including a half-hour for potatoes, an hour for squash, three hours for string beans, and four hours for beets. (The latter in winter, I presume.)

Ultimately, recipe writing, like so many other things, is an idiosyncratic discipline, with writers taking all sorts of approaches in getting across their own interpretations of a dish, and teaching it in their own style. To this day, charcoal grilling calls for an approach similar to the rosaries Willan mentioned; many Southern recipes instruct cooks to count how many "Mississippis" they can utter while holding their hand over the grate, while many of those same recipes still attempt to say how many minutes it then takes to char an eggplant. In a recipe for baked red snapper with grapefruit in *The New York Times Cookbook* of 1961, Craig Claiborne wisely leaves out the minutes it takes to accomplish of one of the first, most basic steps: "In a skillet heat four tablespoons of the butter, add the onion and cook until it is transparent." My style exactly. And then he specifies that the stuffed fish should be baked "until it flakes easily when tested with a fork, about fifty to sixty minutes," a crucial step for which he gives the reader a good testing mechanism. By 1979, though, his friend and frequent coauthor, Pierre Franey, was going in the opposite direction in his *60-Minute Gourmet*, deemphasizing descriptive cues and listing a time whenever possible. It makes sense; as more and more women were leaving domestic life behind in favor of the workplace, our cooking culture was becoming ever more focused on speed and convenience. Perhaps Franey's approach was to some degree a way of helping readers count the minutes and see for themselves that they wouldn't add up to more than the all-important hour he was promising.

After a long downward trend in home cooking, recent years have seen a rediscovery of the kitchen. That's nothing but good news. Yet the standards are different when the target audience includes less experienced cooks, and trying to account for this is where I think we've started to really go off the rails with recipe timing. When I called Sally Schneider, author of *The Improvisational Cook*, to talk about the issue, she said that as much as she tries to write recipes that include many other descriptive cues in addition to timing, she still gets emails and calls from readers asking shockingly basic questions, such as how to tell when that simple sautéed onion is done: "The problem is people these days don't have basic structures in place in their heads."

Writers and editors often think that to make recipes doable by less experienced cooks, they must attach time cues to each and every step, however small, and to weigh or otherwise measure every last smidgen of every last ingredient. The irony, though, is that by trying to account for so many variables, the recipes can become so long-winded that they run the risk of intimidating the very cooks they're trying to appeal to. Even worse, they might be doing a disservice by not helping even the most inexperienced cooks learn what I think they need to learn most: How to make their own judgments. How to interact with their food, to roll with the punches, to develop instincts. How to make mistakes, and recover. How to learn. How to be free. Schneider echoes the old "teach a man to fish" adage when she says, "If you tell somebody how something works, if they understand the workings of it and what its end point can be, it gives them more confidence."

Technology has long tried to come to the rescue of home cooks (most of them women) who had their hands full, whether with other household chores or work outside the home. Generations of slow-cooker devotees have loved the fact that they can close the thing up, head to work, and come home to a meal. That Ronco rotisserie oven hawked on TV has sold gazillions on the promise of its earworm of a slogan, shouted out by Ron Popeil and the audience in chorus: "Set it and forget it!"

But should we forget it, really? As Willan said, cooking has always been about multi-tasking. Nobody's asking you to stand there and do nothing except watch the cake rise in the oven. "But you still have to have it in the back of your mind while you do other things," she said. "It's a skill to be acquired."

I'm no Luddite, but I can't ignore some of the tradeoffs we've made in our dependence on technology. For example, I'm as addicted to my smartphone as anyone I know, and am especially dependent on the built-in GPS to overcome my lack of a natural sense of direction. So when I'm walking or driving and staring at Google Maps rather than at the streetscape around me, I don't really learn where I'm going, I just get there anyway. What's the harm in that, you may ask? Well, putting aside the possibility of running into a parking meter on the sidewalk, or heaven forbid into oncoming traffic, the harm is that this is just one more area where I'm getting a little bit dumber, a little less independent. More than once I've run out of battery before I see where I'm supposed to make a turn, sending me into the nearest gas station or Starbucks to do the old-fashioned thing, and ask for help.

There are countless cooking apps, too, and many feature built-in timers, not to mention voice commands to move from one step in the recipe to the next. Maybe one day Siri will teach everybody to cook, or perhaps she'll do the sautéing herself. But in the meantime, when you're in the kitchen, why not just . . . look up? As author Tamar Adler puts it, learning to cook by interacting closely with your food is a little like learning to drive on a stick shift rather than an automatic. You feel more connected to the process of driving, and therefore you understand it a little better.

Adler's book *An Everlasting Meal* calls for a return to instinctive cooking, and she tells audiences and students and readers that they can make their own decisions about recipes, that they don't need to be slaves to any instruction, timing included. And she says they are surprisingly quick to respond. "At first they feel incredibly unmoored and unsupported, and they say, 'That's all well and good for you, because you know how long everything takes, and the processes, so you're not nervous, but what about me?' I always say, 'I learned this by standing over the pan and paying attention.'"

You may have heard this before, but I'm going to say it again: Recipes—mine and everyone's—are road maps. Throw away the stone-tablets idea, and you'll eventually be a better cook.

The more I think about this issue, the more committed I become to making sure my own recipes give readers something more than just a bunch of numbers. I have long insisted that my own recipes in the *Washington Post* put the time cue last in a sequence, the hope being that if readers read that the eggplant should be baked "until it blackens and collapses, about an hour," rather than the other way around, they'll be more attuned to the blackening and collapsing part of the equation. When I initially sent the recipes for this book to testers, I asked for feedback on the plethora of time references, to make sure as much as possible that the ranges I was giving were working for others, and I used that feedback to make sure they did. But then I made another decision: in many of the instructions, particularly the ones about sautéing an onion or anything else that happens relatively quickly—and exceedingly variably—the time references have come out altogether. In their place, I'm trying to describe to you as best I can how to tell what's happening with the food and, therefore, how to really cook it.

The result, I hope, is that you might find your own cooking rhythms and realize the point of all this: that what you see, hear, smell, and feel happening is the only thing that matters. I think it might be easier for single cooks to get there than others. If your primary consideration is your own craving and nobody else's, you can learn more naturally to listen to your instincts as you cook, and to let them lead the way—hopefully to something that satisfies you. No matter how long those onions took to soften.

Meals from a Hunter

By Steve Hoffman

From the Minneapolis Star Tribune

Juggling various roles as a freelance writer, tax
preparer, real-estate agent, beekeeper, hunter, and
dad, Steve Hoffman isn't wrapped up in foodie fads
and gourmet snobberies. But that doesn't mean that he
doesn't think profoundly about how—and why—we eat
what we do.

I t was certainly the best meal I've ever eaten while sitting in snow.
Maybe one of the best meals I've eaten anywhere.

A friend and I had spent a January morning ice fishing, then an
afternoon with shotguns slung across our backs, snowshoeing the
cedar-lined shore of one of those Boundary Waters lakes that look
like claw scratches along the Canadian border.

The day's result: Zero fish. One snowshoe hare.

Back in camp we balanced a soup kettle on a teetering propane stove, melted some snow and slowly defrosted a frozen block
of venison stew. By headlamp, in the late afternoon darkness, we
scooped olive oil, turned gelatinous from the cold, into a camp skillet, browned the skinned and butchered hare, then added the thighs,
shoulders and saddle to the bubbling, wine-rich stew.

An hour later, squatting outside a glowing tent, we improvised a
table from an upside-down enamel pot in the snow, set the kettle of
stew on top of it, and ladled out two steaming bowlfuls. Clouds of
our own breath drifted through the cones of our headlamps, as we
forked up gravy-glazed carrot and onion, and big, dripping cubes of
venison shoulder, our forks clanking against the metal bowls with

our shivering. We peeled fat shreds of glistening hare from the bones with our brittle fingers, and agreed that there was really nowhere else we'd rather be.

The dish failed every test of Food Styling 101. This was not fine dining.

But it was many other kinds of fine, seated as we were at a stock-pot table, under a frozen dome of stars, as guests of that gruffly hospitable country, tasting meat that had been flavored by the willows and cedars rocking in the wind around us, before it had been flavored by garlic, red wine and a mirepoix.

It was a reminder, sometimes obscured by talk of gear, techniques and trophies, that hunting is not an end in itself, but a means to an end. And that end is the table—whether a turned-over cooking pot in a snowbank or candlelit white linen.

A reminder, as well, of what wild game can be when cleaned immediately, cooled quickly, butchered with care, and cooked with gratitude—not just lean and healthy, not just full of Omega-3s, not just ecologically sensible, but to many of us, quite simply, the best tasting meat in the world, and the most complete expression of our connection to wild places.

A Local World-Class Gift

During a recent extended stay in rural France, I was able to observe the hunter-cook connection at its most intimate. One day our neighbor, Jean-Luc, came home with a double brace of snipe from an undisclosed local wetland. He spent 15 minutes in the middle of the street, describing every detail of how he would roast them en brochette, as their long necks swung loosely from his hand.

Another day, I found myself leaning against a truck after a morning's mushroom forage with two hunter-farmers who would, in their way, fit seamlessly into a Stearns County bar. They were parsing the precise preparation of each type of mushroom in their baskets, arguing heatedly over whether lactaire mushrooms grilled over a vine-wood fire were best served with, or without, a persillade of finely chopped parsley and garlic.

That kind of thing doesn't happen in the Midwest as often as our game deserves.

Well cared for, the game of Minnesota is a world-class gift. Even a brief tour among its species might lead a culinary traveler past such wonders as seared wood duck breast with foie gras, pheasant cacciatore, cottontail hasenpfeffer, squirrel pad Thai, roast wild turkey stuffed with Honeycrisp apples, sautéed woodcock with chanterelles, a daube of whitetail venison or minted grouse breasts with wild mushroom risotto.

I merely mention these things. Of course, boneless, skinless chicken breasts are fine, too.

From Field to Kitchen

But let's be clear. "Well cared for" means you can't heave a gutted four-point buck in the back of your pickup and drive for four hours through the slush of Interstate 35. You can't walk trails all day with that morning's grouse in your vest pocket. And you can't leave a bag full of soggy mallards on the garage floor for very long and somehow expect to work a little Thomas Keller magic when you get to the kitchen.

Here, along those lines, are some very personal and noncomprehensive rules.

- Warmth in the field is the enemy of taste at the table. Put the gun down for just a minute, O Nimrod Son of Cush, and field-dress your animal right away. Meat lockers are cold for a reason.
- Save the heart and the liver. No, seriously, it's all concentrated right there. If you just can't bring yourself to eat them whole, mince them and add their rich flavor to a pan sauce.
- Use really short cooking times, or really long cooking times. Either medium-rare, or braised until it falls off the bone.
- Cook legs and thighs (furred or feathered) long, rich, wet and slow.
- Duck breast looks like steak. Cook it like steak.
- Venison looks like steak. Cook it like steak. That medium-well backstrap medallion that feels like a flexed quadricep and looks like a hockey puck? Yeah, it's gonna taste like a hockey puck.
- Wine is good.
- Grilling is good (but it isn't the only way).

Remember: They've been doing this for a long time in Italy and France.

They've been doing this for a long time in Mexico.

They've been doing this for a long time in the hills of Vietnam, Laos and Thailand.

We can all still learn a thing or two.

Back in the Woods

About 400 years ago, a party of pretty quirky Brits, somewhat newly arrived, took matchlocks and fowling pieces and headed into the New England woods with their native hosts. I'd like to think it was a congenial hunt, with flat November light filtering down through the beeches and chestnuts. I'd like to think there were some jocular insults tossed back and forth, and taken the right way, and that there was time afterward to lean against whatever the 17th century had to offer in the direction of a pickup truck, in order to talk over the day's events.

Such talk, I'm certain, would have been heavy with more or less accurate recountings of soft-footed stalking, sharp reflexes, misfires and cold toes.

But it's worth noting that history has forgotten the particular exploits of the hunters on that occasion. It has not forgotten the work of the cooks.

Which leads me to the second best wild meal I've ever eaten—the tenderloin of a Michigan whitetail, grilled and served medium-rare on an ancient table in a white cedar cabin with no electricity. The chef was a Marquette hunter and friend, who cares to get things right.

There were six or eight of us at the table. Not a particularly sentimental crew. But we did know instinctively what word to use at the end of the meal.

It's not a bad word to have in mind when thinking about good cooks. Or about the deer you're eating. Or the snowshoe hare. Or their wild, native country. Or, for that matter, about olive oil and garlic. Or thyme and rosemary. Or chile peppers. Or lemon grass. Or the wanderers who brought such things with them from so far away, and then decided to stay and add their flavor to the communal pot.

At the end of the meal in Michigan, we turned to the cook and said, "Thanks."

THE MAN MACHINE

By Oliver Strand

From Fool

Though he's based in New York City, food writer Oliver
Strand covers a worldwide java scene for the *New
York Times* and other publications; he just may be the
universe's preeminent coffee writer. In this essay from
a beautiful new Swedish food magazine, his reflections
on the current coffee scene could apply to all our foodie
fetishes.

I once asked the manager of one of those small, influential shops
where groupies Instagram their drinks, to describe his ideal customer. We were a few beers into the afternoon and he took a moment to collect his thoughts before giving a description of a generic
somebody with urbane tastes (good palate, good income) and an
open mind (willing to try anything once, even coffee without milk).
Then I asked him to describe his nightmare customer. He shot back:
"An old Italian man who thinks he knows everything about coffee
just because he was fucking born in Italy."

The moment that old Italian man places an order, the manager
said, the lectures start: hold it like this, there's too much of that,
there's not enough of this, it should taste like that, you're doing it all
wrong. At some point, the old man grows exasperated and fatherly
and tells the staff that if they want to understand the soul of espresso,
they need to go to Italy.

The way the manager told it, that was the punchline. Conventional wisdom might hold that the coffee in Italy is an art form, but

that's just folklore—nobody at the cutting edge of the coffee industry cares about the coffee in Italy.

To be sure, there's a reverence for illycaffé—the official if unnecessarily slickly branded name for the company better known as illy— and their ability to produce quality coffee on a large scale. (*Espresso Coffee: The Science of Quality* by Andrea Illy and Rinantonio Viani, a dry, textbook-like tract of detailed information, is required reading for any serious professional.) But that's it. There's no interest in other big coffee roasters, or small coffee roasters, or coffee buyers, or coffee bars or baristas. This rising generation of coffee artisans looks to Melbourne, Oslo or San Francisco, not Milan, Rome or Turin.

In part, it's because the mystique of espresso has faded. A well-made shot is always a pleasure, but it's no longer thought of as the highest expression of the roasted bean. Instead, we're living in an age of filter coffee, and the tastemakers who are reshaping the industry tend to be more interested in how the brilliant clarity of a simple cup of brewed coffee illuminates the strange, delicate flavors you can find in the beans from a particular region, or farm, or lot on that farm, than in a syrupy espresso. If a roaster or buyer travels to origin (industry speak for the countries where coffee is grown), and goes through the trouble and expense of sourcing high-quality ingredients, it's with the goal of presenting a coffee that's distinctive, unusual, maybe even challenging. You go halfway around the world and sample 400 coffees in a week in search of something beautiful and unique, not familiar and safe.

But even if you take filter coffee out of the picture and only look at espresso, the scene in Italy is ossified, the coffee a relic from an era that might have been at the apex of quality and flavor back when televisions used antennas nut that hasn't evolved much since. Mystery blends, regional roasts, beans stored for months or even years: this was fine when Americans were drinking watery swill from a percolator, and the Swedes used coffee as a mixer for their morning aquavit, and the British had to take a hovercraft to Calais to see an espresso machine, but the world caught up, and then it moved on. Go to The Coffee Collective in Copenhagen, or Heart Coffee Roasters in Portland, or Coffee Lab in São Paulo, and you'll have a shot so elegant and floral that it will bend your mind and reshape your understanding of what you can find in an espresso; go to the peach-colored marble counter of a coffee bar in Verona, and you'll enter a flavor time machine set to 1975.

Although if you do go to The Coffee Collective, or Heart Coffee Roasters, or Coffee Lab and you order an espresso, it won't be prepared on a machine made in Denmark, or in the United States, or in Brazil. It will be pulled on an Italian machine, with beans pulverized by an Italian grinder. Faema, Mazzer, La Marzocco, Nuova Simonelli, la Pavoni, La San Marco: these are the names of manufacturers so admired that they end up on t-shirts and in tattoos. In the convoluted relationship that high-end coffee has with Italy, nobody follows Italian coffee, but everybody pays close attention to Italian machines.

Last October, the manufacturer Nuova Simonelli unveiled a prototype called the Black Eagle 0388, the newest model in the Victoria Arduino line. It's a handsome object. While many espresso machines have the boxy silhouette of an air conditioner, the Black Eagle has the low-slung profile of a fast, jumpy car: slim chassis, lattice side panels, wishbone legs. It's two axles and one drivetrain away from going for a couple of laps around a test track.

Of the number of improvements hiding behind the mirror-polished hood—temperature stability, boiler capacity, recovery time—the most significant breakthrough is built into the drip tray. Called the "gravimetric system," it consists of a drip tray equipped with hyper-sensitive scales to weigh each espresso as the liquid flows into the cup. If you come across a machine after they roll out later in 2014, peek around the side to see if the barista doesn't finger the grates to test the scales in a gesture that might be considered mildly obscene.

The gravimetric system is the first time a manufacturer has responded to what the best shops are already doing, namely measuring an espresso by weight, not volume. Right now, if a shop pulls shots by weight it means rigging up a jewelry scale sensitive to at least 1/10 of a gram and watching two sets of numbers—the timer and the weight—so that you stop the machine at the right moment. It works like this: the director of coffee will work out a recipe for a particular espresso (example: 19g dose of coffee; 27-second extraction; 35g yield of espresso), and it's up to the barista to tweak the grind, watch the scale and keep an eye on the timer so that the numbers all line up.

It's a labor-intensive process. You place the portafilter on a scale, set the scale to zero, dose the coffee, check the weight, add or subtract more coffee, flush the machine, lock the portafilter into the machine, place a demitasse on a scale on the drip tray, set that scale to zero, start the shot, keep an eye on the timer (which is above the portafilter), keep an eye on the scale (which is below the demitasse), and stop the machine just when you feel it hits the sweet spot. Then you bang out the puck, wipe out the filterbasket, flush the machine and do it all again. In a busy shop, you might repeat those steps a thousand times in a day.

The software that runs the Black Eagle 0388 is supposed to respond to use and be able to read what happens in a busy shop, with autocorrect-like functions that keep the readouts from getting too twitchy. Program the machine to pull a 35g shot, and the pump will shut off at just the right moment so that last fraction of a gram trickles into the cup. It's the little things that count.

If it seems excruciatingly wonky, it is. But that's where we are in coffee, or at least that's where the most interesting figures are to be found. One of those is James Hoffmann, the co-founder of London's Square Mile Coffee and the winner of the World Barista Championship in 2007. Hoffmann was a consultant on the Black Eagle, and pushed for the gravimetric system. "I've been bothering them about it for almost two years," Hoffmann said. "I think I just wore them down."

That Victoria Arduino, a brand that first started manufacturing machines in 1905 (the triassic period for espresso: Luiggi Bezzera registered what is considered the first patent for a true espresso machine in 1901), turned to Hoffmann, a Londoner who commutes on a tastefully urban bicycle and whose speech was polished in boarding school (words such as "whilst" and "thrice" come easily to him), isn't as odd a mashup as it might seem. In fact, it's a feedback loop that reflects the state of coffee. The innovative baristas might not be in Italy, but the manufacturers are.

What might surprise coffee's true believers is that the Italians still have a thing or two to teach the rest of the world.

•

A couple of years ago, I was standing in line at one of New York's better hardcore coffee bars. When it was my turn, the barista recognized a friend standing farther back in line and curved his eye contact around me like a free kick. The friend was served and fist-bumped before the barista bothered to ask me what I wanted.

The coffee that morning was better than anything I've ever tasted in Italy, but the masterful roast and skillful preparation didn't make up for the low-frequency rage simmering in me all morning. I was delayed maybe three minutes, but that's a long time to seethe.

I like most baristas—I'm not one of those haters who catalogs a few slights and castigates the whole profession—but in the thousands of interactions I've had over the last five years, there have been a number of instances when the delicious coffee was spoiled by a sullen barista.

It doesn't have to be a shitshow to ruin the fun. Indifference is enough of a turn-off. When a transaction is nothing more than an exchange of money for goods and services, it doesn't matter how magnificent the espresso might taste to an objective judge. When you get the sense that the barista would rather be anywhere other than facing you, you'd rather be anywhere than facing that barista.

In 1994 I lived in Venice while I was interning at the Collezzione Peggy Guggenheim. The following year I returned to work at the Biennale, and I stayed in one of the apartments that were circulated among the art professionals who came to town before the dealers and the tourists arrived. It was a converted storage room on the ground floor of a palazzo on the Grand Canal that had been carved into more than a dozen apartments for the branches of a fallen noble family.

The terrestrial side of the palazzo faced onto a narrow street directly across from a pink building with a marble balcony. The ground floor housed Bar da Gino, a caffé that was the unofficial clubhouse for the Guggenheim staff. Later, the museum opened its own caffé, but at the time Bar da Gino was the closest place we could get a drink or a bite. It was where you had your morning coffee, your mid-morning coffee, your lunch, your afternoon coffee and your first after-work aperitivo.

Like many caffés in Italy, Bar da Gino had a three-tiered price structure. You paid one price at the bar, another at a table and a third if you sat outside. Like many caffés in Venice, there was a second layer of prices: one for tourists, one for locals. It was an important day when I was given the local discount; it was an even more important day when my mother came to visit, and she overhead the cashier tell the waiter that she should get the lower price because she was "the mother of that boy who lives over there."

I went back to Venice a few years ago, well before I started writing about coffee. When I stepped through the door of Bar da Gino, the waiter saw me, put down her tray and gave me a hug. Then the cashier came over, then the bar man, then the other waiter. Service stopped. I teared up, and so did they, and when the momentum of the morning returned I found myself outside at a table with a cappuccino and a cornetto and a waiter who refused to let me pay.

I don't think I was a remarkable customer. I was a familiar face for two blocks of time, an American with enough Italian to order quickly and politely, but that was enough to leave an indelible impression. The espresso at Bar da Gino was equally unremarkable—it seemed fantastic then, although I'm sure that I would taste all kinds of faults were I to try it now—but I will remember it long after the detailed impressions of the exquisitely-prepared coffees I've had in Los Angeles, New York and Portland will have dissipated. The intellect can be fickle; it's the heart holds onto memories.

That old man might get most things wrong, but he gets one thing right, at least in part. If you want to master espresso, you can learn the craft in a number of countries, but that will only take you so far. If you want to understand the soul of espresso, you need to go to Italy.

COOKING AS THE CORNERSTONE OF A SUSTAINABLE FOOD SYSTEM

By Kim O'Donnel

From CivilEats.com

Sustainability matters deeply to Kim O'Donnel,
a Seattle-based cookbook writer (*The Meat Lover's
Meatless Cookbook*), longtime food blogger (the
Washington Post, EcoCentric), and founder of the
Canning Across America collective. But sustainability,
she argues here, isn't just about what happens on a
farm.

"How cool is this!" Susan, a 68-year-old retiree from Philadelphia, was on her maiden voyage with her new toy, a salad spinner.

As she pulled the spinner's retractable cord, the room filled with a rattling hum, similar to a washing machine at the end of its cycle. She was visibly pleased that after just a few pulls, the lettuce leaves tucked inside the colander-like basket were nice and dry. She marveled at how she could both wash—"Wow, there's a lot of dirt in these leaves"—and dry salad greens with just one tool.

This was just one of the many ah-ha moments for Susan, who signed on to take an immersion cooking course with me earlier this summer. Over the course of a week, we met in her kitchen each day with one primary objective: Getting a handle on the bare essentials of cooking.

With beautifully washed and dried greens before us, the next logical step was to make some salad dressing. This would be another first for her record books, a stark departure from decades of lining the inside door of the refrigerator with an array of store-bought bottles of Thousand Island, Ranch, and Creamy Italian.

She could hardly fathom, as with the salad spinner, the low-tech simplicity of the DIY version. Surely there was more to salad dressing than a few tablespoons of olive oil, the juice of a lemon, salt, pepper, and maybe a smidge of strong mustard. "That's it and you just shake it all together in a little jar?"

You see, during the 20-plus years of raising three children, Susan put dinner on the table with minimal chopping, slicing or dicing. Instead, she opened cans, unsealed jars and unzipped seasoning envelopes, as per the directions on the back of a box, and within minutes, voilà, dinner was ready. With so many heat, reheat, and quick-serve options on supermarket shelves, Susan, a young mother of three in 1971, felt no need to learn how to use a kitchen knife, and it certainly never occurred to her to make salad dressing. In her mind, Susan fulfilled her job of putting a hot meal on the table for her family. Nobody ever starved, she noted.

Susan is right. Her kids did eat three "square" meals a day. But they each went out into the world without knowing how to prepare one.

I should know. I'm her daughter.

I was 21 when I graduated from college, the same age Susan was when she gave birth to me. I bought my first cookbook (*The New Basics* by Sheila Lukins and Julee Rosso) and fumbled my way through my first-ever apartment kitchen. Cooking dinner, I quickly learned, was a practical way to stretch my measly paycheck. But it also set me on a path of personal discovery. Cooking was a way to learn about the world and find my place in it. It helped me grow up and grow into a kinder, more nurturing version of myself. Far from a great cook was I, botching and burning and under seasoning with great frequency. But it hardly mattered, I was cooking dammit, and I felt alive.

Learning to cook reminds me of discovering my true love for reading. I was six years old, the lucky recipient of a brand new hardbound copy of *Charlotte's Web*, a gift from cousins on my mom's side. I laid at the foot of my bed, on my stomach, and cracked open the book, reading out loud so that I could hear the words, proof positive that I could read, yes indeed. It marked the beginning of a lifelong love affair; reading took me places I longed to go and helped me to better understand the world, even at the age of six.

At the stove, my world similarly expanded. Even when I screwed up a dish, I learned something new: Maybe math or chemistry, botany or history, or a hard-fought lesson in patience. Looking back now, with the perspective that comes with a culinary degree and a 17-year food career, I still believe deep in my bones that cooking, which marries the practical with the magical, can be the greatest teacher of all, and that it's never too late to learn.

It was in this spirit that I approached Susan about the kitchen project. Nothing too cheffy or complicated, I said to her over the phone, simple tricks and techniques like washing and drying salad greens and making legumes.

Legumes. What are those?

You know, lentils.

Oh yes. And can we make some quinoa? I would like to learn how to make some quinoa salad. I love the one that's on the menu at Terrain.

Sure. And maybe work on some knife skills, you know, how to dice and slice.

Ugh, my knife is so dull. Maybe we need to buy a new knife.

Secretly, I hoped she would have so much fun and feel so empowered and wowed by her food that she would forget about what she had never learned and instead celebrate what she would come to know. As with reading, cooking is all about diving in and just doing it.

Our adventure began, as it did every day, with warm-up exercises that went something like this: "Okay, ready? Heel, tip. Heel, tip. There you go. Glide, glide. Twenty times on each side."

You might think we were working out to a Jane Fonda tape. Instead, we were honing our knives with a sharpening steel. A long metal rod used to maintain the edge of a knife, the steel is one of the first things I learned to use in culinary school, but unfortunately it rarely sees the light of day in most home kitchens.

Use the steel on your knife every time you cook, I said. Think of it like flossing, daily maintenance that doesn't replace annual dental checkups but makes them easier. A knife left unhoned goes dull very quickly.

From honing, we'd transition to actual chopping. Susan was particularly excited about the "half moon" cut (also known as the crescent), which gives her quick-cooking thinly sliced vegetables. With the half moon, she saw many possibilities within easy reach: Caramelized onions, sautéed zucchini, and melty-thin potatoes for a frittata.

By our fifth day, Susan had prepared two kinds of lentil dishes, boiled quinoa ("wow, it took only 15 minutes!"), seasoned the quinoa with her newly beloved salad dressing in a jar, and stuffed that quinoa into bell pepper halves. We cruised the supermarket bulk section and comparison shopped for lentils, walnuts and oats, and we bought just-harvested asparagris (her word) from a local farm stand that we roasted and topped with lemon zest and grated Parmigiano.

The point of this little tale isn't to self-congratulate the teacher or to boast the number of dishes that the student mastered. The point is that Susan showed up, all five senses engaged, and she jumped off the sidelines.

I'm sure some of you are asking how this sweet little mother-daughter cooking story has any business appearing in a serious publication about the food system.

The thing is, home cooking is serious business. It is a conscious decision to turn raw ingredients into a meal to nourish ourselves and the people we love. The food system is more than crops and livestock; it's what we humans do with them.

In these disheartening times, when we're asked to make sense of mega farms, antibiotic-resistant foodborne outbreaks, and poverty-driven obesity, cooking is a beacon. It gives us purpose when we want to throw our hands up in the air in despair and it's something positive that we can do—me, Susan and you, you and you. It is a call to action that is both self-sustaining and sustainable.

Back in 1966, a woman named Margaret McNamara founded Reading is Fundamental (RIF), a nonprofit dedicated to eradicating illiteracy. To this day, RIF pro-actively puts books in the hands of millions of children who otherwise wouldn't have access.

RIF points out on its Web site that "Literacy—the ability to read and write—is essential to developing a sense of well-being and citizenship."

Couldn't we say the same thing about the ability to prepare a simple meal? Cooking is as fundamental as it gets—to our personal health and nourishment, and to the well-being and longevity of our communities, culture, and society. It can be *the* cornerstone of a sustainable food system, if we give it a chance.

In the words of the African-American proverb: "Each one, teach one."

See you in the kitchen.

How to Boil Water

By Irvin Lin

From Eatthelove.com

Irvin Lin is a San Francisco food-scene Renaissance man—an award-winning photographer and graphic designer; he's also a self-taught baker, recipe developer, and food blogger. Readers may come to his blogsite for the dazzling photos, but they're just as likely to return for his irrepressible wit, as with this April Fool's Day post.

I woke up this morning utterly parched with thirst. It was one of those cold mornings in San Francisco, gloomy and gray. Even though the blankets were wrapped around me, I was shivering and AJ had gone to work already.

I laid there in bed, trying to figure out if there was any substance at all that could help quench my dry throat. Then it hit me. I knew exactly what I so desperately needed, what would warm me up like nothing else. I needed hot water to drink. But how do I boil water? It's such a difficult thing to make at home! Or is it?!?.

The first thing I did was do my research. I grabbed my iPhone, next to my bed, and skipped Facebook and Twitter and Instagram and Pinterest and Google+ (ha! like anyone ever checks G+ on their phone) and launched my browser. I hit up America's Test Kitchen, then Saveur and then Bon Appetit. But none of them seem to have a recipe for how to make boiling water at home.

Then I visited my favorite popular food blogs: Simply Recipes, The Pioneer Woman, David Lebovitz, Gluten Free Girl. Nothing. I mean, boiling water is naturally GLUTEN FREE Shauna! Get on that. Even the apparently misnamed Steamy Kitchen seemed to not have a recipe for boiling water. The site is called STEAMY KITCHEN! Boiling water produces steam . . . oh Jaden, how you missed a golden opportunity. Even when I broke down and checked Pinterest it disappointed me as there were NO moody dark underexposed photos of boiled water that I could find. PIN FAIL.

Clearly someone needed to show the internet how to boil water. So I got out of bed, while still wearing my Faded Glory (a private label version of Fruit of Loom if you must know, because I'm not fancy) sleepy plaid flannel pants and nearly worn through oversized t-shirt that had a faded burger printed on it with a word bubble coming from it that had the words "I want to be inside you" lewdly hovering above it. I hauled myself into the kitchen and started to experiment with water and how to boil it.

After all, if I was going to go through all the trouble of figuring out how to boil water, I needed to make sure I created a recipe that was utterly foolproof. A recipe perfect for summer. And Winter. And Spring, and Fall (though really, San Francisco really has messed me up in terms of the seasons as we don't really have them). I needed a recipe that is the best ever, utterly amazing and completely delicious. Most importantly, I needed a pin-worthy recipe. The DEFINITIVE recipe on how to boil water. And after 27 attempts, I think I nailed it. Let me know what you think. And ABSOLUTELY let me know if you have any problems with this recipe. Like all food bloggers, I totally LOVE it when I get comments telling me how the recipe doesn't work . . . especially when the reader who tried it substituted different ingredients. Those are the best comments ever.

How to Boil Water

A gluten-free, grain-free, paleo-friendly, meatless Monday friendly, cane sugar-free, soy-free, peanut and nut tree–free, egg-free, dairy and casein-free, vegan, vegetarian, local and organic recipe. NOT water-free though. So if you are allergic to water, you're out of luck.

By Irvin Lin

Forget all those "uni-tasker" items that take up so much

space in the kitchen like the novelty whistling tea kettle (it whistles when the water boils!) or those hot water dispensers that are always sitting on your sassy-but-slightly-obsessed-with-wearing-sunscreen-all-the-time Asian friend's counter. Making boiling water is as easy as buying $4 toast and way easier than making a Kouign Amann or a Green Shamrock Shaped Guinness Infused Potato Irish Cheddar Bread Corned Beef Sandwiches with Orange Mayonnaise. And, it's just as much fun!

Now there are a million variables in boiling water, but I'm not going to get all persnickety and tell you how you need to use a scale to measure out the right amount of water to use. Nor am I going to tell you that you have to use that copper All-Clad pot or that you need the TOP notch ingredients like the spring water drawn from the remote part of Canada which takes three days travel just to get to the location where it's sourced. No, amazingly delicious perfect boiling water can happen with just basic everyday water and any old pot. Seriously. Just follow my easy step-by-step instructions . . . to make sure you don't make any mistakes in making the absolutely gorgeous fun-to-drink super-fun-to-make cup of boiling water!

Directions

1. Find the perfectly sized pot for your water to sit in. The size of the pot is going to limit the amount of water you boil, so make sure to pick one that will hold the right amount of boiling water that you want.

2. Locate the sink in your kitchen and bring the pot to your sink. Turn the faucet to the "on" position, which means water will be running out of the faucet. If you are pushing the handle or turning the knob and no water is coming out, you are pushing or turning in the wrong direction. Try pulling or twisting the other way.

3. Run the water until it gets cold, as the end result will be better. I taste-tested cold water, lukewarm water and hot water myself then decided to run a focus group blind taste test with 25 of my favorite food blogger friends and all but one of them picked the boiling water that started with cold water. I later

found out that Sean, the sole dissenter, had a sinus cold and stuffy nose so his taste buds were totally off. Why he didn't tell me up front, I don't know. I'm never inviting him to one of my taste test focus groups again.

4. Fill the pot up with as much water as you would like to boil. There is no right or wrong answer to this. This is not a trick question. Just fill the pot up.

5. Turn the faucet off and walk the pot to your stove. Place the pot on stove top, over one of the burners. If you have an electric stove just place the pot on one of the circles on the glass that specify where the heat comes on (or if you are old school electric, place it directly on the electric coil itself). If you have an induction stovetop I hate you and you're on your own.

6. Turn the heat up to high for the burner or electric circle/coil that you placed the pot on. You can certainly use medium or even low heat to boil water, but high heat is definitely recommended. You want to make sure to really sear the water surface initially with the high heat. This is called the Maillard reaction and it really gives the final boiling water a lovely flavor and color.

7. Now cover the pot with a lid. If you've lost the lid or the lid is so bent up that it doesn't fit over the pot properly, then either grab a sheet pan or metal cookie sheet and cover the pot with that, or just skip covering the water. Just be forewarned that the water may take longer to boil, and the resulting water may be more concentrated in flavor because some of it will have evaporated in the heating process. But if you like a more concentrated water flavor, then by all means, don't cover the pot.

8. Now wait for the heat to do its job. If you covered the pot, you can periodically check underneath the lid to see if the water is boiling. Just be aware that the more you uncover the pot, the slower it will take for the pot to boil. So check JUST frequently enough to see if the water is boiling, BUT not frequently enough that you slow down the heating process. The range of checking usually is between 2–5 times but sometimes is more and occasionally less. Just try not to go over 8 times because then you look like an impatient fool. Plus the whole "a watched pot" thing . . .

9. The water is boiling when large rapid bubbles are vigorously appearing and are coming up from the bottom of the pan to the top of the water surface. If you only see small tiny bubbles, you haven't fully reached the boiling point and you need to let the water heat ever so slightly more. Once the rapid large bubbles appear, you can turn the heat off. You have boiling water!

BONUS STEP

10. Carefully pour the boiling water into a drinking container of your choice. Mugs with handles are the preferred drinking container, but you can use glasses, or other heat proof drinkware, even cute mason jars wrapped in baker's twine or polka dotted ribbon. Be careful that you don't spill the boiling water on yourself or pick up the mason jars immediately because the boiling water is hot and will burn you.* Let it cool a bit to pick up or to drink.

Makes exactly 3 2/7ths cups of boiling water.

* I am not responsible for any burns you may suffer from drinking boiling water. Please check with your doctor or health care provider if burns do happen. This post was not sponsored by First Degree Therapeutic Burn Cream as I have never used it before because I practice common sense when it comes to drinking boiling water. All opinions are my own.

Special thanks to Sabrina of The Tomato Tart for loaning me baker's twine, as I do not own any and really didn't want to buy any for this post. The stripey paper drinking straws are my own though. I stole a handful of those from a friend of mine's wedding.

This has been a special April Fool's edition of Eat the Love. I write this disclaimer because inevitably someone will believe that this is a legitimate recipe for how to boil water and try to correct me about the Maillard reaction listed above. To that person, I say . . . you are a fool. Good day.

THE LIONS OF BANGKOK STREET FOOD

By Matt Goulding

From RoadsAndKingdoms.com

Exotic travel, music, politics, food—it's all fair game for
the digital magazine Roads and Kingdoms. Co-founder
Matt Goulding, a former *Men's Health* food editor,
needs no excuse to jump on a plane, especially if there's
adventurous eating at the other end. Note: Check out
the full online version, where Singapore and Saigon are
added to the street food mix.

T he worst meal I ever ate in Southeast Asia was at a beautiful
candlelit restaurant in Bangkok. The waiters wore sarongs and
offered lemongrass-scented towels to wash off the day. Back in the
kitchen, the chef, a young European, had taken to reinterpreting traditional Thai food, adding modern twists and foreign "refinements"—
replacing chicken with duck confit, daubing noodles with foie. It was
twice as expensive and half as good as any other meal I ate on that
trip (including the tame farang fare of the island bungalow circuit).
Later that same night, I went out and ate the dishes the young chef
was trying to approximate and promised myself to never eat inside a
real restaurant in this part of Asia again.

That experience, coupled with other letdowns over the past decade of travel to the Far East, helped form the basis of what I'll call the
Pretty=Shitty Postulate: That is, the more attractive the restaurant in
Southeast Asia, the less likely it is to serve delicious food. There are,
of course, exceptions to the rule, but they are shockingly scarce. No,
to eat well in this part of the world, look for the establishment with

the tiny plastic stools, the gathering insects, the fluorescent glare of a hospital waiting room.

While you're at it, might as well skip the place with the credit card machine and the his and hers bathrooms. And there's really no use for that team of waiters. Or even a menu. Come to think of it, what you're really looking for is a stretch of cement with just enough room for a few plastic stools and a raging fire. That's where the good stuff is.

Street food is big news these days. Guidebooks dedicate entire sections to street food safety, tour operators take westerners to not-so-secret locations to observe this exotic style of eating, and vast blogging communities busy themselves with mapping out the best of a city's sidewalk offerings. All the while, the Western world tries to find a way to make it theirs. Some people buy trucks and pass black bean burgers and Korean tacos through the window. The more ambitious ones, the chefs with names you might recognize, make the pilgrimages to these cities, often with their team of underlings in tow, where they eat and eat and eat. Back in their spotless kitchens, they set about recreating the stars of the street scene with impressive precision and first-class products. They add that garnish of fried shallots they tried in the Chiang Mai market; they serve their shrimp with lime and black pepper like it's done in Hanoi. But when you bite into that $19 "small plate"? It is fine. It is perfectly satisfying.

But it isn't street food. Not even close.

The first thing I do in Bangkok is the first thing everyone does when they come to Bangkok: I get lost.

I spent weeks doing research, emailing experts, marking maps, setting up interviews—doing what I would normally do before eating my way though a town. Only, when the bus doors open and spit me out into that cauldron of spice and sin, all of the preparation evaporates into the warm city air. In Bangkok, where the best places to eat come without names or addresses, you can't Google your way to the promised land; you just need to feel it out.

As someone accustomed to planning Thursday's lunch before Monday's breakfast is fully digested, this takes time and patience and a considerable surrendering of compulsive behavior. But once you accept the reality, there is something deeply liberating about intuiting your way to a good meal.

It's well past noon and my hunger burns as hot as the midday sun. I come across a sad set of stands under a freeway overpass, but just before dismissing this shabby collection, I spot two tables of well-dressed men, all silently attacking the same dish. I follow the smell and the breath of the wok until I come upon the tiny old woman responsible for the small crowd. She stares up at me blankly from behind her wok. I point to the men behind me. She turns around and goes to work.

Ninety seconds later, out comes a heartbreaking version of *pad kha-prao*: roughly ground pork and wilted leaves of holy basil, spiked lavishly with chilies and a beautiful sheen of fish sauce, a violently fried egg resting atop it all. Whatever expectations I have for the meal come not from the months of reading books and blogs before the trip, but in the seconds between ordering and eating.

With even the most rudimentary skills of observation you can sniff out an astounding meal on any block of the city. A few clues: Is that wok firing especially hot? Is she cooking to order, rather than scooping out the warmed-over creations cooked hours prior? (The latter is, of course, the only way to serve many of Thailand's great dishes—jungle curries, tom yum—but if it's a dish that comes from the wok or the fryer, it should burn your lips with the first bite). Is the cook's prep area well stocked with vegetables, herbs and protein? Is the menu short? Better yet, is there no menu at all?

When it comes to density and intensity, Bangkok is unrivaled in the world of street food. Next to the wild tastes of Bangkok, the hawker flavors of Singapore seem domesticated. Take my 3am nightcap at the Huay Kwang Market. After a round of beers and sundried pork that has a sweetness and chew stranded perfectly between satay and jerky, I order a plate of raw prawns. The fat crustaceans are plucked live from a fish tank, summarily executed, shelled and butterflied on the spot. They are then slathered in what looks like pesto and buried under tufts of fresh herbs and nickel-size circles of raw garlic. Everything looks so fresh and innocent . . . and then you bite down. First, a rush of sweetness from the shrimp, then a sharp hit of garlic, and finally, blackout levels of spice from the puree of green chilies painted onto the crustaceans. It takes two large Chang beers to extinguish the fire.

Thai food is a high-wire balancing act, one that pits salty, sour, sweet and hot against each other in equal and opposite measures. Ever wonder why you find yourself so consistently disappointed with Thai food in places that aren't Thailand? Out of fear of offending sensitive Western palates, the kitchen holds back on the heat, they pull back on the fish-sauce punch, and the whole dish falls apart.

But it's not just the impossible juxtaposition that makes Thai street food so special. Thai street cooks, like great restaurant chefs, know the value of the little touches that take a dish over the top: the leaves of crunchy fried holy basil that add texture to a salad, the crust of coconut encasing molten chunks of fried bananas, the drizzle of vinegar infused with chilies and lemongrass that makes your whole body buzz.

To take those little touches one step further, street vendors empower eaters with a table full of condiments, turning you into a sous chef of sorts. Too spicy? A squeeze of lime and a dusting of sugar should curb the burn. Lacking punch? A splash of fish sauce and a spoonful of fresh chilies should fix that right up. It's an unspoken agreement between cook and eater: I give you these tools, if you promise me you won't fuck up my creation.

It's one of my favorite parts of eating on this side of the world: I find myself constantly tinkering, dusting a midnight pad thai liberally with dried chilies, cutting the funk of a breakfast bowl of boiled offal with a few squeezes of lime, goosing a Chinese-style stir-fry of water spinach and pork belly with spicy vinegar and fish sauce.

A few meals into a trip to a place like Bangkok you begin to wonder how it ever got so good, how they cracked the code on one of gastronomy's most enduring challenges: how to make food fast, healthy, inexpensive and unthinkably delicious all at the same time.

It starts with the fact that these countries have the building blocks: fresh produce of exceptional quality, cooking techniques developed and refined over millennia, potent condiments that can be combined in thousands of different ways to create vastly different effects. But just having the right paint isn't enough to make a work of art. The proliferation of street food—in Thailand and Vietnam, just like in ancient Rome and Athens—is, by definition, an urban adaptation. When the bulk of Thailand's population lived in rural villages, most meals were cooked and eaten at home, but as people began to swarm towards the cities in the mid to late 20th century, domestic life underwent radical changes. Urban kitchens were ill equipped for family cooking and busier lifestyles left little time to stand around the stove. Plus the economies of scale made eating out every bit as cheap as eating in. And while Mom might make a mean green curry or tom yum, it's tough to compete with the legions of street cooks who dedicate their lives to making the same dish over and over until its part of their identity.

On my last afternoon in Bangkok, standing in front of a dizzying number of street vendors besides Siam Center, I decide to play a game. With a bus to catch in 20 minutes and unable to find my preprogrammed location, I set out to deposit my remaining 300 baht (about $10) into the hands of as many cooks as possible. I start with dessert: an old man covers a flattop with a dozen mini crepes, toasting them to a rich mahogany brown. The crepe itself is as thin and crunchy as a candy shell, the warm savory filling evoking the sweet, salty comfort of an American diner breakfast. A few stands down, a plump middle-aged woman cooks chicken meatballs: smooth, pale orbs threaded onto bamboo skewers, grilled until gently charred on the surface, then dipped into a crimson vat of sweet chili sauce and served with a few slices of cucumber. Next stop, *som tam*, the ubiquitous northern Thai salad of green papaya, chilies, and dried shellfish, pestle-pounded into an electric mix of spice and sweet and ocean umami.

If the game is to eat one of the best meals of my life for as little money as possible, I've already won, but I keep going: I still have a wad of bills in my pocket and the last stand in the line of vendors is the most enticing of the lot. A mother and daughter work in a tight formation, pulling chicken parts from their fish-sauce marinade, dredging them in flour, then dropping them into a vat of burbling fat. The chicken emerges with a craggy coat the color of maple syrup. By the time I board the bus five minutes later, it's still too hot to handle without a napkin.

And so I sit there, lips blistered with chicken crackling, fingers singed with pounded capsaicin, watching the whole of Bangkok sink into the horizon behind me, smilingly stupidly, wondering what to do with the last 150 baht.

Context and environment have a profound impact on how we experience food, but there is something else that makes this way of eating so vital, something beyond the scooter cries and the tiny stools and the mugs of iced beer. It's the fate of the wok that has seared millions of meals into submission. It's the fact that not one motion is wasted in transforming that pile of vegetables and meat into a beautiful plate of food. It's the years of cooking the same dish over and over until the pan handles and the spatula rivets have worn away at your skin like a river rounding out the edges of a stone. That doesn't travel; that doesn't translate.

That stays on the streets, exactly where it began and where it belongs.

How to Cook a Turkey

By Molly Watson

From TheDinnerFiles.com

As a freelance food writer, recipe developer, and columnist (Serious Eats, About.Com), Molly Watson is immersed in the rich local food culture of her adopted hometown San Francisco. But sometimes, the down-to-earth Minnesotan in her bursts out—like, say, in the midst of a crazed Thanksgiving dinner.

I've cooked several lifetimes worth of turkeys. Being a food writer will do that to a person. Such vast experience has left me with no desire to cook one ever again. It has also left me with a remarkable ability to cook a turkey—blindfolded if necessary—and to do it well. Like, really well. People say things like, "Holy shit, this is the best turkey I've ever tasted," and, "Why is this turkey so much better than every other turkey I've ever eaten?" and, "Molly, will you marry me?"

It seems wrong to keep this precious knowledge to myself, especially in November, when so many people are suffering, overwhelmed by what they mistakenly think is the Herculean task of cooking a turkey. That's their first problem: they let the turkey get into their head. Like dealing with your drunken aunt's insults at the dining table, cooking a turkey is primarily a mental game and you need to start from a position of confidence, with a take-no-prisoners attitude. Then, do as I do, and be the boss of that bird:

1. Salt the Shit Out of the Turkey

I know, you've heard all about this brining thing. If you want the hassle of creating gallons of brine and figuring out a place where your turkey can simultaneously be submerged in the brine and kept cold, knock yourself out. I stopped brining turkeys years ago. I just salt them. It's easier, it makes a crazy delicious and moist bird, and you don't risk overdoing it and ending up with something more sea sponge than poultry. On Monday, I work gobs of salt into every part of the turkey. I salt it inside and out. Instead of letting the turkey get under your skin, get salt under its skin. Then I plop it in a pan, cover it, and stick it back in the fridge. On Wednesday, I uncover it, pour off any liquid in the pan, and put it back in the fridge uncovered so the skin can dry out—all the better to crisp up! Early on Thursday I take it out to let off any chill, which helps it cook more evenly. Cooking a cold bird is the primary cause of The-Breast-Is-Dried-Out-But-The-Thighs-Are-Bloody syndrome. Food safety experts will tell you not to leave the turkey out for hours; you may want to listen to them or you may want a delicious turkey. The choice is yours!

2. Layer On Some Fat

Here's another reason to let the turkey de-chill before cooking: an ice-cold bird is near impossible to slather with butter, and turkey rewards me with moist meat and crisp skin in exchange for said butter massage. If newspaper food sections and television cooking segments are to be believed, people around the country live in mortal fear of a dry turkey. I figure I'd mention this easy work-around.

I've also been known to lay slices of bacon or pancetta all over the breast to give it a bit of protection from the heat. This tactic also results in crackling turkey-flavored bacon for me to nosh on while finishing up the feast. You may choose to share it, but that's fucking insane—Who's watching football? Them! Who's making this bird? You! So who gets the bacon? It's simple math.

3. Put the Turkey Someplace Crazy Hot

For most of you, this is an oven. For me, it's a grill. Wherever it is, make it hot. Really hot. The someplace hot may, if you're a bit nuts, be a giant vat of oil because you've decided to deep-fry your turkey. Color me impressed.

Note: Grilling the turkey frees up valuable oven space for roasting brussels sprouts and re-heating all those crap dishes your guests insisted on bringing to "help." If you've put the bacon slices on like

I told you to, your yard and possibly even your neighborhood with be perfumed with the scent of cooking bacon and you'll have something pithy to say if you're gathered with people who insist everyone at the table say what they're thankful for. I know I'm always thankful that "I'm grateful for a deck that smells of bacon" keeps me from saying, "I'm grateful for all the times I haven't had to go around the table like it's kindergarten saying what I'm grateful for."

4. Cook the Turkey Until It Is Done

But how long do I cook the turkey, you're asking. You're pleading. You're emailing and texting and tweeting me all Thursday morning. Such a question forces me to state the obvious: you cook it till it's done. If you're into gadgets, go buy a fancy digital thermometer. But while your fix-it friend is busy figuring out how to replace the batteries, you can just wiggle the leg. Does it feel loose? Like your son could pretty much rip it off and gnaw on it Henry VIII-style? The bird is done.

How big the turkey is, the temperature and size and altitude of your oven are all going to factor into the magical, mystical equation. Another important factor will be how often you and your nosey relatives open the oven door to check on its progress.

5. Give the Bird a Break

After all the salting, butter-massaging, roasting, and wiggling, your turkey is exhausted. The key to being a good boss is knowing when to push and when to let up. Let the bird hang out for awhile before you attack it. Give it at least half an hour. Yep. Just let it sit there and mellow under a cozy blanket of foil. The turkey will think all the fuss is over, relax, and let all its yummy juices settle back in place after their frantic attempts to escape the protein as it cooked. Plus, it will give you time to eat that bacon, pound back a Manhattan, and try to remember why all those damn people are in your house.

Home Cooking

AND BABY MAKES FREE-FOR-ALL

By Adam Sachs

From Bon Appétit

Bon Appétit contributor Adam Sachs—a.k.a. the
Obsessivore—is also a travel writer for *GQ* and *Travel
and Leisure*; he comes naturally to a globetrotting
perspective on food. But when there's a new baby in the
house, sometimes just going to the food market seems
like a major expedition.

"**S**it," the boy commanded.

I thought I detected an unfamiliar note of concern and tenderness in his voice. But my powers of detection were blunted by an
interrogation level of sleep deprivation. It was a time of happy chaos
within our growing household: The boy, not quite two years old, had
just been joined by a girl whose age we still measured in days.

We sang nonsense songs all night and ate ice cream for breakfast.
For a week, nobody went outside or wore pants.

Sensing a frayed fabric of life in need of mending, my son stopped
me as I leapt by him on the way to fetch something infant-related in
the kitchen.

"Dada, sit," he said, indicating the seat opposite his high chair. He
sounded serious. So I sat.

Typically at this point, he would ask to honk my nose or demand
a Lego train car. But now he fixed me with an arresting look, forgiving but firm. We need to have a little chat, it said. Pay attention.

I recognized it as the kind of look I'd no doubt use on him in
fatherly negotiations ahead. But now my son had the floor and was
ready to make his case.

"Dada," the boy said, "I want to have eat-eat."

I was impressed. Nobody around here, least of all the nearly two-year-old, was in the habit of using full sentences.

And I knew what he meant. "Eat-eat" was more than the sum of its repetitive parts. It wasn't food as fuel. Eat-eat, I'd come to understand, was a proper family meal. It was togetherness at the table, the boy sharing what we ate.

It was civilized—healthier and more fun than the kind of disjointed perma-snacking we'd fallen into. He wanted to yell "Cheers!" and clunk his milk cup into my wineglass.

We all wanted eat-eat.

The directive was clear, the tone urgent: Venture forth into the sunny world to hunt and gather (or at least shop and schlep) something nice for dinner.

So we all put on pants, except for the little girl, who dozed in her pastel muumuu-straitjacket. And we set out toward the farmers' market with two strollers and bed head and a bag of wipes.

When the boy had first arrived, I'd been flush with joyful mania—and the need to make myself useful somehow. The miniature, mother-focused creature asked little of me in those early weeks, so I set my euphoric enthusiasm loose in the kitchen. I cranked up the oven and churned out piles of pizzas for visiting grandparents and friends. I made chicken salad for the new nanny and heaping bowls of nutty farro salad with tiny halved tomatoes and sweet beets for the new mom. I simmered and froze great quantities of chicken stock and meat ragouts for our bright and homebound future.

This time around, confidence had bred complacency. Until my son reminded me of the central importance of making sure we all ate well.

The question, then, was what to make? What to feed a growing gang when you've got work deadlines to meet and a son who knows you're phoning it in; when it's also brain-meltingly hot out and everybody's already a little goofy from lack of sleep?

The answer is, you want something stabilizing that can be assembled—in stages—ahead of time without too much sustained attention; something that easily scales to mass quantities and can be repurposed for days.

At the market, I saw crates of green and wavy purple lettuces, peppery mizuna, and esoteric leafy things whose names I would never remember even when rested. Typically I'm not a salad craver, but I'd been living on ginger ice cream, lemon sorbet, and adrenaline, and these leaves, man, they were lookin' real good to me. Across from the lettuce monger was the duck dude. He pulled some nice-looking smoked magrets from his case, and I knew we had the makings of a kick-ass eat-eat.

I spent a hot week in the Périgord region of southwestern France a few years back. Every lunch consisted of some variation on the salade Périgourdine, which roughly translates as "all the delicious things you can think of thrown together in a louche, duck-and-goose-fat-laden manner not at all resembling austere American notions of a salad."

My version, adapted to what I found at the market, may not be traditional, but it is true to its spirit. Not quite a recipe, it's simply a reliable combination of things that shine together: sturdy, flavorful greens brightened by a mustardy vinaigrette; the sunsetty yolks of good eggs; the earthy heft and salt of the duck, thinly sliced; the crunch of walnuts; a bit of crumbly blue cheese.

The nice thing about a salad like this is that you can cook the eggs, wash and dry the greens, and whisk your vinaigrette whenever you want. (While others are napping, say.) Then assemble it—at room temperature—for lunch, dinner, or anytime in between (or after).

The nicer thing about a salad like this is that when I served it to the mother, whose soul had also been silently crying out for leafy things and smoky-salty protein and the satisfying crunch of bread nuggets crisped in duck fat, she let out a low purr of approval. Her look said, Now you're pulling your weight around here.

My son inhaled the greens, hand to mouth, a natural. He ate the egg, cut up. I tore off a piece of the smoked magret and told him, "Duck."

"Duck," the boy said, taking it and seeming satisfied. After a thoughtful chew, he appeared to remember a bedtime book about lost ducklings and said again, a little scandalized, "Duck?"

"Cheers!" I yelled to change the subject. That was a conversation that could wait. The boy clunked my glass with his milk cup. Beside us in her cradle, the girl slept on, quietly. The important thing was that we were here together, seated and finally sated.

A French-ish Salad to Feed an Expanding Household

An assemblage of delicious things to be deployed in necessarily inexact proportions.

Leafy greens, the more peppery the better.

A mustardy vinaigrette. Whisk 2 tablespoons red wine vinegar with 1 teaspoon each Dijon and grainy mustards. Gradually whisk in ½ cup olive oil.

Fresh farm eggs. Slide into already-boiling water, cook for about 7 minutes, then put straight into ice water.

Smoked duck breast. Trim off some fat for frying the croutons, then thinly slice the meat against the grain. Order at *dartagnan.com*.

Toasted walnuts

Slivered red onion

Croutons. Fry torn bread in a combo of olive oil and rendered duck fat until crisp.

Crumbled blue cheese

Now, arm yourself with enough ingredients to feed everybody for a few meals. Toss some greens with vinaigrette. Top with the duck and halved eggs. While snacking on the croutons, scatter some around. Sprinkle the cheese, onion, and walnuts over the top; finish with Maldon salt and pepper. Bask in the admiration of your loved ones. Nap. Repeat.

SENSE OF SELF

By Erin Byers Murray

From FoodThinker.com

Ah, the underappreciated day-to-day job of cooking for a family. Growing up, Erin Byers Murray (managing editor of *Nashville Lifestyles* magazine, author of *Shucked: Life on a New England Oyster Farm*) took her mother's kitchen routine for granted. And then fate intervened.

While I was growing up, my mother was a get-folks-fed, functional kind of cook. A teacher and mother of two, she always managed at least one meal (though it was usually three) each day, constructing well-balanced plates with a thoughtful array of proteins, vegetables, and starches. She was careful to avoid the things she knew we would reject (lima beans for me; steamed broccoli for Dad) and loved to toss in treats (butterscotch pudding for everyone). Lunches were made for school. Holiday dinners were a three-day affair that started with the heady scent of sautéed onions and ended with the sweetly fragrant spices layered into her pumpkin pie.

Half of the time she worked from a recipe—her collection of Southern Living Annual Recipes books were a favorite go to—but the other half, she worked "by the seat of my pants," she'd say. There were a handful of favorite dishes she knew by heart, and usually measurements were an afterthought. "I season by taste," she'd say and dip a finger into a bowl of mashed potatoes, pausing to taste its contents, eyes looking upward as she pondered what might be missing. She cooked constantly—not for pleasure or to let off steam, but to get dinner on the table—and always produced tasty meals.

But that was all before the accident that stripped my mother of her taste and smell. That was before the years she spent avoiding the kitchen, avoiding food, and avoiding her fear of making something over-salted, undercooked, or completely inedible. It was also long before she overcame all of those fears and restrictions, started experimenting, and learned to fall in love with the joy of cooking.

My mother doesn't remember much about the accident. She had been on a train from New York to Wilmington, Delaware, where we lived at the time. When the train pulled into the Wilmington station, she quickly gathered her things and ran to the exit to jump off. Just as she was stepping down, the train lurched forward, and the motion of the beast spun her around. She fell, smacking the back of her head against the concrete platform.

It was late June and I had just finished my junior year of high school. Being very busy with my teenage life, it took me a minute to digest my sister's words. Mom. Accident. Hospital. She had a concussion and a fractured skull. Thankfully, the doctors told us, she would be ok. But there was no way of knowing what the long-term effects might be.

Mom was discharged a few days later with a very tender head and some serious nausea. Within minutes of arriving at home, she asked my dad for a Diet Coke—she consumed anywhere from three to five on a daily basis. But with one sip, she told us it was flat. Another one? Flat. A ginger ale? Also flat. "It's just not right," she said.

"Well, that might go away," said the doctor who'd treated her. "It's typical to have that reaction when you suffer from the kind of concussion you did." The olfactory nerves, which sit at the base of the skull, had likely been damaged, he said.

Some time passed and Mom still couldn't taste or smell anything. We started to realize that her condition could be permanent, and to keep from annoying her, we stopped asking if it was getting better. She saw a neuro-psychologist who eventually recommended an appointment at the University of Pennsylvania's Smell and Taste Center, one of only two in the country, where there was a six-month waiting period.

Earlier that year, Dad had been transferred to Houston, Texas and was already spending most of his time at the office down there. Mom was planning to join him as soon as I graduated, but until then, with my sister away at college, she and I were on our own. By now, I was busy being a senior in high school. I tested her lack of smell by going out and smoking cigarettes. She never once noticed. And even though eating together at the dinner table had forever been a family ritual, I suddenly had plenty of reasons to avoid it.

Mom, meanwhile, had plenty of reasons not to cook. Besides her fear of creating something inedible, she just wasn't interested in spending time on a meal she couldn't enjoy. The smell of chopped garlic, the peppery bite of a well-made vinaigrette—with those basic pleasures gone, what use was the effort? We muddled through dinner with take-out and trips to our favorite sub shop. And if I wasn't around—an increasingly common behavior—she wouldn't eat and quickly started losing weight.

A few months into the ordeal, I finally picked up the slack. With her guidance, I learned to throw together a few easy meals: baked, stuffed manicotti, homemade pizzas. They were simple projects that really only required some assembly, but it was my first experience understanding the sense of gratification that comes from feeding someone else. I became interested in the inner workings of our kitchen—why it was organized just so; how to put together a grocery list; seeing, probably for the first time, the simultaneous order and chaos that occurs when chopping, shredding, baking, and plating. While Mom sank further into a culinary void, I felt my first spark of romance with food.

Six months after the accident, we celebrated my 18th birthday. As she had done for every birthday of my life, and my grandmother had done for every birthday of hers, my mom woke up that morning and started baking an angel food cake. There was no forethought; she simply pulled out the ingredients and got started. Cake flour. Sugar. Egg whites. Almond and vanilla extracts. She pulled out her old, overused tube pan and her mixer, then beat the egg whites and cream of tartar together before adding the sugar.

As she worked, she thought about her mom's angel food cakes and remembered how the sweet smell of almond extract would waft through the house, signaling yet another family birthday. "I could tell an angel food cake from ten miles away," she says today. Folding the extract into my cake, she wanted so badly to smell that sweet, pungent scent. To feel that sensation of home.

And then, just like that, it hit her. Earthy nuttiness. Sweetness. Aroma. She sensed almond in the air. She couldn't smell anything, of course. But a smell memory had returned. "And that was the beginning of just saying, 'OK. I know what that smells like,'" she says.

At long last, she had her appointment at the Smell and Taste Center, and they determined that her olfactory nerves had been severed. They called it anosmia: the inability to smell, which was ultimately affecting her sense of taste. She could differentiate salty and sweet and, to lesser degrees, bitter and tart. They recommended that she never live alone in case of a gas leak and to pay very close attention to milk carton expiration dates. Other than that, there was nothing they could do.

I eventually left for college, and Mom and Dad made their way to Houston. They took advantage of their empty nester status and ate out frequently. When Mom did cook, she held onto the idea of her sense memory and imagined the many scents and flavors she was missing. She enlisted Dad to help her overcome her fear of seasonings (he was more than happy to assume the role of house guinea pig) and began to appreciate the construction of a bite: the sensation of the food and its texture, the color of various foods on the plate. Instead of protein, vegetable, starch, she created dishes that had crunch, vibrant color, and two of her favorite detectable palate notes, salt and sweetness. Tomato Caprese salads; simply baked fish over a bed of asparagus spears; quickly stir-fried vegetables.

No longer confined to cooking to feed a brood, Mom started to cook for fun, pulling recipes out of magazines or cookbooks, buying kitchen tools and testing out new gadgets. Food and cooking became a hobby, something she looked forward to daily. During my breaks from college, Mom would enlist me to help in the kitchen. Whether it was decorating a batch of Christmas cookies or helping her prep for Thanksgiving, I was usually eager to get to work (dorm cooking left plenty to be desired). Especially since I knew I would pick up a few tips along the way.

The holiday before I left to spend a semester studying abroad in London, where I would live in my first flat, she helped me plan a meal from scratch and took me shopping. We scoured the aisles in search of our ingredients and I marveled at her appreciation for the variety of colors and textures. She wasn't seeking sustenance, that vital but mundane purpose she once survived on—now she was seeking pleasure. To this day, I can't go into a grocery store without hearing her voice in the back of my head, calling, "Ooh! Grab some parsley and lemons. We need some color to go with all of those browns on the plate."

She and Dad developed a close-knit group of friends who started their own gourmet group. They called themselves "Ten Chefs Too Many," and each couple took turns hosting dinners, always challenging themselves to create elaborate, complicated menus. The theme would vary, from one particular cookbook to a specific country's cuisine. Mom and Dad started cooking together more often—and always purely for fun. One club dinner they hosted involved a complex menu of Chinese dishes, including Mom's favorite, Kung Pao Prawns in Bird's Nests. She and Dad spent two days testing the dish, practicing the dexterity required to remove the thin noodles of the "bird's nest" from the piping hot oil in one piece. Dad tested the seasonings while Mom perfected the visual elements of the dish. And despite the fact that she couldn't taste their final creation, Mom swears she savored every bite. "It had all the essential elements," she says. "Crunchy, salty, fried, and fattening."

The Utley Family Angel Food Cake

The unforgettable scent of almond is what still makes this a family favorite. When we were growing up, we would usually have our angel food cakes "naked." However, if Mom prepares it for somebody else, she glazes it.

> 1 ¼ cups cake flour
> ½ cup sugar
> dash of salt
> 1 ½ cups egg whites (about 12)
> 1 ¼ teaspoons cream of tartar
> 1 teaspoon white vanilla extract
> ½ teaspoon almond extract
> 1 ⅓ cups sugar

Heat oven to 375°F.

In a medium bowl, sift first 3 ingredients together.

In a large mixing bowl with an electric mixer, beat egg whites and cream of tartar until foamy. Add 1 ⅓ cups of sugar and beat on high speed until mixture holds stiff peaks. Fold in vanilla and almond extracts.

Sift in about a quarter of the flour and sugar mixture. Gently fold in. Continue sifting remainder, a quarter cup at a time, until the flour mixture is incorporated into the egg whites.

Pour batter into 10-inch ungreased tube pan. Take a knife and gently cut through batter to remove large air bubbles. Bake for 35 to 40 minutes.

When you remove from the oven, immediately invert the pan and stand on a tall bottle. Let cool upside down.

When cake is completely cool, take a knife and loosen cake from the sides and the inner tube. Remove cake to a cake plate.

Creamy Lemon Glaze

⅓ cup butter
½ teaspoon grated lemon peel
2 cups powdered sugar
2 to 4 tablespoons lemon juice

Over low heat, melt butter in saucepan. Add lemon peel, powdered sugar, and 1/2 tablespoon of lemon juice. Stir in additional lemon juice, 1 tablespoon at a time, until it's thin enough to pour but not too wet. Pour glaze over cake and let cool until firm.

The Ghosts of Cakes Past

By Monica Bhide

From ModernSpice.com

In her 2009 cookbook, *Modern Spice*, engineer-turned-food writer Monica Bhide creatively reinterpreted the cuisine of her native India for the modern American kitchen. One thing she quietly left out: desserts. Now she confesses why.

I don't bake. Let me clarify that: I cannot bake. I did not grow up in a house where anyone baked. I grew up around spiced curries, smoked kebabs and fried milk but never around the smell of a freshly baked cake.

So, usually when I am upset, I try to cook. When I have a decision to make, I go in the kitchen and lose myself in my spices, in the sizzle of the hot oil, in the smell of the sautéing ginger, in the rumble of the boiling rice. And yet today, as I am faced with a very difficult decision, I decide to bake. A cake no less.

I am not sure what I am doing here surrounded by flour, eggs, butter, brown sugar, vanilla. I stare at them and all the ghosts of cakes past stare back. They are laughing at me. The overcooked and burned cake I made a year ago, the soufflé that never rose, the three-tier cake that ended up in the trash, the cookies that could change the game of hockey forever: edible pucks, anyone? A chill runs down my spine as I recall all the bad decisions I have made in the past. What if this time is no different?

I am torn about what to cook.

I stare at the familiar yellow turmeric. The powder in the small transparent bottle looks like warm sunshine on sunny day. The cumin calls my name. The cinnamon beckons to be added to the lamb in my fridge.

I close the spice cabinet.

I am going to bake a cake. God help us all.

I begin by reading the instructions and I can almost hear cookbook author Nancie McDermott talking to me. I met her at a conference this year. Her vibrant spirit and her contagious laughter attracted me to her. I am cooking from her book. Perhaps I am trying to channel her and have her here with me. She looks like the kind of person who could make hard decisions easily.

Not me.

I begin by opening the bag of flour. It spills all over the counter and the floor. The fine white powder covers the newly cleaned hardwood floor. I want to clean it up. Instead I simply stand there. It is how I feel. My spirit is covered in dust and I cannot seem to shake it off.

I bend down and clean the flour. But it seems I have just made a bigger mess. Funny how it seems like my life now. I plug one hole to have another one open up. Noah, your ark has nothing on me.

I begin to read the instructions again and it asks to boil some milk and butter. I can do that. I think. The weight of my decision is hurting me so much that I cannot function. I hear the kids in the living room playing a game of carom. It is a fun game, if you haven't tried it. It is like playing pool except it is on a flat board and there are little "coins" instead of balls and a larger coin called a striker to strike them with (instead of a cue).

The kids, they hear me rattling around the kitchen, and come to see what all the fuss is about. The older one offers to break the eggs in a container so I can proceed with this monumental dish. He looks at the recipe photo; it is stunning, "Wow, mom. This looks amazing. Look at all the caramel on this cake!"

Oh, right, have I mentioned that I have never made caramel icing before?

He breaks the eggs as I stand and watch him. I haven't created too many amazing things in my life but he is one of the best ones yet. He smiles at me. "You look tired," he says and then begins to help me clean the floor.

I stand back and watch him. He is cleaning while his four-year-old brother is standing there, quietly, throwing more flour on the floor. They make me laugh, these little miracles.

They run back to their game and I begin to continue my cake or what I hope will be a cake.

As the milk and the butter meld together on the stove, I begin to look for the cake pans. I know I have them somewhere. I begin to look in earnest for the pans. I spot an old plate a friend had given me, a old jar that hosted a shrimp pickle I once made and a broken spatula that holds heavy memories.

How did I get myself into this mess? Why do I have to make this decision? Why can't decisions make themselves? Better yet, why can't things go back to the way they were, when we were all strangers to each other, when there was no familiarity, when there was no relationship, when there was nothing that could hurt.

My husband of eighteen years wanders into the kitchen. I want to go and hug him. He knows I am struggling with this decision. He comes over and hugs me and as gently and kindly as possible whispers, "Don't worry. Don't try so hard. Let it be." I know he is right. But I don't feel it yet. I am not ready to let it be.

He leaves to watch a football game. I return to my hunt for the cake pans.

Much to my dismay, I find the pans.

This means I will have to go on.

I sift, I measure, I pretend to know what I am doing.

I have been doing that all last year. Pretending.

I cannot pretend anymore, I am no good at it. I am stuck between a rock and a hard place, and only the right choice will help me.

What is the right choice? How does one know when a decision will heal and when it will hurt more?

I don't know. I seem to be saying and writing that a lot lately: I don't know.

My four-year-old complains about that. He asks how planes fly, why the wind only blows on our face when the windows are down in the car, how plants eat, how the little people get inside the TV, why the sky is blue, why the grass is green, why butter is so delicious, why rice can be red. I say I don't know. Then I hug him. I am tired. The choices I have to make have made me tired. But he makes me laugh as he makes up answers to his own questions.

He comes in and stares at the baking cake in the oven, through the little glass window on the door. We smile at each other. A sweet, warm smell has filled my tiny kitchen. A reassurance that there is peace to be found in the small things in life.

He runs off to find his brother.

I begin to make the caramel icing. I read the instructions again. I can do this. The brown sugar, the butter, the milk begin to fall in love with each other in my pan and meld together to become a gorgeous brown crème.

The cake has cooled on the rack and does not look like a volcano exploded. In fact, it looks like a fairly decent pound cake. Nancie would be proud. Perhaps, it is too early to say that. No one has tasted it yet.

I need a spatula to spread the icing. I cannot find it and as I peek in the pan on the stove, I notice the icing hardening.

I sit down and stare at the kitchen. It is a mess. I am a fairly clean cook and yet today I have made it look like my husband was cooking, unsupervised.

I make myself some coffee and sip it as I taste the cake, hardened icing on the side.

Did I really do it? Did I just bake a two-tier cake with almost icing on it?

My eyes are moist. I have wandered through unknown territory and come out the other end. Mostly unscathed.

I still don't know what I am going to do. But then, perhaps, there is the point. I don't have to know. It is like my younger son and his questions. My husband and I never seem to have adequate answers and yet he trusts us. He makes up his own sometimes. But more importantly, he trusts that we will guide him to the right answers when the time is right.

I have to trust that things will work out as they are meant to be.

Perhaps some people are only meant to be in our lives at a certain time and not at another. It does not mean that friendships are lost or lives have to be ruined. It is just time to move on.

Trusting in the process is hard; believing that the right answer will come out the other end is harder.

And yet, here I am with a gorgeous caramel cake, a family that is praising my non-existent baking skills, and a feeling that everything is going to be just fine.

Bread and Women

By Adam Gopnik

From The New Yorker

Adam Gopnik covers many topics as a staff writer
for *The New Yorker*, but he returns again and again to
food—or more precisely, as the subtitle of his 2011 book
The Table Comes First puts it, "France, Family and the
Meaning of Food." Baking a loaf of bread, though? That
was a new challenge altogether.

Like many men who cook a lot, I'm good at doing several things
that look hard but aren't—béarnaise sauce, tuna au poivre—and
not very good at doing some things that are harder than they look.
I can't make a decent vinaigrette, anything involving a "salt crust"
baffles me, and, until quite recently, I had never baked a loaf of bread.
For years, I told myself that I didn't bake bread for the same reason I
don't drive a car: it's a useful skill, unnecessary in New York. In New
York, you don't drive because you can take the subway practically
anywhere, and you don't have to bake bread because there are so
many good bakeries. Even at the supermarket, there are baguettes
from Tom Cat and cinnamon-raisin loaves from Orwasher and Eli's
empire of sourdoughs.

Just a few weeks ago, though, going through heirlooms that had
been left by my wife's ailing ninety-three-year-old mother when she
moved out of the family house in Montreal, we found a beautiful
hand-lettered, framed recipe for something called Martha's Bread. It
was a long, very seventies-looking recipe, samplerlike in style, with
instructions and ingredients—including lecithin granules and millet

and oats and honey—surrounded by a watercolor border of leaves and falling petals and pumpkins.

"Martha's Bread!" I cried. (Martha is my wife.) "When did you bake bread?" To say that I was incredulous doesn't capture it. One way to describe Martha is to say that she looks like a woman who has never had a loaf of bread named after her—perfumes, dresses, and dances, perhaps, but not oat-and-honey bread. "No Loaves" might be the title of her personal manifesto, as "No Logo" is of Naomi Klein's.

"When I was a teen-ager," she said. "I sewed all my own clothes and I baked all my own bread."

This puzzled me. I knew her in her teens, and she never baked bread. She didn't sew her own clothes, either, not that I could see. She ate matzos with bits of canned asparagus on top, and she dressed, beautifully, in Icelandic woolens and Kenzo dresses and lace-up boots. So I was genuinely curious to see what she looked like baking a loaf of bread. After many years of marriage, you tend to focus your curiosity not on the spectacular moments that might yet happen but on excavating the stranger, smaller ones that did: your partner punching down dough at sixteen. As Proust knew, all love depends not just on current infatuation but on retrospective jealousy; lacking a classy old lover, a Marquis de Norpois, to be jealous of, I was jealous of the men in Montreal health-food stores who had sold her millet and lecithin granules.

"So why don't you make your bread?" I asked.

"My bread's not that easy," she said loftily. "I have to get a big earthenware bowl to make this bread. And a big wooden breadboard. I used to have them at home. I used to make this bread with my friend Rachel. She's the one who illuminated the recipe. We would bake all day in aprons and then drink tea and eat our bread with honey." The thought of her in an apron surrounded by all that homey seventies blond wood was so intoxicating that, to shake the spell, I resolved to start on a loaf that night. I lighted upon the now legendary "No-Knead Bread" recipe I clipped from the *Times* half a dozen years ago. Invented by Jim Lahey, of the Sullivan Street Bakery, this is bread that sort of makes itself. I ran across the street, bought some Fleischmann's yeast, and followed the directions for mixing it with water, salt, and flour. I left the dough to rise overnight and, in the morning, put it in the Le Creuset Dutch oven I normally use only for lamb and beef braises, and then into a four-hundred-and-fifty-degree oven.

An hour later, out it came. It was—bread! It wasn't *good* bread—it didn't have many of those nice, irregular bread bubbles, and I must have put in too much yeast. It was oddly bitter. But it was bread, and I can't explain how weird and pleasing this was. It was as if you had put a slosh of stuff in a bowl and it had come out a *car*, with a gleaming front and a good smell inside.

For the next couple of days, I became, for the first time in my life, acutely bread-conscious. *So many breads!* I marveled as I stared at the bread counter at Dean & DeLuca. I thought of the bread I loved to eat. There was the big, round *pain Poilâne* at the bakery in Paris, sour and stiff and yet yielding to the bite; Montreal bagels, sweet and sesame-rich; and real croissants, feathery and not too buttery. Could you really *make* these things?

"If you're so interested in bread-making, you should apprentice with someone big," said Martha, who had declared herself *hors de combat*, waiting for her wood. "Someone who yells at you a lot and teaches you what's what. You know. Every writer does that now."

I wouldn't want to learn just one thing, though, I mused. "It would have to be someone who had range, so I could learn how to bake *pain Poilâne* and Montreal bagels and croissants, and—"

I stopped in mid-sentence. The larger implication of what I had been saying hit us both. We looked at each other balefully, as those on whom the implacable hand of fate has fallen.

"I'll call her," I said.

When I got my mother on the phone a few hours later—you often have to leave a message, because she and my father are always out in their fields, building things—she was delighted at the idea of a bread-baking-master-class weekend. "Yes, yes, dear," she said. "It's so funny you called. I'm just working on a new series of water-buffalo-milk ice creams. You'd love trying them. Do come for a visit as soon as you can. I'll show you how to bake anything in the world you like."

A week later, I found myself once again in the back seat of my parents' all-purpose child-mover and S.U.V. My parents live these days on a farm in what their six children think of as remote rural Ontario—a designation my parents emphatically reject, pointing out that it is only a three-hour drive from the Toronto airport, not seeing that a three-hour drive from the Toronto airport is *exactly* what their six children mean by "remote rural Ontario." They retired a decade ago to these rather Berkshire-like hills, after a lifetime as college professors.

The vibe of their property, one of their kids has pointed out, is somewhere between "A Midsummer Night's Dream" and "The Island of Dr. Moreau." Bosky though their woods are, within them are a host of strange new buildings that my mother has designed and she and my father built, laboriously, with local lumber, responding to their own unaltered eccentricities and the changing passions of their grandchildren. There is a Japanese tea house, complete with a little Hiroshige-style arched bridge; an Elizabethan theatre, with a thrust stage and a "dressing house" above; a garden-size chess board, with life-size pieces, made when my own son was in the midst of a chess mania, now long past; a Tempietto, modeled on Bramante's High Renaissance design; and a Pantheon, a domed building lined with niches, in which sit portraits, with quotations, of my mother's heroes—Galileo, Shakespeare, Darwin, Emily Dickinson, and Bach among them.

My parents, you might gather, are unusual people, although, to be honest, "unusual" is not really an unusual enough word to describe my mother. One of the first women in North America to earn a Ph.D. in mathematical logic, she became a notable linguist and (as she would be the first to tell you) also reared six kids, for whom she cooked a big French-ish dinner every night. We have a complex relationship. I know that I am more like her than I am like anyone else on earth, for good and ill. Like her, I cook every night. Like her, I offer hyper-emotional editorials to the television at moments of public outrage. Like her, I look accusingly at my children when they fail to devour some dish that, backed into a corner, they had acceded to at seven in the morning. ("What do you want tonight, salmon or capon?" "Uh, whatever. Salmon.")

I even inherited some minute portion of her creative energy, which once launched a thousand shapes—from doll house to linguistic theory—so that, coming home after an eight-hour family trip (during which I, like her, will have left all the driving to my spouse), I can actually enjoy whipping together a big meal, with a hot dessert, for the gang. I once realized, with a sense of fatality, that I have written long essays in praise of nearly every hero in her pantheon up there on the Ontario hill—only Bach and Emily Dickinson had escaped my attention, or her gravitational pull. Into one of her areas of particular mastery I didn't even try to follow her: baking bread. As a kid, I never left for school without being equipped with croissants or pain au chocolat or cinnamon babka or sticky buns, often in combination; on the morning before a big holiday, the kitchen always looked like a Left Bank bakery.

As we pulled up onto the property, my mother turned around. "Did you see our new building, dear?" she asked.

"Sure," I said. "Last visit I saw it." I thought she meant the Pantheon, or maybe the Tempietto.

"Oh, no, not *that*," she said, as though a Pantheon were as commonplace as a lawnmower shed. "I mean our Erechtheion!"

Alarmed by the name, I peered out the left-hand window, and, insanely enough, there it was: in wood and plaster, a nearly full-scale model of the Porch of the Caryatids from the Acropolis, with its six Ionic columns and six draped female figures supporting the roof. The Greek girls were about six feet tall, and, in the Ontario farmland, they looked pretty impressive, though something about the way the figures were incised gave them a demure Canadian quality.

"It's beautiful, Mom," I said, feebly.

That night, we sat down to a dinner mostly of breads—sketches of the weekend to come. I recognized most of them from childhood, but there was a dinner roll that was the best dinner roll I had ever eaten: flaky and rich and yet somehow reassuringly simple and eggy.

"Oh, that's my *broissant*," she explained gaily. "It's my own invention. It's brioche dough given a croissant treatment—egg dough with butter folded in in layers. Do you want to try it? We'll do it tomorrow."

My stomach filled with gluten, I took the books on bread baking and bread history I had brought with me, and went back to my old bed.

At this point, there should be a breath and a space and a new paragraph and lots of stuff about ancient yeasts, the earliest known instances of bread, bread-in-Sumer-and-Egypt lore, and then a joke or two about the Jewish invention, on the lam, of the unleavened kind. I will spare the reader this, for, turning the pages in my books, I decided that the worst of modern food bores is the bread bore. The very universality of bread, the simple alchemy that makes it miraculous, can also make it dull to discuss.

But, as I was reminded the next morning—with my mother wearing her flour-resistant "Monaghan Lumber" T-shirt—bread, though perhaps unrewarding as an analytic subject, is fascinating as a practice. It is probably the case that these two things often vary inversely: activities that are interesting to read about (science experiments) are probably dull to do, while activities that are dull to read about (riding a bike) are interesting when you attempt them. What makes something interesting to read about is its narrative grip, and stories are, of necessity, exercises in compressing time. What makes something interesting to do is that—through repetition, coordination, perseverance—it *stretches* time.

Fortunately, my mother is also an expert in-depth explainer, although her children have been known to run for doors and leap out windows when she starts up with "Well, studies show that. . . ." I have a fond summertime memory of her explaining Gödel's Proof to me; I wish I had retained it, though I recall an indecently vivid picture of sets struggling, in vain, to contain themselves.

Yeast, my mother explained now, is really just a bunch of bugs rooming together, like Oberlin grads in Brooklyn—eukaryotic organisms of the fungus kingdom, kin of mushrooms. "When you mix the little bugs with carbohydrate—wet wheat is a good one—they begin to eat up all the oxygen in it, and then they pass gas made up of ethyl alcohol and carbon dioxide." The alcohol they pass is what makes spirits. The carbon dioxide is what makes bread. The gas they pass causes the dough to rise. It's what puts the bubbles in the bread. If you bake it, you trap or fix the bubbles inside.

As we mixed and kneaded, the comforting sounds of my childhood reasserted themselves: the steady hum of the powerful electric mixer my mother uses, the dough hook humming and coughing as it turned, and, in harmony with it, the sound of the Canadian Broadcasting Corporation in the background, offering its perpetual mixture of grave-sounding news and bright-sounding Baroque music.

(A certain kind of Canadian keeps the CBC on from early morning to bedtime, indiscriminately.)

Like most good cooks, my mother is sweet-tempered in the run-up to cooking, short-tempered in the actual event. (Her quick, sharp "Gop!," instructing my father to do something instantly, is as familiar to her children as birdsong.) For all its universality, bread's chemistry; or, really, biology, is a little creepy. "The longer it takes the little bugs to eat up the oxygen, the better the bread tastes," she went on. "The high heat of the baker's oven simply kills off the remaining little bugs, while leaving their work preserved in place. It's all those carbon-dioxide bubbles which become fixed as the nice spongy holes in the crumb of the bread." The tasty bites of your morning toast, I realized, are all the tombs of tiny dead creatures—the Ozymandias phenomenon on a miniature scale. Look on my works, you mighty, and eat them with apricot jam.

We turned to the *pain Poilâne*, whose starter she had made earlier; it now luxuriated under a plastic bag in the sink. You can mix up water and wheat, she explained, put it out in the air, and wait for all the wild yeast that's drifting around in the schmutz of the kitchen to land on it and start eating the carbohydrates. This yeast tends to have more character than the yeast that you buy in the store, because, as every dog knows, the schmutz on the kitchen floor has more flavor than anything else. Well-kept schmutz of this sort provides the sour taste in sourdough bread. (San Francisco has a distinctively sour kind of schmutz, so distinctive that it has a scientific name: Lactobacillus sanfranciscensis.) The long-cherished deposit of ancient schmutz—a spongy mess that you can use day after day and even decade after decade, and whose exigencies you, as a baker, basically can't escape—is called, no kidding, "the mother."

"Bread is very forgiving," my mother said, as she turned over the *pain Poilâne* dough. "In the books, they fuss endlessly, and, you know, I used to worry and weigh, but now I know the bread will forgive. The secret of bread is that bread is much more forgiving than non-bakers know."

We took out the breads that we had prepared the night before. "The broissant is essentially a brioche egg dough with butter folded into it," my mother said. "Now, the trick, dear, about laminating butter is to get the thickness of the butter *exactly* the same as the thickness of the dough." We cautiously beat down the butter into layers. "Then you fold it over in exact thirds, like *this*." She showed me.

We began to fold. And fold. And fold again. As I tried to fold, she frowned ferociously. "You have to even it out so that you don't have these budges at the corners," she said. The CBC rose in the background. As luck and life would have it, a mildly alarmed Canadian-style piece about gluten allergies and gluten-free diets was on. In a slightly prim tone—as my sister Hilary points out, Toronto is the last big town where "hygienic," a holy word, is pronounced as though it had five syllables—it told of how many people had given themselves a diagnosis of celiac disease, and how our bread-addicted society might be ending.

"That is so stupid," my mother bristled. She went on to rattle off facts about the incidence of celiac disease and the follies of self-diagnosis. But beneath it, I knew, was the simple love of bread. I imagined my mother and myself as the last bread-heads, the final gluten addicts, sitting in a stifling, overheated basement room somewhere, stuffing ourselves with broissants.

We spent two days mixing water and yeast and different flour, and then we waited for different lengths of time. We did the *pain Poilâne*, dark and crusty and dependent on a long, long resting period, we did bagels—real bagels, as produced in the Montreal bakeries, with a large hole, a bright sesame glow, and a sweet, firm bite. These had to be rolled, and my mom was impatient with my rolling, since unless you do them just right they bounce back yeastily to their original form.

I was taken by the plasticity of every sort of dough, its way of being pliable to your touch and then springy—first merging into your hands and then stretching and resisting, oddly alive, as though it had a mind of its own, the collective intelligence of all those little bugs. Bread dough isn't like dinner food, which usually rests inert under the knife and waits for you to do something to it: bread dough sits there, respiring and rising, thinking things over.

Then, there are the smells. There's the beery, yeast-release aroma that spreads around the kitchen, the slowly exuding I'm-on-my-way-smell of the rising loaf, and the intensifying fresh-bread smell that comes from the oven as it bakes. The deepest sensual pleasure of bread occurs not when tasting but when slicing, cutting into softness that has suddenly gained structure: the pile of yeasty dough, after its time in the hot oven, turned into a little house, with a crisp solid roof and a yielding interior of inner space. Bread is best seen in cross-section, and each cross-section is different. Each bread has a beautifully different weight and crumb as the knife cuts into it. The *pain Poilâne* style almost squeaks as you cut into it, the sourdough, or levain, that gives it that nice acid bite seeming to protest under the knife; the bagel's firmer flesh is made less resistant by that hole; the broissants crumble, with a spray of soft crumbs, under the lightest touch, the many layers you fold into the puff pastry turning into a house of a hundred floors under your command. And greed can sometimes lead you to tear off the end of the softer breads, in a gesture satisfying in itself, even before you bite. (And if all this sounds a touch Freudian for a man baking with his mother, well, the Oedipal dramas we enter knowingly leave us better sighted, not blind.)

As one project followed another, I realized why I had not been drawn to bread baking in the first place. Stovetop cooking is, at a first approximation, peeling and chopping onions and then crying; baking is mixing yeast and water with flour and then *waiting*. The difference between being a baker and being a cook is whether you find waiting or crying more objectionable. Waiting is anathema to me, and activity is essential to my nature—a nature I share with my mother. But then it occurred to me that my mom is that anomalous creature: an impatient baker. She fills the gaps created by enforced waiting by being active, so that each bread, as we put it down to wait for it to rise, was succeeded by another bread in need of mixing or punching or rolling. The kitchen of my childhood had filled up with bread as she waited for the rest of the bread to be ready.

On Monday morning, I packed the loaves and broissants and bagels in my overnight bag. I would take them home to study and share with my own children. I gave my mother a hug. "It's such fun to bake with you, dear," she said. "Of course, I spent years making you bread every morning. We always had croissants and muffins and—oh, dear, I *always* had so many things out for you."

Was there, after all these years, a just discernible note of exasperation, a regretful sense that her children's appetites were not equal to their bafflement at her avidity? I realized that I had never once thanked her for all that bread. On the long drive to the airport and the short flight to LaGuardia, with all her bread in my bag, I reflected that the thank-yous we do say to our parents, like the ones I hear from my own kids now—our over-cheery "Great to see you!"s and "We'll catch you in October!"s; our evasive "Christmas would be great! Let's see how the kids are set up"—are never remotely sufficient, yet we feel constrained against saying more. (We end phone conversations by saying "Love you!" to our parents; somehow, adding the "I" seems too . . . schmutzy, too filled with wild yeast from the hidden corners of life, likely to rise and grow unpredictably.) We imagine that our existence is thank-you enough.

Children always reinterpret their parents' sense of obligation as compulsion. It's not *They did it for me* but *They did it because they wanted to.* She wanted to bake that bread; you told those bedtime stories every night, really, for yourself. There'd be no surviving without that move, the debt guilt would be too great to shoulder. In order to supply the unique amount of care that children demand, we have to enter into a contract in amnesia where neither side is entirely honest about the costs. If we ever totted up the debt, we would be unable to bear it. Parents who insist on registering the asymmetry accurately (the Jewish mother in a Roth novel, the Japanese father in an Ozu film) become objects of frantic mockery or, at best, pity for their compulsiveness. "All I do is give and give and what reward do I get? You never call!" the Jewish mother moans in the novel, and we laugh and laugh, and she is right—she *did* give and give, and we *don't* call. She is wrong only to say it out loud. In the market of emotions, that sacrifice is already known, and discounted for, as the price of life.

When I got back to New York, Martha was at last ready to make her bread. She had found the right kind of earthenware bowl, and the right kind of wooden board, and even the right kind of counter scraper. After my weekend with my mother, I offered to show her how to use the dough hook on the Sunbeam, but she looked at me darkly. "My kind of bread isn't made in an electric mixer," she said.

"There's a certain aesthetic to baking my bread," she went on. "Everything has to be clean and nice." She had, I noted, put on a black leotard and tights for the occasion, so that she looked like a Jules Feiffer heroine. She mixed together all the good natural ingredients—the brown flour and the millet and the organic honey—and then laid a length of white linen over the earthenware bowl. "It's not a sweet bread, but it has sweetness in it," she explained.

At last, in the silent kitchen, the dough had risen, and we all gathered around to watch. Her kneading startled her family. She kneaded in a domestic fervor, a cross between Betty Crocker and a bacchante. There was no humming mixer, just a woman and her dough. Then she began to braid three long rolls of dough together, expertly.

"Mom, this is, like, such a *big* bread," our fourteen-year-old said. "It's like bread you would bring to Jesus."

It was, too. And suddenly, crystal through the years, I saw Martha at nineteen, on one of those bitter, beautiful Canadian mornings, eyes turned almond by the cold, fur hat on and high collar up, carrying ... a braided loaf, in a basket, tied with a shiny purple ribbon. She *had* baked bread, this very bread, and brought it to me, too. And it had been lost in the family kitchen, surrounded by too many croissants and sticky buns and too many chattering and devouring mouths.

"You brought a loaf like this over to my house!" I said. "I see it now. But I can't remember how it tasted." It was an anti-Proustian Proustian moment: memory flooded back in the presence of something that I had forgotten to eat.

"Of course not," she said. "No one noticed. It was just, 'Oh, how nice! Put it there.' I don't think you even ate any. Your mother's whole French thing was so different. It overwhelmed my loaf. I think it was the last time I made my bread."

When it was baked, sixty minutes in a slow oven, her loaf looked beautiful, braided like the blond hair of a Swedish child. The next day, I buttered a slice of it, delicious and long-deferred toast, and had it with my coffee. As toast always will, it seemed morning-bright, and clean of complications. Women, I thought, remember everything. Bread forgives us all.

The Science of the Best Chocolate Chip Cookies

By J. Kenji López-Alt

From Serious Eats

⌒⧼⧽⌒

Science class was never this much fun. In his weekly
Food Lab column, J. Kenji López-Alt meticulously
dissects recipes and cooking techniques, concocting
(hopefully) foolproof instructions for classic foods.
It was about time he got around to America's favorite
cookie.

"Stop making cookies."
I'm sorry, what was that dear?
"I said, **stop making cookies.**"
That's odd, I thought to myself. *Why would she be saying that? Wouldn't
any wife be pleased to be married to a husband who fills the house with the
aroma of warm butter, caramelized sugar, and gooey chocolate? Indeed, wouldn't
any human being in their right mind **yearn** to be constantly surrounded by
sweet, crisp-and-chewy snacks?*

Then, as I glanced around the apartment, wiping chocolate-specked
hands against my apron, running a finger across the countertop and
tracing a line into the dusting of white powder that coated every surface in the kitchen, eyeing the dozens of bags of failed experimental
cookies that blocked the television, opening the refrigerator door to
discover that more than half of its contents were batches of uncooked
cookie dough in various stages of rest, I thought, *maybe she **does** have
a point.*

For the past few months, I've had chocolate chip cookies on the brain. I wake up in the middle of the night with a fresh idea, a new test to run, only to discover that my 10 pound flour bin has been emptied for the third time. Did I really use it all up that fast? I'd put on my coat and walk out in the cold New York winter night, my sandals leaving tracks in the snow as I wander the neighborhood, an addict searching for a convenience store that will sell me flour at 3 in the morning.

You see, I've *never* been able to get a chocolate chip cookie exactly the way I like. I'm talking chocolate cookies that are barely crisp around the edges with a buttery, toffee-like crunch that transitions into a chewy, moist center that bends like caramel, rich with butter and big pockets of melted chocolate. Cookies with crackly, craggy tops and the complex aroma of butterscotch. And of course, that elusive perfect balance between sweet and salty.

Some have come close, but none have quite hit the mark. And the bigger problem? **I was never sure what to change in order to get what I want.** Cookies are fickle and the advice out there is conflicting. Does more sugar make for crisper cookies? What about brown versus white? Does it matter how I incorporate the chocolate chips or whether the flour is blended in or folded? How about the butter: cold, warm, or melted?

So many questions to ask and answers to explore! I made it my goal to test each and every element from ingredients to cooking process, leaving no chocolate chip unturned in my quest for the best. 32 pounds of flour, over 100 individual tests, and 1,536 cookies later, I had my answers.

How Cookies Crumble

Most traditional chocolate chip cookie recipes start with the same basic ingredients and technique: butter and sugar (a mix of white and brown) are creamed together with a touch of vanilla until fluffy, eggs are beaten in one at a time, followed by flour, salt, and some sort of chemical leavening (baking soda, baking powder, or a bit of both). The mixture is combined just until it comes together, then spooned onto a baking sheet and baked.

When you bake a cookie, here's what's going on, step-by-step.

- **The dough spreads:.** As the butter warms, it slackens. The cookie dough begins to turn more liquid and gradually spreads out.
- **The edges set:** As the cookie spreads, the edges thin out. This, coupled with the fact that they are fully exposed to the heat of the oven and are constantly reaching hotter areas of the baking pan, causes them to begin to set long before the center of the cookie does.
- **The cookie rises:** As the butter melts and the cookie's structure loosens, this frees up water, which in turn dissolves baking soda. This baking soda is then able to react with the acidic components of brown sugar, creating gases that cause the cookies to rise up and develop a more open interior structure.
- **Egg proteins and starches set:** Once they get hot enough, egg proteins and hydrated starches will begin to set in structure, finalizing the shape and size of the finished cookie.
- **Sugar caramelizes:** At its hottest areas—the edges and the underbelly in direct contact with the baking dish—sugar granules melt together, turning liquidy before starting to caramelize and brown, producing rich, sweet flavors.
- **The Maillard reaction occurs:** Proteins in the flour and the eggs brown along with the sugar in a process called the Maillard reaction—the same reaction responsible for giving your hamburger or bread a brown crust. It produces nutty, savory, toasted flavors.
- **The cookie cools.** Once it comes out of the oven, the process isn't over yet. Remember that liquefied sugar? Well as the cookie cools, that liquid sugar hardens up, which can give the cookie an extra-crisp, toffee-like texture around the edges. Meanwhile, the air inside cools, which causes the cookie to deflate slightly, though when fully baked, the structure lent by eggs and flour will help it retain some of its rise.

It's a simple technique that hides more complicated processes underneath. So how do you decipher what's going on? My first course of action was to test out these basic ingredients one at a time in order to determine how they affect the final outcome.

Butter

Butter is where most recipes begin, and it provides several things to the mix.

It keeps cookies tender. When flour is mixed with water (such as the water found in eggs), it develops *gluten*, a tough, stretchy network of interconnected proteins that set up as they bake. Gluten can't form in fat, thus butter will inhibit its overall formation, leading to more tender results. The higher the proportion of butter to other ingredients, the more tender your cookie will be (and consequently, the more it will spread as it bakes). I found that a ratio of 1 part butter to 1 part sugar to .8 part flour was about right for a cookie that spreads moderately but doesn't end up cakey.

COOKIE FACT #1: MORE BUTTER = WIDER SPREAD AND MORE TENDERNESS

Butter is essential for **flavor**. Substituting butter with a less flavorful fat like shortening, lard, or margarine yielded sub-par cookies. Butter is about 80 to 83% butterfat, 15% water, and 3 to 5% milk protein. These proteins brown as the cookie bakes, adding nuttiness and butterscotch notes to the final flavor of cookies.

COOKIE FACT #2: BUTTER GIVES THE MOST FLAVOR

Because of shortening's different melting qualities (and the fact that it has no water content), shortening-based cookies come out softer but more dense than those made with butter.

How butter is incorporated can also **affect texture**. In the early creaming stages of making a cookie, cool butter is beaten until it's light and fluffy. During the process, some air is incorporated and some of the sugar dissolves in the butter's water phase. This air in turn helps leaven the cookies as they bake, giving them some lift. Melting butter before combining it with sugar and eggs leads to squatter, denser cookies.

COOKIE FACT #3: MELTED BUTTER = DENSER COOKIES, CREAMED BUTTER = CAKIER COOKIES

I asked myself: if browning milk proteins provide extra flavor to cookies, how could I boost that flavor even more?

My friend Charles Kelsey, the man behind the fantastic Brookline, MA sandwich shop Cutty's, developed a simple chocolate chip cookie recipe for *Cook's Illustrated* magazine back in 2009. In his recipe, he made the ingenious discovery that browning the butter before adding it to the mixture would give the cookies a much more pronounced nuttiness.

But this created some other problems. Since the butter can't get hot enough to brown milk proteins until all of its water content has evaporated, **brown butter adds no moisture to dough.** This produces a couple of interesting results. Without water, sugar that is mixed into browned butter cannot dissolve (sugar molecules are highly *hydrophillic* and will dissolve readily in water, but not in fat), which makes it subsequently more difficult for them to melt into each other as the cookie bakes. The cookies ended up missing out on some of that caramelized toffee flavor I was after.

COOKIE FACT #4: LESS DISSOLVED SUGAR = LESS CARAMEL FLAVOR

With less water, you also end up with less gluten development, thus a cookie made with browned butter is softer and more tender than one made with creamed or plain melted butter. Soft and chewy is good, but I wanted a slightly better balance.

COOKIE FACT #5: CREAMED BUTTER = LIGHTER AND FIRMER, MELTED BUTTER = DENSER AND CHEWIER

So how do I get the flavor benefits of browned butter while still allowing for sugar to dissolve and caramelize properly? The answer turned out to be in the eggs.

Eggs

Before we jump to the solution, let's take a quick look at what eggs have to offer in a cookie.

Egg whites provide a good amount of water, as well as protein.

Egg proteins are particularly good at trapping and retaining bubbles of air or water vapor. The higher the proportion of egg white in a cookie, the more it rises during baking. Because of the extra water, you also get more gluten formation, which again leads to a taller cookie (provided you use enough flour to absorb that extra water). Other than the small amount in the butter, eggs are the main source of water in a cookie dough recipe.

Egg yolks also provide some moisture and protein, but more importantly they provide a well-emulsified source of fat. When cooked, egg yolk forms a tender protein coagulum that can keep cookies tender and fudge-like. A high proportion of egg yolk leads to a more brownie-like texture in a finished cookie.

By keeping the total mass of egg added to a dough the same but altering the proportion of white to yolk, you can achieve a variety of textures.

COOKIE FACT #6: EXTRA EGG WHITES = TALLER COOKIES. EXTRA EGG YOLKS = FUDGIER COOKIES

Turns out that the combination I like best is actually a 1 to 1 ratio of egg whites to egg yolks, which conveniently is exactly how eggs naturally come. Ain't that something?

Going back to my initial problem of wanting the flavor of browned butter but disliking the way it prevented sugar from properly dissolving, I asked myself, what if I were to flip the script for these cookies: instead of creaming sugar and butter and adding eggs, why not beat together the eggs and sugar then add the butter?

I tried it, beating brown sugar, white sugar, and vanilla with whole eggs in a stand mixer until the mixture became pale, aerated, and ribbony, with a nearly completely smooth texture. To this, I added my browned butter, which instantly cooked the eggs and curdled them, turning the mixture into an oddly sweet and vanilla-y scrambled egg custard. Lesson learned: let that browned butter cool before adding it.

My next attempt with cooled brown butter fared better, but the finished cookies ended up with an oddly uniform texture and a relatively smooth top rather than the cragginess I'd been getting earlier.

Turns out that you actually want a balance between dissolved sugar and undissolved sugar to keep things texturally interesting.

COOKIE FACT #7: TOO MUCH DISSOLVED SUGAR = UNIFORM TEXTURE AND LESS CRACKING

I settled on beating half of the sugar with the eggs until it completely dissolved, then incorporating the rest when I added the brown butter. The degree to which the butter is cooled before adding it to the mix can also affect how well it holds air when being mixed with the eggs. Warm butter flows very easily and doesn't trap bubbles well. The cooler it is, the more viscous it becomes, and the better it can trap air. Even a few degrees can make a difference. By letting my browned butter cool down until it was almost at room temperature, it became firm enough to beat into the egg and sugar mixture without deflating it.

COOKIE FACT #8: THE WARMER THE BUTTER, THE DENSER THE COOKIE

In order to get my browned butter to chill a little faster and to add back some of the moisture that's lost in the browning process, I discovered that whisking an ice cube into it after cooking killed both birds with one stone.

Sugar

There's more to sugar than just sweetness! The type of sugar you use and its method of incorporation can have a profound effect on the finished cookies. **White sugar** is crystallized sucrose, a complex carbohydrate consisting of a fructose molecule and a glucose molecule linked together. It is mildly hygroscopic (that is, it likes to retain moisture), and relatively neutral in pH.

Brown sugar is *mostly* crystallized sucrose, but also contains a good amount of glucose and fructose, along with trace minerals that give it its flavor and a slightly acidic pH. Glucose and fructose are far more hygroscopic than sucrose.

If you bake cookies that are made 100% with white sugar or brown sugar, you can clearly see the difference in spread. This happens because the baking soda in my cookie recipe is a powdered base, and needs some form of acid to react with in order to create the bubbles that leaven the cookie. Slightly acidic brown sugar causes cookies to rise higher when baking, which limits their spread. You end up with a cakier end result. White sugar, on the other hand, adds no leavening power, so you end up with a cookie that spreads wide. Because white sugar-based cookies more readily give up moisture, they also end up more crisp.

COOKIE FACT #9: WHITE SUGAR = THIN AND CRISP, BROWN SUGAR = TALL AND MOIST

A mixture of the two provides a good balance, and as I noticed in my egg tests, dissolving too much sugar can lead to a texture that's too uniform. With sugar left in distinct grains, the pockets of melted sugar that caramelize within the cookie as it bakes remain irregular, giving the cookie more textural interest.

But brown sugar has another advantage over white: it caramelizes more readily, leading to more intense flavor. I wondered: could I bump up the intensity of the toffee flavor while still maintaining a good white and brown sugar balance by pre-caramelizing some of my white sugar?

I tried it, heating my white sugar up in a pot until it was a golden amber before adding cold butter to rapidly chill it and then incorporating it into my dough.

No dice. First off, it's a mess trying to scrape hot caramel out of a pan and prevent it from hardening into a single massive clump. Secondly, it made my cookies far too soft and chewy (I recalled that in the process of caramelizing sucrose, it breaks down into glucose and fructose, acquiring their hygroscopic properties).

A much simpler way was to blend only the white sugar with the eggs so that it was pre-liquefied, giving it a little jump start on caramelization, then adding in the brown sugar later on with the melted butter.

Incidentally, if you want the absolute chewiest, most uniformly textured cookies, try replacing some of the white sugar with corn syrup, a sugar that is even more hygroscopic.

You end up with wide, flat cookies that stay soft and flexible even when completely cooled. Not only that, but since corn syrup is made up of simpler sugars than granulated sugars, it caramelizes more readily, leading to darker overall color.

COOKIE FACT #10: CORN SYRUP = SOFT, WIDE, DARK, AND FLEXIBLE COOKIES

Corn syrup is so darn powerful, in fact, that even a small amount of it will completely alter the texture of your cookie.

Next up: baking soda and baking powder.

Leavening

Leavening—the introduction of air to the internal structure of baked goods—can come in many forms. In bread, it's the carbon dioxide produced by yeast. In a cream puff, it comes from expanding water vapor. In the case of cookies, we get it from egg proteins capturing expanding gases, creamed butter, and most importantly, chemicals, namely baking powder and baking soda. What's the difference between the two?

Baking Soda is pure sodium bicarbonate—an alkaline powder (aka, a base). When dissolved in liquid and combined with an acid, it rapidly reacts, breaking down into sodium, water, and carbon dioxide.

Baking Powder, on the other hand, is baking soda with powdered acids built right in. In its dry state, it's totally inert. But once you add a liquid, the powdered acid and base dissolve and react with each other, creating bubbles of carbon dioxide without the need for an external acid source. Most baking powders these days are **double acting**, which means that it contains two different powdered acids. One that reacts immediately upon mixing with water, and another that only reacts after it's heated, giving cakes and cookies a little boost early on in the baking phase.

Making cookies with varying degrees of both soda and powder, I found that baking powder generally produces cakier cookies that rise higher during baking, producing smoother, shinier tops, while soda yields cookies that are craggier and denser in texture

COOKIE FACT #11: SODA = CRAGGY AND COARSE, POWDER = CAKEY AND SMOOTH

Cakey cookies are not for me, and the brown sugar I was using in my cookies provided plenty of acid for the baking soda to react with. I landed on ¾ teaspoon as the right amount. Moreover, because the Maillard reaction takes place more readily in mildly alkaline environments, baking soda has a powerful effect on how rapidly foods darken and develop browned flavors. Browning is a good thing when it comes to cookies.

Flour

The main differences in flour varieties comes down to protein content. Cake flour contains a relatively low amount, which leads to less gluten formation. Cookies made with all cake flour will be very soft, almost mushy, even when you've cooked them to what would normally be a beyond-crisp stage. All-bread-flour cookies, on the other hand, come out ultra-chewy. Alton Brown has a recipe called The Chewy which utilizes this effect.

COOKIE FACT #12: MORE BREAD FLOUR = CHEWIER COOKIES, MORE CAKE FLOUR = SOFTER COOKIES

The infamous Jacques Torres recipe from the *New York Times* calls for a mixture of low-protein cake flour and high-protein bread flour in an attempt to balance the two. I found that by working carefully with the ratio of other ingredients, you can get away with using regular old all-purpose flour with no problem.

Since flour provides the bulk of the structure in a cookie, the amount you use can alter the texture of the cookie. A small amount of flour compared to butter (a ratio of 1 to 1 or less) will give you cookies that spread out into a wafer-like lace cookie. Extra flour (a ratio of 1.3 to 1 or higher) will give you cookies that barely spread at all as they bake, with centers that stay dense and dough-like, even after being almost fully cooked.

This may be a good thing for some folks, but I like my cookies to have a nice balance between the two. I settled on a ratio of 10 ounces flour to 8 ounces of butter.

COOKIE FACT #13: LESS FLOUR = LACIER COOKIES, MORE FLOUR = DOUGHIER COOKIES

Turns out that how you incorporate that butter also makes a difference (are you sensing a theme here? When it comes to cookies, apparently EVERYTHING MATTERS).

I tried really working the flour into the butter and egg mixture before subsequently folding in the chocolate chips. It comes out very smooth and it bakes into correspondingly smooth cookies. Because extra kneading creates a stronger gluten network, the cookies also end up rather tough.

Much better is to barely work the flour in, folding it or mixing it with a stand mixer until it just pulls together into a dough. I incorporate the chocolate half way through this process, so that I don't accidentally overmix the dough while trying to fold the chocolate in.

COOKIE FACT #14: LESS KNEADING = CRAGGIER COOKIES AND BETTER TEXTURE

The resultant scoops of dough should have a natural cragginess to them even before baking.

The Chocolate

When I first started testing, I figured that the only real question when it came to chocolate would be what brand and what cacao percentage. Turns out that how the chocolate is incorporated can *also* affect texture.

Chocolate chips produce the most regular cookies, with small, melty pockets of chocolate. **Chocolate discs and chunks** will cause some degree of layering in the dough, creating a flakier cookie with larger sections of molten chocolate. **Chopped chocolate** produces the most contrast—the small bits of debris and chocolate shavings get dispersed throughout the cookie dough, disrupting its texture and giving a nice chocolatey flavor to the whole affair, while larger chunks still melt into large gooey pockets. The only way to get this effect is to hand-chop whole chocolate bars with a knife.

COOKIE FACT #15: HAND-CHOPPED CHOCOLATE = MOST INTENSE FLAVOR AND INTERESTING TEXTURE

Hand chopping also gives you control over the exact size of your chocolate chunks. I quickly discovered that I like quite a bit of chocolate (a full 8 ounces), and I like it in large, ½- to ¼-inch chunks.

Fixing Flavor

Ok, we've been at this for a while. **Time for a quick recap**. So far we've covered butter, sugar, eggs, leavening, flour, and chocolate. As far as covering the major chemical and physical players in the cookies' final outcome, we're done.

Here's what we're working with so far: White sugar is beaten into whole eggs until it dissolves. Butter is browned and chilled with an ice cube to add back lost moisture and hasten its cooling, before being beaten into the egg mixture, along with brown sugar and. Flour and baking soda are folded in very gently, along with chocolate.

Salt (and quite a bit of it) is essential to balance the flavor of caramelized sugars, and a good amount of vanilla is a must (though, as our recent taste test has shown, even imitation vanilla flavoring will do just fine).

COOKIE FACT #16: COOKIES NEED MORE SALT THAN YOU THINK

COOKIE FACT #17: INEXPENSIVE VANILLA IS INDISTINGUISHABLE FROM FANCY

Even with regular salt mixed into the dough, I like adding a little sprinkle of coarse sea salt to the tops of the cookies, gently pressing it in right as they come out of the oven for little crunchy bursts of salt that pop with each bite.

With flavor and ratios out of the way, it's time to talk thermodynamics.

Taking Temperature

We've already seen how the temperature of the dough can affect how chocolate is incorporated, but it can also affect how it bakes. Both the starting temperature of the dough and the oven temperature have an impact.

I baked cookies at various temperatures in 25°F increments ranging from 250°F up to 450°F. When baked at a lower temperature, the dough has more of a chance to spread out, leading to flatter, wider cookies. Conversely, cookies baked at higher temperatures spread less. Even a difference of as little as 50°F makes a big difference.

Moreover, the lower the oven temperature, the more evenly the cookie bakes, with less of a contrast between the edges and the center. In fact, when the oven temperature gets low enough (around 275°F and below), you completely lose any contrast, producing a cookie that's more or less homogenous across the board.

COOKIE FACT #18: COOLER OVEN = WIDE COOKIES. HOTTER OVEN = COMPACT COOKIES

Beyond oven temperature, starting temperature of dough also affects the outcome.

Cookies cooked straight from the fridge will stay a little more compact, while those that are allowed to warm will spread more. By adjusting the starting temperature of the cookie dough and the temperature of the oven, you can create a wide variety of textures and contrasts.

COOKIE FACT #19: WARMER DOUGH = WIDE COOKIES, COOLER DOUGH = COMPACT COOKIES

I like the flexibility that being able to cook cookie dough straight from the fridge lends you, so my recipe is designed to make cookies from dough that starts at 40°F. I found that baking in a 325°F oven until the edges are nice and toasty brown will leave you with a cookie that's still plenty soft and chewy in the center.

Giving It a Rest

You still here? I haven't bored you with cookie talk yet? Good, because we're coming round third base and into the home stretch here. But not so fast. We gotta take our time with this one. Literally.

Back when the *New York Times* published that Jacques Torres recipe in 2008, I'd never heard of the concept of resting a cookie dough, yet Mr. Chocolate himself insisted that it was the secret to better flavor. Since then, I've talked to several pastry chefs and cookie experts who all agree: letting your cookie dough sit overnight in the refrigerator produces better tasting cookies.

It seems a bit finicky (and honestly, who wants to wait for cookies?), but after trying it dozens of times, the results are absolutely undeniable.

If there's one single thing you can do to improve the flavor of your cookies, it's to let the dough rest. They bake up darker and more flavorful. That butterscotch note that was barely hinted at when you baked the dough right after mixing? It'll blow you away with its intensity and complexity by the second day.

So how does it work? Harold McGee explains it in *Keys to Good Cooking*. Turns out that during the resting process, both flour proteins and starches break down a bit. How does this help improve flavor?

It helps to think of proteins and starches as large LEGO structures. During the process of browning, those large structure are broken down into smaller parts and individual pieces and subsequently rearranged. Sort of like destroying that LEGO castle so you can build a dozen spaceships. Now, both of these phases—the breaking down and the reconstruction—take time.

By resting the dough, you give the deconstruction phase a head start. It's as if you left your LEGO castle sitting out over night and your annoying little sister came by and smashed it all, King of Tokyo-style. With the pieces separated, building your spaceships is much faster.

It's really the same thing, except instead of LEGOs, you've got proteins and flour. Instead of an annoying sister, you've got enzymes. And instead of awesome spaceships, you get awesome cookies. How awesome? We're talking, oh, a million puppies on the moon wearing superhero underpants under their little doggie spacesuits levels of awesome.

COOKIE FACT #20: AN OVERNIGHT REST YIELDS SUPERIOR FLAVOR

And while it's tough to be patient, awesomeness is something worth waiting for in my book.

When all is said and done, my final recipe has ended up combining some unique techniques from a couple of my favorite recipes—the browned butter from Charles Kelsey's *Cook's Illustrated* recipe and the resting from Jacques Torres' *New York Times* recipe—along with a couple of my own novel twists—dissolving half the sugar in the eggs and chilling the melted butter with ice before incorporating—to produce a cookie that hits all the right notes. A deep, rich, butterscotch-and-toffee flavor, crisp edges, and a soft, chewy center, an irregular crumb structure with a craggy top, and a mix of chocolate dispersed through the cookie in fine threads and big gooey pockets, all with a nice sweet-and-salty balance.

Are they the simplest cookies in the world? No way. Are they worth the extra time and effort? *I* certainly think so.

"This is the last batch, I promise," is what I told my wife about a week ago. Since then I've gone through another 10 pounds of flour. Heck, if you want to know the truth, I've baked four batches of cookies *while I was writing this article*, which means that even as I hit that "publish" button, this recipe is already obsolete, a work in progress. My wife went to bed over 5 hours ago and left by giving me a gentle hug from behind and a soft whisper in my ear: "*Please* stop making cookies."

The beauty of understanding how ingredients interact with each other is that even if my definition of the "best" chocolate cookie isn't in line with yours, if you've come along this far, then you know what you need to do to adjust my recipe to suit your own tastes. Like your cookies chewier? Substitute some of that all-purpose flour for bread flour. Want your cookies to rise up a little taller? Add a touch of baking powder or replace the yolk of one of those eggs with an extra white. You like your chocolate in distinct pockets? Just use chocolate chips instead of hand-chopped. Want your cookies more flexible and chewy? Just replace some sugar with a touch of corn syrup.

You get the idea. Doesn't that make you feel all empowered and stuff?

"STOP MAKING COOKIES!"

I promise I will, dear . . . After this batch.

The Best Chocolate Chip Cookie

Ingredients

8 ounces (2 sticks) unsalted butter
1 standard ice cube (about 2 tablespoons frozen water)
10 ounces (about 2 cups) all-purpose flour
3/4 teaspoon baking soda
2 teaspoons Diamond Crystal kosher salt or 1 teaspoon
   table salt
5 ounces (about 3/4 cup) granulated sugar
2 large eggs
2 teaspoons vanilla extract
5 ounces (about 1/2 tightly packed cup plus 2 tablespoons)
   dark brown sugar
8 ounces semi-sweet chocolate, roughly chopped with a
   knife into 1/2-to 1/4-inch chunks
Coarse sea salt for granish

Directions

Melt butter in a medium saucepan over medium-high heat. Cook, gently swirling pan constantly, until particles begin to turn golden brown and butter smells nutty, about 5 minutes. Remove from heat and continue swirling the pan until the butter is a rich brown, about 15 seconds longer. Transfer to a medium bowl, whisk in ice cube, transfer to refrigerator, and allow to cool completely, about 20 minutes, whisking occasionally. (Alternatively, whisk over an ice bath to hasten process).

Meanwhile, whisk together flour, baking soda, and salt in a large bowl. Place granulated sugar, eggs, and vanilla extract in the bowl of a stand mixer fitted with the whisk attachment. Whisk on medium high speed until mixture is pale brownish-yellow and falls off the whisk in thick ribbons when lifted, about 5 minutes.

Fit paddle attachment onto mixer. When brown butter mixture has cooled (it should be just starting to turn opaque again and firm around the edges), add brown sugar and cooled brown butter to egg mixture in stand mixer. Mix on medium speed to combine, about 15 seconds. Add flour mixture and mix on low speed until just barely combined but some dry flour still remains, about 15 seconds. Add chocolate and mix on low until dough comes together, about 15 seconds longer. Transfer to an airtight container and refrigerate dough at least overnight and up to three days.

When ready to bake, adjust oven racks to upper and lower middle positions and preheat oven to 325°F. Using a 1-ounce ice cream scoop or a spoon, place scoops of cookie dough onto a non-stick or parchment-lined baking sheet. Each ball should measure approximately 3 tablespoons in volume and you should be able to fit 6 to 8 balls on each sheet. Transfer to oven and bake until golden brown around edges but still soft, 13 to 16 minutes, rotating pans back to front and top and bottom half way through baking.

Remove baking sheets from oven. While cookies are still hot, sprinkle very lightly with coarse salt and gently press it down to embed. Let cool for 2 minutes, then transfer cookies to a wire rack to cool completely.

Repeat steps 3 and 4 for remaining cookie dough. Allow cookies to cool completely before storing in an airtight container, plastic bag, or cookie jar at room temperature for up to 5 days.

HOW TO COOK CHICKEN CUTLETS, AND GIVE YOURSELF A REASON TO KEEP LIVING

By Albert Burneko

From DeadSpin.com

❧

Gawker Media's brash sports website DeadSpin makes
a perfect home for snarky food blogger Albert Burneko.
His often-foulmouthed FoodSpin column redefines
Guy Food, slipping in gems of cooking advice while
happily stirring up a media storm or two. (Cincinnati
chili dog fans are *still* pissed off . . .)

These are dark times, friends. Literally! It's dark as hell all the time, because it is winter, and everything is polar vortices and bitter bullying winds and frostbite and uncontrollable sobbing and making a fort out of couch cushions and hiding inside the fort shrouded in sweaters and jackets and layers upon layers of paper towels and burning the paper towels for warmth, and sobbing. You go outside and your whole goddamn face chips off and shatters on the sidewalk, and you think to yourself that maybe that is a good thing, because at least now you look kind of happy, because skulls always look happy. Skulls. Why can't we all be them.

How will we live? How will we want to live? The answer: We will make tasty things to eat, things that remind us of the warmer months, and we will eat them. Like, for example, today you are cooking and eating chicken cutlets, which, I mean, chicken is not really all that summery—but you are *also* cooking a quick, fresh-tasting tomato sauce for your chicken cutlets, and you are using fresh herbs if you can find them anywhere without freezing to death. And this will be your reason to live, for a time anyway. Until the next time you run out of tissues (from the sobbing), venture outside in pursuit of some, and turn into a goddamn snowperson.

Now, if your ears pricked up at the mention of chicken cutlets and tomato sauce, you may be wondering whether we are making chicken parmigiana—the chicken version of the layered-and-baked dish more famously made with eggplant or cutlets of veal—and whether, if that is what we are making, we couldn't have just said so, like in the title or something, *I mean don't you people have editors for chrissakes,* and so on. The difference between what we're doing here and chicken parmigiana is that we're going to stop at breading and frying the chicken cutlets, and skip from there to the part where we pair the cutlets with tomato sauce and eat them, which means cutting out the part where we layer the cutlets with sauce in a casserole dish and bake them for a long time. Couple reasons for that. First, the layering-and-baking routine, with chicken at least, tends not to accomplish much beyond letting the cutlet's crispy-fried breading absorb a bunch of liquid and get soggy, which is a bummer. Second, goddamn it, this is the middle of fucking winter; we need hot food, fucking *stat.*

So, yeah, this is gonna turn out to be kind of a weird half-assed amalgam of chicken parmigiana, chicken Milanese, and a straightforward friggin' breaded chicken cutlet. It's also going to taste very, very good, which you'll agree [stares daggers] is much more important than what an internet food person tells you to call it. I mean, call it Steamed Rat Dick if you want. It's your food, after all, you goddamn weirdo.

To begin, before you get around to handling any bird parts, whip out a medium-sized saucepot and **start a basic tomato sauce.** Cook some chili flakes and chopped onions and garlic in oil for a few minutes; dump a big can of whole tomatoes (San Marzano if you can find 'em; um, *not* San Marzano if you cannot find San Marzano) on top of the aromatics, break up the tomatoes with a wooden spoon, chuck in some tomato paste and a few glugs of cheap red wine, and let this stuff simmer in the background while you cook everything else.

And now, **produce chicken breast cutlets.** You can go about this a couple of different ways, and are of course free to choose for yourself: Whether to acquire some packaged cutlets that have been pounded and cut already, or to acquire some whole boneless, skinless chicken breasts and pound and cut them yourself. For the purposes of this preparation, we will proceed as though you have indicated a preference for enacting grisly violence upon some poor bird's dismembered boobs, and then we will back away from you slowly while placing a call to the local authorities.

In the meantime! Here is how to turn a large chicken breast into four flat cutlets. Lay the breast on top of a sheet of plastic wrap on a cutting board; holding your biggest, sharpest, and most frightening knife on its side (so that the blade is parallel to the surface of the cutting board), slice through the breast horizontally, cutting it in half. Place one of these halves between two sheets of plastic wrap (to prevent spattering salmonella juice) on top of the cutting board, and pound the ever-loving shit out of it with the mallet, that, ha ha, you do not own a mallet, you are not fooling anyone. Use the side of that sad can of Dinty Moore beef stew that your grandfather left you in his will.

Really wallop that goddamn chicken, like you would if it suddenly started speaking in Jay Mariotti's voice, until it is roughly a quarter-inch thick all over. (The chicken breast will spread out as you do this.) Examine the result, and pretend that in its general outline you are able to perceive a rudimentary squareness; now, with your very frightening knife, slice this "square" in half so that you are left with two vaguely rectangular, quarter-inch-thick flaps of chicken. Cutlets. There. Set these aside, and repeat the beating-and-slicing with that other half of the chicken breast. You have now turned a breast into four cutlets. You can tell your cellmate all about it, you fucking lunatic!

(You should assume that each person who will taste one of these cutlets will be possessed by a desire to taste at least one, or maybe four, more of them. Some very sophisticated non-linear mathematical equations indicate that this means you should assume no less than half a chicken breast per person, and also that there are NSA radio transmitters in your teeth. Plan accordingly.)

So now you've got your cutlets all pounded out and ready to go. This grim exercise of violence has left you with a sheen of sweat, the wild, feral eyes of a madman, and a potent, carnal musk. Actually your wrist hurts from swinging a goddamn stew-can for a half hour and you wish you could just have a nice bowl of soup and go to bed. But no! You are not finished yet. **Heat up some olive oil** over medium heat in a wide skillet. Maybe, oh, three or four tablespoons? That sounds good. I mean I have no idea how big your skillet is. Maybe you are Paul Bunyan and your skillet is an acre across. Use enough oil to coat the bottom of the skillet without pooling together in one spot and leaving the rest of the skillet naked.

While the oil is heating, **apply breading to cutlets**. Set up three stations: a dish filled with dry flour, a bowl of beaten eggs, and a wide bowl or storage container filled with a 2:1 mixture of unseasoned breadcrumbs and grated Pecorino cheese (and maybe some fennel seeds and dried thyme and cracked black pepper, or not, it's your damn food). That last bowl is the breading; the other stuff is there to help the breading adhere to the chicken.

So, here's how to apply breading to a chicken cutlet (and also to other things that need to have breading applied to them) in the manner of a clean person even though you are not one of those and never will be. You (probably) have two hands; for the purposes of this procedure, designate one of them your Dry Hand, and the other one your Wet Hand. With your Dry Hand, drop one of the cutlets into the dry flour; flip it over and move it around until it is completely covered with flour, touching it only with your Dry Hand; with your Dry Hand, lift the cutlet from the flour and give it a vigorous shake to get rid of any excess; drop it gently into the beaten egg bowl *without allowing your Dry Hand to touch the liquid egg*. Now, with your Wet Hand, lift the cutlet from the liquid egg and let the excess egg run off the cutlet back into the beaten egg bowl, and then lower the cutlet into the breading *without allowing your Wet Hand to touch the dry breading*. With your Dry Hand, scoop some of the breading on top of the cutlet, and flip the cutlet over and scoop some more onto it so that it is completely covered, and let it sit in there for a minute so that its coating can become sticky before you cook it.

Now, **cook cutlets**. (Actually, this will be a bit more like an assembly-line affair: You'll bread one or two or three cutlets, move them to the skillet, and while they're cooking you'll get the next few cutlets breaded, and then move them to the skillet when the first batch is done cooking, and so on.) The skillet and its oil are pretty hot and the cutlets are very thin; they shouldn't take more than two or three minutes per side to turn golden-brown and crispy. When that first batch gets there, move them to a cooling rack (Note: This can be an oven rack or grill grate positioned on top of a baking pan, if that's the best you can do) or a paper towel, and **top each of them** with a leaf or two of fresh basil (if you can get it) and then, on top of that, a slice or two of provolone cheese. The cheese will melt a bit while the cutlets wait for you to cook their brethren; the smell of the warm basil will fill your kitchen and lungs and soul and remind you of the summer whose eventual return is your sole reason for continuing to live.

Repeat, until all your chicken cutlets are cooked and basiled and cheesed and ready. Check the pot of tomatoes and (figurative) shit you've had simmering in the background this whole time: By now, the tomatoes and aromatics have broken down and combined with the wine and tomato paste into a modestly and appealingly chunky but still fresh and vibrant-tasting *sauce*. Turn the heat off under the pot, and stir in some rough-chopped fresh basil (if you can get it) and finely chopped fresh oregano (also if you can get it). Lean your head over the pot, close your eyes, and inhale deeply through your nose. Mmmmmmm oh man oh man, *oh man open your eyes no no no don't dunk your face in the scalding-hot tomato sauce.*

This is where, if you were committed to going all the way with the basic parmigiana outline of the steps you've taken so far, you would spend a buncha goddamn time layering all this shit in a baking dish (maybe with some sliced mozzarella) and sticking it in a preheated oven and waiting forever for it to be "done," even though it's all "done" now, in the sense that everything is already cooked and edible and good-tasting, and also in the sense that it is the middle of goddamn winter and you may very well die of sadness and despair while you wait for your food to complete an entirely unnecessary final step of cooking. Fuck that shit! It's time to eat!

You've got a couple of options, here. You can stick one or two of your chicken cutlets on a plate by themselves, or with a salad, and scoop some of that sauce on top of them, and eat them, and that will be a very pleasant meal indeed. Or, you can do that same thing, only on top of a bed of cooked pasta that has been tossed with a small amount of the tomato sauce—this will also be very enjoyable.

Or! Best of all! You can crank open an Italian sandwich roll, sock one of those chicken cutlets in there with an immodest, improbable quantity of sloppy tomato sauce (and if you should happen to misplace a thick slice of mozzarella in there, that's OK, too), squeeze that fucker shut, and fire it directly into your head, crunchy and juicy and tart and salty and oh so satisfying, leaving great glorious gobs of hot tomato all over your happy rosy cheeks, and wash it down with big Dionysian gulps of more of that cheap red wine, and wipe your face with your hand or your sleeve or your outraged cat, and make a grotesque and wonderful and blissful *Aaaaaaahhhhhhh* satisfied noise, and have another, and another, and another, and live to welcome spring with open arms and a beatific smile and a belly stuffed with things that are hot and nourishing and happymaking and good.

Do that. It will be warm where you are, and you will be the warmth.

SMELTED

By Sara Bir

From FullGrownPeople.com

❦

Essayist, recipe tester, librarian, cooking teacher, CIA graduate, and ex-punk-rock journalist Sara Bir now lives with her husband and young child in small-town Ohio, after stints in the Bay Area and Portland, Oregon. So what do you do when you're in a place in life where foodie thrills are few and far between?

It was going to be a treat. I'd bought the fish at the discount grocer's seafood counter, which usually offers semi-thawed Thai shrimp or filets of tilapia brightly flecked with some snazzy marinade that steadily works on its flesh until, when you get home, the fish cooks up pasty and mealy. But the smelt was wild-caught and, at $2.49 a pound, a steal. They looked so recognizably marine and vital in their plastic pan of chipped ice, the largest of them no more then eight inches from silvery snout to tail. As a part-time vegetarian plotting a quick relapse, I wanted the satisfaction of eating an identifiable animal.

The plan was to pan-fry the smelt and serve them with mashed potatoes and spinach salad, what one of my chef friends calls a three-point landing: protein, starch, and vegetable in their assumed sections on the plate, the protein filling three o'clock to nine o'clock (protein always gets plated closest to the diner) and the starch and veg claiming the remaining two quadrants.

Ever since I stopped eating and cooking meat, the three-point landing had all but vanished from our dinner table. I missed making pan sauces with the *fond* clinging to the bottom of my favorite skillet after properly sautéing a cutlet. I missed the hiss of chicken

stock and vermouth hitting a searing metal pan. I missed artfully ar-
ranging components on a plate just so, letting the rusty bones of my
expensive culinary school training perform some deeply ingrained
but long dormant acrobatics. I liked knowing that I could still pull
off classy restaurant-caliber food at home. We never go out to eat,
often because I'm disappointed with the food at the upper-mid-range
places in town everyone fawns over; we carefully select the locations
of the once-a-year splurges and then I realize my $23 trout is served
with only three spindly spears of asparagus and a blood orange *buerre
blanc* that's underseasoned. Better to stick to take-out veggie burritos
or cheese pizzas once a month; we know what we're getting, and no
sitter required.

The smelt was an opportunity to please Joe with both my talent
and my thrift. How fun it would be to sit with a bottle of $5 rose and
lift the spiny string of intact bones from our fish, to crunch through a
tiny browned tip of a fin! We couldn't go to the earthy, broadly smiling locals of some anachronistic European village and bask in their
hospitality, eating lusty, rustic foods; we couldn't go to cozy places in
Portland that hoped to offer a simulacra of the same sunny Mediterranean thing right here under our own oppressively grey dome or
our damp skies. But we could pull off the coup of having that meal
in our own dump of a rental house as our toddler sighed the sighs
of early evening sleep in her crib just two rooms away. No sitter, no
corkage fee, no showy tattoos of pigs or chef's knives on the tensed
forearms of our posturing servers.

I'd never cooked smelt before. They'd appealed to me at the store in
part because of their immediacy, the hint that we could have caught
them ourselves on some rejuvenating fishing outing. Joe doesn't fish.
Daniel, my boyfriend many years ago, once took me to his family's
cabin deep in a West Virginia holler where we fished for trout in a
clear, frigid stream using canned yellow corn for bait. Our catch was
modest but enough to reasonably feed two. We fried them up using
the Country Crock margarine from the cabin's dormitory-sized refrigerator, and Daniel deftly lifted the rear fin of the fish to release
the filet on one side, then the other, the perfect chain of bared bones
resembling the cartoon skeleton a cartoon cat would dig up from a
trash can.

That trip, it must have been Daniel who cleaned the fish. The few times I'd bought farmed trout, their bodies came eviscerated, their guts missing. But, newly examining the smelt I'd so breezily brought home, I find they are not gutted. It's a decent pile of little fish, a baker's dozen. After clumsily slitting open a few with my chef's knife, I open up their cavities and scoop out the slimy brown organs and mushroomy red gills with my finger, just as the *Joy of Cooking* I'd looked at earlier during Frances's nap advised me to. It's tiny, stinky work.

The smelt give off the perfume of algae and barnacles clinging to the filthy blue foam float under a bobbing wooden dock, a smell of simultaneous life and decay. Yes, the disembodied segments of salmon filets I rarely allow into the house have fishy aromas, too, but they entail no liquid eyes or gritty digestive tracts to deal with. The smelt are wet and cold, and my fingers act up, turning numb and yellow-white.

Mid-gutting, a naked and baby-fresh damp Frances pads to the kitchen, her hands clasped expectantly behind her back. These post-bath visits to the raging inferno of dinner prep are one of the few times she behaves demurely. "Mama, mama!" she calls, reaching out. With my fishy, frigid hands immobilized, I still can't help but scoop her up using the crooks of my elbows. I kiss her and point her back to her father, who reads books to her in a marathon bedtime session peppered with explosions of shrieks and giggling.

I read to calm her; Joe reads to delight her. I like to time the cooking so that dinner hits the table just as Joe creeps out of her bedroom, but usually I get to the end of my prep and sense that he won't emerge anytime soon. I'll tap on the door and say, "Ten minutes and we're eating." Sometimes he won't come out for another twenty; he lingers in there searching for some kind of elusive peace, hoping Frances will fall asleep in his arms and open a portal to her carefree non-adult world and invite him along to stay forever.

Even with the window cracked to the chilly March air and the feeble but noisy vent fan on, the cooked smelt assert their presence throughout the house. Joe makes his way from Frances's room just as I remove the second batch of fish from the pan, and he scowls. "Whoa! It stinks in here."

Yes, I agree, it does. It's the exact duplicate of the cooked fish stench that haunted the stairwell of the sublet apartment where we stayed in Queens the summer of our doomed and ultimately aborted move to New York City. A Greek family lived on the second floor of the three-floor building, and the residue of the seafood they fried hung heavily in the humid city air. Joe constantly complained of that family, of the way the dubiously employed adult kids who still lived there constantly slammed the door. "So those are it? The smelt?" he says, looking skeptically at the tangle of heads and fins I just heaped on his plate. He says "smelt" the way you'd say "chum" or "chub." He shirks, repulsed. "How are we going to eat those?"

"Like I'd told you, the meat falls right off the bone. You just lift the spine out like a chain. I can do it for you, if you like."

"Uhhh . . . I don't think I can eat this. It's just . . . you know."

The day before, when I'd bought the fish, I'd told him my plan, how we'd be eating these little fish like they do in trendy restaurants. He'd seemed into it then, unless he hadn't been listening, or hadn't understood. I guess I talk about cooking food a lot, using terms that don't have any meaning for a person who doesn't cook food. I guess it's easy to tune me out. It's certainly no effort for me to tune him out.

"These have faces. They look like fish." He's trying to excuse himself, to extricate his feelings from my hostility, but it's only digging him in deeper. People who gladly eat dead animals but don't like to be reminded that they are eating dead animals are not people I have much patience for.

"Okay, so don't have the fish. You can have mashed potatoes and salad for dinner." Mashed potatoes and salad is what a kid who's not into what Mom made for dinner eats. I feel like I'm Joe's mom a lot of the time.

"Mashed potatoes and salad?" he says. "That's not very exciting."

"So make yourself something else." He does not. Joe eats a modest serving of unexciting salad and mashed potatoes, and by that point I'd be happier if he'd slapped together a peanut butter and jelly sandwich instead, because at least he'd be proactive about getting what he wants.

I find I no longer want my smelt, either, but I gamely eat a few ounces. The flesh does fall right off the bone. The caper sauce is excellent. I drink most of the rosé. Before we opened it, I had been thinking maybe we'd have sex later that night, but right then I wasn't even interested in being in the same house with Joe.

A few days later, I made smelt salad with a dab of the caper sauce and the leftover flakes of smelt—rich and fishy and still with some stray bits of crispy skin, fin, and needle-thin bone. I ate this at work atop long pieces of toasted rye and cornmeal bread I'd made myself, interspliced with nibbles of a kosher pickle I'd pickled myself. It was a splendid lunch, serendipitously Scandinavian. All it needed was some pickled beets. And while it's no feat to make no-knead bread, or to make kosher pickles (that it's all a matter of letting cucumbers and garlic cloves sit forgotten in salt water for a few days seems like an April Fool's joke), I thought to myself, "I am awesome." I wanted Joe to be saying this, and for the same reasons I was thinking it: that I made things that tasted good, that I figured out how to on my own, that I so shrewdly navigated our little family's constantly ailing finances through cruel storms into civilized ports of comfort and even occasional refinement.

Daniel—Daniel of the trout and the remote Appalachian cabin—loved my food. It enthralled him, as did nearly everything about me. Only once was he less than thrilled, at a dry and chewy noodle kugel I'd baked using thick Amish egg noodles instead of the lighter supermarket kind, and even then he tactfully said he didn't think this misguided Amish-Jewish fusion ranked among my culinary triumphs. I broke up with Daniel because I eventually found that I was not capable of being adored so much by one person. He spoke French and rebuilt motorcycles engines and split wood with an ax and won awards for his journalism. He thought everything I did was wonderful, and I left him.

Which I don't regret. On paper the relationship was ideal, but in practice the responsibility of being idolized smothered me. Now I try to please the man I did marry by being who I am, and it backfires. Even when I set out with lovely intentions, I have to cook on my terms. To love me is to love my food. For him, I do not slice onions but dice them; the limp, stringiness of cooked onions reminds him of worms, the sight of which makes him retch. For him, I eschew spaghetti and fettuccini and linguini for the same reasons. For him, I buy Tofurkey sausages. There are far greater concessions.

When I was a teenager, you could have knocked me over with a feather if you told me I'd someday marry a skateboarder who plays drums and makes art, so elated would I have been. Skateboarding is the thing Joe slips away from the house for on Sundays, leaving me alone with Frances to cope with a pile of smelt and a cold, muddy playground calling her name. Then he goes to band practice. Then, after dinner, he washes the dishes and complains about how difficult it is to clean a sheet pan in our shallow sink, and about the amount of dishes there are to wash, even though I never reach for a utensil or pot without first thinking, "Do I need this? How can I go about this prep in such a way as to minimize cleanup?" because that is what working in professional kitchens and graduating from one of the top cooking schools in the country will pound into you. Then, after the kitchen is acceptably immaculate, Joe gets out his colored tape and works away at his art. The sight is so familiar by now that I don't even notice him. He shows me a new piece and I can't come up with convincing enthusiasm if I do like it; if I don't like it, I just say "hmm" or "ahh," then retire to the bedroom with a book.

Would that have happened with Daniel or someone else, that after more than ten years together he'd wander in from the garage, black grease under his short-clipped nails and an industrious evening of manly repairing and improving under his belt, and I'd grunt in indifference? Would the oily cling of cooking smelt put him in a grumpy mood once he set foot in a kitchen thrumming with the energy of a meal in unstoppable progress?

A week later, we still have some of the caper sauce. I cook two decent-sized artichokes in the pressure cooker to serve with it. It's taken me years, but I finally figured out that artichokes taste best when you cook the hell out of them. I put them on a plate, one for me and one for him, and set an empty wooden salad bowl next to it for us to put the leaves in.

The artichokes are rich and meaty, more so as we work towards their gray-green hearts. Cleaning an artichoke is involved, about as much work as gutting a fish, though it's not nearly as slimy or fishy. Eating an artichoke is work, though tasty and relaxing work. We obliterate our artichokes, dipping them in caper sauce and leaving behind only a thorny pile of spiny scraped-up leaves, and Joe gladly works his way toward his favorite part, the rich and tender area toward the center of the base and stem, and I realize you can't count on everyone to be satisfied with making a meal of artichokes, or to think of such a thing as a special occasion, and I decide to let the smelt thing slide.

Stocking the Pantry

A Green Movement

By Jane Black

From Dark Rye

∞

As a reporter and columnist for the *Washington Post*, *New York Times*, Slate, and *New York* magazine, Brooklyn-based Jane Black dives into issues of food politics, sustainability, and the vagaries of foodie trends. Who better to explicate how 2013 became the Year of Kale?

Had you been a foodie at the dawn of the twentieth century—though, of course, no one would have called you a foodie then—you very likely would have followed the teachings of Horace Fletcher. A wealthy businessman, who lived in a grand thirteenth-century palazzo on Venice's Grand Canal, Fletcher was neither a scientist nor a chef. Nonetheless, his prescription to chew each bite 32 times, a technique soon dubbed "Fletcherizing," was widely accepted as a key to good health. "Nature will castigate those who don't masticate!" he warned. His adherents, who today might be called celebrity endorsers, included John D. Rockefeller, Henry James and U.S. Army Chief of Staff Gen. Leonard Wood.

The concept, of course, seems ridiculous today. But each food fad is a reflection of its age. Fletcher, who also advocated more sensible practices such as eating less meat and only eating when hungry, was keen to cure upper-class ills such as gout and dyspepsia. More recently, doctors have prescribed low-fat, low-carb and vegan diets (to curb obesity), while chefs have brought us nose-to-tail eating (to save the planet), Korean tacos (to redeem fusion food), and cupcakes (ostensibly to promote equal parts nostalgia and portion control).

And now, we have kale: glamorous but respected; sexy but not in a cookie-cutter way. The Cate Blanchett of vegetables. Like any starlet that has hit the big time, kale is everywhere. It has bumped romaine out of Caesar salads. It curls across pizzas and alongside locally raised pork chops. It's the muse for *50 Shades of Kale*, a cookbook and love letter too. "I hold her leaves in my hands," writes author Drew Ramsey. "Her fine, iridescent dust glimmers. I am invincible. Immortal. Potent." It is even the inspiration for American Kristen Beddard's crusade to enlighten the French who, despite their claims of gastronomic superiority, remain oblivious to kale's appeal.

Why kale? The question echoes across the blogosphere. But kale's powerful allure on this side of the Atlantic is hardly a mystery. While most trendy foods appeal to only one camp of obsessives—acai is for health nuts; bacon is for food fashionistas—this most humble member of the cruciferous family is a crossover act: a uniter not a divider.

To the fashionistas, kale is the poster child of the chic farm-to-table movement. Led by chefs such as Alice Waters and author Michael Pollan, its adherents prize "authenticity" and yearn for a simpler, more connected way of life. To its credit, kale has a vibrant history. It was farmed in ancient Egypt, Greece and Rome. By the Middle Ages, it had become so popular in England and Scotland that the word actually meant "dinner," just as "tea" did later in the nineteenth and twentieth centuries. During World War II, Britain urged home gardeners to grow kale for its "Dig for Victory" campaign, a historical moment that prompted *New York* magazine to cheekily note that "kale did its part in the defeat of fascism."

But more important, kale offers to those who cook it a badge of honor. Sure, they could buy foie gras or truffles. But that would be too obvious—too "one percent."

To make something delicious out of kale demonstrates pluck, a trait prized by those who also raise chickens out back. Rightly or wrongly, it also signals a cook's commitment to farm-to-table values, like buying local and, of course, eating your vegetables.

That kale is versatile is another plus. Kale salads have a monopoly on trendy restaurant menus and the charity circuit. But kale can be eaten raw, steamed, sautéed, baked or deep-fried. Cooks can present it "authentically" with white beans and sausage or, creatively, as cornmeal and kale spoon bread. In *50 Shades of Kale* there are recipes for kung pao kale, kalejitos with rum, lime and mint, and chocolate-kale fudge pops. (Perhaps 25 shades would have been enough.)

Healthy eaters, in turn, love kale for its nutrient density.

One cup of kale has just 33 calories but packs nearly 700% of the recommended daily dose of vitamin K, more than 200% of vitamin A and 134% of vitamin C. Plus it's got so much iron that some are calling it the "new beef." A salad of kale, avocado and quinoa—today's trendiest grain—is hard to beat. No wonder it's the most popular item on salad bars at Google's corporate offices.

With every fad, though, comes the inevitable backlash. Curiously, the first attacks have been lobbed, not at kale's pretensions of grandeur, but at its health credentials. Writing in the *Huffington Post*, the respected author Nina Planck argued that raw kale—even baby leaves—are too tough to chew. Moreover, cooking it—and cooking it with fat—is what gives kale its superior nutrition.

Like all crucifers, kale, Planck explains, contains high concentrations of a family of toxins called oxalates, which interrupt the absorption of potassium and calcium. You need heat to destroy oxalates. Meanwhile, the vitamin A in kale is in fact beta-carotene, which the body must convert to a useable form in the presence of fat. Likewise, calcium is best absorbed with fat, saturated fat in particular. "That's the nutritional wisdom behind the pairing of greens and ham in the American South," Planck concludes.

Such a critique is worthy. And it could do kale's stellar reputation some damage. America is a country built on immigration and, as such, it lacks the deeply rooted food cultures of countries like France, Italy and China. That, combined with the peculiarly American belief that what is new is always better, dooms us to lurch manically from one culinary fad to another. Before kale was the "it" vegetable, sundried tomatoes, arugula, portobello mushrooms and celery root each wore the crown.

Still, the backlash, such as it is, isn't changing people's minds about kale yet. There's a petition on Change.org to make the first Wednesday of October National Kale Day (though to date it has fewer than 700 signatures). Vermont folk artist Bo Muller-Moore is locked in a trademark battle with fast-food giant Chick-fil-A to allow him to keep selling T-shirts that read: "Eat More Kale." If the ubiquitous raw kale salad proves not to live up to its nutritious and culinary promise, perhaps the solution is to mix and match culinary fads. Anyone ready to Fletcherize?

THE 16.9 CARROT

By Dan Barber

From The Third Plate: Field Notes on the Future of Food

⁂

Chef/owner of New York City's Blue Hill restaurant
and its farm-to-table sister Blue Hill at Stone Barns,
Dan Barber is a gifted and thoughtful cook, continually
pondering big-picture questions about food and the
environment. His new book is equal parts memoir,
eco-science, and rousing call-to-arms.

O ne day, during an especially cold stretch of winter in 2006, a
few years after Blue Hill at Stone Barns opened, Jack came
running into the kitchen, smiling big. Jack has curly hair and—
especially back when his beard was still full and flowing—the look of
a man who works closely with nature. You might say (although he
wouldn't) that he's sort of a cross between Paul Bunyan and a young
Bob Dylan.

On this particular day, he held two big handfuls of bunched carrots, their green tops waving in the air like pom-poms. It's hard not
to be taken by Jack's electric good cheer in moments like these—
showing off a new variety, or a perfectly ripe vegetable. You'd think
such displays would happen often in a kitchen that's connected to a
working farm, but the truth is that we tend to ignore one another, the
farmers and the cooks, precisely because we're so close. The morning harvest arrives, it gets organized in the receiving room and stored
in the coolers, and by the end of dinner service it's gone.

"We're sort of like a marriage," Jack once said. "We need to do
one of those date nights every week just so we can actually talk."

Jack placed the carrots on a cutting board and took a step back, allowing us to admire his work. The last time he'd displayed his wares like this, it was an exotic variety of ginger, and before that an "extra dwarf" bok choy that fit into my palm. But carrots? They were always growing—in the field during the spring and summer and in the greenhouse most of the winter and spring. They were usually good carrots, sometimes exceptionally good, but did they deserve such swagger?

"Sixteen-point-nine, pal," he finally said. "Sixteen-point-freakin'-nine."

"Sixteen-point-nine?" I repeated, not understanding. "Brix," Jack said, removing a small handheld refractometer from his pocket as evidence. Refractometers, which look like high-tech spyglasses, are popular tools for measuring the Brix, or amount of sugar present, in a fruit or vegetable. They've been used for years to verify levels of sweetness in grapes, helping winemakers determine ideal harvest times.

But Brix also indicates the presence of healthy oils and amino acids, proteins, and—this is key—minerals, those ingredients that Albrecht recognized were so critical for flavor. A 16.9 reading means the carrots were 16.9 percent sugar—and bursting with minerals. It's an extraordinarily high number, which Jack made sure I understood, even as the cooks, being cooks, drifted away to get back to work.

"Off-the-charts high," Jack said, watching me take a bite. He wasn't kidding. The variety, mokum, had been shown to reach a Brix of 12, a fact Jack discovered before his visit to the kitchen. So the astonishingly delicious mokum carrots I tasted that day were, in fact, off the charts. . . .

The 16.9 mokums lasted only a few services, but the small harvest left a big impression. Which is why, the following week, early on a frigid January morning, I stood with Jack in front of a row of future 16.9's incubating in the rich soil of the greenhouse. He had offered to explain to me in detail how the carrots had come to be so delicious.

The 23,000-square-foot greenhouse was calm and quiet, save for the soft hum of the overhead fans. Jack wore a look of pride as he surveyed the rich black soil that spanned the building. The soil came from the excavation of the Stone Barns parking lot, which partly explains Jack's fondness. After the construction crews unearthed the virgin soil, Jack rescued it from the dumpster. Then he created a recipe for the highest-quality compost, mixing it in to build up the soil's organic matter. He applies a wheelbarrow of his compost to every new row of vegetables.

I was familiar with the power of compost (what I understood of it) and impressed by the quality of Jack's personal blend. So I had a sense of how, after several years of building fertility, the soil could now nurture a carrot with a Brix of 16.9. But how exactly?

Jack pointed to the soil. "There's a war going on in there!"

"War" seemed a funny way to put it. The process had always struck me as extremely cooperative: Leaves and needles and grasses eventually die, forming a brown carpet of carbon on top of the soil. Herbivores (such as cows) and birds (chickens) periodically disturb the surface, allowing soil organisms (worms) to reach up and pull this organic material deeper into the dirt, where it—along with other material such as dead roots—is broken into nutrients available to the plants.

Jack went on to explain this war, which is when my understanding of the soil organisms' shared objective—the notion that everyone works together for the betterment of the soil community—became more complicated. There is a whole class system. First-level consumers (microbes), the most abundant and minuscule members of the community, break down large fragments of organic material into smaller residues; secondary consumers (protozoa, for example) feed on the primary consumers or their waste; and then third-level consumers (like centipedes, ants, and beetles) eat the secondaries. The more Jack explained it, the more it started to sound like a fraught, complex community. Organisms within each level may attack a fellow comrade (say, a fungi feeding on a nematode—or vice versa), or any of the tiny eaters can, and often do, turn on their own kind.

All of this subterranean life, Jack explained, is forced to interact—"cooperatively, yes, but also violently and relentlessly to maintain the living system."

As we left the greenhouse, Jack acknowledged that the precise mechanics of flavor creation are still mysterious. He realized this many years ago, after experimenting with brining olives. At first he chose distilled vinegar, which, when used as a brine, produced a predictable olive—delicious, but uniform in flavor. "Then I used a live vinegar," he said, "and after six months to a year, with all the fungi and bacteria in there, some olives would turn out sweet like fruit, some smoky, some had a roasted flavor almost. It was wild! The same thing is true for soil. You have different things going on, catalyzing new flavors, reaching the full potential and expression of the plant. It's the action that's important. But who really knows what the hell is going on in there?"

The admission took me by surprise, if only because Jack always seemed to know exactly what was going on in there. But eventually I realized he had it just right. I thought of Sir Albert Howard, who, writing in 1940, could not have named the full roster of microorganisms. Nor would he have known a phytonutrient if he saw one. Nor could he have described the chemistry behind well-composted soils—even though he was a chemist, and the father of compost. He didn't need to. I suppose that, like Jack, Howard was fine with not knowing. Where there is a bit of mystery, respect—even awe—fills the void.

A little ignorance keeps us from wrongly thinking it's possible to manipulate the conditions for every harvest. It's humbling to not know the how, and in the end it's probably a lot healthier. In the words of ecologist Frank Egler, "Nature is not more complex than we think, but more complex than we can think."

If a great-tasting carrot is tied to the abundance of soil organisms, a bad-tasting carrot comes from the absence of soil life. Which is the big distinction between organic and chemical agriculture. The nutrients in compost are part of a system of living things. They are constantly absorbed and rereleased as one organism feeds on another, so they're continuously available as plants need them. The supply to the plant comes in smaller quantities than it does with fertilizer, but it comes in a steady stream. It's slow release, versus one heavy shot of chemicals. The disparity is enormous.

To administer the heavy shot, soil is bypassed. Synthetic fertilizer, in soluble form, is fed directly to the plant's root. "It's a fast system," Jack said. "Whoosh! Water and nutrients are just flushing through. You can get your crops to bulk up and grow very quickly."

This is one of the reasons conventional salad lettuce—iceberg lettuce from the Salinas Valley of California, for example—often tastes of virtually nothing. It's almost all water, and the nitrates saturate the water, leaving no room for the uptake of minerals.

Thomas Harttung, another of the Fertile Dozen farmers at Laverstoke and founder of the largest organic farming group in Europe, has compared it to cooking: "Imagine a wonderfully balanced Italian main course full of herbs and other fresh ingredients. You then drop the salt bowl into it—rendering it totally inedible. The other taste notes 'die.'" Industrially produced grains, vegetables, and fruits taste of almost nothing because the nitrates have crowded out the minerals.

To bypass the network of living things is to deprive the plant's roots of the full periodic table of the elements the soil provides. But it also deprives the soil organisms of their food source. When Klaas said the number of organisms in his fistful of dirt was greater than the population of Penn Yan, he added, "That's a lot of community life to feed." He meant it as an obligation. "What kind of soil life are we going to promote in our fields, and what kind of flavor are we going to get in our mouths, if we feed soil life garbage?"

Why limit the hand that feeds you? As Eliot Coleman once said, "The idea that we could ever substitute a few soluble elements for a whole living system is like thinking an intravenous needle could administer a delicious meal."

Late one afternoon the following November, Jack finished his carrot tutorial by excavating a three-foot ditch in the vegetable field next to the fall crop of mokums. We climbed into the trench to examine a cross-sectioned wall of black dirt. It reminded me of the glass-enclosed ant farms I studied in seventh-grade biology. But in the dim light, this soil looked both exposed and secretive. Jack, my subterranean escort, pointed with a small stick to the exposed earth, hoping to illustrate once more how flavor starts in the soil.

"You should see this, because everyone talks about the chemistry of soil, or the biology," Jack said, running his hand along the wall, "but without the right physical structure, say goodbye to chemistry and biology. Nothing works."

The root systems created what appeared to be small highways

and back roads, allowing organisms the freedom to move around. It brought to mind the interior of a well-made loaf of bread—moist, textured, and filled with irregular bubbles. The miles of white, wispy root hairs clenching the dirt in Jack's trench looked like the strands of gluten in bread that allow it to expand in the oven. Unhealthy soil, by comparison, resembles cake mix—dry and packed down, with no spaces for air to circulate or organisms to maneuver. . . .

Back in the kitchen, Jack brought out his refractometer to test another batch of mokums. They scored well again, with Brix readings between 12 and 14. Someone pulled a case of stock carrots from the refrigerator. Grown in Mexico, these workaday carrots are large, uniform, and fast-growing, which makes them cheap fodder for vegetable and meat stocks.

I asked Jack if adding soluble nitrogen to his mokum carrots would make them grow faster. "No way. You'd just end up burning the shit out of everything," he said. "Adding Synthetic N is like adding a bomb—I mean, bombs are N, the same ingredient, so think what happens if you were to drop a bomb in the middle of a community of soil organisms."

"So let's say I'm a mycorrhizal fungus . . . "

"Kiss your ass goodbye," Jack said, chopping the air. "Gone, goodbye. N is ammonia, as in ammonia. It's burning, like the stuff you wash your floors with, only it's double, triple that in strength. If you're fungi, you're hightailing it out of there."

The Mexican carrots were from a large organic farm, an example of what Michael Pollan calls "industrial organic" and Eliot Coleman once described as "shallow organic." Such farms eschew chemical fertilizers and pesticides and technically abide by organic regulations, but they use every opportunity to operate in the breach. They grow in monocultures, they look to treat symptoms instead of causes, and, to cut to the real offense, they don't feed the soil.

"Carrots like these are all grown in sandy soils," Jack told me. "It's sand, water, and fertilizers." Organic fertilizers are the tools of the shallow organic farmer's trade. Like chemical fertilizers, they are applied in a soluble form, feeding the plant but not the soil.

Jack squeezed the juice and read the refractometer. "Whoa," he said.

"What did you get?" His expression had me imagining the Mexican carrot registering 20.9.

He shook the refractometer, squeezed more juice, and stared at the monitor. "Holy cow . . . zero."

"Zero?"

"Zero point zero," he said, flashing me the screen. "There's no detectable sugar."

"I didn't know a zero-sugar carrot was possible," I said.

Jack was silent a moment, holding the carrot up to the light as if it were a lab experiment. "Neither did I."

He said the Brix discrepancy could be attributed to several factors. Mokums were bred for outstanding flavor, for one thing, giving them a hereditary leg up on the Mexican organic variety, which was likely conceived for high yields or better shelf life. So comparing the mokum with the Mexican vegetable wasn't actually comparing carrots with carrots. And then there's the mokum's stress response, in this case to the cold snap we were experiencing. Freezing temperatures kick-start a carrot into converting starches to sugars. This neat physiological trick raises the internal temperature and prevents ice crystallization, helping the carrot survive another day. The Mexican carrots, in contrast, hadn't lived a day under a balmy sixty degrees.

But none of these excuses could disguise the essential difference between the two carrots. Jack's carrots were satiated with nutrients; the others were starved. By afternoon's end on this chilly fall day with Jack, I'd come to another paradigm-shifting realization about soil. Until then, I had held on to a remarkably simple misconception about conventional agriculture: that chemical farming kills soil by poisoning it (which it can) and that ingesting chemicals is unappetizing and harmful (which it probably is). But both miss the larger point if you're after a 16.9 carrot. Chemical farming—and bad organic farming—actually kills soil by starving its complex and riotous community of anything good to eat.

Monsanto Is Going Organic in a Quest for the Perfect Veggie

By Ben Paynter

From Wired

∽◌∾

Business, technology, food, sports, science—Ben
Paynter energetically reports on them all, for
publications including the *New York Times*, *Wired*, *Fast
Company*, *Bloomberg Businessweek*, *Outside*, and *Men's
Health*, where he's a senior editor. It's like hitting a
trifecta when those topics intersect, as they do here.

In a windowless basement room decorated with photographs
of farmers clutching freshly harvested vegetables, three polo-
shirt-and-slacks-clad Monsanto executives, all men, wait for a special lunch. A server arrives and sets in front of each a caprese-like
salad—tomatoes, mozzarella, basil, lettuce—and one of the execs,
David Stark, rolls his desk chair forward, raises a fork dramatically,
and skewers a leaf. He takes a big, showy bite. The other two men,
Robb Fraley and Kenny Avery, also tuck in. The room fills with loud,
intent, wet chewing sounds.

Eventually, Stark looks up. "Nice crisp texture, which people like,
and a pretty good taste," he says.

"It's probably better than what I get out of Schnucks," Fraley responds. He's talking about a grocery chain local to St. Louis, where
Monsanto is headquartered. Avery seems happy; he just keeps eating.

The men poke, prod, and chew the next course with even more
vigor: salmon with a relish of red, yellow, and orange bell pepper and
a side of broccoli. "The lettuce is my favorite," Stark says afterward.

Fraley concludes that the pepper "changes the game if you think about fresh produce."

Changing the agricultural game is what Monsanto does. The company whose name is synonymous with Big Ag has revolutionized the way we grow food—for better or worse. Activists revile it for such mustache-twirling practices as suing farmers who regrow licensed seeds or filling the world with Roundup-resistant superweeds. Then there's Monsanto's reputation—scorned by some, celebrated by others—as the foremost purveyor of genetically modified commodity crops like corn and soybeans with DNA edited in from elsewhere, designed to have qualities nature didn't quite think of.

So it's not particularly surprising that the company is introducing novel strains of familiar food crops, invented at Monsanto and endowed by their creators with powers and abilities far beyond what you usually see in the produce section. The lettuce is sweeter and crunchier than romaine and has the stay-fresh quality of iceberg. The peppers come in miniature, single-serving sizes to reduce leftovers. The broccoli has three times the usual amount of glucoraphanin, a compound that helps boost antioxidant levels. Stark's department, the global trade division, came up with all of them.

"Grocery stores are looking in the produce aisle for something that pops, that feels different," Avery says. "And consumers are looking for the same thing." If the team is right, they'll know soon enough. Frescada lettuce, BellaFina peppers, and Beneforté broccoli—cheery brand names trademarked to an all-but-anonymous Monsanto subsidiary called Seminis—are rolling out at supermarkets across the US.

But here's the twist: The lettuce, peppers, and broccoli—plus a melon and an onion, with a watermelon soon to follow—aren't genetically modified at all. Monsanto created all these veggies using good old-fashioned crossbreeding, the same technology that farmers have been using to optimize crops for millennia. That doesn't mean they are low tech, exactly. Stark's division is drawing on Monsanto's accumulated scientific know-how to create vegetables that have all the advantages of genetically modified organisms without any of the Frankenfoods ick factor.

And that's a serious business advantage. Despite a gaping lack of evidence that genetically modified food crops harm human health, consumers have shown a marked resistance to purchasing GM produce (even as they happily consume products derived from genetically modified commodity crops). Stores like Whole Foods are planning to add GMO disclosures to their labels in a few years. State laws may mandate it even sooner.

But those requirements won't apply to Monsanto's new superveggies. They may be born in a lab, but technically they're every bit as natural as what you'd get at a farmers' market. Keep them away from pesticides and transport them less than 100 miles and you could call them organic and locavore too.

John Francis Queeny formed Monsanto Chemical Works in 1901, primarily to produce the artificial sweetener saccharin. Monsanto was the family name of Queeny's wife, Olga. It was a good time for chemical companies. By the 1920s, Monsanto had expanded into sulfuric acid and polychlorinated biphenyl, or PCB, a coolant used in early transformers and electric motors, now more famous as a pernicious environmental contaminant. The company moved on to plastics and synthetic fabrics, and by the 1960s it had sprouted a division to create herbicides, including the Vietnam-era defoliant Agent Orange. A decade later, Monsanto invented Roundup, a glyphosate-based weed killer that farmers could apply to reduce overgrowth between crops, increasing productivity. In the early 1990s, the company turned its scientific expertise to agriculture, working on novel crop strains that would resist the effects of its signature herbicide.

Now, breeding new strains of plants is nothing new. Quite the opposite, in fact—optimizing plants for yield, flavor, and other qualities defined the earliest human civilizations. But for all the millennia since some proto-farmer first tried it, successfully altering plants has been a game of population roulette. Basically, farmers breed a plant that has a trait they like with other plants they also like. Then they plant seeds from that union and hope the traits keep showing up in subsequent generations.

They're working with qualities that a biologist would call, in aggregate, phenotype. But phenotype is the manifestation of genotype, the genes for those traits. The roulettelike complications arise because some genes are dominant and some are recessive. Taking a tree with sweet fruit and crossing it with one that has big fruit won't necessarily get you a tree with sweeter, bigger fruit. You might get the opposite—or a tree more vulnerable to disease, or one that needs too much water, and on and on. It's a trial-and-error guessing game that takes lots of time, land, and patience.

The idea behind genetic modification is to speed all that up—analyze a species' genes, its germplasm, and manipulate it to your liking. It's what the past three decades of plant biology have achieved and continue to refine. Monsanto became a pioneer in the field when it set out to create Roundup-resistant crops. Stark joined that effort in 1989, when he was a molecular biology postdoc. He was experimenting with the then-new science of transgenics.

Monsanto was focusing on GM commodity crops, but the more exciting work was in creating brand-new vegetables for consumers. For example, Calgene, a little biotech outfit in Davis, California, was building a tomato it called the Flavr Savr. Conventional tomatoes were harvested while green, when they're tough enough to withstand shipping, and then gassed with ethylene at their destination to jump-start ripening. But the Flavr Savr was engineered to release less of an enzyme called polygalacturonase so that the pectin in its cell walls didn't break down so soon after picking. The result was a tomato that farmers could pick and ship ripe.

In the mid-1990s, Monsanto bought Calgene and reassigned Stark, moving him from Roundup research to head a project that almost accidentally figured out how to engineer flavor into produce. He began tinkering with genes that affect the production of ADP-glucose pyrophosphorylase, an enzyme that correlates to higher levels of glycogen and starch in tomatoes and potatoes. Translation: more viscous ketchup and a French fry that would shed less water when cooked, maintaining mass without absorbing grease. And he succeeded. "The texture was good," Stark says. "They were more crisp and tasted more like a potato."

They never made it to market. Aside from consumer backlash, the EPA deemed StarLink corn, a new biotech strain from another company, unfit for human consumption because of its potential to cause allergic reactions. Another genetically modded corn variety seemed to kill monarch butterflies. Big food conglomerates including Heinz and McDonald's—which you might recognize from their famous tomato and potato products—abandoned GM ingredients; some European countries have since refused to grow or import them. Toss in the fact that production costs on the Flavr Savr turned out to be too high and it's easy to see why Monsanto shut down Stark's division in 2001. Large-scale farms growing soy or cotton, or corn destined for cattle feed—or corn syrup—were happy to plant GM grain that could resist big doses of herbicide. But the rest of the produce aisle was a no-go.

Furthermore, genetically modifying consumer crops proved to be inefficient and expensive. Stark estimates that adding a new gene takes roughly 10 years and $100 million to go from a product concept to regulatory approval. And inserting genes one at a time doesn't necessarily produce the kinds of traits that rely on the interactions of several genes. Well before their veggie business went kaput, Monsanto knew it couldn't just genetically modify its way to better produce; it had to breed great vegetables to begin with. As Stark phrases a company mantra: "The best gene in the world doesn't fix dogshit germplasm."

What does? Crossbreeding. Stark had an advantage here: In the process of learning how to engineer chemical and pest resistance into corn, researchers at Monsanto had learned to read and understand plant genomes—to tell the difference between the dogshit germplasm and the gold. And they had some nifty technology that allowed them to predict whether a given cross would yield the traits they wanted.

The key was a technique called genetic marking. It maps the parts of a genome that might be associated with a given trait, even if that trait arises from multiple genes working in concert. Researchers identify and cross plants with traits they like and then run millions of samples from the hybrid—just bits of leaf, really—through a machine that can read more than 200,000 samples per week and map all the genes in a particular region of the plant's chromosomes.

They had more toys too. In 2006, Monsanto developed a machine called a seed chipper that quickly sorts and shaves off widely varying samples of soybean germplasm from seeds. The seed chipper lets researchers scan tiny genetic variations, just a single nucleotide, to figure out if they'll result in plants with the traits they want—without having to take the time to let a seed grow into a plant. Monsanto computer models can actually predict inheritance patterns, meaning they can tell which desired traits will successfully be passed on. It's breeding without breeding, plant sex in silico. In the real world, the odds of stacking 20 different characteristics into a single plant are one in 2 trillion. In nature, it can take a millennium. Monsanto can do it in just a few years.

And this all happens without any genetic engineering. Nobody inserts a single gene into a single genome. (They could, and in fact sometimes do, look at their crosses by engineering a plant as a kind of beta test. But those aren't intended to leave the lab.) Stark and his colleagues realized that they could use these technologies to identify a cross that would have highly desirable traits and grow the way they wanted. And they could actually charge more for it—all the benefits of a GMO with none of the stigma. "We didn't have those tools the first time around in vegetables," Stark says.

Also in 2005, Monsanto bought the world's largest vegetable seed company, Seminis. Think of it as a wholesale supplier of germplasm. It turned out Seminis came with another benefit: something in the pipeline that Stark could turn into his division's first test product. A decade prior, swashbuckling plant scientists had discovered on the limestone cliffs of western Sicily a strain of *Brassica villosa*, ancestor of modern broccoli. Thanks to a gene called *MYB28*, this weedy atavist produced elevated levels of glucoraphanin. Stark's team bred further enhancements to that antioxidant-increasing compound into a more familiar-looking plant—good old broccoli.

In 2010 Monsanto started test-marketing the new crop, calling it Beneforté. The strategy was coming together: enhanced premium veggies for an elite buyer. Beneforté broccoli came in a bag of ready-to-cook florets—so convenient!—labeled with a bar graph telegraphing how its antioxidant levels stacked up against regular broccoli and cauliflower. It sold, but Monsanto researchers knew that future veggies would need a more compelling hook. Everybody already knows that they're supposed to eat their broccoli.

Stark's group had one last angle: flavor. In produce, flavor comes from a combination of color, texture, taste (which is to say, generally, sweetness or lack of bitterness), and aroma. But the traits that create those variables are complicated and sometimes nonobvious.

For example, Monsanto created an onion—the EverMild—with reduced levels of a chemical called lachrymatory factor, the stuff that makes you cry. That wasn't too hard. But making a sweet winter version of a cantaloupe took more effort. Stark's team first found genes that helped a French melon keep from spoiling after harvest. Through crossbreeding, they learned to keep those genes turned on. Now farmers could harvest the melon ripe, and it stayed ripe longer with full aroma. But the researchers didn't stop there—they also made sure the fruit had the gene for citron, a molecule associated with fruity and floral aromas. They called the final product the Melorange.

Figuring out these relationships takes place at a sophisticated sensory and genetics lab perched amid hundreds of acres of experimental farmland in the rural, sun-scorched outskirts of Woodland, a farming town in California's ag belt. White-coated scientists hover amid tubs full of fruits and vegetables in a lab, probing them with the intensity of forensic investigators. Penetrometers measure squishiness. Instruments called Brix meters track sugar content. Gas spectrographs, liquid chromatographs, and magnetic resonance imagers isolate specific aromatic molecules and their concentrations.

Eventually volunteers eat the experimental foods and give feedback. In one tasting session, sensory scientist Chow-Ming Lee passes out five plastic cups filled with bite-size squares of cantaloupe, harvested from outside and brought in from a store, to a dozen melon growers and distributors. Each cup is labeled with a three-digit code. Score sheets have two columns: "Sweet/Flavorful" and "Juicy."

After sampling each batch and writing down their assessments, the participants punch their scores into devices that connect to Lee's laptop, which plots the room's general sentiment on a screen along a four-quadrant grid ranging from low to high flavor on one axis and low to high juiciness on the other. None of the melons manage to crack the upper corner of the far right quadrant, the slot Monsanto hopes to fill: a sweet, juicy, crowd-pleasing melon.

In the adjoining fields a few hours later, Monsanto breeders Jeff Mills and Greg Tolla conduct a different kind of taste test. There they slice open a classic cantaloupe and their own Melorange for comparison. Tolla's assessment of the conventional variety is scathing. "It's tastes more like a carrot," he says. Mills agrees: "It's firm. It's sweet, but that's about it. It's flat." I take bites of both too. Compared with the standard cantaloupe, the Melorange tastes supercharged; it's vibrant, fruity, and ultrasweet. I want seconds. "That's the shtick," Mills says.

Of course, sweeter fruit isn't necessarily better fruit, and it's perhaps no surprise that critics of Monsanto are unconvinced that this push toward non-GM products represents good corporate citizenship. They question whether these new fruits and vegetables will actually be as healthy as their untweaked counterparts. In 2013, for example, consumer-traits researchers prototyped their Summer Slice watermelon, designed with a more applelike texture (to cut down on the dreaded watermelon-juice-dripping-down-your-chin phenomenon that has scarred so many childhoods). But the denser texture made it taste less sweet. So Stark's team is breeding in a higher sugar content.

Is that unhealthy? No one really knows, but it's certainly true that the law doesn't require Monsanto to account for potential long-term effects. (The FDA considers all additive-free, conventionally bred produce to be safe.) Nobody has ever tinkered with sugar levels the way Monsanto is attempting; it's essentially an experiment, says Robert Lustig, a pediatric endocrinologist and president of the Institute for Responsible Nutrition. "The only result they care about is profit."

Monsanto, of course, denies that charge. Make fruit taste better and people will eat more of it. "That's good for society and, let's face it, good for business," Stark says.

Monsanto is still Monsanto. The company enforces stringent contracts for farmers who buy its produce seeds. Just as with Roundup Ready soybeans, Monsanto prohibits regrowing seeds from the new crops. The company maintains exclusion clauses with growers if harvests don't meet the standards of firmness, sweetness, or scent—pending strict quality-assurance checks. "The goal is to get the products recognized by the consumer, trusted, and purchased," Stark says. "That's what I really want. I want to grow sales."

But he gets coy about the company's longer-term agenda. "I'm not sure we ever really projected what kind of market share we'll have," he says. The vegetable division cleared $821 million in revenue in 2013, a significant potential growth area for a $14 billion-a-year company that leans heavily on revenue from biotech corn and soy. More telling is the company's steady stream of acquisitions, which suggests a continuing commitment to the produce aisle. It owns a greenhouse in the Guatemalan mountains, where the dry, warm air allows three or four growth cycles a year—great for research. In 2008 Monsanto bought De Ruiter, one of the world's biggest greenhouse seed companies, and in 2013 it picked up Climate Corporation, a big-data weather company that can provide intel on what field traits might be needed to survive global warming in a given region. Mark Gulley, an analyst at BGC Financial, says the company is following the "virtuous cycle" approach; it spends heavily on marketing and pours much of the proceeds back into R&D.

The new crops keep coming. In 2012 Monsanto debuted Performance Series Broccoli, a conventionally bred line that stands taller, enabling cheaper, faster mechanical harvesting as opposed to hand-picking. Breeders are also growing watermelons with the green-and-white-striped rind patterns familiar to US consumers but also the tiger-striped variety favored in Spain and the oval jade version loved by Australians. "It's supposed to remind you of where you grew up," says Mills, the Monsanto melon breeder. That suggests the division plans to be a player in the trillion-dollar global produce market.

For his part, Stark hopes that when Monsanto's affiliation with some of its best sellers becomes more widely known, the company might win back some trust. "There isn't a reputation silver bullet, but it helps," he says. In that basement dining room at Monsanto headquarters, he waxes rhapsodic about the lettuce long after he has cleaned his plate. During a recent trip to Holland, where Frescada is gaining popularity, Stark saw folks peeling leaves straight off the heads and munching them without dressing, like extra-large potato chips. "People just ate it like a snack, which was not the intent, but . . . " Stark trails off and looks around the room. His napkin is still on his lap. He's savoring the potential.

The Flavor Man

By Laura Taxel

From Edible Cleveland

Every city should have a local food champion like
Laura Taxel, dean of Cleveland food writers (*Cleveland*
magazine, *Edible Cleveland*, ClevelandEthnicEats.
com), who always seems to have the inside scoop on
hometown chefs, markets, eateries, recipes—and one-
of-a-kind artisans like Kevin Sheuring.

Kevin Scheuring has a lot on his plate. A character, by every
measure and definition, easily spotted thanks to long blonde
dreadlocks, tattoos, lip ring, and earrings of a gauge that makes most
mothers squirm, he lives a food-focused life. Memorable both for
his appearance and his outspoken, expletive-laced style, Scheuring
is the founder and sole employee of SpiceHound, a mobile retailer
of quality spices, herbs, chiles, and natural salts, and the barely paid
manager and passionate advocate for the Coit Road Farmers Market
in East Cleveland.

He believes food is the most important purchase we make and
that everyone would be better off choosing it thoughtfully and preparing it from scratch. "You eat 1,000 plus meals a year," says Scheuring, "Cook most of them yourself. Be bold, fearless, and creative and
don't be afraid to screw one up now and then."

That's advice he follows himself, constantly experimenting with
everything from making sausages and sauerkraut to canning tomato
sauce and baking bread, and prompting his wife to once pose the
rhetorical question, "Why am I married to an old ethnic woman?"

He didn't start out this way. "I played guitar and bass in a rock band," Scheuring says. "I ate tacos from a boxed kit. Never in my wildest dreams did I see myself as a guy who would sell spices and be seriously into food."

Things changed after he got married. The couple bought a house in Collinwood, where he'd lived since 1988 and "a neighborhood," Scheuring notes, "populated with other poor musicians just like me." He became interested in eating well and became a regular shopper at the nearby Coit Road Market, whose roots reach back to 1917, when a group of local farmers began selling food from the backs of their trucks.

In 1932, the farmers formed a cooperative, bought property, and erected the long enclosed shed and covered arcade that's still in use today. It is Northeast Ohio's only permanent, enclosed, year-round farmers market. The place has survived economic hard times, white flight, the deterioration of the surrounding community, and the loss of many farmer member tenants. It almost closed in the 1990s. A last-minute rescue pulled it back from the brink and put it in the hands of a nonprofit, the East Cleveland Farmer's Market Preservation Society.

"This market is underutilized," says Scheuring, "but it's so important that it is here for people. It's a part of Cleveland history, and I actually think the original model—farmers banding together and running their own permanent market site—is a good one for the future."

Once he began messing around in the kitchen, Scheuring developed a fascination with various ethnic cuisines and found himself driving all over town to get many of the spices he needed. A light went on. He saw an opportunity in his obsession and decided to become a spice vendor and set up shop at Coit Road. In the ensuing 10 years, he proudly announces, he has never missed a single market day.

He now orders in bulk from 20 different suppliers and offers an international array of products that include the familiar—garlic, sweet smoked paprika, onion powder, dill, mustard seeds, and cloves—and rarer, more esoteric items such as preserved lemons, Himalayan pink salt, dried habaneros, African Bird chilies, star anise, sumac, ground galangal, fennel pollen, and juniper berries. He can talk knowledgeably and at length about the specific characteristics of cinnamon from Vietnam and why it's best to get nutmegs whole.

There is, he admits, a certain contradiction in being a self-described "hardcore locavore" and a seller of spices sourced from around the world. But we still want pepper, he says by way of explanation, and other flavorful ingredients that simply cannot be grown or produced in this area. And that's okay. So he has no problem seasoning the meat, poultry, vegetables, and fruits he gets from area farmers with Tasmanian pepperberries, Mexican oregano, and Madagascar vanilla beans.

Everything is packaged in small $1 bags: quantity varies rather than price. Scheuring does this to keep things simple and affordable. The approach also encourages customers to experiment and discourages overbuying. "Old spices lose something. It's best to use them up quickly." The packets are set out in 216 compartments in a display case he built himself (it has that look). It was supposed to be a prototype, but he never seems to find the time to craft a finished version. When Coit Road is closed, Scheuring folds up the whole thing and carts it around to other farmers markets.

But the East Cleveland location is his priority. He took on the role of market manager in 2006. He keeps things running smoothly, manages the EBT program (Electronic Benefits Transfer that provides subsidies for shoppers), works tirelessly to promote the place, and does cooking demos. He helped establish a small urban farm and community garden on an adjacent plot of land and is trying to get a co-op up and running to house chickens that will supply participants with eggs. It is not, he admits, the most profitable use of his time, but he tells me "there are things that just need to be done, whether you get a paycheck or not."

It was Wednesday afternoon at closing time when we met to talk. He had just finished cooking stuffed poblano peppers in the market's "demo kitchen"—propane and butane burners, countertop convection ovens, no plumbing—for the dinner he'd share with his wife, Lynne, later. It speaks to the consistent theme in all that he does. Whether he's selling spices, manning the office at Coit Road Farmers Market, or whipping up a meal, Kevin Scheuring is always thinking about how to make sure there's something good to go on the table.

Spicehound Says

Spices go stale. **Buy in small quantities,** and use within a couple of months.

To **test for freshness,** crumble or rub spices and herbs in your hands. Sniff. If the smell isn't vivid, pleasing, and strong, the product is past its prime.

Put a small amount of each spice and herb on the tip of your finger and **taste it.** This will give you a better idea of how it will impact a dish, and whether you want to use a little or a lot.

There are no rules about what spices go with which foods. Flavors are like colors—choose what you like. If a combination works for you, then it's good.

Season incrementally to avoid going overboard.

Most spices are better added early in the cooking process. Fat is an excellent carrier of flavor so sautéing in oil, butter, or ghee at the start brings out their best.

Cauliflower Tomato Tarka

By Kevin Scheuring

One of the challenges of selling spices is the reality that most folks will never grind them and therefore never experience the superior flavor of fresh-ground spices. The other side of this is how often people don't consider using whole spices, well, whole. We accept whole caraway in bread, whole fennel in sausage, and whole anise in cookies, but don't consider whole spices much beyond that.

The tarka technique is a good way to play with whole spices. It's nothing more than frying some whole seed spices in oil (or ghee) to release their flavor and then adding the contents of the sauté pan to what you're cooking.

2 pounds fresh tomatoes (or canned equivalent)
1 head of cauliflower cut into florets
2 teaspoons ground coriander
1 ½ teaspoons whole cumin
1 tablespoon black (or brown) mustard seeds
1 teaspoon caraway seed

1 tablespoon pequin chilies (Feel free to add more or less to
taste or use any other small dried red chili.)
2 tablespoons oil or ghee
1 teaspoon garam masala
Salt to taste

Combine tomatoes, cauliflower, and coriander in a pot and
begin heating. Meanwhile heat oil in a small skillet. Once the
oil is moderately hot, add the cumin, caraway, mustard, and
chilies. Heat them gently until they become fragrant and the
mustard seeds begin to pop. Add the spices and oil to the tomato mixture and stir. Cook until the cauliflower is tender.
Taste and add salt and the garam masala. Cook 10 more minutes. Serve over rice—or not.

YELLOW DUTCH

By Rick Nichols

From Edible Philly

∽∾

Pulitzer Prize–winning *Philadelphia Inquirer* writer Rick
Nichols nowadays covers a locavore food beat, focusing
on his native Philadelphia and Pennsylvania Dutch
country. For the new *Edible Philly* magazine, Nichols
chronicled how one man revived his family's spice
business, and with it a proud immigrant history.

O ne day last fall, not long after his saffron crocuses bloomed and
their spindly stigmas had been hand-plucked—one by one—and
dried, Justin Hulshizer showed up at the city's Reading Terminal
Market with his packets.

He had a hunch, maybe a hope is more like it, that there might
still be a niche for the stuff. There was plenty of imported saffron
around, increasingly from Afghanistan, but from Italy and Greece,
too, and certainly Spain, where it famously yellows the paella.

But not a blessed thread was to be had anymore from the Pennsylvania Dutch lands west of Philadelphia where Hulshizer grew up
and still lives, and where saffron was a kitchen-garden staple of his
Swiss Mennonite forebears, and once—lucratively—widely farmed for
export.

Pennsylvania saffron commanded top dollar. In the early 1700s,
in fact, its price per ounce—still the highest of any spice—equaled
the price of gold on the Philadelphia commodities exchange. And
back then it was the Spanish in the West Indies who were hot to get
American saffron, not the other way around.

The last local saffron farmer of any commercial bent in recent years had been Martin Keen of Landisville, whose patch of local saffron got boffo reviews—in *Cook's Illustrated* in 2001 for its richness; in the *New York Times* for a potency that was easily, as Philadelphia Magazine reported, "as intense as the Persian."

Then seven years ago or more, Keen stopped returning phone calls from his biggest wholesale customer in the city. Soon after, his trademark tubes of M & J Greider Saffron dropped out of sight.

Some say it was hungry voles marauding from a field gone fallow next door that chewed up his saffron bulbs.

Justin Hulshizer did not know much about that. He was not even a farmer, actually. He was a drug and alcohol counselor for troubled kids. He once had to send a 13-year-old to rehab for heroin addiction. But he was also a home gardener who six years ago started tending an organic micro-crop of saffron in the raised beds—16 by 24 feet long—he'd wedged between the cement tracks of his Wernersville, Berks County, driveway.

He had grown up in northern Lancaster County, a few miles south, obliviously eating "yellow Dutch," which meant that the soul foods of his once-Mennonite (now Lutheran) family typically shone with saffron's buttery tint: "I didn't know that potpie wasn't [always] yellow," he says, "until I was 22."

Now he wanted to test the waters, to see if Michael Holahan at the Reading Market's Pennsylvania General Store would be able to move the $8 packets he'd dropped off, each one with a pinch of his threads, enough for about two heaping bowls of saffron noodles.

But when he talked about his project, he talked more about it as a sentimental journey. His saffron bulbs—technically, corms—came from the flower bed he had tended as a boy for his late grandmother, a revered school nurse named Merla Shirk Hulshizer.

The saffron crocus (*Crocus sativus*) is a botanic nonconformist, its bulbs multiplying by dividing, its blooms coming exclusively in the fall, the opposite of the ornamental springblooming crocus.

So every October, Merla would linger by her back door, and when the flowers finally opened, she'd shuffle outside, down the steps and promptly pick the cup-shaped lavender blooms. Then she'd pinch out the three dainty stigmas—antenna-like crimson strands—and dry them on the sunny sill of her kitchen window.

That's the way Hulshizer wrote up the story in the packets of

Shirk's Saffron that he had brought to the market. But in the weeks that passed, the narrative itself started multiplying and dividing, the unexpected postscript threatening to overtake the original tale.

As 2014 dawned, Justin Hulshizer found himself giddily contemplating, at age 38, whether there might be more to this saffron business than he'd banked on.

Before things started to heat up—before he got the eager call from Eli Kulp, the chef at Philadelphia's cutting-edge Fork bistro, and a nibble from a baker at Judy's on Cherry, a café in Reading, and inquiries from historic sites—Hulshizer had promised to cook me a lunch "yellow Dutch."

So we convened in his modest kitchen in small-town Wernersville, a few yards from his repurposed driveway, down Gaul Street from the local fire hall, 20 minutes west of Reading.

His wife Louise was out of town for the day, and his kids' parakeets—Rainbow Tail and Megalodon—were looping around. Redware pottery was stacked willy-nilly. On one wall was a framed vintage poster: "FOOD," it said. "1. buy it with thought 2. cook it with care 3. use less wheat & meat 4. buy local foods 5. serve just enough 6. use what is left. don't waste it."

It dated from the U.S. Food Administration, circa 1917, which is to say World War I.

Hulshizer had already put a chicken in the oven to roast, and broccoli on the stove, and crimped the crust on a deep-dish apple pie. Now he folded a square of paper into an envelope, sprinkled in red threads, and on the counter top, rubbed them into powder with the edge of his thumb.

This is how you start to turn even store-bought noodles into saffron noodles. He added the powder to warm broth, and soon its sunny, marigold blush emerged.

It is the same blush that announced the chicken-corn soup every year at the fireman's carnival in Schoeneck, a few miles south, where Hulshizer used to live, and near where his Shirk ancestors owned 2,000 acres of farmland long ago bought from William Penn's sons, Richard and Thomas.

It is the blush that colored the filling (as stuffing was called) in the Thanksgiving turkeys, and the interior of the Pennsylvania Dutch delicacy known, rather indelicately, as stuffed pig stomach.

But most commonly it defined the potpies of the yellow Dutch, who are, simply, those who held on to a saffron cookery whose roots go back to their European homeland. "Yellow" doesn't necessarily connote Amish, or any other sliver of the diverse German-Swiss descended community. Hulshizer is Lutheran. Some Catholic Dutch are yellow. Some Reformed Mennonites don't touch the stuff.

And across the Lancaster-area country where it was once farmed, and in Kinzers and White Horse and Gap, and where auctioneers still offer, on occasion, 19th-century folk-art saffron boxes painted with strawberries, it is hardly universally celebrated. Or, in many cases, even remembered.

Still, the historian William Woys Weaver sees it as a revealing benchmark. You can conclude a great deal by dissecting a potato potpie. Look at one once served with chicken salad and fried oysters at Lutheran church suppers: "With its layers of pasta and potatoes and local-harvest saffron and spice," he writes, it's hard to imagine it surfacing "anywhere else but Pennsylvania."

Hulshizer puts the bronzed chicken and broccoli and yellow noodles on the table.

But I'm at a loss to pin down the aroma (hay-like? metallic honey?) and the flavor.

Maybe it's a mildy floral note with an undertone of earthiness. But saffron is a creature of its terroir, so elsewhere it is said to confer a nutty taste, or toasty, bitter, or pungent flavor.

I look to Hulshizer for a little help. He has the bulk of James Gandolfini, his hair thinning, his shirt untucked from a pair of relaxed-cut jeans.

How would he describe the taste of a bowl of saffron noodles? "It tastes," he says, "like it's supposed to taste."

Merla Shirk Hulshizer's saffron apparently liked the move to Wernersville. Rabbits were a threat. They could gnaw its grassy blades down to the nub. And root rot was a constant worry.

But the first time Hulshizer dug up the bulbs to clean and dry their roots—normal maintenance every three years—they'd gone gangbusters underground, multiplying and dividing. "Like crazy," he says.

It was as if an unseen hand had been watching over them, urging them on. He started to cry.

He figured there are 3,000 or so bulbs now, a pittance in the larger saffron world. But still he was starting to consider—in a few years—adding new raised beds back in Schoeneck, on the street where he once lived, where his brother still resides.

Then the saffron started to sell, albeit modestly, at the Reading Terminal Market. A handful of inquiries trickled in from gift shops at historic sites. Hulshizer knew someone who knew a purchasing manager at Winterthur, which houses a world-class Pennsylvania Dutch collection. Wouldn't his heirloom saffron packets be a good fit?

And then there was the nibble from Judy's on Cherry, the ambitious café in Reading's former farm market. And, in early January, the call from Eli Kulp who wanted a sizable supply of his saffron for a locally themed tasting menu he was putting together.

Kulp had already lined up a handful of other small-time, local suppliers—Highbourne Deer Farms in Dallastown, which raises red deer for venison; an older lady who had a stash of hard-to-find hickory nuts ("similar to, if not better, than a pecan"); Castle Valley Mill in Doylestown, which sources grains from Bucks County and grinds them with cool, old stones; and Hodecker's celery farm on Esbenshade Road in Manheim, one of the last family operations still trench-growing sweet, tender, golden celery hearts.

The very notion of it all, and Kulp's enthusiasm, got Hulshizer thinking about moving up his timetable. Maybe he'd shoot for this spring to expand his crop, put five more raised beds on the old homestead in Schoeneck, push for a total of 10,000 bulbs.

There was south-facing space with full sunlight all day there, more than the six hours a day he routinely got in the Wernersville driveway. Kulp was keen on creating a special dish. Hulshizer mentioned the pesky affinity that rabbits had for his saffron.

And that's how it came to pass that at Fork, for much of last winter, there appeared on the menu a dish of stewed and roasted rabbit with smoked buckwheat dumplings, a golden pond of saffron broth lapping triumphantly at its edge.

It was called, pointedly, Saffron's Revenge.

THE FORGOTTEN HARVEST

By Jack Hitt

From Garden & Gun

Jack Hitt brings a yarn-spinner's droll humor to his
non-fiction articles for the *New York Times*, *Harper's*,
Rolling Stone, and radio's *This American Life*. His 2012
book, *Bunch of Amateurs*, looks at America through
the lens of its tinkerers and inventors—men like this
homespun crew from Hitt's native South Carolina.

I t is a truth universally acknowledged that a bunch of men standing
around a fire must be in want of some banter. There were about
a dozen of us gathered deep in the Carolina woods, and the fire
blazed. When I asked one of the older men what his role was here,
he said he was a project "consultant," which, he explained, "means
I ain't doin' a lick of work." A burst of laughter cleared the glade of
squirrels.

One guy kicked the dirt and confessed that he didn't really understand a whole lot about what we were doing. To which another consultant started in on a story—about a young fellow, newly hired at a
stable, who confessed to the foreman that he didn't know a lot about
horses. "Yeah," said the foreman, "stay around here long enough and
you'll find out how little all these other people know." Once again,
the squirrels bolted for the far woods.

Yet it was probably around a fire like this one a few aeons back
where the first mysteries of cooking dinner blazed into revelation.
And if that's the case, then not much has changed except the location. It was a brisk fall morning, and we were way down a dirt road
beneath some oaks and tall pines on Lavington Plantation in South

Carolina's Lowcountry. The rowdy fire howled inside a brick hearth built to support a massive kettle—five feet in diameter and weighing about three hundred pounds—bubbling with eighty gallons of sugar-cane juice, which would take some five hours to boil down to eight gallons of cane sugar syrup. The process involved a lot of watching. At various moments throughout the day, the whole lot of us some-times just stood there, staring into the rolling boil, seized by a silent reverie Herman Melville might recognize.

It's hard to say which is more mesmerizing, the reddish depth of the juice bursting onto the surface in an amber lather, or just the ket-tle itself. I say "kettle" but that somehow puts in mind a cauldron one might see in a high school production of *Macbeth*. There is no good English word for the simple beauty of this stunning object. It is pure cast iron and shaped like an outsized cereal bowl. You could wash a couple of children in this thing or use it as a birdbath for pterodactyls. The curve itself is enough to pull you in, a shape that grabs the eye like the slope of a horse's back or the gunwale of a schooner.

Four hundred years ago, the European longing for the sweetness in this kettle got the first colonial economy going, and was part of what set the slave trade in the Americas on a trajectory that would last for centuries. There is a lot of history in this kettle. But for much of the last hundred years, cane sugar syrup was the main source of sweetness in small communities when everything else was too ex-pensive. By lunchtime, we were all looking into the foaming broth to catch that magic moment when the concentrated liquid would quickly thicken into syrup, but honestly, I was looking to see if there was anything else in that kettle besides nostalgia.

My friend Jimmy Hagood and I have, off and on, been poking around old Charleston recipes and fading cooking techniques, mostly for fun, looking to find old flavors that somehow got lost. Hagood used to be an insurance agent, but one thing led to another and now he's one of the Lowcountry's leading pit masters, and his company, Food for the Southern Soul, sells all kinds of mainstays from grits and rice to Charleston specialties like benne wafers and Jerusalem artichoke relish. A while back, for instance, he started fooling around with jerky. When I joined him in the kitchen one time, it was a revela-tion to learn just how much has been lost between what everyone's grandparents used to make and that crud dangling by the cash register at the gas station. A lot. Real jerky was once the vehicle for a host of complex marinades and spicy vinegars and varieties of smoke—before it got streamlined into a greasy finger of sodium nitrite.

This time, Hagood invited me out to his uncle's place, where once a year they boil the juice into syrup. And that syrup is said to be milder and more complex than the potent bullet of sweet that is granulated sugar. So, I wanted to know, was there something real here, something different in that kettle that our grandparents might recognize? Or was this just an exercise in old-timey fun?

By the time I showed up, the general task of the day was already half accomplished: A quarter acre of sugarcane, about a thousand stalks, had been cut in about three hours the day before by the manager here, Ben Ferguson. He was one of three—as I counted them—head cooks in charge of this brew. "When I grew up, every year the whole community would come together and make cane syrup," he told me. "For a lot of people there was no granulated sugar, and if there had been, they couldn't afford it." After the stalks were cut, they were run through a cane press—two heavy iron drums with just a crack of daylight between them hooked up to a tractor engine. The cane was mashed and then the juice strained through a T-shirt laid atop a croker sack and into a bucket. By mid-morning, the juicing was done and the eighty gallons from the thousand stalks were in the kettle.

The third cook on this endeavor was David Maybank, who owns these woods and has been the motivating force behind making the syrup since the late 1990s."I was in Brazil, and the drink of choice turned out to be cane juice," Maybank told me. "On every street corner there was a small cane mill running off a little three-horsepower gasoline engine." They poured it directly over ice. "It beat out Coca-Cola two to one."

At eighty-two, Maybank is a soft-spoken man whose Geechee lilt is perfect Charlestonian, rare to hear these days. He wore a cap out of which sprouted an unruly head of hair, still with traces of red. His easygoing manner belies a stubborn sense of determination. In his late sixties, he talked up his desire to sail around the world, and then one day in 1997, he and some friends weighed anchor, returning the following spring, in 1998.

While they were moored in Salvador, Brazil, he encountered the syrup, and Maybank remembered old-timers in South Carolina who used it during the Depression. "It was the only way to sweeten your coffee," he said. But he actually loved the taste, so he bought one of those street-corner presses and shipped it back to Lavington. He planted his own cane, and he and Ferguson have since been learning the nuances of making cane syrup. "We probably made every mistake you can make," Maybank said.

Ferguson was eager to explain the process. Sugarcane is a perennial, but the cane starts to lose its sweetness in about the third year, so you have to buy new seed cane and lay it down. Each section of a cane stalk has a little eye in it. Seed cane is, simply, fresh-cut stalks laid end to end and buried. Each eye sends up a fresh stalk. "You have to overlap them a little bit because the end pieces aren't reliable," he said, in a tone suggesting that every tidbit he knew about cane was learned the hard way, by trial and error. A lot of people nourish their cane with nitrogen, but Ferguson said, happy to spare me a world of pain: "I top dress it with cottonseed meal."

After returning from Brazil, Maybank tracked down a few folks in Reevesville, South Carolina, who made syrup the old-fashioned way, growing their own cane and cooking it down once a year, usually around Thanksgiving. They gave him some pointers and got him started. For him, it wasn't about nostalgia but about taste.

"I actually just like to put it right on my grits," he said, almost sheepishly, as if he were giving away a state secret.

Another senior syrup consultant, Stewart Walker, who occasionally contributed a blue joke to the fire, said, "Putting it on biscuits is heaven." Hagood looked up from the kettle and said, "Well, Stewart, that's as close to heaven as you're ever gonna be." (And the squirrels were gone.) Afterward, another senior consultant leaned in confidentially: "I cannot stand the stuff." Maybank later told me that one of his best friends, Rufus Barkley, who was the leading force behind the Reevesville expeditions and getting the entire annual operation going, declared cane syrup on par with a really fine "axle grease." So opinion is divided.

Cane "syrup" is another term (like "kettle") that sets the mind off in the wrong direction. We think of maple syrup and that sticky texture and candied density. But cane syrup is naturally thinner and only mildly sweet. It doesn't share with either maple syrup or Dixie crystals that tooth-aching bolt of super-refined sugar. The five-pound bag one buys in a store involves a series of processes required to extract and condense the sweet into those intense granules. But cane sugar syrup, the first boiling of cane juice, is where it all starts. "What molasses is," Hagood said, "is the second cook. You cook it again to extract the sugar out, and that's why molasses is not as sweet. And what blackstrap molasses is, is a third cook."

The simplicity and naturalness of just boiling cane juice into syrup have begun to attract the folks promoting healthy foods. On various websites, you can already catch wind of a pro-syrup sentiment, noting that diabetics can allegedly consume cane syrup without a problem, while sugar crystals can set off diabetic shock. The century-old Steen's syrup out of Louisiana has managed to still hold on, but so far, making cane hasn't attracted a sizable artisanal crowd. There is no outlet to buy equipment, no Food Network series, no reality show (*The Real Chefs of Lavington Plantation*). Yet.

Not long ago, when an old but more powerful cane press came up for sale nearby, Maybank bought it even though it lacked one essential part: a *mule*. In the center of the gears was a pin that was to be attached via a long pole to a "sweep mule," which would walk around in a slow circle to turn the gears. Instead, Maybank connected that part to a tractor motor, which has sped up the process considerably.

Once put to a boil in the kettle, the bubbling spume started to throw up the impurities that somehow made it through the T-shirt. "So we remove all that with skimmers," said Hagood, who pulled a homemade sieve through the amber bubbles. It's a tin bowl poked full of holes wired to a broomstick. Like everything else, the equipment is purely DIY because the Williams-Sonoma catalog doesn't sell, say, three-hundred-dollar mahogany-handled syrup sieves.

"You can't let the syrup get too hot," Hagood explained, grabbing another homemade tool. He dipped in a five-gallon bucket—also poked full of holes and fastened to a broomstick—and then let the cooling juice rain back into the kettle. The juice was in a rolling boil, and just as boiling grits will foam up and spill over the stove, the juice can do the same.

"The reason you don't want to cook it too hot," Hagood said, pointing to the inside lip of the kettle, "is the juice can scorch right here where it meets the metal, and that later leaves a sediment in the syrup." The chore for the afternoon was to keep the juice just at the boiling point before it foamed over. By late afternoon, the once-full kettle had dropped by two-thirds of its volume. Then that edge of the kettle, where the thickening syrup touches the air, started to change. Now the syrup lapping at the edge left smudges of light brown cream. Hagood snapped a small stick from some kindling and scraped some goo from the side.

"Don't eat it yet," he said. "It's two hundred and twenty degrees. Let it cool." A few minutes later, I was holding a Mary Jane–like candy hardened at the end of my stick.

The real trick to making cane syrup is figuring out just when it is approaching the perfect thickness. "In the old days," Hagood said, "they would dip a pan into the syrup and watch how it dripped—looking for what they called scaling." It's an inexact science, best left to very experienced syrup cooks. A few years ago, Maybank decided to upgrade by buying a hydrometer. It looks like a jumbo thermometer, and it gauges specific gravity. "What it really measures," Hagood said, "is viscosity."

To test for that quality, we needed to pull out some syrup so that we could drop the hydrometer in. Its ability to float in the liquid gave us a number. In one test, it was thirty. "The magic number we want is thirty-two," Hagood said. The container used last year had broken, so Maybank found an old but enormous campfire coffeepot, one that held more than a gallon, easy. "We practically have to empty the kettle to measure it," Hagood said.

The crucial point arrived at the end of the day, and it happened fast. As the liquid boiled off faster and faster, we approached that special moment. A tension filled the air. From a nearby bench Maybank watched. "If you pull it off the fire too early, it's too watery," he said. "But if you pull it off too late, you end up with candy."

"When it gets to thirty-two, we want to pull the fire," Hagood said, "and then at thirty-four we transfer it from the kettle to that container and then let it cool down for jarring." The trick is to get it off the heat just before, so that the hot syrup will continue to cook to precisely the right consistency. "I had this one guy here once," said an anxious Ferguson, "and he knew everything. He watched us, and he never said a word—so I'm assuming we were doing it just right." But he sounded less like a man reporting a truth than one trying to convince himself of it.

The consultants stood back as Hagood and Ferguson roamed the kettle's edge, nervous. They dipped a pan into the syrup old-school and looked for scaling, called for another hydrometer measurement, tasted the edge of the syrup. They sampled another smear of Mary Jane candy. The two paced about like expectant fathers. The consultants crossed their arms in deep concern. Melville's ghost reappeared. There was lots of talk: I'm not sure it's ready. I'm pretty sure it's ready. I'm not sure it's ready.

At a certain point the anxiety in the air became overwhelming, and, suddenly, Ferguson cried out, "I'm calling it! Pull the fire!" His son kicked open the hearth door and began raking about a bushel of flaming heart pine out from under the pot. That's the other thing. You cannot take a three-hundred-pound kettle off the fire, so you have to pull the roaring fire out from under the three-hundred-pound kettle.

The eight gallons in the kettle were quickly ladled out by bucket brigade and poured into a fresh cotton sheet stretched over a steel box, drizzling through like a tin-roof rain. At a far corner of the box was a spigot, and not long afterward, we had jarred thirty-two quarts of cane sugar syrup.

Maybank produced a plate with a few pieces of cornbread on it and poured hot syrup on top of the small squares. Everybody sampled, and even the most skeptical consultant saw that it was good. In fact, the batch was declared the best batch they'd ever cooked—a realization that, according to Hagood, miraculously got realized at the end of every batch.

The next day, Hagood and I met in his kitchen and decided to try the syrup in every possible configuration we could come up with. His mother-in-law had earlier made some peanut brittle from the syrup for us to sample. We cooked skewered shrimp brushed with syrup on a grill, and made a salad dressing from syrup. We improvised a bourbon cocktail we christened a Lowcountry Pomegranate

Smash. We grilled some elk and some duck breast as well as pheasant and dove that Hagood had shot earlier.

The meal was extraordinary, and it underscored what has been lost in the four-century-long race toward sweeter and sweeter sugars. I'm not knocking sugar crystals. But the more-is-better pursuit of sweetness has driven us to forget the virtues of the milder sugars back down the sweetness scale. I especially found this with the meat and the booze.

Our Pomegranate Smash was fairly tasty, but that was probably because Hagood made it with Pappy Van Winkle. Later I tried the syrup in several variations of julep. All my life, a julep was made with a simple syrup derived from boiling sugar crystals in water. My guess is that somewhere in the past, the original addition *was* cane syrup. A julep made this way is not as sugary, but it complements the natural smoky sweetness of a good bourbon—and is a drink with numerous, layered flavors. I'll plant my flag here: The modern julep—made with lots of granulated sugar—is, frankly, a grown-up's substitute for a college kid's bourbon and Coke. I still have to work on the color because cane syrup can be dark or light, depending on the batch, and so sometimes the resulting julep looks muddy. Maybe the answer is to stick to the old-timers' insistence that all juleps be served in cotton-napkin-cosseted silver goblets or not at all.

The other lost flavor was found in the meats. Brushed on, the syrup nicely enhanced the sweeter meats, especially the fowl. Modern efforts to work with the natural sweetness of some meats typically involve dry rubs with brown sugar added. (Brown sugar, by the way, is white granulated sugar cooked in molasses.) I experimented with a number of approaches.

I slathered a beef tenderloin in cane syrup and improvised a rub made out of fine-ground espresso beans, chile powder, paprika, dry mustard, salt, pepper, ground ginger, and garlic powder. Normally, these dry rubs include a hefty shot of brown sugar. I skipped that part because I had coated the meat in syrup. I heated up an empty cast-iron skillet until it was smoking hot and seared the tenderloin. I moved it to my grill, where a really hot charcoal fire was already glowing. I threw a handful of pecan shells on there every few minutes, creating a dense pecan fog. After a few minutes on each side, in direct heat and full smoke, I pulled the tenderloin off when the internal temperature hit 125 degrees—super rare.

The thing about the syrup is that it held the rub onto the meat so that a hairline crust had formed, redolent of coffee and spices combined with a distant hint of sweet and very prominent pecan smoke. The folks who ate this went berserk.

Two days after that first batch at Lavington, we reconvened in the woods to make a second. This one would be different because it would include some sour cane.

"If you cut the cane after the first frost," Ferguson said, "then the cane is a bit sour." He offered a jar of the juice alongside some pre-frost juice, and the difference was remarkable. But once it started cooking and by the end of the day, I'm not sure I could tell the difference.

One of the consultants, Charlie Ratliff, decided to solve the hassle of pouring gallons of liquid into a coffeepot every time we wanted to use the hydrometer. In the intervening forty-eight hours, he had manufactured a perfect aluminum viscosity ladle. It's a long metal pole ending in a metal cylinder about two inches in diameter—just big enough to let the hydrometer bob without requiring a lot of liquid.

I was sitting on the bench when Hagood and Ferguson were trying to remember another tiny detail of the cooking procedure and, what the hell, they just decided to wing it. "That's part of the fun of cooking cane syrup," Maybank said. "You can never quite remember all the things you learned the last time you made it."

Someone's in the Kitchen

THE LEADING LIGHT OF PASTRY

By Alex Halberstadt

From Food & Wine

Let the West Coast have its $4 toast; in New York City,
2014 was the year of the Cronut™, and who better to wax
eloquent about it than music writer Alex Halberstadt
(check out his bio of the great songwriter Doc Pomus),
a savvy judge of pop trends—or at any rate, a man with a
sweet tooth.

The next time you read about Dominique Ansel, the pastry chef
of the moment, don't envy him. During the several days we
spent together, I began to think of him as a kind of confectionary Van
Gogh—a pioneering artist molested by a capricious destiny. Over the
course of our brief acquaintance, Ansel taught me about the quick-
ening power of the Internet, perseverance and the passive-aggressive
behavior of the first couple of France.

I first scoped out the Cronut™ frenzy in front of Ansel's epon-
ymous Soho, New York, bakery on an early morning in October.
At 6:45 it was still murky, but the line had wound its way along the
chain-link fence of the Vesuvio Playground and around the corner,
onto Thompson Street. Among the youngish, drowsy Cronut™ hope-
fuls, the savvy had brought friends, and lounged in folding chairs or
on discreetly placed cardboard; others stood, drawn up in the chill,
their downturned faces lit by the bluish glare of smart-phones. The
reason for the commotion was, of course, Ansel's croissant-doughnut
hybrid—laminated, glazed, heightened to beehive-hairdo proportions,
fried in grapeseed oil and injected with a filling of the month, like
Tahitian vanilla cream and caramelized apple.

Ansel chose pastry making because he's always enjoyed the scientific rigor of the craft, and emulsifying custards and laminating paper-thin doughs afforded him opportunities to calculate and measure. He's worked at Fauchon, the Fabergé of sweets on the Place de la Madeleine in Paris, and for six years was the executive pastry chef at the restaurant Daniel. Ansel—who is 36 but looks 28, with milk-chocolate eyes and a forehead of professorial elevation—sleeps barely five hours a night and is happiest tracing precise vectors with a bag of ginger-infused crème anglaise. He is soft-spoken and mild and organically averse to notoriety. Which is why there exists considerable irony in Ansel becoming the custodian of the world's most viral dessert, a situation that has forced him to hire Johann, a security guard shaped like a Coke machine, to discourage line-cutting, peddling and scalping outside the shop. The Cronut™ has impelled him to submit to thousands of personal questions, and to be photographed surreptitiously on the premises of Manhattan dry cleaners, and to be told by glucose-addled strangers, on an almost hourly basis, that he has changed their life. You have to feel for the guy. It's as though Henrik Ibsen had written *Fifty Shades of Grey.*

The Cronut™ cult, like Presbyterianism, has spread rapidly across the land. For Ansel, who grew up poor in France, counting coins on the floor of his apartment, the culmination of his unbidden fame was a recent visit from Valérie Trierweiler, the soignée girlfriend of France's president François Hollande, who swept into the bakery with a detail of bodyguards and consular workers. She wanted to meet the chef she'd been hearing so much about in Paris. She handed Ansel her phone. "It's the President," she said. On the other end, Hollande told the dumbstruck Ansel how proud France was of his accomplishments. Trierweiler also expressed pride because "the Cronut™ is French." Ansel began to say that his invention was as much American as French, but she interrupted. "It's French because you're French," she said, bringing their confab to a close.

At this juncture, I'd like to address a possibly distracting typographical issue about Ansel's best-known creation. He introduced the Cronut™ on May 10, 2013, and nine days later, on the advice of his attorney, filed an application with the US Patent and Trademark Office. The USPTO has since received 12 applications—from parties other than Ansel—attempting to trademark the indelible name, and his attorney has been busy mailing cease-and-desist letters to supermarket chains, industrial bakers and other entities that have attempted to bask, extralegally, in the croissant-doughnut bonanza. In any case, the spelling of Cronut™ is no longer a lexical whim but a matter of international law, enforced in more than 30 countries under the Madrid Protocol by the World Intellectual Property Organization in Geneva.

Little about Ansel's biography foretold his present eminence. He grew up an unlovely hour north of Paris, in Beauvais; with its hives of public housing and teenage gangs, it's almost certainly the single most blighted city in France. Three siblings, his parents, grandmother and a cousin shared two rooms with him in the local projects. Ansel let on that his mother wasn't the thriftiest with the family budget, and by month's end, he would sometimes dine on stale bread soaked in milk and heated in the oven. At his first job—the 16-year-old Ansel washed dishes and swept floors at a family restaurant—a sous-chef heated a metal spatula over the gas range and used it to brand Ansel's forearm. The only cooking classes he could afford were offered by the city and entailed preparing food in the kitchen of a nursing home. His ticket out of Beauvais was the mandatory draft—he enlisted a year before it was abolished—and he spent a year at the Republic's least popular military outpost, in the humid rainforest of French Guiana. He said his quick way with the regional dialect and a job in the kitchen were all that averted the death threats that greeted him at the army base; nearly every enlisted man was a local of African descent, and some weren't too keen on their colonial masters. "But when you work with people's food," Ansel added, "they generally don't mess with you."

Back home, he traded his savings for an elderly Renault coupe and drove to Paris, where he knew no one. He worked his way up from a neighborhood bakery to a holiday-help stint at Fauchon; only one of the 32 seasonal workers would be offered a permanent job, and Ansel won it. He went on to hold nearly every position at the Parisian institution, eventually opening new shops abroad when the company decided to expand. In Moscow, he single-handedly trained a group of novice bakers to make some of the world's most filigreed pastry—speaking Russian. His interpreter disappeared on the second day, so Ansel bought a dictionary. One morning, he noticed several young cooks in his kitchen wearing particularly vivid makeup; they said they had applied it the previous night, before heading to their other jobs as strippers.

In 2006, Ansel arrived in New York City with nothing but two suitcases, to take over the top pastry job at Daniel. The situation in the restaurant's kitchen turned out to be rather unlike the choreographed service in the dining room. "When Daniel [Boulud] got in my face, I yelled back at him. A few times we really got into it, and I remember chasing him through the kitchen and the cooks around us scattering. But we always smiled and shook hands the next morning."

All along, Ansel planned to open his own, considerably less French operation. Instead of Fauchon, with its coiffed, suited salespeople, he envisioned a casual shop with a lunch trade, good coffee and "nobody with a French accent to give you attitude." He opened his doors in Soho in 2011. In addition to traditional staples like macarons, cannelés de Bordeaux and his DKA (a shrink-ray version of the Breton pastry kouign amann), Ansel began to think up increasingly strange and original inventions, many inspired by American flavors like peanut butter and sweet potato. The most theatrical was the Frozen S'more: a vanilla-flavored core of elastic frozen custard—inspired by Turkish dondurma—in a chocolate feuilletine wafer under a layer of marshmallow, stabbed with an applewood-smoked willow branch and torched to order.

Though he may be the most inventive pastry chef going, Ansel isn't forthcoming about what drives him to invent; he spoke to me about creativity the way NBA players speak to play-by-play announcers about "stepping up." But he was surely on to something when he remarked that at least one of his pastries was inspired by dreams. Consider his disconcertingly mimetic Apple Marshmallow. A whipped vanilla marshmallow with the texture of Champagne foam, a blood-colored milk chocolate shell and an unexpected center of salted caramel, it contains more than a sprinkling of dream logic.

On the morning I visited the bakery, I arrived a few minutes before the first batch of customers would be let in, and Ansel was conferring coolly with his counter staff, some of whom had the sunken-cheeked look of people anticipating severe trauma. Ansel opened the doors and greeted the waiting before they were ushered into another, shorter line along the counter by a young woman with an air-traffic-controller manner. Soon, they discovered the small glass room in the back where two chefs were injecting Cronuts™ with the business end of a pastry bag; a volley of flash photography ensued. Ansel shot me a smile and a shrug before he was borne away for photos and testimonials, and I sat at a table on the terrace with my own personal Cronut™, cut it in half, and took a bite. It was pretty good.

CHEAPSKATES

By Sarah Henry

From Edible San Francisco

Based in Berkeley, California, Australian-born
journalist Sarah Henry writes about food, health,
and social justice; she blogs at LettuceEatKale.com.
Navigating the Bay Area's plethora of world food
options, Henry kept facing one nagging question: Why
should ethnic food always be typed as "cheap eats"?

Richie Nakano likes to stir things up—and not just his food. Nakano runs Hapa Ramen, a noodle soup stand at the weekday Ferry Plaza Farmers Market, where his brothy bowls brimming with locally sourced organic produce and free-range meats normally sell for $10–$14.

Nakano keeps things fresh: He also hosts pop-ups so he can play with his food. A stirrer in social media circles who goes by the moniker @linecook, Nakano enjoys the professional challenge of taking it up a notch on the culinary front.

Last December, at a pop-up at Wing Wings in the Lower Haight, he served his soups oozing umami with as many high-end products as he could muster. We're talking white truffle, duck confit, fois gras, Kobe ribeye and sea urchin. Who doesn't enjoy a little seasonal indulgence? For anyone who ordered all those add-ons, the tab came to $88.

"It was ridiculous and it was a bit of fun," says Nakano, a California Culinary Academy graduate who has worked in the kitchens at Sushi Ran, Va de Vi and Nopa. "One guy had just gotten his holiday bonus and was headed home to the Midwest, where he knew he wouldn't be eating anything like this for a couple of weeks. He just wanted to treat himself."

And he was not alone: Several eaters loaded up with the works.

A stunt? Maybe. And out of reach or unfathomable for many? Sure. But Nakano wanted to make a statement: Even the most modest of dishes can reach rock star status with the right marriage of ingredients, techniques and attention to detail in both preparation and presentation. And why, argues the soon-to-be owner of a brick-and-mortar joint in the Mission, should his ramen be slapped with the stigma of that cheap, instant packaged soup, anyway?

Nakano has a point. American diners have long balked at paying big bucks for so-called ethnic food. Ramen for 99 cents or less. Tacos for a buck and change. A bowl of pho for a few dollars, tops. Everyone loves a bargain bite.

Many adventurous eaters on the hunt for authentic global flavors expect to find cheap "ethnic" eats in urban enclaves like San Francisco and Oakland. It's a cornerstone of city living, a plethora of mom-and-pop shops and divey diners repping diverse cultures from around the world, slinging seriously tasty stuff for a fraction of the price it costs—and the effort it takes—to make at home.

We bite into that bánh mí with mystery meat or chow down on Chinese dumplings made by kitchen hands who may earn less than minimum wage—ignoring, oblivious to or unperturbed by what we're participating in as we eat. We're just jonesing for great grub on the run, provenance of raw materials or exploitation of food service people, many of them immigrants or people of color, be damned.

Who cares what goes on behind the kitchen door when food this cheap tastes so good?

But why should "ethnic" food be inexpensive? What the hell is ethnic food anyway? And who gets to decide what's so-called ethnic and what's not?

Enter a new breed of upstart chefs and restaurateurs, many of them with origins in other lands, who are reimagining "ethnic" eating and educating diners hungry for traditional tastes with far-flung roots about the true cost of Mexican, Indian, Thai, Chinese and Korean cuisine. Bon appétit.

Why Pay More When You Can Get It for Less?

Here's the deal: Quality ingredients cost more money, plain and simple. Given the current food system and economies of scale, organic produce, grass-fed beef, free-range chicken and sustainable seafood are more expensive than factory-farmed meat and conventionally farmed crops.

Likewise, it costs more—in both raw materials and labor—to make food without convenience products or cutting corners. Whether condiments and sauces made from scratch or tortillas and noodles prepared by hand, there's a ton of time and people power in all that prepping, planning, chopping, crafting and cooking.

Nakano knows that from firsthand experience.

"When we started Hapa Ramen in 2010 we made all the noodles in-house for about six months. It was brutal," says Nakano, who plans to bring back noodle production at his restaurant, scheduled to open on Valencia Street in July.

These days, his noodles come courtesy of a Japanese noodle maker in San Jose. "It was one person cranking out noodles for 10 hours straight. They could barely stop."

And don't get him started on what else goes into his bowls. Take his veggie version.

"The broth alone is expensive—it has a ton of vegetable purée. There are so many different vegetables in the bowl and they're all cooked differently, so the labor alone on veg prep is huge," he says. "You might get cabbage that's been shaved, kale that's been roasted, blanched chard, deep-fried Brussels sprouts, roasted or baked carrots, squash, broccoli and cauliflower."

It ticks off Nakano that there's a common notion that so-called ethnic food should be cheap. Ever since he opened this chef has fielded complaints over the price of his ramen. "People don't think anything of paying 20 bucks or more for a bowl of spaghetti," he says, noting that Italian and Mediterranean food is no longer considered "other." Similarly, some of the same people who recoil at spending $10 on soup have no problem, he says, plonking down $9 for fresh-squeezed juice or $11 for a cocktail with in-house infusions.

The dining public often views foods with Asian and Latin origins differently, says Nakano, who is of mixed Anglo-Japanese heritage.

"Chinese food comes in little white boxes that your parents get delivered on a night they don't feel like cooking dinner. You hit the Mission for tacos," says Nakano, whose paternal grandfather ran a restaurant. "These are fast casual places, not necessarily sit down, not taking up the nicest real estate. People's perception is that it's food you shouldn't have to pay much money for."

But the true cost of food is hidden from view. "Our bowl of ramen is a couple of pounds of food, there's a ton of nourishment packed in there. We should really charge people $22 for what we serve."

Businesses like Hapa Ramen are trying to do something different. Nakano sources from local, organic farmers and ranchers, and aims to keep his food costs around 30% of his overall expenses. Labor accounts for another big chunk of his budget. He says he pays his employees "way above" minimum wage ($10.74 in San Francisco, currently the highest in the country).

"You have to pay your people well, at least a living wage, otherwise you can't keep them," says Nakano. "It's expensive here, it's a competitive market, and if you want a loyal, hard-working, nice team, it's what you need to do."

The small business owner is considered a success, so newcomers want his insights. "People come and tell me they want to open their own ramen place and I tell them: 'Don't do it. It's a crazy amount of work and you're not going to make that much money.' We're doing OK, we're not scraping by, although for the first year we were," says Nakano, who supports a family of four. "I could complain but the truth is we make our rent every month and pay our bills. But we can't take a vacation."

Luckily for Nakano, he cops it on both ends of the dining spectrum from lay critics like Yelpers. He's been dissed as not "ethnic enough" and dismissed as a ramen master wannabe. His food falls into what other chefs in a similar situation call the middle ground. They're not dishing up suspect stuff made with questionable ingredients at a greasy spoon. They're also not assembling fancy-pants plates at a white tablecloth place catering to the 1%.

They're trying to do the right thing while they do their own thing.

Move Over, Ethnic Eats. Hello, Culinary Mashup

Across the bay at Juhu Beach Club in Oakland, Preeti Mistry is another example of this new style of American chef/owner with immigrant roots. With their mashup menus, craft beers and cocktails and groovy, casual interiors, these restaurants are totally different beasts from the unassuming first-generation immigrant holes-in-the-wall of the past. Mistry, who is of Indian heritage, grew up in Ohio and moved to San Francisco at 19.

She has her own issues with the "ethnic" food label.

"The term is so ingrained in American culture it's hard to escape. It's outdated and it annoys me," says the former San Francisco dweller, who hosted a Mumbai street food–inspired pop-up in that city before opening Juhu. "When people first started writing about Juhu they called it an Indian restaurant. I hadn't thought about it like that," says the restaurateur of her year-old dining place in the Temescal neighborhood. "I ate at Frances the other day. Nobody refers to it as a French restaurant. Nobody calls Delfina an Italian joint. What's with that?"

Like Nakano, Mistry found customers whining about the prices on her menu when she opened.

"Some people complained about $14 for a chicken leg. It's marinated for 24 hours, we use fresh ginger and garlic and a spice mix I make from hand," she says. "It's braised, it comes with three condiments that we make in-house. We use organic vegetables. And yet people are outraged because Indian chicken curry should be cheap."

Here's where Mistry goes out on a limb. "That's really where racism comes in, this idea that that thinking is OK."

She shares an anecdote to illustrate her point: "I recently ate at an Italian restaurant I love. I had eight pieces of tortellini with pork mousse inside and a clear broth for $21. I understand the skill and talent involved in making the mousse and pasta," she says. "There's this respect and reverence for the technique and talent. I bet nobody goes into that Italian restaurant and says: 'At Olive Garden I can get an all-you-can-eat pasta bowl for $7.99, why are these $21?'"

The takeaway for Mistry: Her food isn't considered as serious, important or worthy as someone else's of European influence.

"It's almost like non-European food goes into this box and what's championed is the greasy dive and not that that cuisine could have a level of technique and innovation that could elevate it to something else," she explains. Still, she's glad that, a year out, the people who

Juhu is the right restaurant for found her, and relish the opportunity to eat her spicy sliders known as pavs. They don't flinch at the price ($13 for three) either.

"Funnily enough, now we get feedback about how value-driven we are for what you get. The portion size is generous. Nobody leaves Juhu Beach Club hungry."

Some disagree with the racism charge.

"It's the price point. Period," wrote home cook Chris Juricich, a Berkeley resident who foregoes paying $15 for a bowl of ramen or $13 for Indian-style sliders based purely on the numbers. "This doesn't mean I don't wish them well, and I expect those who are well-heeled . . . will continue to keep these places afloat. Bottom line: I can't afford it . . . regardless of the pedigree of the chefs or their sourcing of quality ingredients."

That's a sentiment likely held by many, and yet these restaurants and pop-ups continue to attract diners who willingly fork out for this fare.

Mistry concedes that race is just one factor here. "Sometimes it's a lack of education about what we're doing in terms of sourcing—and equally important, a lack of education about what some other places aren't doing in terms of where their food comes from," she says. "I'm a chef who is in the kitchen every day trying to articulate on the plate a reflection of who I am as a person of Indian background who has lived in London and the U.S. My menu is an expression of all my experiences."

Rather than getting stuck on the outdated "ethnic" food label—or, worse, the concept of authenticity—Mistry sees a lot of chefs like herself of different ethnic heritage exploring a more diverse definition of what it means to be American, an American chef, and what it means to serve American food.

In the end, it boils down to this for Mistry: "You get what you pay for. There's a population in the Bay Area who give a shit about what they eat and won't go to places where they don't know where the meat comes from. People here will pay for that."

Hidden Human Costs, Too

Pim Techamuanvivit, who recently opened the Thai restaurant Kin Khao, has a similar philosophy to Mistry and Nakano. She's all about sourcing, craft in the kitchen, paying a living wage, culinary integrity and attention to detail at her new, high-rent, street-level space in downtown San Francisco's Parc 55 Hotel. The chef at Kin Khao, Michael Gaines, has cooked at fine-dining favorites Manresa and Central Kitchen, so this is not your typical corner Thai food joint and it has prices to match. The tell-it-like-it is Techamuanvivit puts it this way: "You won't find frozen prawns grown in antibiotic slush and flown here from Vietnam in our food."

Consider the restaurant's curry bowls ($18–$26). "Our Massaman curry is a whole shank of natural, locally sourced, antibiotic-free, sustainable beef with bone marrow in the middle. The paste has 19 ingredients and each one is treated differently: Some are toasted, some are burned, some are fried, some are fresh, everything is done by hand, everything is ground for the day's use," says the restaurateur, who developed a following for her small-batch jams under the Chez Pim label.

Techamuanvivit doesn't expect to please everybody; diners won't find pad Thai on her menu at all. Like other local chefs, she's cooking traditional and family dishes from far away through the lens of the local farmers' market. Her foray into jam making was instructive.

"People can spend $3 on a big-arsed jar of Smucker's jam or they can pay $14 for my artisanal jam made by hand with the best ingredients I can find," she says. "There are people who can see and taste the difference and are willing to pay for that. But I'm not going to win over the people who spend $3 for jam."

Talk of the price of labor makes Techamuanvivit prickle; she's hiring and service workers applying for positions have been open about earning less than minimum wage and no overtime at other area Thai restaurants. "It's appalling," she says. "If you pay $5 or $6 for a bowl of curry or pho you have to understand what you are complicit in. It's not just the cheap ingredients. It's cheap labor too."

The new restaurateur also notes that at many area Thai or Chinese restaurants diners will find the same menu made from convenience products, such as premade curry pastes, sourced from the same distributor. Unsurprisingly, much of it tastes the same, she says.

"We have people come in, look at the menu and they say to us, 'What, you don't have any tom kha gai?' and we suggest the restaurant across the street. The price is right and it's the food they're familiar with and want to eat. It's a generic Thai restaurant; it's not bad, but it's not doing anything different and that's not what I'm interested in." That well-known Thai soup sets customers back $8.50 at that particular place.

Kin Khao is striving to make a splash. "I wanted to open a restaurant and cook the food that I wanted to eat: Thai food with the quality of ingredients that I'd find at the Ferry Building farmers market," says Techamuanvivit. "This is not a place where the menu invites you to pick a protein and a carbohydrate and you tell me how spicy you want it. That's not our kind of food."

And so far—at press time the restaurant had been open about a month—diners have been lining out the door.

"I thought I might have an uphill battle with my menu but that hasn't been the case," she says. "I'm happy to be in San Francisco; I don't have to really explain why we're doing what we're doing. The people who come to the restaurant just get it."

Perhaps no one is as well equipped to see both sides of this equation as Gonzalo Guzman, the chef at Nopalito, who immigrated from Veracruz, Mexico, to San Francisco in 1997. He came here hungry for work and looking for culinary experience. He landed a job in a kitchen, washing dishes in exchange for food. From there, he gradually worked his way up the kitchen hierarchy, accumulating an impressive resume along the way with stints at restaurants like Kokkari, Boulevard and Nopalito's sister restaurant, Nopa.

Now, he oversees two Nopalito locations, in NoPa and the Inner Sunset, where his carnitas, pozole and mole (27 ingredients) receive rave reviews. Guzman learned about the importance of the pedigree of raw products at Nopa and applies that sensibility to his regional Mexican cuisine. The masa for tortillas and tamales comes from house-ground organic corn. Chorizo sausage and queso fresco—also in-house. This is not a burrito joint but a celebration of slow-cooked rustic dishes from south of the border featuring complex, layered flavors that's a rarity even in the Bay Area. And the most expensive items on the dinner menu cost 18 bucks.

Guzman got his big break as a restaurant chef when he was tasked with preparing the evening family meal for the staff at Nopa, fashioning craveworthy dishes made with leftovers and lots of heart. Let's give him the last word.

"There's a lot of labor going on in our kitchens; everything is fresh, organic and made from scratch," he says, echoing his fellow chefs. "I'm trying to bring the authentic flavors from my country and represent home-style Mexican food in ways I don't see happening much here and I'm doing it with the best ingredients available. I'm grateful that the people who come to eat in our restaurants see the value in that."

Sherry Yard's Sweet Independence

By Besha Rodell

From LA Weekly

⌘

After moving from Atlanta to succeed Jonathan Gold as
restaurant critic for *LA Weekly*, Besha Rodell has been
cast in the position of new girl in town. No wonder her
interest was piqued in the story of this female Wolfgang
Puck pastry chef, poised to step out on her own.

Sherry Yard is large in personality and small in stature. Blond, Brooklyn-born, 5 feet 2 inches tall, Yard is one of the most respected pastry chefs in the country and, in her trademark bubble gum–pink coat, one of the easiest to spot. But standing in the gaping 4,000-square-foot space at the Helms Bakery complex that soon will house her new venture, Yard looks especially small, and her personality seems especially large. Because what she's talking about, what she envisions for this giant empty space, is one of the most ambitious food projects in L.A. history.

Best known as the longtime pastry chef at Spago, Yard worked for 19 years with Wolfgang Puck in that restaurant's kitchen, and also on many other projects in his massive restaurant empire. In that time she wrote two cookbooks, won a James Beard Award and mentored or influenced an entire generation (or three) of pastry chefs, who now fan out all over the world.

She is finally striking out to do something of her own. With Sang Yoon, chef and owner of Lukshon and Father's Office, Yard is planning to redefine the old Helms Bakery complex.

Next January, Sherry Yard will turn 50. Her gift to herself will be Helms Hall and Bakery.

In an industry where male chefs who work with savory ingredients get the lion's share of the glory, Los Angeles is somewhat unusual. There is a strong maternal line in the history of our best chefs and restaurants, and it goes right back to the pastry kitchen at Spago.

Spago's first pastry chef was Nancy Silverton, who went on to open La Brea Bakery and Campanile with then-husband Mark Peel and, after that, her Mozza empire with Mario Batali and Joe Bastianich. Later, in the Spago kitchen, Sherry Yard trained an incredible number of chefs, from Karen Hatfield, who now owns and operates Hatfield's and Sycamore Kitchen with her husband, Quinn Hatfield, to Food Network personality Giada De Laurentiis. It's hard to find a well-regarded chef in L.A. who didn't go through the kitchens of Spago or Campanile, and harder still to find one who wouldn't admit to being influenced in some way by Silverton and/or Yard.

You could read up on all of Yard's accolades, her many awards, her best-selling cookbooks, her badass reputation. But what might be more illustrative, what might give you a better idea of why she has all these accolades, would be to spy on her at the farmers market as she talks to a farmer about Ring of Saturn peaches.

Yard: "You only have three cases? I want all three."

Farmer: "No, you can only have one. I need to save some for the other chefs."

Yard, in the tone of a hustle, quick-tongued, full of passion and bravado: "No, no, you can have all of them. Keep them. Tell me the person that's going to do something better with them than me. He can have them; she can have them. But if you say sorbet, pie, cobbler or crisp, they're automatically out. Because how could they not respect the fruit? How could you not look into it and say, 'What is it meant to be?'"

She picks up a peach and pries it open. She talks about its perfume; how, at this point in the season, it doesn't smell like almond. It's too young, so it smells like pistachio. She says she'll take the peach and blanch it, dip it in flour, then dip it in egg, then dip it in biscotti crumbs because they have pistachio and anise in them. She'll bake them in the oven, to order.

She gets all three cases.

•

The first time you eat a Sherry Yard dessert, the experience may be somewhat stupefying.

You may have heard of Yard's raspberry chocolate-chip soufflé at Spago, but you'd still be unprepared for the almost childish sugary glee of it, the hot pink mousse-y interior, the melted chocolate, the extra chocolate sauce poured over this insane, puffy ode to sugar. This is dessert with a point of view, but it's the antithesis of the self-serious architectural creations offered by other famous pastry chefs. There's no turning away from the idea that dessert is meant to be fun, that at its heart it's an indulgence and therefore shouldn't become too solemn. This is a celebration of the part of us that, as children, would have risked life and limb—or at least stern punishment—to get our hands on that sweet sticky stuff, and it is the purest expression of that notion (without falling into the trap of mawkish, saccharine overkill) you may ever encounter.

Restaurant critics often hear readers complain, "Why don't you write more about desserts?" The problem is that generally there's only so much you can say about creme brulee and flourless chocolate cake and fruit tart. More often than not, any given version is just like everything else everyone else is serving. The highly technical stuff lacks heart; the rustic stuff you could often make yourself at home. Week after week, it's hard to come up with exciting new ways to say something emphatic about another bread pudding.

But Yard's work is different. When Spago reopened after its latest renovation, the savory food and the stylish new decor both were striking, but what made you stop and pay attention and actually feel something were Yard's desserts. Playful, surprising and intensely technically accomplished, they seared themselves into your sense memory like nothing else at Spago, and as very little else has the capacity to do.

Sherry Yard grew up in Sheepshead Bay, Brooklyn, the daughter of a firefighter. Her grandparents were a fishmonger and a turndown maid at the Waldorf Astoria Hotel. She was the second of four girls. You can see some of that Brooklyn firefighter still in Yard's demeanor and attitude; she has the swagger, the twinkle in the eye and the no-bullshit bearing of Sheepshead Bay. Yet so much of what influenced her earlier in life was what she calls the "simple pageantry" of her grandmother's rituals.

"She had Czechoslovakian china, which she served our eggs on in the morning. Our juice was served in crystal glasses," Yard says. "We lived in a house in Brooklyn that was two steps above a shanty, but she gave us this sense of glamour. Because she was a turndown maid, everything was about doing things properly. Setting the table properly. I learned that things taste better on pretty plates."

Yard also credits her grandmother with teaching her how to taste. "She would blindfold us and get us to taste and tell her if she'd put coffee in the ice cream, or what kind of soda she'd bought. She'd say, 'What does it taste like?'"

Yard went to a Catholic girls school and received a scholarship to nursing school at 18, but her mother told her, "Give it back. This is not who you're going to be, and you're taking it from someone who can use it."

She worked at catering halls and at McDonald's and at a dentist's office and at a medical center, and along the way she started baking for people. But she didn't really get bit by the restaurant bug until the mid-'80s, when she went to apply for a job at the newly opened Rainbow Room, during a time she was taking classes at New York Technical Institute. They hired her, first as a cigarette girl, then as a waitress; when she confessed to pastry chef Albert Cumin that she wanted to be a pastry chef, he offered her a spot in the kitchen. "I went to the back of the house and made as much in one week as the pastry wench as I had made in one day in the front of the house."

Over the next decade, Yard went to culinary school three times (dropping out once, graduating twice), received a scholarship to study in London, worked at some of the best restaurants in New York and then San Francisco, met and worked with and rubbed shoulders with almost every legendary chef you've ever heard of, and made a very good career for herself as a pastry chef. But none of that prepared her for a phone call she got out of the blue in 1994.

She was working as pastry chef in Napa, at Jan Birnbaum's Catahoula. "I got a phone call from some guy with an Austrian accent." She assumed it was a prank call. "I thought it was my crazy friend Bob from back East. I called Bob and he said, 'You're drunk.

Don't drink and dial me.' I played the message back, I took down the phone number. It was Sunday night—I called the number and they said 'Spago,' and I hung up the phone."

On Monday morning she got up the nerve to call back. Wolfgang Puck told her a mutual friend had said she was looking for her next gig. And he needed a pastry chef. "He asked me when my next day off was. I told him we were closed Monday and Tuesday and he said, 'OK, I'll see you tomorrow. Hold on.' See you tomorrow? But he got me on the phone with his assistant, and she said, 'There's this flight out of Oakland tomorrow, we've got your ticket, and we'll have someone pick you up at the airport.' They picked me up at the airport, and 19 years later. . . . "

But there was more to it than that. Yard had long been fascinated by Austria, and had traveled there and obsessively studied the culture. When she showed up in L.A., she apologized for not bringing a résumé. What she did have was little cards with color drawings of her desserts, which she had laminated in order to show people in the kitchen how to plate them. She spread the cards out on the table for Puck to see and his eyes lit up. He grabbed a menu to show her his own colored drawings of dishes, which decorated Spago's menus in those days. "They looked identical to mine," Yard says. "There was a pear tart on mine, and a pear tart on his. He said to me, 'I have crayons, I have markers. You can share.'"

For his part, Puck says he had no idea when they first met how well it would work out—much less that their collaboration would last 19 years. "It's like with anything," he says. "You can fall in love with someone, and then a week later it's over—it's the same with finding people to work with. But the main attribute that I always appreciated, from the beginning, was her enthusiasm and her spirit."

He gives that spirit a lot of the credit for why they worked so well together for so long, as well as the fact that he tries to give everyone who works for him the freedom to be creative and successful.

But Puck and Yard very much share an enthusiasm for the customer-service side of the business. "Sherry's personality is fantastic," Puck says. "When I wasn't there in the restaurant, she was happy to go out and talk to the customers, make them something special, be that face of the restaurant. She was really my No. 2 for many years in that respect. There are many people who can make great desserts, or are great cooks. But she's not only a great pastry chef, she has an amazing passion for hospitality."

Sherry Yard and Sang Yoon have known each other for years, since the days when Yoon worked as a cook at Chinois, Wolfgang Puck's Santa Monica fusion restaurant. They share many things in common: their initials, their love of Champagne, their lucky number (11). They are both left-handed but both play sports with their right hands. These things are important to Yard—she's a strong believer in fate, in things feeling right.

Two years ago, Yard and Yoon ran into each other at the James Beard Awards in New York City. Yard was on the verge of signing a lease for the spot in the Grove that is now Umami Burger, and she told Yoon about her plans for a bakery. "It dawned on me—holy shit, she's actually leaving Spago," Yoon says. "So I told her about the space at Helms, about how I had always wanted to open a bakery there." Yard told him she'd do it with him. They pinkie-promised. "She told me, 'My pinkie promise is better than a written contract.'" When she returned to L.A., she called off the deal at the Grove.

"If Sherry hadn't agreed to do this with me, I might not have wanted to do it at all," Yoon says. "But if Sherry Yard says she wants to do something with you, you do that thing."

At first, it was just going to be a bakery. That alone made a nice headline: "Sherry Yard and Sang Yoon Bring Baking Back to the Historic Helms Bakery." But somehow, in the two years since that first pinkie promise, the project has morphed into something else entirely. Yes, there will still be a bakery.

"My initial thought was, this used to be a grand bakery, so let's mass-produce some things and be really well known for one thing— maybe it's a cream puff, maybe it's a doughnut," Yard says. "Then I got an office at Helms. Once I got an office on-site, and I really started to get to know the neighborhood, I started to look and say, 'What do they need here?' And the truth is: How much can I bake? How many people are going to walk through the door? When I started to do the math, with all my experience in catering and mass production, I can do a lot of baking in a very small space. So, with 4,000 square feet, to create a bakery, I realized that a lot of that product is going to have to go out the back door," meaning wholesale rather than retail.

"I don't want that," she says. "I'd rather bake 14 times a day than bake one time a day and have all the bakers go home and then everything's 14 hours old by the time anyone eats it. No."

So her plans for the kitchen space began to change, to shrink. She realized that part of what the neighborhood needs is somewhere to eat. She wanted a great sandwich. She wanted a place to sit down.

Somehow, over the months, that conversation between Yard and Yoon led to a plan not just for a bakery where you can get a great sandwich but also a full-blown food hall. Helms Hall and Bakery will be a bakery, yes, but right now the plans are for it to also have a coffee and pastry bar, a deli, a wood-fired oven, hot and cold stations, a rotisserie, a carving station, seating, a long cookie and confections counter, and over in one corner a beautiful little glassed-in dinette. The dinette, which Yard giddily describes as being "like a three-star Michelin restaurant but a diner," will be open for breakfast and lunch. The rest of the hall will be open from early morning until 8 or 9 p.m.

The original Helms Bakery operated from 1931 to 1969. Started by Paul Helms, a New York baker who had moved to Southern California, the bakery began with 32 employees. Helms products were never sold in stores; instead they were distributed fresh each day by trucks called "coaches." The coaches operated much like ice cream trucks, driving through neighborhoods and sounding a whistle. They also stopped at houses: People displayed blue "H" signs in their windows to alert drivers to stop. There were 11 routes in 1931 when Helms opened—at the height of its success in the 1950s, Helms served more than 950.

Many things lead to the demise of Helms—the advent of the supermarket, women joining the workforce, the rise of cheaper, mass-produced breads. Despite the fact that Helms ceased operations in 1969, the brand name, building and trucks remain powerful symbols for people who grew up in Los Angeles, who remember that whistle and its promise of cream puffs and doughnuts and bread baked that morning.

In 1971 the Marks family, led by Wally Marks Jr., bought the complex. In the past 40 years, it has held everything from an antiques mall to a jazz club.

In recent years, Wally Marks III, Wally Jr.'s son, has made a concerted effort to expand the complex, curate tenants and create a space for design and food. In 2005 HD Buttercup, the largest furniture store in Los Angeles, opened in what had been a giant antiques store. The following year, Yoon opened Father's Office, his temple to beer and upscale bar food. Since then, many more furniture and design stores have opened, and in 2010 Yoon opened Lukshon, a sleek, modern take on Southeast Asian food.

Father's Office and Lukshon have given Helms some serious food credibility, but the Helms Hall and Bakery could make the place a food destination on a whole different level, getting people to think of Helms in food terms the way they currently think of it in design terms: as one of the city's major hubs.

Yoon admits he's nervous about taking on such an ambitious project. "We're trying to look at it like it's five separate food businesses under one roof, each of them separate, individual pieces. When you look at it that way, it's a divide-and-conquer thing. But yeah, it's a big thing to take on no matter how you look at it."

Not only is the food hall a lot of different moving parts, but Yard and Yoon also envision the bakery aspect somewhat differently from a regular bakery. "Sherry hates what she calls the 'adoption process,' where there are a bunch of cakes and pies sitting out waiting to be adopted," Yoon says. "It breaks her heart. She's invested in doing everything fresh."

Yard echoes this, saying, "If someone wants to order a cake, I might say, 'OK, when do you want to eat it? What time are your guests arriving? Six p.m.? So you might be done with dinner around 8:30? Fine, you can pick up the cake at 4. Any earlier than that, it won't be good, it won't be fresh.'"

What isn't as clear is how she plans to do this for every single item in the bakery, from cookies to bread, pies to cream puffs. Talk to her about any single item they plan on serving in the hall and Yard gets worked up about how things should be done, about the history of that item, about the ways she will do it better. She can talk for 10 minutes straight and a mile a minute about toast—about how thick toast should be cut, about how toast should be buttered, about why no one ever gets toast right. Oh, and she plans to mill her own flour on-site. "I'm trying to learn and absorb everything I can right now about grains," she says.

The most interesting thing about Helms Hall and Bakery might be how these two perfectionists will handle a giant operation with so many moving parts, 50 employees and three reputations—hers, his and the Helms complex—resting on their success.

So what took Yard so long to strike out on her own? Someone with so many ideas, so much passion and the force of personality to drive a hundred successful businesses—why did she stay with Puck for so long?

"I still have the original red file folder from 1995, when Wolfgang and I were going to open a bakery together," she says. "From the very beginning, he said to me, 'You love bread so much. I'll help you open a bakery.'"

It wasn't that he wasn't serious, either; it's just that every time an idea, a location, a plan was put into place, for some reason it fell through.

Five years ago, Yard had to get some work done on her teeth and one of the dentists at the practice caught her eye. "The next time in, I asked the receptionist, 'Is Dr. Ines single?' She said he was, so I asked him out."

Three months later, they were engaged. Maybe it was her marriage that got her thinking about creating something of her own.

Or maybe it was just time: time to remember the pastry chefs. Time to indulge our sweet tooth a bit. And high time Sherry Yard got her due.

A Day on Long Island with Alex Lee

By Francis Lam

From Lucky Peach

As a food writer, Francis Lam has hit many heights—
articles for *Gourmet*, the *New York Times*, and Salon.
com, a judge slot on TV's *Top Chef*, an editor-at-large
gig at Clarkson Potter books. In this profile of a once-
hot chef's thoughtful next chapter, Lam seems to have
found a kindred spirit.

It was a February night in the back room of Gramercy Tavern, at
a dinner for Ed Behr and the *Art of Eating*. Every guest—writers,
chefs, editors—was a household name for American food nerds. All,
except for one: an Asian man, maybe in his late forties, with close-
cropped hair and a sturdy look. He smiled graciously but had a vis-
itor's air amidst the cheek kissers. Every once in a while someone
called him "Chef."

We introduced ourselves eventually. "I'm Alex," he said as we
shook hands. Alex . . . Alex . . . a name I'd only read before jumped
into my mind, and I could feel my eyes grow wider. "Alex *Lee*?" I
asked.

Way back, before Daniel Boulud was President of the Restaurant
Universe, when he was still just a young star with a lot of promise,
when he'd just left Sirio Maccioni's Le Cirque to strike out on his
own, Alex Lee was right there with him. He was trained by Ducasse
in Monte Carlo, by a grandmother in Italy (a grandmother who
happened to have three Michelin stars at Dal Pescatore), and by his
own Chinese grandmother. He spoke perfect French with long Long
Island o's and, straddling the divide between Boulud's French and

American cooks, became Restaurant Daniel's first chef de cuisine. He was one of the first chefs to braise pork belly in American haute cuisine, to season roasted lobster with soy sauce in the foie-and-truffles world. But this was 1993, before the Food Network made chefs into living-room fixtures, before Tony Bourdain made them into pirate heroes, before the Internet made them buzz. Back then, it was really just work. Work, and, if you cared, craft. Alex Lee cared.

He poked and prodded every box of ingredients that came into the restaurant, constantly writing ideas and combinations on his clipboard, making eight or nine specials a night in a restaurant where diners might come only once in their lives. He giddily called cooks around to show them a new squash he'd grown on his rooftop, and he destroyed their mise en places—and maybe them—if they were doing it wrong. Daniel's kitchen was a constant hurricane as it cooked furiously for its fourth *New York Times* star, and he stood at its center. He pushed and yapped and yelled and willed it into the most celebrated restaurant in New York, blowing 200 minds a night and training a whole generation of brilliant, steeled chefs in the process.

And yet there was, I guess, a reason that I didn't even know what he looked like. He ran the kitchen at Daniel with seemingly no sense of ego. He didn't seek out reporters to give interviews, rarely even went into the dining room. Daniel did that; Daniel mastered that. Alex stayed with the cooks. And then, ten years later, he was gone: decamped back to Long Island, to run the kitchen of a country club, to grow vegetables, to be with his family. When I called him to tell him I wanted to write a story about him, he said, "I love talking about food, so if there's anything I can tell you about, I'm happy to help you out." I wanted to say to him, "No, man, the story isn't about food; it's about you." In a world where we cover and cover and cover chefs—who's hot this morning and who's hotter this afternoon, plywood reports and blogs shedding each other's blood to get the scoop on someone's off-duty eating habits—he's like a ghost.

Glen Oaks is the kind of country club where members decide in the morning whether they feel like coming in for some golf or just to play the day's round on their own personal courses. Its dining rooms rival anything in Manhattan for grand comfort: rich woods and clean lines, hushing upholstery, and light that makes everything glow slightly gold. If a member would like, Alex will prepare a tasting menu—seasonal, refined, lovely—but the club's kitchen is strictly big-kitchenesque: a cook fed heads of cabbage into a buffalo chopper, shooting ribbons of coleslaw-to-be into a massive bowl set in a garbage can. Dozens of chickens sat brining in tubs big enough to bathe triplets, and a few feet away was a rack of sweets, an orgy of pies on stainless steel, ready for Summer Sunday Barbecue Night on the veranda.

Sitting amidst all this was a cart of vegetables, arranged with obvious affection: the tomatoes gently pressing on one another, the yellows and greens of squashes peeking from their crates, eggplants so plump they seemed to be smiling, a bouquet of sunflowers. It was like a cartoon of a farm stand, a postcard of the good country life.

Alex Lee was cutting tomatoes. I walked over to him, reintroducing myself. "I was just making a dish for you," he said, as if that's the normal way bare acquaintances greet each other. I glanced at the plate he was working on: a perfect rectangle of twelve tiles of tomato, every one different—one the lusty pink of ripe watermelon, one striped white and green, one cooked-carrot orange, one so dark it looked like dried blood . . . and then I was stunned with a sudden recollection: I once read that when Ruth Reichl came into Daniel, Alex made her a mosaic of his tomatoes. That was how he greeted the queen of the VIPs, and I flashed through four feelings: flattered to be in that company, thrilled to taste what that life is like, nostalgic for a time in a restaurant I never lived through, and then worried that I might be too entranced by Alex's past. At some point, you have to let the quarterback be more than the touchdown he threw in high school, right?

He put down his knife and came to shake my hand, walking with rigidity, an ex-boxer's gait. "I don't know what you want to talk about, but I can talk anyone's ear off about food," he said. We decided to sit down in his office, to affect something like a formal interview, and for the next hour, I went tubing on a stream-of-consciousness exaltation of country cooking ("I love country cooking . . . how do you capture the flavors of country cooking? . . . We need to preserve country cooking . . . Ducasse was so great about concentrated flavors, country flavors . . . "); gardening ("I've had gardens since I'm thirteen. If I wasn't a chef, I would have wanted to be a farmer, but boy, do they work hard"); *Desserts Traditionnels de France* by Gaston Lenôtre ("I love that book, because he's this amazing pastry chef, but the book is all about country pastry"); his management style ("Believe me, I was very tough in the kitchen. But I always thought I could get people to work harder for me than anyone else. I guess because I also always made time for them; I always showed my interest in them"); and his favorite Haitian restaurant ("I've learned so much about food from cabbies"). He talked about his grandmother, how he remembered being in the kitchen with her while she made four shrimp stretch to feed six. "She was frugal, and she was a magician. I don't want to sound cheesy, but that was her greatest joy. That type of nurturing became important to me. I love to feed people."

During a pause, he decided to show me a Japanese cucumber he grew. "Let me get some salt," he said, but then stopped himself and instead grabbed a pair of scissors.

I followed him to his herb garden, right outside the kitchen, and there the random-access memories he'd been calling up began to take a kind of shape, a logic. He saw the lemon verbena—*la vervaine*, en français—and started telling me about arriving in his first French kitchen and being made to break stock bones for seven hours, then cleaning seven cases of squid the size of your fingertip. "But the cooks were so polished. They had so much reverence. Believe me, I could watch the staff set the tables for an hour. Everything was such a ballet," he said. We got to the basil, and he told me about working in Italy, at Dal Pescatore, where the chef, Bruna, would wake him up, open a book on the traditional cooking of the region, and show him what they would cook that day. "Then her son would go out fishing and bring back what we'd need," he said. "It was the most moving experience." For him, every ingredient carries stories, and just laying eyes on one calls them up. The entire time we talked, he never referred to them as "product," the way all chefs do. They were always "ingredients," they were always individual and real, not abstracted and at arm's length.

A group of Hispanic men suddenly stopped their golf cart beside us. One got out to get a closer look at the garden, and then sheepishly pointed toward the patch of chilies. Alex spoke with them in Spanish; they were on a golf course maintenance crew brought in to work for a few weeks. They'd love a few peppers for their dinner, and, as soon as they said that, Alex sprang into the plants. He snipped from three varieties of peppers, and came out with his hands full for them.

They drove off, a million Scoville units richer, and Alex pointed to a plant he was now standing next to. "This is a Kyoto eggplant," he said. "Traditionally, they would take off the top, broil them, and punch holes in them for the moisture to escape. They they'd finish them with some miso and broil them again, and it would get so soft, you'd just eat it out of the skin, like a custard." I wanted that, more than I'd ever wanted an eggplant before. "I love to grow specific varieties of vegetables and find out where they come from, what people did with them," he said. "I think you have to know the history of a food when you make a dish with it."

Eventually, we got to a tiny calamansi tree, taking some for our cucumber back in the office, its fate held hostage to another hour of downloading Alex's food brain. He talked about the floral acidity of calamansi, when he might use it in place of lime in a marinade. Then his eye caught a small pot of young bay leaves, more fragile than I'd ever seen. I said they smelled a little like vervaine. Alex smiled: yes, exactly. He looked intently at them for a moment. "I could imagine these in a delicate custard, very simple, just to show that aroma," he said. His brain is always putting flavors into form.

Finally we returned to the office and tasted the cucumber. It was quietly astonishing—sweet and grassy, with an almost melon-like scent. It crunched with integrity, like a radish. It was the proudest cucumber I have ever had. Then it was back to his station in the kitchen, where the tomatoes waited, and Alex pointed to one of his cooks, a strapping dude who looked like a cover model from a grocery-store romance novel, wrapped in what seemed like a child-sized apron that didn't quite reach his knees. "The chicken he makes is tremendous. Fried chicken, barbecued chicken. They call him the Chicken Man. And the ladies love him. Believe me." I imagined his face embossed on a paperback: *The Farmer's Daughter and the Chicken Man—A lust created by nature, forbidden by men.*

Alex piled a full sturgeon generation's worth of caviar on his cutting board. He formed it quickly into a thick row, then laid it down the center of the tomato mosaic. It was the exact right length, the gunmetal eggs cropped close to the tomatoes, as if they'd been cut from the same stroke. On each tile he placed a touch of herb: a small burst of fennel flowers for this one, that one a tip of spearmint, two splinters of chive for another.

"The caviar brings out the nuances of the tomato," he said plainly. I took my time eating it, every bite different from the others: this one sweet like fruit, the next savory and deep. The unexpected cool of mint brushing up against the brine of caviar, red tomato tartness cruising overhead. Butter, nuts, seaweed. Licorice candy and peaches. Raw meat and fish belly. It looked like the most no-brainer of a dish you'd ever seen, but it went in a hundred directions. I'd like to say that the dish was an education in the flavors a tomato can take, but honestly, I was so knocked over by what was going on that the lesson washed over me. My palate wasn't worthy of Alex Lee's version of a tomato salad. I wondered if that's how Ruth felt when she had it at Daniel's gastronomic temple on 65th Street. I wondered if this is something his guests now enjoy, smelling of sunblock after a round of golf, a glass of iced tea sweating onto the table, a platter of the Chicken Man's chicken on the way.

Over lunch—he made us the greatest diner-style Spanish omelet in history, with square yellow cheese because "nothing melts like American, man"—he told me how he came back to New York after his time in Europe. He'd been working, like an ox, at Alain Ducasse's Louis XV. "They put me up in the Hotel de Paris—an amazing, beautiful place!—and one day Ducasse knocked on my door, saying, 'There's someone here to see you.' So I went out to the lobby, and Daniel was sitting there. He wanted to talk about his new restaurant." I chewed on my omelet. "And then the next day, Ducasse knocked again. 'There's someone here to see you.' And it was Sirio. He wanted me to come back to Le Cirque."

Did it really go down that way? Did the greatest chef of his generation come to Monte Carlo to recruit Alex one day, and did the greatest restaurateur of his generation come the next? I almost didn't even want to write that down. Origin myths are not meant to be fact checked.

Alex wanted to take me to see where our omelets' tomatoes and peppers came from, and ten minutes later, we pulled into the Rottkamp Brothers Farm. It's a fourth-generation farm, sixty-five years in the game, on property someone would probably kill to turn into a stand of mansions. Instead, it's a cornucopia laid out on dusty earth: green beans, watermelons, half a dozen kinds of eggplants, and the full family tree of tomato varieties. Squashes, pumpkins, and a football field of callaloo, grown for Caribbean markets in the city. An unreal row of beets, as if staged for a photo shoot: their leaves proud, rigid, and deep green, their single red vein diving down into perfectly round roots, gently nestled in the soil.

Alex put his feet in the dirt and beamed.

"If I see you serving a tomato from a thousand miles away when this is right in your backyard," he said, "I just don't see why I would need to ever come back to your restaurant again."

Anne Marie, one of the owners, rushed over to greet him. He spoke with her in French, and they caught up: she's well, and her husband—one of the namesake brothers—is out cutting the callaloo. It's been a good season; the tomatoes have been fantastic, haven't they? The corn is coming to the end, but it's been a great year for it too.

She turned to me, saying, "You know, when Alex calls, they all go into the field and pick whatever he wants. We could be so busy, but everyone will run out, and they all say, 'But it's for Alex!' He has such a great heart. They all love him." He looks a little bit away, into the fields, as if to avoid hearing.

Anne Marie took us through her crops, and Alex pointed out patches of purslane she didn't even know she had. He talked about Ducasse's favorite stuffed zucchini, with *poulet roti*, truffle, and parmesan. He recalled three preparations of every vegetable we walked past, every herb from every dish. It's like he remembers everything he's ever cooked, everything he's ever eaten, and it needs to come out. The herb garden was one thing, but walking through an actual farm with Alex Lee was a little like staring at the sun.

But then we got to one of the barns, and Alex was stunned silent. There was a gray, ancient tractor, a Ford, from 1952. Richard, one of the Rottkamp brothers, found it abandoned in a stand of shrubs. It had the round, bulging nose of old cars from that era, a kind of warm muscularity. "He fixed it up himself! He looks so happy when he rides on it," Alex said. "I love asking him about it, because he's so proud of it. But his life is so hard. These people, they work so hard."

It occurred to me that Alex talks about hard work almost as much as he talks about country cooking. I watched him chat with Anne Marie and Richard. He offered to cook them some of that callaloo, which they've only grown, never eaten. I thought about what he'd told me earlier, about making time for the people who worked so hard for him. At first it sounded like a strategy, something you put in a best-practices guide for business managers. But seeing the way Alex swelled with a kind of pride looking at this farmer's fixed-up tractor, I don't think it's a tactic. I think it's just him.

We said goodbye to the Rottkamps. Driving back to the club, I asked Alex how he came to his job there. It wasn't exactly the question I was supposed to ask, I guess—the question anyone would want to ask of the guy who spent ten years building one of the best restaurants in New York, one of the best restaurants in the world: "Why did you leave the game?" I didn't want to ask that question. I didn't want to ask this man something that would sound like I was questioning his honor or his commitment. But that might have been the question he heard anyway.

We pulled into the parking lot. "I like growing, I guess," he started. "Watching plants grow. Watching people grow. I love cooking, but the balance of my life wasn't so good anymore.

"In the restaurant, you feel like it's a fight when you walk in the door. You're fighting the purveyors, you're fighting during prep, you're fighting to be perfect in an imperfect system. Then service is a battle. There's a lot of yelling and screaming. Whether it was me or someone else, I always talked to people after to make it good. It takes so many people to put on that show, and everyone's important: the dishwasher, the coffee guy, the bread guy. I tried to make myself available to them, but it just got too crazy, to be between my family, my staff, the menu, the ordering . . . In life, all these things are tradeoffs. I do miss sometimes the energy of the city. Cooking is performance, and I enjoy the aspect of creating for people, especially when other chefs, critics, real foodies are coming through. I love feeding people."

He paused, and I couldn't tell if he was looking for words or getting emotional.

"At a restaurant like Daniel, you work so hard. I would be there eighteen hours a day, especially in the beginning, standing there and scrubbing down steel with my cooks after service. Believe me, you're punishing the cooks. I guess I eventually just felt like I couldn't ask that of them anymore if I wasn't always going to be there for them, too."

We decided to call it a day. It was hot, and his dinner service was starting. Casual millionaires were taking their seats for the barbecue on the veranda. The sushi station was set, the carving station was going up. Alex asked if he could get me a bottle of water for the road.

I waited a few minutes for him to come back out with the water, and his words turned in my mind. Alex Lee left the city for himself, for his family, but, just as much, because he was committed to the notion that if he couldn't sacrifice everything of himself for his cooks, he shouldn't be there at all. Could it be that he really had so little ego? Could it be that, after ten years of his life, after all the stars in the dining room and all the stars in the reviews, he didn't think he should be doing it with his own name on the door?

A few days later, he will tell me over the phone that, just a few months ago, Daniel texted him out of the blue to say that the happiest he'd ever been in the kitchen was when he was cooking with Alex. And before I can follow up with a question, Alex will quickly change the subject and I will let it be, because some people want to keep their pride for themselves.

When Alex didn't appear in the parking lot, I assumed he got stuck in service. I found him inside, by the Chicken Man's fried chicken. He was munching on a drumstick, putting a few pieces into a box for me. He wanted to make sure, before I went, that he could feed me one more time.

SAVORING THE NOW

By John Kessler

From the Atlanta Journal-Constitution

As dining critic of the *Atlanta Journal-Constitution*,*
John Kessler usually has to judge a restaurant on the
basis of its food. But he has also been a restaurant cook
himself; he knows what it takes to get that food on the
table. Who better to tell the story of a talented young
chef with a dream, racing against time?

O n a warm afternoon in late September, Ryan and Jen Hidinger
show visitors around a red brick two-story building on Edge-
wood Avenue in Old Fourth Ward. This handsome structure dates
to 1906, and it will be everything to them.

The Hidingers speak in the imaginary future-inflected present—
a verb tense known only to people with fantastic architectural plans.
"So these are steps," Jen says, pointing to a perfectly flat expanse of
floor. "After guests walk down, they meet the hostess," she continues
with hands outstretched, outlining a standing desk or perhaps a very
short hostess.

Ryan takes over. "Here's the kitchen pass," he says of thin air, the
spot where cooks give finished plates to hovering waiters. "Guests
are sitting here," where he runs his hands over the smooth surface of
a phantom counter facing the kitchen.

Ryan and Jen, who've been married for nearly eight years, pass the conversation ball back and forth with ease; you barely see the hand-off, hear the pause, as one takes a breath and the other continues the tour. They walk their visitors through the middle of an imagined dinner service at their busy not-yet restaurant called Staplehouse. In the back courtyard, invisible guests sip drinks under the shelter of a weeping white oak, its fall leaves rustling on brick pavers underfoot. Meats roast in the open fire pit along the back wall.

At the front of the building upstairs lies the nexus of the whole operation—an office for the Giving Kitchen, the nonprofit philanthropic foundation that helps restaurant workers who can't afford medical treatment when faced with an illness or catastrophic accident. The Giving Kitchen is Ryan and Jen's life's work, their gift back, their payment forward. Private donations and money collected from fundraising events—not to mention every penny of Staplehouse's profit—will flow into it. Because of what they've been through in the past nine months, the Hidingers find themselves able to dream up such an audacious enterprise and convince everyone it will work.

Had the Atlanta restaurant community not rallied to raise funds when Ryan got the worst possible news, they wouldn't be here. Rather than merely accepting the support, they kept the discourse going. They thought bigger.

The Hidingers lead their visitors back to a patio, Ryan's favorite spot, by the concrete wall spiderwebbed with a dark filigree stain left by the ghost of a creeping vine. A guest asks to take their picture. "Like this?" asks Jen, striking a Betty Boop pose, a k a the proto-twerk.

"How about full nudity?" Ryan asks, hand on the brim of his ball cap, ready to expose his chemo-whitened crown of hair.

You go right ahead," she laughs. "I'm keeping my clothes on."

Love and Food

Ryan Hidinger (pronounced "HIGH-dinger") first noticed Jen Wells in the Indianapolis market where she was bagging groceries in 2000. She looked a bit like Penelope Cruz—huge brown eyes, high cheekbones and long chestnut hair so dark it verged on black. He bought a pack of gum in her checkout line and asked her out. She looked this tall, earnest, 22-year-old catering cook up and down and said no.

The next week he tried again. She thought for a second, pressed the button on her cash register until it spat out a length of receipt paper and wrote her store beeper number down. "Call me here," she said, thinking it seemed cool to have a beeper.

She didn't reveal she was only 17 and a high school senior.

When Jen told her tradition-minded Spanish mother she had a "formal date" with a culinary college graduate, Mary Carmen Wells shrieked loudly and insisted that he come over so the family could meet him. "Ryan showed up that night, and we went to the family room and sat him on the couch and started questioning his intentions," Wells said. "Ryan called it the Spanish Inquisition."

He charmed the family that night and got the blessing to date Jen as long as he didn't interfere with her college education. While she took classes at Indiana University 50 miles away in Bloomington, he traded out his catering gig for a job at a restaurant called H20 Sushi. Greg Hardesty, who supervised Ryan in the kitchen there, saw an instinctive quality in Hidinger that escapes so many young hotshot chefs. "He puts the dish ahead of himself. He's not the star, it's the food that's the star, and his job is to coax it."

Once Jen graduated, they got engaged and took off in his Volkswagen Golf for a whirlwind cross-country trip. They drove west across the Rockies, down the coast, through the Southwest arriving at Ryan's brother's house in Atlanta with no money and an empty gas tank. Atlanta. It was as good a place as any to pitch a tent.

Ryan soon landed a job as a line cook at Bacchanalia, Atlanta's top-rated restaurant. It wasn't easy. Hierarchy, intense pressure: that's the way high-level kitchens operate. When asked about the job, Hidinger says, "I wouldn't trade that experience for anything in the world. It gave me everything I needed."

Ryan persevered, got promoted and soon moved to a management position at sister restaurant Floataway Cafe. But he wanted that feeling of family back, and so he and Jen began talking about opening their own restaurant. Nothing fancy, just a sandwich shop. But a really good one, with quality ingredients. Ryan even had a name—Staplehouse, a portmanteau he made up and then turned over often in his mind to admire its facets of meaning.

Ryan looked around Atlanta for the best example of the concept he had in mind, which led him to Muss & Turner's in Smyrna. The popular gourmet deli was starting to improve its wine and beer lists and morph into a dinner destination. It felt perfect—the place where Ryan might find his Atlanta family.

A Dream Takes Form

Ryan Turner remembers how unlike other chefs Ryan Hidinger seemed when he applied at Muss & Turner's that day in 2006. "He was very humble, very quiet, just a Midwest good guy who played basketball and ate chicken wings," recalls Turner. "He was not the punk rock kind of chef." Ryan had neither tattoo nor piercing on his 6'4" frame, showed meticulous knife skills, paid attention to seasonal produce and could take or leave pork belly.

Turner hired him right away. The management-level position paid a typically low foodservice salary but would entitle Ryan to benefits on the restaurant's group health plan.

Within six months, he was running the kitchen. He oversaw the menu's shift to the new open-ended format that was changing American dining—more small plates and shareable appetizers, a peaceful coexistence of sandwiches and knife-and-fork entrees, a suggestion that cutting-edge cooking could happen in low-key, comfy places that encouraged guests to relax. In the kitchen he encouraged calm voices, teamwork and opposing opinions from his staff.

The experience made Ryan rethink Staplehouse; maybe it should be more than a sandwich shop. One day at work he pulled Turner aside to share his idea. "I want it to be a restaurant but not a big one. Fifty seats, that's all—a neighborhood place," he said. "Larger restaurants get so contrived. With a smaller place you can make more personal connections, attract the right kind of people."

Turner wasn't buying it. "You're not going to make any money with a 50-seat restaurant," he said flatly.

"If I wanted to make money," Ryan sighed, "I wouldn't be in the restaurant business."

In 2009, Ryan and Jen started a supper club called Prelude to Staplehouse. "We knew we wouldn't be able to open a restaurant that had legs without doing it," said Jen, who sensed their brand must be built on a foundation, and their literal foundation was their Grant Park bungalow. "It was the only way to gain respect and value" for Ryan as a signature chef.

They figured they could fit 10 people max—four at the kitchen counter, six around the white Ikea dining room table. They offered tickets on a blog and sold four the first week. The diners filed in on Sunday, Ryan's night off.

As word spread, they began selling out—often within minutes of putting the tickets online. Guests arrived slightly freaked by the transitional neighborhood a few blocks west of Zoo Atlanta. They walked into a tiny living room to the strains of the Pixies from an iPod speaker and a waiting glass of wine. Soon they were sitting down to five-course dinners with dishes such as homemade duck sausage with cornbread and local greens. By the time they left, the guests had moved from polite conversation to an exchange of bear hugs and phone numbers, their bellies full of the Hidinger brand of hospitality. Jen's gregarious quick wit and eye for setting the stage proved as much of a draw as the food. Reporters and bloggers helped spread the news about not only the supper club, but also the would-be restaurant, Staplehouse.

Did they have a location yet? An opening date? Not yet, the Hidingers said, we're still working at it.

While Ryan and Jen had no problem raising the capital of community goodwill, banks and investors refused to bite. The rejections came—ceaseless, almost comical, eventually depressing. All they wanted to do was open a little restaurant, and it was proving impossible.

Between the job and the supper club, Ryan worked without taking a break. Colleagues began to notice he seemed stressed out and sullen. Sometimes he went in the back office to sit at the desk with his head down on his arms.

Jen thought he needed a jolt, something that would bring the hopeful Ryan back. On their seventh wedding anniversary in December, she gave him a plane ticket to New York. She couldn't afford a ticket for herself or the cost of a hotel room, but she could give her husband one whirlwind day in New York stuffing his face. He had never been. Ryan Smith, the chef at Empire State South who was dating Ryan's sister, Kara Hidinger, decided to join him for some quality bro time.

The day was a gustatory orgy of Moroccan lamb sausages at one stop and spicy rice cakes at the next. They slurped dozens of oysters with absinthe cocktails, feasted on octopus slicked with pork fat, drank shots of Blue Bottle espresso and ordered more rounds of beer than they could count. They only felt queasy in the cabs that shuttled them from restaurant to restaurant, but otherwise they rode through the city on a cloud of limitless appetite.

A New Purpose

Ryan, who never got sick, stayed home from work the day after the trip. And the next day, too. It seemed like the flu. He went back to work but felt like hell. At night his stomach cramped. Sharp pains. He couldn't sleep.

The following week he visited his doctor, who recommended an ultrasound. It showed "liver abnormalities." The doctor scheduled an MRI, magnetic resonance imaging, for a more accurate picture. After the MRI, Hidinger headed back to work, feeling guilty for taking so much time off. But a member of the radiology team intercepted him by phone and asked him to return as soon as possible to a different address on the Emory campus to go over the scan.

Hidinger plugged the address into his iPhone and was stopped cold. The word that lit up on his phone stabbed him like a knife. He called Jen. He could barely talk. "The Winship Cancer Institute," he cried. "That's where they want us to go."

The doctor was blunt, pointing to scattershot white spots and masses. He needed a biopsy to make the official call but felt 99 percent certain they were looking at images of late-stage gall bladder cancer. Metastasis to the liver. A spot on the lung. "This is a bad diagnosis," the oncologist said. Ryan and Jen wept and held each other.

"Usually patients with this cancer have six, maybe up to 12 months," the doctor said.

The news made Jen's head spin and she grasped at thoughts, any thoughts, to anchor herself. A weird one came to her overactive mind: That day's date was Dec. 21, 2012–Mayan End Days. She was 30, the good man next to her was 35, and it felt like their end days.

Gall bladder cancer is exceptionally rare, less than 1 percent of all cancers. It typically shows up in Asia, where parasites are believed to trigger it. Environmental issues might also play a role.

Ryan could count on his group health policy at work to pay for treatment, but the co-pays alone might cost more than he and Jen could manage.

That is when the extended Atlanta restaurant community, in breathtaking fashion, swept into play. The day after New Year's, dozens of the biggest names in the Atlanta dining community showed up to plan Team Hidi, a fundraiser for the Hidingers. "It was an amazing collaboration," says Turner. "All these so-called competitors came together to help one of their own." Among them, chef Anne Quatrano led a small army from Bacchanalia and Floataway Cafe.

Three weeks later nearly 800 people filed into the King Plow Arts Center to eat, drink and offer support. The event raised more than $275,000. The turnout overwhelmed Ryan. "It's not like I save lives or anything," he said. "All I do is cook."

The Hidingers decided to seek treatment at Cancer Treatment Centers of America, a new facility in Newnan. According to CTCA oncologist Brion Randolph, the center focuses on "the genome or the genes of the cancer itself, and figure out what kinds of mutations this person's tumor might have."

Ryan slept a lot those first weeks and stayed home as the chemo stripped weight from his body and verve from his soul. More than anything he felt sad, just bone-weary with the ache of it.

He was lying in bed when the sun shone in one day, and with it came a prickly January breeze. Jen had left the back door open for their dogs, Vida and Camper. It was, he says, a "distinct moment." The breeze touched his face, and the sadness was gone.

He knew then he needed a purpose.

The night after the Team Hidi event, Turner couldn't sleep. He couldn't sleep the next night, either. He got up at 5 a.m. and poured his heart into an email addressed to Ryan. "I can't stand the thought of you sitting at home with chemo running through your veins," he wrote.

He spelled out a plea: "'All I do is cook' is what you keep saying and you are right and you need to keep 'cooking.' Replace the word cooking, with 'creating.' That is what you do Ryan. You take ideas and inspiration and with food you create dishes that bring people joy and deep admiration. You don't need food to create, BUT you need to keep creating and contributing. STAPLEHOUSE is your ultimate creation that embodies everything important to you and Jen. It is time to start 'cooking again.'"

In the words that followed, Turner laid out the structure for Staplehouse and the Giving Kitchen—a restaurant where Ryan could release his long-bottled creative spirit. All of its profit would feed into a foundation to help restaurant workers in need. He promised to get his partners behind the financing and management. And at 8:39 a.m., an hour past sunrise, he hit "send."

February and March were months of forward motion for the Hidingers as they turned Turner's letter into their Magna Carta. Jen quit her job at a children's clothing store and assembled a group of friends and colleagues for the board of the Giving Kitchen Initiative. Coxe Curry & Associates, the Atlanta-based consulting firm, helped them fast-track 501c3 nonprofit status. The board began granting funds from the Team Hidi event, which raised more than Ryan needed, to various restaurant workers throughout Atlanta.

More than 13 million people, about a tenth of the U.S. labor force, work in restaurants, yet few receive health benefits. A study conducted by the nonprofit Restaurant Opportunities Center shows that 88 percent of food service employees polled try to work through injury and illness because they can't afford the time off.

Ryan Smith and Kara Hidinger, brought closer by these events, decided to marry, and Smith quit his high-profile job cooking at Empire State South to join Hidinger as co-chef at Staplehouse. Jen and Ryan started a crowd-sourced online donation campaign on Indiegogo to solicit funding for Staplehouse—the for-profit restaurant that would donate all proceeds to the Giving Kitchen. In a month, they collected more than $100,000.

Ryan's stomach pains subsided and his tumor markers decreased. The treatment appeared to be working. He felt stronger.

Jen kept their lives busy, filled with crowd-sourced love. She gathered 75 friends and relatives for a surprise 36th birthday for Ryan, a bus ride to Buford Highway for banh mi sandwiches eaten in a parking lot under the stars. The Staplehouse team cooked a feast at the acclaimed Nashville restaurant, City House, raising funds for the Giving Kitchen Initiative. Ryan had never felt such happiness.

Looking for Answers

In July, Ryan and Jen went to CTCA for a PET Scan. It's an advanced imaging procedure that uses radioactive isotopes of sugar injected into the bloodstream to create an accurate accounting of the size and density of cancerous tumors.

Ryan's first PET Scan 12 weeks earlier showed numerous liver tumors, and the Hidingers and their oncology team drew up battle plans to focus treatment on the organ. The second scan six weeks later showed a 90 percent decrease in tumor size—a result so hopeful that the staff snapped a picture of the medical team with the Hidingers lined up in the garden, their fists pumping in victory. This next PET scan would be pivotal. If the tumors continued to shrink, then Ryan would be able to discontinue Erbitux, a bi-weekly chemo infusion that leaves him sick and listless for two days after treatment.

The center sits just off the highway and looks like a palatial version of a traveler's hotel—like a Courtyard by Marriott re-imagined as the Bellagio in Las Vegas. Visitors walk past a pond with a gazebo and arrive to a smiling concierge behind a marble counter in the grand foyer. A broad carpeted corridor leads to a fancy gift shop, a cafeteria and doctors' offices. In the very back of the corridor lies the large waiting area for imaging. There are sofas, work carrels, a wide choice of coffee pods. Families camp out here.

"You go off to 'Star Trek,'" says Jen, giving Ryan a peck and settling into an overstuffed armchair with a clamshell of salad from the cafeteria. She cracks open her ever-present binder and her laptop to schedule a meeting about light fixtures for Staplehouse. She nervously rubs her wrist right by her tattoo, the state of Indiana with a tiny heart marking home in Indianapolis. Jen has never gone back to the PET Scan area and doesn't want to see it.

The imaging tech leads Ryan through a vault-thick door to a reclining chair in one of the five windowless pretreatment rooms. "I sort of meditate," says Ryan of the hour he must sit motionless in the dark as the radiation seeps like vapor into his organs to paint its shadowy picture. "That's part of my mental attack on cancer. I focus on visualization that it's not in my body anymore." Ryan can wear his street clothes but he must hold his arms uncomfortably over his head during the PET scan, as the detector ring passes around his torso, trailing green laser beams. The tech plugs an iPod into a portable device and presses PLAY. "Is this good?" she asks as Gotye's "Somebody That I Used to Know" fills the aural space. "Sure," says Ryan.

Forty-five minutes later, he is back in the bright waiting area. "Are you radioactive?" Jen asks, slamming shut her laptop. "Can't hang out with any kids today," he retorts.

The next day Ryan and Jen return to hear the results. They will either head home to celebrate or stay for a late round of Erbitux. They stand in the hallway outside Dr. Randolph's office and make small talk. Jen attempts one of her quick, brilliant smiles but it melts off her face as her eyes widen and well up. She holds her binder in one hand and rubs her forehead with the other. Rubs and rubs it like a spot on a rug. Ryan sneaks an arm around her back, kisses the top of her head. The urge to cry subsides. Thank you, she conveys tacitly, nuzzling her head briefly against her tall husband's shoulder. The corners of her mouth turn up.

They are escorted to Dr. Randolph's empty office to wait for a few minutes. Jen, jumpy, gets up to take care of some quick Staplehouse business. Ryan appears calm. Is he? "I mean, we'll manage this or we won't. Something's going to happen. But I'm not worried about me. It's her. Your friends and family."

Jen returns and Dr. Randolph pounds into the room—a life force, loud, cheerful, full of hugs. "You're smiling, cut to the chase," says Ryan. "Is it good news?"

Randolph pauses an instant. "It's good news still, but not as good as I want it." The PET scan suggested that Ryan's therapy may have plateaued—the chemo has lost its efficacy. Randolph floats the idea of a radiation treatment. Jen listens with a dim, unwavering smile plastered on her face.

"Is this a good thing?" Ryan asks.

"It's a neutral thing," answers the oncologist. "Do you have any questions?"

"Do you have a new liver?" Ryan asks.

"I'll take it between two buns," Jen jokes.

That night Ryan goes upstairs to the chemo infusion center to receive the Erbitux. He sits in the waiting room to check in and tries to take the news in whatever passes for stride. He looks up at the wall-mounted TV, broadcasting the Maury Povich show. A woman in a too-tight dress and too-high heels totters to the stage, and Povich incites the crowd. Catcalls and wolf whistles ensue.

Ryan is quietly crying, his eyes transfixed by the screen, deep with sadness. "I think about how much I and everybody else takes life for granted. This," he says, staring at the poor woman making a spectacle of herself, "is weird. It's an alternate reality." He talks evenly in a shallow voice, not sobbing, yet the tears keep falling, separate from his voice. He is sad for all of us.

"I'm completely comfortable with the whole soul and religion part of it," he continues. "It's just that this is such a cool experience. I don't want to leave it. I'm so lucky and privileged to have the life I've had up to this point. We're lucky to be Americans, to have all this." The Midwest good guy.

Healing Power of Food

A plateau flattens out, not as far as the eye can see but for a moment of uncertain calm before the elevation changes. For Ryan, the slope has not been going in the desired direction since that July PET scan. His tumor markers have been rising, a little at first, then faster. The cancer, as Jen writes in one of the letters she routinely sends out to family and friends "is doing what it's supposed to do—it's growing."

Ryan has since discontinued Erbitux in favor of a cocktail of five new chemo drugs. "It is a plan," he says flatly. "That's what we need."

As health permits, there are outings—to a Kentucky bourbon distillery, to North Georgia to run around Burt's Pumpkin Farm with Ryan's dad. In her weekly letter, Jen called the farm "Ryan's favorite place on earth." On Sundays, he and Smith like to shop the Grant Park farmers market and then go home to make lunch. The chemo has dulled Ryan's taste buds; he needs more acid and salt to make food taste right. Since his diagnosis, he has been following a paleo diet and has been scrupulous about eating organic and local produce. "Food is your first medicine," he realizes **now**. "What you eat has everything to do with your personal health."

Smith—famous for his house-cured meats and sausages at Empire State South—has changed his diet, too, and has shed considerable weight. As Jen says, he's "juicing like a [expletive]."

The two Ryans spread their shopping haul across the kitchen

counter. Smith cuts eggplants next to a jar of pickled ring bologna—an Indiana specialty that Ryan wants to reproduce at Staplehouse. Next to that are Resveratrol tablets, an antioxidant found in grape skins, and Afinitor, an FDA-approved drug for advanced cancers.

Ryan cuts an onion the way chefs cut onions, down and sideways and across, the dice so fine as to be translucent, like onion snow. He sizzles these bits in a heavy pan and adds a drop or two of honey that slicks the bottom with erupting bubbles. A dash of apple cider vinegar hisses and deglazes the pan. Another chef might draw attention to the French name—*gastrique*—for this sauce foundation. For Ryan it is a beginning, an invisible step that diners won't be able to put their fingers on but will make them wonder why his food has so much flavor. He adds slivered rainbow peppers from a local farm and a drop of sweet grape barbecue sauce from a canning jar he put up last year.

Ryan knows that some people—particularly ones who lurk at the bottom of comment sections of online forums—have voiced suspicions about the whole Staplehouse/Giving Kitchen model. Does "nonprofit" mean they'll be drawing outsized salaries from the funds raised during their Indiegogo campaign? "I hope people can understand there is no motive here," Ryan says. "The situation sucked so bad, we wanted it to be something good. This is not my retirement job. This is about being sure people are taken care of."

In the garden behind Staplehouse a creeping fig climbs a pitted concrete wall, its vine laden with bell-shaped green fruit. "You can't eat these," says Ryan, breaking one open to reveal spongy, juiceless flesh. "But it's got this great tropical smell—lychee, coconutty. I'm thinking it would make a great infusion for a cocktail." He wants to preserve this essence, have it ready for the restaurant's anticipated February opening.

For Ryan, cooking locally means that he finds potential everywhere, growing all around him.

And cooking seasonally? It means thinking ahead. Ryan knows the seasons will pass, one after the next. As a chef he captures the flavor—the joy—of **now**.

THE TAO OF BIANCO

By Dave Mondy

From Edible Baja Arizona

 Exploring the food culture of his new Arizona home,
Dave Mondy—storyteller, memoirist, and transplanted
Minnesotan—started right at the top: profiling
renowned Phoenix pizza wizard Chris Bianco, facing a
crossroads in his career.

The Best Pizza in America is the best pizza in America, but it's
not the best pizza in America. Does that make sense?

Of course it does, or doesn't. The maker of The Best Pizza in
America could clear this up—but he'd rather not. He'd rather you
just eat his pizza. Let me explain: Chris Bianco, the chef and owner
of Pizzeria Bianco in Phoenix, has been called the best pizza chef in
the United States (by the *New York Times,* by *Bon Appétit*). He's been
called "the godfather of American pizza" (by *GQ*) and an "acknowledged master of his discipline" (by *Gourmet*); he's the only American
pizza chef to win a James Beard Award.

But Bianco himself dislikes the labels, shrugs off superlatives, and
seems allergic to accolades. Of his pizza, he'll say, "I hope it's never
better than your mother's or your favorite." Regarding his plaudits,
he'll reply, "We all get our 15 minutes of fame, and I think I'm overtime on mine."

And yet, he works maniacally to make the best pizza possible—he
still rises at 7 a.m. and works until midnight; still shops for ingredients at the local farmers' market, still makes his own mozzarella, still
kneads the dough. "Oh," he'll tell you, "I need it." He wants things
precise—farmers have been known to hold rulers up to their arugula

because Bianco prefers it to be a certain length (these farmers also happen to love him). The man is casually exacting. The best pizza in America is and isn't the best pizza in America; is a koan; is a paradox; is a palindrome. A man. A plan. A pizza.

Read this sentence. During the time it took you to do so, Americans inhaled more than 350 slices of pizza. As you first glanced at the "R" in "Read"—well, a full pizza disappeared. Americans eat more than 2,500 pizzas every minute. We love it: Tick tick tick, chomp chomp chomp.

And yet, we generally think that eating pizza is unhealthy. We think of it as fast food—a more benign fast food than, say, burgers, but not by much; we'd never call it health food. But what if pizza were a health food? What if, when you ate pizza, you thought, "Well, at least that's one good thing I did for my body today."

Such is the promise of Bianco's product: a pizza that might not only be good for you, but—composed entirely of local ingredients—might also be good for the place where you live?

But that promise requires staying close to home. "I don't want an imitation or a cloned deal," Bianco told the *Arizona Republic* in 2006. "The place is so small and cramped and I'm sweaty and it's loud, but somewhere in the chaos of it all, you find a sense of place." Bianco so loved that sense of place that during his first two decades, he had a hand in creating nearly every pizza at Pizzeria Bianco. Two-hundred and fifty pizzas a night, and Bianco's digits danced over nearly every one, night in, night out—until he eventually acquiesced to excessive demand for his wares. He opened a sandwich shop in 2005. Then he opened a bar next to his original pizza place, to accommodate overflow; then he opened an alternate "Italian restaurant" locale in Phoenix.

But it wasn't until just one year ago that Bianco agreed to create a new Pizzeria Bianco. This time, 150 miles southeast from the original. This time, in Tucson.

"Is this a chain?" an old woman asked. She was asking the bartender this at the original Pizzeria Bianco—an innocent question; she'd simply enjoyed a great meal and wondered if she could have a similar experience closer to her house—and she had no way of knowing that Chris Bianco himself sat a few stools away.

I was interviewing him—or had been interviewing him—but once he'd heard her question, he couldn't concentrate on anything else. "Is this a chain?" he asked himself. "Well, we're not the dog on a fucking leash, I can tell you that. We're just a link in the chain. Hopefully a good link."

How does one become the best pizza chef in America? Let us zoom backward, as if this were a comic book, to see his "origin story." First panel: Rowdy, hardscrabble kids goof around in a back alley in New York—perhaps they play street ball. Next panel, say a third floor window: a saddened child looks down, wishing he could play, too—but he can't; he has asthma. Last panel: Young Chris is slumped in the corner, turned away from the window, knowing he can't go outside—but, curiously, he doesn't look sad. His eyes are somehow bright—he's watching the magic happening at the stove; he's reading his aunt's *Gourmet* magazines.

Next page of the comic book: TEN YEARS LATER! We see a young man-boy Bianco leaving the little shop in the Bronx, Mike's Deli, where he learned to make the magnificent mozzarella that would be a key weapon in his utility belt.

Bianco drops out of high school, but finds salvation in restaurant work. "I started to cook," he told me, "because I felt incredibly insecure. I needed to know, we need to know, that it's all right. That's why we cook, why we break bread, why we offer someone a pint. To feel it's all right."

And then, Bianco's big ticket out was an actual ticket. Bianco won a plane ticket to anywhere in America, and so he chose . . . Phoenix? He still can't say why, but apparently his instinct was well founded. "When I got here, I felt connected."

To finish up this history, a rapid montage: See Bianco making mozzarella in his little Phoenix apartment, then selling it at the back door of various Italian restaurants. See Bianco being offered a small corner at a local grocery—a little corner with a wood-burning stove where he could try to make some pizza. See the pizza sell extremely well. See a thought balloon form above Bianco's head: "I could open my own pizza shop." See Bianco work for a few years as a sous chef. See Bianco travel through Italy, sharpening his skills. See Bianco return to Phoenix.

See him open Pizzeria Bianco.

•

Bianco made such good pizza that after just four years there were lines around the block on Saturday nights. You can still find these lines. The original Pizzeria Bianco hasn't expanded from its original small space, and it doesn't take reservations.

But Bianco is still focused on the present, and on the future. If you want to talk about his past, he'll want to talk about his new restaurant. "It just felt right," he said. "I mean, maybe it's that I'm getting older. I think I start to think about what I want to leave behind."

Right or not, he said that expansion had been "the last thing I wanted to do. [But] it's like with a puppy or a significant other," he said. "When you're looking? Very hard to find. But if you're not looking . . . "

When you're not looking, you find the perfect space in downtown Tucson. "Tucson has always been a place of respite for me," he said. "An incredible concentration of all the things I love, in art, architecture, music—it's a place that's always inspired me. And there's a movement here now, with food—is 'movement' the right word? You tell me, is it a movement? Yeah. Cool. I think so, too."

It's notoriously difficult to pin down a time to talk to Chris Bianco, given that, in spite of his expansion, he still works lunch shifts at the original Pizzeria Bianco. But then again, he's a busy man, all around. "I'm having a child," he said. Then clarified, "I mean, my wife is having a child. Soon." As I walked into the semiconstructed space of his new restaurant in Tucson, I couldn't help but hear the words of my brother-in-law, himself a recent first-time parent: "During the pregnancy, your wife spends all this time with the child, she does all the hard stuff," he said, "but I didn't know what to do with my nervous energy. So I just built the nursery."

Though Bianco and his group have owned the new space for over a year, the opening date keeps being pushed back. "I hear what people are saying, 'When will it open? When will it open?' But it's like with a baby. There's the day of conception, and then the due date [and] there's some time between," he said. "But I guess the good news is that with the baby and the restaurant, I'm in it for the long haul. We're not creating a space just to flip it. We want to do a thing that is forever."

Bianco showed me the small wall in the new restaurant where

he'll display paintings made by his father, a lifelong painter. "He's 86," Bianco said, "but he's still painting!" And so, one wall of the restaurant will display the man's work. "My friend, Bill Steen, has this photo of Churro lambs. Out in the desert. My father loved that photo. So he's painting it. How cool is that? Say we roast a Churro lamb. And serve it on pizza, here? Say people can have a pizza with meat served from the lamb they see painted on the wall? Full circle," he said. More full circling: Bill Steen's son built one of the large tables that diners will soon sit at—a beautiful table, with weird whorls overlaying various veils and veldts of varnish, layers beneath layers.

"Some of the things we revere, the deeper we dig, we find compromise. In origin and intention," Bianco said. "But sometimes we can create things where the deeper you dig, the better it gets."

Then there's the antique Coke sign Bianco plans to mount in the restaurant. Bianco is all about the local, the individual—about the singularly produced. But he likes the Coke sign. Yes, Pizzeria Bianco will be serving glass-bottle Mexican Coke. But mostly, the sign belongs in the space because Bianco loves its worn surface. The patina. "We say words like 'patina' or 'time-worn,'" he said. "But all that means is journey. All these objects have gone on a journey. They show their scars. Maybe it's just me getting old, but I like things that show their scars. Especially as a chef," and he looked at his forearms, where every chef worth his salt bears burns. "The scars are what matter . . . You learned because you didn't listen."

In the middle of the room: A big concrete box, made of bricks, elevated off the ground. "And that? . . ." I said; "That's the epicenter," he replied. He walked over to the newly installed wood-burning pizza oven. He looked at it. He started to say something, then stopped. He fingered a weird corner of the metal—then walked away.

He looked back at it and said, as if in a comic book, a dramatically sparse statement for a man so loquacious: "The fire."

So, is the pizza really that good? is the question you're asked when writing about "the best pizza in America." Hidden implication: Come on, it can't be that good.

We all, generally, like pizza. So what could the "best pizza" even be like? The phrase carries with it an absurd level of expectation.

One expects, at the very least, that one's jaw will be literally blown from one's cranium, since one's taste buds have just exploded.

But when I ate the pizza, it was simply delicious. The first time I tried it, I was on vacation in Phoenix. It was one great part of one great night. The pizza was great. I loved it. But it was just part of the night.

"I hope you're never here to judge," Bianco said, "just to enjoy." He wants the full experience to be enjoyable at Pizzeria Bianco. "Food itself never mattered to me. It's all the stuff that goes into it, every-thing—and everyone—around it. I want you to have an experience."

Bianco's menu in Phoenix—"It'll be the same thing in Tucson, with maybe a funky local thing or two"—is just one page: one starter; a salad or two; and then six pizzas, all of them pretty simple.

For Bianco, it all starts with his sourcing, and he's been advo-cating for local ingredients before the portmanteau "locavore" was ever portmanteauxed. "The biggest thing I had to learn," he said, "growing up when I did? Not everything that tastes good is good for you." That seems obvious to us now, but way back whenever Bianco wanted to create something that was both. Bianco wants his food to be good for you, but "that said, none of that fucking matters if the food doesn't taste fucking delicious." He adds: "Health food stores would have sold a lot more if they didn't call themselves 'Health Food Store'—instead just called themselves 'Good Restaurant.'

"All that said, I hope if someone walks in here and doesn't know shit about shit, just wants pizza . . . he gets it. He eats it and thinks, fuck . . . and it makes him dig deeper." Fuck, yes.

Almost 30 years ago, right before opening the first Pizzeria Bianco, Bianco was in New York and spied a very old Italian restaurant that was going out of business.

"I was looking for stuff for my bar, so I poked my head in," he said. He tracked down the remaining owner—a widow who was ea-ger to retire. "I had to tell her, 'No, no, no, I'm not crazy, I'm just starting a restaurant. I want to know if you're selling anything.'"

"I have one thing," she said, "but it's too expensive." When he asked to see it anyway, she took him into her garage and revealed a beautiful old oak bar. The bar had upheld the elbows of her restaurant patrons since the 1920s—but it was older than that: The widow and her husband had originally purchased it from a New York grocery that had been in business since the 1880s. "It had marks from cigars," Bianco said, from "guys back then."

Bianco rested his palm very briefly on the bar where he sat while telling me this story, in the original Pizzeria Bianco in Phoenix, and I realized we were sitting at the widow's bar. The cigar stain near my own elbow was 150 years old.

"She took pity on me," he said, and sold it to him at the only price he could pay. But I'm not sure it was pity. I think it was that he valued her bar about as much as he valued her (and she could tell this); which is to say, he valued her and her bar very, very highly. She parted with these remnants of her bar, saying, "I hope it brings you good luck."

Bianco loves things—but in the most nonmaterialistic way. Bianco loves things, objects, but loves them merely as tangible representations of moments, people—tangible totems of moments spent with people. Indeed, Bianco loves things that he senses were created by people. People he likes. I think this is what he means when he repeatedly uses the word "authentic."

What it takes to create a restaurant is more than buying equipment and serving food. Of greater importance are the people that contribute, said Bianco. The restaurant is built on relationships.

And this is why Chris Bianco could never create a "chain"—at least not in the modern, American sense. He cares far too much about people. About things. About things as representations of all the people he loves. Each an individual.

A man, a plan, a pizza.

Personal Tastes

FAMILIARITY BREEDS CONTENT

By Frank Bruni

From the New York Times

As a recovering *New York Times** dining critic (2004–2009), it took a while for Frank Bruni to get back to being just another guy eating out at restaurants. In our Yelp-ified, everyone's-a-critic dining culture, maybe we could all learn a lesson from Bruni's mellowing-out experience.

What a cad I used to be, constantly ditching the bistro that had opened only four months ago for the week-old trattoria with an even dewier complexion, callously trading in the yellowtail sashimi that had been so good to me for a hot tamale of unproven charms.

Then, a few years back, the restaurant Barbuto and I settled down. It's bliss. She knows my heart, knows my drill: a gin martini to begin, a seasonal salad for my appetizer, the roasted chicken after.

And I know her. If the weather's nice, a breeze will blow in from the West Village streets that her retractable walls open onto. The kale that she serves me will be sparingly dressed. And the breast meat? As plump and tender as it was the last time around and the dozen times before that.

We don't have fireworks, not this late in the game. But we have a rhythm. Sometimes that's better.

What I'm saying is that I'm a regular there, as I am at the Breslin, whose lamb burger is as true to me as I am to it; at Empellón Taqueria, where I never stray from the fish tempura tacos, which never let me down; at Szechuan Gourmet, where I don't glance at a menu. I don't have to.

I'm no monogamist, that's clear. More of a polygamist, but I dote on my sister wives. I've come to see that the broccolini isn't always greener on the other side of Houston Street, and I'm here to sing what's too seldom sung: the joys of familiarity. The pleasures of intimacy. The virtues of staying put.

What you have with a restaurant that you visit once or twice is a transaction. What you have with a restaurant that you visit over and over is a relationship.

The fashionable script for today's food maven doesn't encourage that sort of bonding, especially not in a city with New York's ambition and inexhaustible variety. Here you're supposed to dash to the new Andrew Carmellini brasserie before anybody else gets there; be the first to taste ABC Cocina's guacamole; advertise an opinion about the Massaman curry at Uncle Boons while others are still puzzling over the fugitive apostrophe. Snap a photo. Tweet it. Then move on. There's always something else. Always virgin ground.

For years, I was dedicated to exploring it, by dint of my duty as *The Times*'s restaurant critic. I was a paid philanderer. It was exhilarating. It was exhausting.

And it wasn't necessarily the best course. I'd think back to my pre-critic days, in Rome, and to the handful of restaurants I kept circling around to. The servers and owners there would exult when I walked through the door, because they understood how to make me happy and they could have a conversation with me different from the ones they had with newcomers, a conversation built on shared history and reciprocal trust, a dialogue between honest-to-goodness friends. I wasn't special. But I was special to them.

I'd think, too, of my food-loving father's approach to dining out. When he found a place with a few dishes and a few servers he adored, and when those servers reciprocated his affection, he stopped looking around. Called off the search. He understood what I've relearned these last few years, with Barbuto and the others: the smiles you get from hosts, hostesses and bartenders who know you are entirely unlike the smiles from ones who are just meeting you. They're less theatrical, less stilted, warmer by countless degrees.

Regulars matter to a restaurant. Though the newcomers drawn there by reviews or Yelp chatter can keep it packed for a while, the familiar faces help it go the distance. That's why some of those fusty, pricey Italian haunts on the Upper East Side outlast the trend-conscious efforts of this "Top Chef" alumnus or that darling of the culinary scribes. They've put extra energy into cultivating a steady clientele, turning themselves into clubs, into tribes.

"It's the only way to do it," said Robert Bohr, one of the owners of the new restaurant Charlie Bird, in SoHo, which is designed, as are Barbuto and so many other restaurants in that general area of downtown Manhattan, to be a repeat refuge for neighborhood folks who like to drop in impulsively. A few tables are informally tagged for such "walk-ins," as they're called in the business, and the menu accommodates snacking as well as feasting.

Mr. Bohr said that he had worked at what he called "destination restaurants," and that while first- and second-timers might keep them humming at peak hours during peak stretches, "it's regulars who support you on off days, in bad weather, during times of the night that aren't prime times."

In return, regulars at most restaurants get extra consideration: a glass of sparkling wine that wasn't asked for, a dessert that just appears, a promotion to the head of the waiting list when the place is full. There's a practical, unemotional reason to join the frequent-flier club. Perks accrue.

Mr. Bohr noted that you can make requests of a restaurant where you're a regular that you'd never make—and that might not be indulged—elsewhere. Because he has lunch as often as once a week at ABC Kitchen, he can place his order the second he sits down and say, "I want to be out in 25 minutes."

"They're welcoming to that," he said, because he's been loyal and he'll be back.

And that's why Charlie Bird doesn't flinch when Stephen Carlin, an investment banker, pops in unannounced at 6 p.m. with his wife and their two children, both under 4 years old. Just three and a half months into its existence, he has already been there some 15 times, he told me.

"They make me feel like family," he said.

Regulars make a restaurant feel a certain way, too.

"It has such a huge impact on the morale of the staff, to see people falling in love with what you're doing," said Eamon Rockey, the general manager of the new restaurant Betony, in Midtown Manhattan.

The diner who comes back again and again is a validation, a vindication. "It changes the culture of a restaurant," Mr. Rockey said, explaining that managers and servers become intent not on razzle-dazzle but on reading diners' minds, anticipating their needs, soothing them.

That's precisely what I value. I'm not a regular at the Breslin, in Midtown, for one of the curtained booths that I'm usually ushered to, the prime real estate that devoted patrons often get. I'm not a regular at Perla, an Italian favorite of mine in Greenwich Village, for the free appetizer sometimes put on the table.

I'm a regular for the solace. The peace. A new restaurant entails stress: Which of these main courses looks like the best one? What did the reviewers say? Is this table in a louder spot than others? How come no one warned me about the noise?

When you're a regular, you're always forewarned, prepared: For the decibels. For the lighting. For the menu. The one at Szechuan Gourmet, in Midtown, is as vast as a continent, but I'm never lost. The crispy lamb with cumin, the wok-fried prawns, the pork dumplings in roasted chile oil. These are the landmarks. These stand out.

And I fit in. There's Simon, the unofficial dean of Szechuan Gourmet's servers, who always takes care of me there. He arches an eyebrow if my partner, Tom, and I deviate from our usual order, and sometimes makes the executive decision to overrule us and bring a dish we neglected to request. He's earned that right.

He's met my father. He's met Tom's sister. He's met Tom's nephews. He's visibly tickled by that. We're tickled in return, and so we bring in more relatives, more friends. It's like taking them home.

To be a regular is to insist on something steady in a world and a life with too many shocks, too much loss. The week can go off the rails. The month can go all the way to hell. Hill Country's brisket is still there, forever fatty, a promise kept.

To be a regular is not just to settle down but to grow up and appreciate that for all you haven't tasted, you're plenty lucky and plenty happy with what you have: Perla's orecchiette, Empellón Taqueria's chorizo-studded queso fundido.

And Barbuto's chicken. Definitely Barbuto's chicken, crisp-skinned and drizzled with herbs.

The restaurant's chef and owner, Jonathan Waxman, told me that he never expected to have the chicken on the menu every single night of the nine and a half years that Barbuto has been in business, but regulars won't go without it.

"That and the kale," he said.

So we get them.

If we're going to commit (more or less) to Barbuto, she's going to be faithful to us.

EVERYMAN'S FISH

By Tom Carson

From Saveur

∞

Novelist (*Gilligan's Wake*) and award-winning movie
columnist (*Esquire, GQ*) Tom Carson has lived in many
initialed cities: DC, NYC, LA, and currently NOLA.
Steeped in American pop culture as he is, he was
actually born in Germany, a State Department brat—and
food was his gateway back into USA life.

Long gone from Washington, D.C., Sholl's Colonial Cafeteria in
1968 was the kind of place that reminded you of everything
pleasant about America's humdrum side. Yet nothing about the
United States was humdrum to me because I was a State Department brat who'd grown up abroad.

Now that we had moved home again (whatever "home" meant),
I had to keep trying new foods if I wanted to eat at all. Sometime
that summer, while my family was camped out at a temporary apartment near Dupont Circle on the taxpayers' dime, I ate my very first
tuna-salad sandwich at Sholl's. It was a classic, meaning basic: mayo
and canned tuna on white bread with a dab of iceberg lettuce. While
most restaurants anywhere north of Sholl's in culinary pride would
consider it unworthy of the dignity of being plated, no tuna sandwich I've eaten since has come close to its thunderous bestowal of
citizenship.

Of course, 1968 was eventful in far more profound ways. That
spring my father, a loyal Democrat, had muttered, "Oh, no" and
wept as Lyndon Baines Johnson announced he wouldn't run for
reelection. Robert F. Kennedy and Martin Luther King were both

assassinated. August brought the Democratic convention, with Chicago cops and protesters swaying in disharmony like a carpet at war with its own patterns. This was my introduction to America.

Amid such unrest, that tuna sandwich represented tranquility. It didn't taste like some confusing assassination somewhere, though the tuna in question might disagree. It didn't taste like splinters from a billy club or life in a hotel. Saying it tasted like color TV is getting closer to the sensation. It was comforting, accessible. It tasted like democracy. One bite turned me American, launching a love affair with tuna sandwiches—and a quest to recover that magic moment—that continues to this day.

As introductions to democracy go, tuna had the right pedigree. In the 19th century, it was immigrant food. Most Americans considered tuna a trash fish. But then sport fishing was invented, as per Andrew Smith's *American Tuna* (University of California Press, 2012), and eventually the gentleman's struggle to tackle one of the ocean's most impressive predators popularized tuna and led to its exploitation as a cheap canned food for the masses.

The lowly tuna sandwich became a common sight in diners and Automats after the turn of the last century, when, amid the burgeoning American mania for convenience, we fell in love with new food-packaging technologies. Though the canneries of the early 20th century went the way of other American industries—offshore— the U.S. today consumes nearly a third of the world's canned tuna. Drained of its own oil to ensure its blandness and packed with water or vegetable oil, tinned tuna inculcated itself into our popular cuisine.

As I look back, my adult love affair with the tuna-salad sandwich falls neatly into three Proustian phases. Back in 1988, having broken up with the girlfriend I'd moved to Los Angeles with three years earlier, I was living near the Hollywood Freeway and coming as close to turning into a barfly as I ever will. Since they were within walking distance, I made the rounds almost nightly of the local dive bars: the Gaslight, the Firefly, the shabby, venerable Frolic Room.

Come closing time, the 7–11 on the way home was my final stop. One night I discovered they had added a new sandwich: the Tuna Laguna, a thing of glory encased in the convenience-store chain's crust-challenged idea of a baguette. In an added touch of elegance— and compared with most bachelor food, tuna salad does become one's operative definition of elegance—two puzzled-looking walnuts sat atop the filling, peering up at me like Dr. T. J. Eckleburg's eyes in *The Great Gatsby.*

Love was what I was looking for at the Gaslight, the Firefly, and the Frolic Room, but since I was not having luck at any of them, I fell in love with the Tuna Laguna instead. Soon I could almost taste those puzzled walnuts as I ordered one more beer while AC/DC's "Highway to Hell" blasted and pretty girls with trashy eyes vied with trashy girls with pretty eyes for the attentions of someone else. Soon I was not waiting until closing time. In short, the Tuna Laguna saved me from turning barfly.

Luckily for me, by the time it was taken off the menu, I was no longer single. At home, my new wife and I were learning to cook, and 7-11s were a dimming memory. The handiest place to get a bag lunch near the office of the L.A. alternative weekly she and I both worked for was a twee shop called What a Friend We Have in Cheeses. Their tuna sandwich was a beauty. Thick sourdough, sprouts, tomato, and the gooiest havarti topped a hefty heap of tuna. I put on ten pounds in two months. That's when I decided that I'd better work at home, but I felt no obligation to lose the ten pounds. I was married, and they were a very *contented* ten pounds.

Flash forward to the present. That marriage is over. But in my capacity as *GQ*'s movie reviewer, my attendance at the Toronto Film Festival is ongoing. Each year I stay at the Metropolitan Hotel, home of Lai Wah Heen, one of the best dim sum restaurants in North America. My oldest film-fest crony loves the place. But he's lucky to lure me there even once; I prefer the Subway around the corner. Every night I place the same order: "A six-inch tuna on Italian herbs and spices. Yes, cheese. Lettuce, tomato, pickles, onions. No, that's it."

By festival's end, the night guy knows my order by heart, and I can tell he thinks I'm weird. I don't care. Movie viewing like this each day is the cinephile equivalent of looking for love at L.A. bars. My six-inch tuna on Italian herbs and spices provides the same comforting hedge against disappointment that the Tuna Laguna did when Ronald Reagan was in office and life and I were on the outs.

Even back home in the States, Subway is my most trustworthy pseudo-Sholl's fix. You have to admit that, when it comes to democratic eating experiences, the franchise is hard to beat, since you're tasting something at once generic and, within limits, customized. It's homely confirmation that the system works.

In the 40-plus years since I first fell in love with that sandwich at Sholl's, have I tried to re-create it? Many times. But I finally gave up, because there always seemed to be an ingredient missing. I've tried many elaborations on the default celery, onions, and mayonnaise. Would pickles do it? Would capers or olives bring back Sholl's?

Through all of these experiments, I've come to realize this about the democratic quality of tuna salad: You can get only so elaborate before you realize that if you're in the mood for something fancy, you should make something else. I can live with some lunatic notions of what an ideal tuna salad should include: jalapeños and lime juice; edamame and miso; fennel and orange and crème fraîche; sriracha and sesame seeds. I've even dabbled in curried and lemon-pepper tuna salads. But I once made a food writer laugh by telling him why I drew the line at adding chopped egg: "That's a *drunk's* idea of tuna salad."

While my love of tuna sandwiches will never die, the truth is that no array of garnishes will ever feature the missing ingredient from Sholl's. I now know what it was and why it's irrecoverable. The missing ingredient is the evidence that even the tumultuous summer of 1968 could be benign. The missing ingredient is that I was a 12-year-old newcomer to my own country. The missing ingredient is that, as I beheld my first tuna sandwich, I didn't yet know what one tasted like.

THE CHEESE TOAST INCIDENT

By Michael Procopio

From FoodForTheThoughtless.com

⚬⚬

In a world of recipe- and photo-oriented food blogs,
San Francisco's Michael Procopio gives us something
delightfully different: Offbeat, irreverent posts that
spotlight how we feel about food, not just how it's made.
As a professional waiter, he knows *exactly* how the food
goes down.

The evening might have gone perfectly, if it weren't for the
cheese toast.

And perfection was what Mrs. Lewis demanded from everyone
the night she and her husband invited Debbie Reynolds to dinner.
They were notoriously hard to please.

It's just a pity she didn't think to demand it of herself.

I spent my college years working for Harry and Marilyn Lewis, a
married couple of advanced but painstakingly-achieved indetermi-
nate age, who made their fortune from a chain of fancy hamburger
establishments and enjoyed the sort of celebrity that sometimes
comes from catering to the truly famous. They sold their small empire and, with some of the proceeds, opened a restaurant in Bev-
erly Hills as bright and large and intimidating as Mrs. Lewis's teeth,
which she was rumored to have designed herself.

My good standing with Mr. Lewis ended the day I expressed alarm
over the raw, salve-covered flesh of his face, asking him if he was
okay and had he seen a doctor. It was also the day I learned about the
existence of chemical peels. And that he had, in fact, seen a doctor.

My good standing with Mrs. Lewis, whose occasional visits to the restaurant were met with a mixture of terror and morbid fascination by most of the staff, began when I summoned the nerve to point out a critical error in her *New York Times* crossword answers. The look she gave me was appropriately puzzling—part "who *are* you?," part "how *dare* you." She stared at me in this way until my life began to flash before my eyes, then returned hers to the crossword, rubbed out a few letters with the eraser on the end of her pencil, and without looking up said, "So what's 26-Down then?"

I wasn't surprised when she chose me to wait upon her important business dinner with Miss Reynolds.

I was initially excited by the prospect of waiting on Debbie Reynolds. After all, she had danced with both Gene Kelly *and* Fred Astaire. And I heard she could swear like a sailor. I prayed she'd tell stories.

But I was also annoyed. Harry and I didn't like each other. Marilyn could be sweet as Splenda to me, but I knew that could change the moment anything didn't go her way. But fortunately, I knew precisely what she expected of me because she had recently blessed the waitstaff with a short series of "service classes" at which she personally imparted her version of the finer points of table service. Serve to the left. Champagne corks should never make noise. Don't say "parmesan cheese"—it's like saying "cheese cheese." We were given a written test to prove that we were listening.

At the beginning of service that night, I told my manager to give away all the other tables in my section—I wanted to devote my full attention to Marilyn, Miss Reynolds, and Harry. I'd be damned if I'd let any cheese cheese within 20 yards of them.

When the threesome sat down to dinner, I offered them drinks. Miss Reynolds would have white wine. For Mrs. Lewis, a J&B on the rocks with a twist. For Harry . . . I don't remember. They chatted. They smiled. I stood back and scanned the table for flaws. Plates of food came to them: crab cakes, salad . . . they nibbled and talked and drank a little more. I poured Miss Reynolds more wine. I brought Mrs. Lewis a fresh J&B without her asking. She patted my wrist approvingly.

Things seemed to be going well. Debbie Reynolds had a hotel in Las Vegas. Harry and Marilyn wanted to open a restaurant inside of it. They made small talk, but the chatter on the Lewis's end seemed as unnatural as their chemical and surgery-altered faces. Everything was *fine*, but the conversation didn't flow. So I made certain the alcohol did. As I leaned in to top off Miss Reynolds's glass, she paused the conversation to pinch my cheek and tell me I was adorable. When she did this, I caught Marilyn's eye. She looked annoyed because I was pulling focus away from her.

So I did what any true professional server would do—I stepped away from Miss Reynolds and the table as a whole. And then I did what any true professional enabler would do—I went straight to the bar to order another J & B for Marilyn—a stiff one. I gently placed the sweating glass in front of Mrs. Lewis as visual proof that I cared more for her than I did Carrie Fisher's mother. But really, I just wanted to see her to get plastered. I brought another drink of whatever-it-was for Harry, too.

It seemed to be working. Marilyn relaxed. Miss Reynolds laughed. Harry seemed less ineffectual than usual. I changed plates for the dinner course as unobtrusively as possible and let the food flow out to the table in slow progression.

The white bean chili was met with success, as were most of the other dishes that landed in front of them. Marilyn leaned back in her chair a bit, scotch in hand. She flashed a smile to expose her enormous designer incisors as she surveyed the room. Everything seemed to be going perfectly.

That is, until she spotted the cheese toast. Harry and Debbie were chatting away, but Marilyn was no longer participating in the conversation. I watched the gradual change of expression on Mrs. Lewis's face. Her painted lips, so recently expressing pleasure, slowly closed like red velvet curtains over the Cinemascope wideness of her teeth. I could feel the whole room going dark. All she could do was stare at the slice of cheddar-topped bread in front of her. Then she suddenly forced her mouth upwards again, but the overall effect this time was more crazed than happy. Harry noticed Marilyn. Debbie noticed Harry noticing Marilyn. The table fell silent and I stood by helpless.

"Excuse me a moment," Mrs. Lewis said quite calmly. She rose from the table in her white pantsuit, picked up the plate of offending toast, and slowly made her way across the dining room to the kitchen expediting station. The cooks saw her coming and scattered like roaches.

"*WHO* MADE THIS?" she screamed. Everyone in the granite and steel restaurant could hear her, but no one dared to respond.

"*WHO. MADE. THIS. CHEESE. TOAST?!!!?*" There was one line cook who didn't run. He seemed to have been so transfixed by her insane stare and her fiery orange mane of hair that he was instantly rendered immobile.

"DID *YOU* DO THIS?" she demanded. "DID YOU?!!!? CHEESE TOAST IS TO BE SERVED HOT IN MY RESTAU-RANT! THIS. . . . *THIS* IS UNACCEPTABLE!!!" As she shrieked those last words, she slammed the plate down onto the counter. The cheese toast bounced from the plate and hit the poor cook in the chest. The plate itself rebounded and smashed on the floor.

But I knew that plate wasn't the only thing that was smashed. Mrs. Lewis, having found an outlet for her expression almost as satisfying as her time spent designing gowns for Marlo Thomas, made her way back across the stunned dining room to rejoin her guest and her husband.

I didn't know the proper thing to do in this sort of dining situation. Mrs. Lewis hadn't covered it in her classes. As I wondered whether or not it would be a good idea to serve them more alcohol, Debbie Reynolds broke the unbearable silence.

She looked directly at Mr. Lewis and said, "I'll bet she's a real *bitch* to live with, isn't she?" He and Marilyn laughed uncomfortably. And then she finished them off in what I can only describe as her Unsink-able Molly Brown voice, "But you know, Harry, I'll bet you're a real pain in the ass, too!"

They didn't laugh at that one, but she did. I excused myself from the table, got my manager to watch over the mess for a minute while I ran outside and around because I knew it wouldn't do for my em-barrassed owners to witness my own, uncontrollable cackling. I re-turned to the table with an appropriately neutral expression.

Debbie Reynolds didn't stay long after the cheese toast incident. She made her excuses, thanked her hosts, and went home. There was to be no dessert. And, thanks in part to a plate of tepid cheesy bread and plenty of Justerini & Brooks on the rocks, there was to be no Lewis-owned restaurant in the Debbie Reynolds Hotel.

From that evening on, Miss Reynolds has been at the top of my list of favorite people. Because, apart from having starred in my *favorite*

Hollywood musical of all time, she managed to do something I'd always wanted to do—call out the appalling behavior of my bosses—and gave me one of the most satisfying laughs of my life as she did it.

For that, I salute her whenever I eat a piece of cheese toast. And when I do eat it, I always eat it cold.

BECAUSE I CAN

By David Leite

From Leite's Culinaria

Founder of the award-winning Leite's Culinaria
website, and author of *The New Portuguese Table*
cookbook, David Leite is an avid and accomplished
home cook. Like any talent, that skill isn't always
appreciated as it should be—but it did give him the
power to settle a not-so-petty score.

The journey that culminated in my realization of the wonder that
is homemade ketchup was long and circuitous, and, as sometimes happens, littered with the body of a friend.

One autumn night in 2000, our friend Geoffrey slunk back in
through our kitchen door, a waft of cigarette smoke trailing behind
him, as he hoped to avoid his wife, Sarah, who was helping The One
clear the dishes from the dining table so we could play cards. Geoffrey leaned against the counter while I washed dishes.

"The lasagna was great," he said.

"Thanks."

It wasn't, actually. It was an anemic imposter, devoid of the beef,
veal, pork, and cheese that define the true Italian diva. Instead, it contained zucchini, peppers, and broccoli rabe layered between spinach
noodles. Geoffrey was in his green-food phase.

Geoffrey was the worst kind of vegetarian. He was the sort of
self-righteous, self-appointed mayor of Meatlessopolis who never
cared how he inconvenienced the unconverted. Whenever he and
Sarah came to dinner, I had to haul out a special skillet, one that had
never experienced the sizzling, seductive sear of cold meat on its

surface, because Geoffrey insisted he wouldn't eat anything cooked in a pan that had touched meat.

On top of all that, he was lactose-intolerant—say hello to dairy-free "cheese"—and also a bit of a hypochondriac. Half an hour or so after we would pour wine, he'd rub his forehead, grab the bottle, and mutter "sulfites" as he scrutinized the label. Then he'd turn his eyes heavenward and shake his head, looking to all the world like one of those beleaguered saints I used to read about in my catechism workbook when I was a kid.

Every time the two of them came over for dinner and cards, which was often, I not only tied myself into knots trying to come up with something to serve him that The One and I could at least choke down with wan smiles, I stomped through the supermarket seeking suitable meat alternatives and scoured the local liquor stores in search of a specific wine no one had ever heard of (and which we'd never, ever be caught dead drinking on any other occasion), all in the name of friendship.

"Oh, and the *sauce*? Fan-*tas*-tic!" Geoffrey turned his back to the sink and nonchalantly cleaned his nails with a toothpick. I, on the other hand, was so angry my back teeth began twerking. I redoubled my efforts scrubbing the nubbins of noodles from The Great Un-Besmirched Pan.

"Yeah, I got some beautiful second tomatoes," I said, trying to keep the conversation going. "So I made a sauce. I'm making home-made ketchup, too. I think it'll make a nice gift."

With that, Geoffrey lowered his head and looked as if he was squinting over a pair of spectacles. Judgment rippled across his face. "Why on earth would you go through all that work for *anyone*?"

Clearly, the irony of the question was lost on him.

I looked at him as if he had asked me, "Why do you eat an entire pint of Ben & Jerry's New York Super Fudge Chunk by yourself?" or "Why do you binge watch TVLand all Saturday?"

"Because . . . I . . . can." It came out quietly, almost whispered, but carried such weight as to shut down the conversation.

During the past 13 years, I learned how to wriggle out of my friendship with Geoffrey, but not how to make homemade ketchup. It was distaste by association.

Two weeks ago, though, The One and I pulled into the old-fashioned gas station just off the center of town in Roxbury,

Connecticut, to buy organic vegetables from our local mechanic, Mark. On the counter were gorgeous globes of love practically rolling off the table and into our basket. But it was the boxes stacked beneath that caught my eye, "Sauce Tomatoes" scrawled across their sides. Always a sucker for the underdog—and alarmingly low on homemade tomato puree—I asked the price.

"A dollar fifty per pound," said Lucia, the salesperson. *A buck fifty? That's incredible!* I thought. I bought 20 pounds, then a few days later I went back for 20 more. And after making and freezing 12 quarts of puree, I still had ten pounds left.

Then I heard it in my head. "I'm making homemade ketchup, too. I think it'll make nice gifts." *Why on earth did I let his offhanded comment stop me from doing something I've wanted to do for more than a decade?* I asked myself. And with that, I began slicing into a beefsteak, its juices squirting across the counter, and simmering, and food-milling, all the while holding a raging one-sided conversation with Geoffrey.

You know, Geoffrey, if you got your head out of your sanctimonious ass, you'd see that making things from scratch is one of the best ways to live.

I grabbed a handful of overly soft Romas and squeezed hard, bleeding them into a bowl.

You may be a strict vegetarian, but you're a food Nazi. Do you hear me? A FOOD NAZI!

I slammed the pot full of chopped tomatoes on the stove and brought the whole thing to a boil.

And ever since you started making millions of dollars, you've become a motherf...

And there it was. The cancerous root of it all. Standing over a pot of burbling tomatoes, I had a breakthrough that would have cost me $250 had I been sitting in my shrink's office.

I understood that I have always felt less than Geoffrey. I've never dressed as if I was a member of the Connecticut Lockjaw Society. I don't have famous actors as friends. I don't throw fundraisers at my home to support state politicians. Instead I dress so messily I startle our UPS driver. I walked away from Meryl Streep just as she was about to talk to me at an event because I was utterly tongue-tied. And I couldn't name a state politician if Mama Leite's life depended on it. I had let his elitism—his militant vegetarianism, his social exclusivity, his higher tax bracket—-cow me.

After the homemade ketchup was cooled, bottled, and tucked away, I considered giving Geoffrey a jar. There would be a certain symmetry to that. But I knew that such a simple gesture would cost me a lot. A hell of a lot more than $1.50 a pound.

Homemade Ketchup

Adapted from Jeffrey Steingarten. *The Man Who Ate Everything.* Vintage, 1998

What I love about this homemade ketchup recipe is that is doesn't taste too homemade. There's nothing worse than ketchup that tastes like tarted-up tomato sauce. There's no unusual ingredients here–no chipotle peppers or paprika made by 17-year-old Hungarian virgins–that now pass for "house-made ketchup" in so many restaurants. You achieve the perfect Heinz or Hunt's sweet-tart balance by using a common jam-making technique: reducing the tomato liquid to a thick, glossy syrup then swirling it into the tomato pulp. **–David Leite**

Special Equipment: Food mill or potato ricer

Ingredients

10 pounds very ripe red tomatoes, preferably beefsteak, cored and roughly chopped
4 garlic cloves, chopped
1 large onion, chopped
¾ cup white vinegar (for a mild taste) or cider vinegar (for a fruity tang)
1 tablespoon black peppercorns
1 heaping teaspoon allspice berries
1 cinnamon stick
8 whole cloves
¼ teaspoon cayenne
¼ teaspoon ground ginger
2½ tablespoons salt
6 tablespoons granulated sugar, plus more to taste

Directions

1. Place the tomatoes in a heavy, wide, nonreactive pan of at least an 8-quart capacity. Cover, place the pan over high heat, and cook for 5 to 10 minutes, stirring every minute or so, until the tomato chunks spill their juice and everything comes to a boil.

2. Working in batches, pour the tomato chunks and juice into a large, medium-fine strainer placed over a 3-or 4-quart saucepan. Gently press and stir the tomatoes with the back of a wooden spoon so that all of the thin liquid but none of the tomato pulp goes into the saucepan. You should have about 2 quarts of liquid. Reserve the tomato pulp.

3. To the tomato liquid in the saucepan add the garlic, onion, vinegar, peppercorns, allspice, cinnamon, cloves, cayenne, ginger, and salt. Cook over moderately high heat until the liquid is thick and syrupy and reduced to about 2 cups. This could take anywhere from half an hour to an hour or even as long as 2 hours or, in the case of 1 tester, up to 4 hours, depending on the type of tomato used. [Editor's Note: Some tomatoes, such as beefsteaks, are more pulpy and mealy, whereas other tomatoes, like Romas, are more juicy. This will affect the final yield of juice and total simmering time.]

4. Meanwhile, transfer the tomato pulp to a food mill fitted with the finest screen to eliminate the seeds and skin. You should have about 1 quart strained pulp. Transfer the strained pulp back to the first pan and reserve the tomato solids that you strained from the tomato pulp.

5. Strain the thick, syrupy, reduced tomato liquid into the tomato pulp, pressing on the solids to extract all the liquid. Stir in the sugar and gently simmer over medium-low or low heat, stirring frequently, until the ketchup is reduced by ⅓, 15 to 20 minutes. Taste the ketchup occasionally, adding more sugar if desired. You should have about 4 cups tomato goo at the end. If the ketchup still seems a little runny, continue to simmer the mixture over low heat, stirring occasionally, until the desired consistency is attained. If the ketchup isn't quite the texture of commercial ketchup and some very vocal dissenters in your

household prefer that, purée the ketchup in a blender or food processor. Let the ketchup cool to room temperature. Transfer the ketchup to glass jars or other containers with tight-fitting lids and refrigerate for up to several weeks.

Solitary Man

By Josh Ozersky

From Saveur

Founder of the Grub Street food blog, a food columnist
for *Time* and *Esquire*, and the author of *Hamburger:
A History*, Josh Ozersky is known for his prodigious
and enthusiastic appetite. It's a sort of birthright, he
explains here, reflecting wistfully on the consolation
his unhappy father sought in food.

David Ozersky, my father, thought about food a lot. He wasn't
frantic and feral about it like I was, but we shared a deep common feeling on the subject, one of our few such bonds. My father,
a brilliant but melancholy man, loved to eat, but I believe he took
more pleasure in talking about eating. He would talk about his last
meal while eating the current one, and soon his talk would turn to
the subject of where we ought to eat next.

In Atlantic City, our home during my teenage years, the options
were gratifying but few: spareribs from a Chinese joint at the local
strip mall, vast flaccid pies from a boardwalk pizzeria, some frozen
rabbit meat from the ShopRite that he would roast up in the oven
with honey and salt. My father never got tired of weighing each
equally banal option, deliberating back and forth while never being
completely sold on his decision.

I didn't register any of this as odd. In fact, the contours of my un-
formed mind molded to his strange monomania, a shape it has kept
to this day. I didn't realize at the time that my father's preoccupation
with food was a form of denial, something he talked about so as to
avoid talking about—or thinking about—other things. But even as a

child I could tell that he always seemed sad. It made me love him more, and feel guilty, and want to try to make him happy. At times, as I grew older, I was able to do that. Often it involved bringing him little surprises: mail-order Katz's salami, a half-eaten carton of Cantonese roast duck.

One of the reasons he was sad, I knew, was that he was a hugely talented painter, and nobody cared. My father was a failure; he knew it, and my mother and I knew it. We didn't blame him; it was understood as the kind of cosmic misfortune that requires stoicism and big sandwiches to bear up to. But it was tragic nonetheless.

My father's paintings of chefs, one of his favorite subjects, hung in our house when I was growing up. They were much happier than his other paintings, whose themes included dead gangsters, the Holocaust, and junkies.

His paintings are charged with feeling, as per the ideals of abstract expressionism. I think he put so much of himself into them that, beyond their formal qualities, they seem to almost seethe with his thwarted, rueful spirit. He was completely unsparing in his painting, and I feel like it was the only place he ever really opened up. He never said anything to indicate it, because he never talked about himself, but I believe he thought of his whole life as the waste product of his art. Which made it so much worse that nobody cared about it. My father's active hopes for recognition as an artist died before I was born.

David Ozersky wasn't a painter as far as anyone was concerned. He was a stagehand at Resorts International Hotel Casino in Atlantic City, a job he held for the last 20 years of his life. He had contempt for the job, which he considered mindless, but it was a cushy one, a union gig that allowed him to work three hours of an eight-hour shift and spend the other five across the street at a lounge inside the Burgundy Motor Inn. He was, I will say, inspired enough by his time at work to create a series of charcoal sketches of showgirls on acid-proof cardboard. "I'm going to go do my Edgar Degas routine," he would say mordantly, trudging up the stairs to the spare bedroom he used as his studio.

The one subject he kept coming back to in his paintings was food. It was a constant in our pre-Atlantic City days, back in the 1970s, when we lived in the groovy sun-dappled decadence of South Miami. That was before things turned really bad. I was five or six years old, and my father spent much of his time volunteering in the kitchen of a popular Italian restaurant called Raimondo's. His real job was working in his father's hardware store, which he hated but was obliged to do, because he was otherwise unemployable, for reasons I never thought to wonder about. During his time with Raimondo, he created elaborate menus and worked the line. That's when he first started painting chefs.

We went out to many restaurants back then, but my father cooked at home a lot as well. I remember him going through a soufflé phase, when he would make the fluffy desserts every night, beating the eggs with a whisk furiously, and then pulling them at full height from the oven with a triumphant expression my mother and I otherwise almost never got to see.

The chef paintings stopped in 1978 when we moved to New Jersey and he landed the job at Resorts. Those were dismal times, with my mother—isolated, depressed—in even worse shape than my father. His closed-off sadness became even more airtight in 1982, when he came home from work one night to find my mother overdosed on Dilaudid, a potent prescription narcotic. I woke up; he told me to go back to sleep. I did. But when I got up in the morning, she was dead. We didn't talk about it.

We talked about food. For the next few days we talked animatedly about why some potato skins weren't crispy enough (they had too much potato still on them) and why Katz's pastrami was so great (it had to do with hand slicing). We began to eat more too. I remember cooking steaks on our porch, wood-fired New York strips on a little hibachi, served up with buttered onion rolls. Afterward, we sat quietly in that nowhere, and then he said, sheepishly, "Maybe we should get some ribs from the Chinese place." Why not?

His mood eventually stabilized, but there remained a certain wry, morose quality to his eating. The summer I was 16, I manned the grill at Pizza Haven on the boardwalk. One day my father wandered up after a show at Resorts, dressed in black pants and a black long-sleeved shirt, his stage tech garb, killing time before heading to the Burgundy. I made him a double cheesesteak with pizza mozzarella melted into the vinegar peppers. He ate it absentmindedly, then stood around, trying to figure out what to do next. "Maybe I should have a sausage sandwich," he said, in a glum, half-questioning way. I wanted to cry, but I did make him a sausage sandwich, and he did like it.

His story isn't wholly a depressing one. In the early '90s he quit drinking and took up with someone who truly understood and loved him—someone who had known him most of his life. They began to spend a lot of time in New York. He had discovered Jean-Georges Vongerichten when the French chef was still at the Lafayette Restaurant at the Drake Hotel. And when he opened JoJo on the Upper East Side in 1991, my father became such a loyalist that the chef would try things out on him. One Christmas, Vongerichten even presented him with a foie gras terrine, a mark of special favor. My father was astonished by the chef's conviction as an artist, and I think it reawakened something in him. ("Who else would have come up with *white pepper ice cream*?" he'd ask me, rhetorically, over and over again.) He became aware of his torpor; he felt guilty about it, and was moved to start a second series of chefs, many of whom looked suspiciously like Jean-Georges.

When the chef's big luxe restaurant in the Trump Tower received a four-star review in the *New York Times* from Ruth Reichl in 1997, my father had it silk-screened onto shower curtains, which he then painted over in a Warholian manner, the only time I ever saw him depart from his figurative, emotional style. I think he was grateful that the chef had made him so happy in the only way he allowed himself to be happy, and helped him, in some small way, to start painting again. Nobody saw or cared about the paintings, then as before; but he opened up a little in middle age and would occasionally say revealing things in his own sardonic way, like "I beat three major addictions in my life, but I can't stop buying cheap shoes." He would mock his own dark cast of mind, saying his motto was "Let them get you down." But when he said it I knew it was no longer completely true, and that made me feel good.

David Ozersky died in 1998 at 58 from a cancer that had been diagnosed four days earlier. He never saw it coming. He thought he had a backache. He was going to chiropractors. When I got back from the hospital—on Father's Day, no less—there were still some leftover pork chops in the refrigerator from the Malaysian restaurant Penang on the Upper West Side, which, it turned out, had been his last meal. I finished them, of course; there was never any chance I wouldn't.

TOMATO PIE

By Ann Hood

From Tin House

Novelist Ann Hood (*Somewhere Off the Coast of Maine,
The Knitting Circle*) has always fashioned fiction from
strands of her own life; she totally *gets* how favorite
foods become synonymous with the scenes and settings
of our lives. Case in point: tomato pie.

It is that time in summer when the basil starts taking over my yard
and local tomatoes are finally ripe, red and misshapen and so juicy
that after I cut into one I need to wipe down the counter. In other
words, it's the perfect confluence of ingredients for tomato pie. And
not just any tomato pie, but Laurie Colwin's tomato pie, a feast of
tomatoes and cheese and basil baked into a double-biscuit crust.

I first discovered this recipe back in the nineties, in a long-ago
Gourmet magazine. I ripped it out and took it with me for a week
with my parents and assorted relatives in a rented house at Scarborough Beach in Narragansett, Rhode Island. There, in the hot,
outdated, Formica-linoleum-avocado-green 1970s kitchen, I made
loads of tomato pies, maybe even dozens. The recipe got splattered
with tomato guts and mayonnaise—yes, mayonnaise is an ingredient,
too, but only one-third of a cup—the words smearing in spots. But
it didn't matter, because by the end of the week I knew the recipe by heart: You place a layer of biscuit crust in a pie pan, cover it
with sliced fresh tomatoes, sprinkle with chopped basil, and top with
shredded cheddar cheese. You then pour a mixture of mayonnaise
and lemon juice over the filling, cover it all with the second crust,

and bake until it's browned and bubbly. The smells of that pie on a hot summer day make you feel dizzy, so intoxicating are they.

No one in my family knew just how important that tomato pie was to me. Not just because it used the freshest ingredients at their prime deliciousness. Not just because eating tomato pie is something akin to reaching nirvana. Not even because it made me popular and look incredibly talented. No, this tomato pie was important to me because it wasn't just anybody's recipe.

Can there be people out there who do not know Laurie Colwin's writing? Yes, she wrote a *Gourmet* magazine column in the nineties, but she also wrote eight books of fiction, both short stories and novels. Back in the late seventies and early eighties, when I was working as a TWA flight attendant and dreaming of becoming a writer, Colwin was one of my heroines. This was before she began doing food writing, when her stories would appear like little jewels in the *New Yorker*. When I would read lines like these from "Mr. Parker": "He was very thin . . . but he was calm and cheery, in the way you expect plump people to be." Or: "As a girl she'd had bright red hair that was now the color of old leaves." I would smile at just how apt her descriptions were, and at how perfectly she captured real people. "'I don't work. I'm lazy. I don't do anything very important . . . I just live day to day enjoying myself,'" a character tells us in Colwin's 1978 novel, *Happy All the Time*.

To me then—and now—Colwin was a kind of Manhattan Jane Austen. Her novels and stories examine ordinary people and ordinary lives, the very kind of writing I wanted to do. Even though she tackles themes like marital love and familial love, themes that might be construed as sentimental, Colwin appreciates and plumbs the ambiguities of relationships with a sharp eye. In *Happy All the Time*, at a dinner party with her new husband, her character Misty thinks: "How wonderful everything tasted. . . . Everything had a sheen on it. Was that what love did, or was it merely the wine? She decided that it was love." But just when Colwin appears to be veering perhaps too near sentimentality, she throws a dead-on observation at us. Misty says to her husband: "'You believe in happy endings. I don't. You think everything is going to work out fine. I don't. You think everything is ducky. I don't.'" She then goes on to explain: "'I come from a family that fled the Czar's army, got their heads broken on picket lines, and has never slept peacefully anywhere.'" Colwin does this again and again in her fiction. In *A Big Storm Knocked It Over*, her posthumously published 1994 novel, the character Jane Louise observes of other women: "Their pinkness, their blondness, their carefully streaked hair, nail polish, eyelash curlers, mascara, the heap of things . . . that Jane Louise never used made her feel they were women in a way that she was not." She is generous to her characters. And funny. And honest.

The first time I saw her was in the eighties, long before I baked a tomato pie. I was writing what I thought were interconnected short stories (they later become my first novel). Colwin and Deborah Eisenberg were reading at Three Lives bookstore, not far from my Bleecker Street apartment. In those days, the *New Yorker* ran two short stories a week, and sometimes the writers read together at Three Lives. I remember it as a January or February night, cold with an icy sleet falling as I made my way to the reading. I arrived late, or maybe just on time: they had not yet begun to read but a hush had already fallen over the packed store.

For a moment, I paused in the doorway and stared at the two women sitting together at the front of the crowd: Eisenberg, skinny and dark-haired, her legs folded up like origami; Colwin curly-haired and plump and grinning at the audience. She looked up and, I swear, in that moment, I thought she was grinning at me. I thought—and this sounds crazy, I know—but I thought she was beckoning me in, not just to the little bookstore, but into the world of words and writers. A woman, annoyed, in charge, began waving her arms at me to come and sit. And then the irritated woman pointed at the only place left to sit, which happened to be right at the feet of Laurie Colwin.

Although my family did not flee the Czar's army or get our heads broken on picket lines, we were—like many in Colwin's fiction—a waiting-for-the-other-shoe-to-drop family. There was an aunt dead during a wisdom-teeth extraction. An uncle dead on a dance floor on Valentine's night. But also like Colwin's characters, who find "the experience of having a baby exactly like falling madly in love," as Billy does in *Another Marvelous Thing*, we love fiercely. And those weeks in those rented beach houses in the early nineties could have, in many ways, stepped right out of *Happy All the Time*: "We're all together. We're a family and we're friends. I think that's the best thing in the world."

We have always been a public beach kind of family—no pool clubs or private cabanas for us. Growing up, I spent most of my summers sweating in our backyard or watching game shows on TV, sitting in front of a fan and eating root-beer popsicles. My mother worked at a candy factory, stuffing plastic Christmas stockings with cheap toys and candy all summer. But she got Fridays off, and she and my aunt would load us kids into one of their station wagons and drive down to Scarborough Beach, where my cousin Gloria-Jean and I sat on a separate blanket and pretended not to know the rest of the family. We had plans, big plans. To leave Rhode Island and our blue-collar, immigrant Italian roots behind. Even at the beach, we toted Dickens or Austen, big fat books that helped the hot, humid summer pass.

I did escape. First to college, where I waitressed every summer at a tony beach club and studied how the women there held their fancy drinks—Brandy Alexanders and Lillet with a twist of orange peel. I studied how they held themselves, too, the way they shrugged their sweaters from their shoulders directly into a man's waiting hands. The way they looked, a combination of boredom and amusement. I studied their children, who learned how to play tennis and how to dive, how to order lunch from the guy at the grill and sign their parents' names and membership numbers on the bill.

In 1978 I became a flight attendant, a job I held for the next eight years, serving mostly businessmen in first class. I was trained to carve chateaubriand, dress lamb chops in foil stockings, mix a perfect martini. I developed a taste for the leftover caviar and the champagne from duty-free shops across Europe. Eventually I settled on Bleecker Street in New York City and fulfilled a dream I'd had since I read *Little Women* in second grade—I became a writer.

Even after I began publishing, I often thought of that reading at Three Lives. I believe Colwin read from what would become *Goodbye Without Leaving*, her novel about the only white backup singer in a touring soul group. But the memory is fuzzy. I mostly remember the smells of steam heat and wet wool, the way the audience listened, rapt. I remember wanting to say something to Colwin, something about how her generous heart came through on the page, how happy I felt when I saw a new story by her. But I was too shy. I stood and watched people line up to speak to her and to Eisenberg, to get books signed and shake hands. And then I left.

As I walked back through that cold icy night, something settled in me: I could do this. I could be a writer. No. I *would* be a writer. And as corny and impossible as it sounds, Laurie Colwin's smile, the one she sent to me that night, made it so.

As is often the case, with success came a longing for home. How I longed for the taste of my mother's meatballs; the casual way I would flop on the couch beside my father, dropping my feet into his lap; the noisy nights around the kitchen table with all those loud, Pall Mall–smoking, black-coffee-drinking relatives; the long sandy beaches of Rhode Island with the smell of Coppertone and clam cakes frying in oil mingling with the salty air. Of course I loved where I had landed, in a small apartment on Bleecker Street, my books on bookstore shelves, my days spent writing, my nights at parties or readings, just as I'd imagined, or maybe hoped, when I'd dreamed of a writer's life. But I wanted home too, and when I offered to rent a house at the beach, my parents assumed it would be at Scarborough.

I brought lots of recipes with me that first summer and for the dozen or so that followed. But it was the tomato pie that became a symbol of those weeks in that split ranch house across a busy road from the crowded beach. The more local tomatoes that appeared at the Stop & Shop, the more pies I made.

We ate the pies on the back deck of those houses—we never rented the same exact one, yet they were all identical, located in a treeless development called Eastward Look. We ate tomato pies with grilled cheeseburgers and hot dogs and Italian sausages, my father manning the grill with a cold beer in his hand. There were often dozens of us at dinner—cousins and aunts and uncles and the women from my mother's Friday night poker club. At some point, pasta (we call it "macaroni") would be served. And meatballs and my Auntie Dora's Italian meatloaf. The tomato pie appeared at lunch with the cold cuts and sometimes even at breakfast, heated up.

The soggy recipe page returned with me to Rhode Island and the rented beach house every summer, growing more faded and smudged over time. That was okay; I needed only to glance at it to remind myself what temperature to set the oven (400 degrees) and how many lemons I needed to add to the mayo (just one). My father marveled at that pie. As a midwesterner, he always ate apple pie with cheddar cheese, and he liked that this pie had cheese in it. I admit, some of my relatives didn't like the tomato pie, or at least remained suspicious of it. But the beach house was so crowded, so full of family, of aunts and uncles and cousins and old friends and new husbands, that the response to the naysayers was just *More for us, then!*

Over time, we stopped renting those beach houses at Scarborough Beach. My father got lung cancer, got sick, then sicker, then died. My aunts and uncles died too. And my mother's Friday night poker club dwindled from twelve to nine to four as the women too died. Cousins moved away. New husbands became ex-husbands. And that recipe, the one torn from a long-ago *Gourmet*, got lost in the move from one apartment to another, or perhaps one city to another. And then I read somewhere that Laurie Colwin had died suddenly at only forty-eight from heart failure—much as Mrs. Parker in Colwin's 1973 short story "Mr. Parker" dies suddenly, in October, of heart failure. Wrapped up in the heartbreak of a failed romance, I learned about it months later, in winter. Had it been summer, had I still owned that faded recipe, I would have made tomato pie the day I heard.

In the two decades since then, I have found and lost love and found it again. It has turned me to mush. I've published over a dozen books. I've had three children, and lost one suddenly and horribly when she was only five. My heart has broken again and again, and miraculously it has healed. There have been so many things I didn't take good enough care of, or hold on to tight enough, because we don't really believe we will lose them, do we? Somehow we are always stunned that things go away, disappear, die. People, too. They leave us and, despite knowing better, their leaving is always a surprise.

One summer day, I line up farm tomatoes on my windowsill, I glimpse the basil taking over my yard, and I have one thought: tomato pie. Is it too much to hope that the recipe had found its way to the Internet? I type in *Laurie Colwin* and *tomato pie* and just like that I have it again, my beloved recipe, still the ripe tomatoes, still the basil and double-biscuit crust, and, yes, still one-third of a cup of mayonnaise.

•

I preheat the oven to 400 degrees. I cut into the tomatoes, letting their juice spill everywhere, and I remember that long-ago winter night when I stood in the doorway of Three Lives bookstore and Laurie Colwin smiled at me. I am smiling now, at her, wherever she is, at all the people and all the things I lost, because in this moment I feel that maybe we never really lose the things we love. Maybe they are still, somehow, close. I go into the yard and pluck the greenest, most tender leaves of basil and I hold them to my nose and breathe in, deep. In that instant, I am back at Scarborough Beach and the women in my mother's card club are all there, ready to throw their pennies onto the table, and my aunts are complaining about putting tomatoes in a pie and my father is grinning because there is cheddar cheese in it and the recipe is smeared but still readable and the tomatoes are so fresh and so red that I swear, there has never been anything that red since.

Laurie Colwin's Tomato Pie

Crust

2 cups all-purpose flour
4 teaspoons baking powder
8 tablespoons (1 stick) butter
Approximately ²/₃ cup milk, less if it's a very humid day)

Filling

¹/₃ cup Hellmann's mayonnaise
2 tablespoons lemon juice
2 pounds fresh tomatoes
3–4 tablespoons chopped basil, chives, or scallions or a
   mixture of all 4
1¹/₂ cups grated sharp Cheddar cheese

Heat oven to 400 degrees. In a bowl mix flour and baking powder together. Cut butter into flour with a pastry blender until it resembles coarse oatmeal. Stir in milk a little at a time until dough forms a ball. Knead gently only until dough is completely blended. Roll out half the dough on a floured surface and line a 9-inch pie plate with it.

In a small bowl, mix mayonnaise with lemon juice. Blanch the tomatoes in a large pot of boiling water for 20–30 seconds and transfer immediately to a sink full of cool water. Peel and slice very thin. Cover the bottom of the crust with two layers of tomato slices. Sprinkle ⅓ of the herbs across tomatoes. Add another layer of tomato slices, sprinkle with ⅓ of the herbs and ½ the grated Cheddar. Drizzle with ½ of the mayonnaise mixture. Layer the rest of the tomato slices on top and scatter remaining herbs over the last layer. Top with remaining Cheddar and mayonnaise mixture.

Roll out the remaining dough, fit it over the filling, pinch the edges of the dough together to seal them. Cut several steam holes in the top crust and bake the pie for about 25 minutes, or until crust is golden and filling is just bubbling.

Extreme Eating

THE INVASIVORE'S DILEMMA

By Rowan Jacobsen

From Outside Magazine

In books such as *American Terroir, Shadows on the Gulf,*
and his new *Apples of Uncommon Character,* journalist
Rowan Jacobsen has carved out a very specific beat:
scrutinizing the environmental impact of what we eat.
Here he proposes what could be an elegant solution—
but it's not as easy as it sounds.

B un Lai is rolling rocks in the dark along a craggy coastline, claw-
ing on all fours after the little crabs that burst like roaches from
underneath, stuffing them into a bucket.

With his spotlight and his pail and his perfect snap-on hair, he
looks like an action figure. We are on a clandestine mission that began at 10:30 P.M. at Miya's, Bun's New Haven, Connecticut, sushi
restaurant, where I asked him who did the foraging for the restaurant, which has become famous for serving invasive organisms.
"You're looking at him," he replied.

So here we are, at low tide on a steamy summer night, scrabbling
around a closed Connecticut beach park. When the crabs bolt, you
must quickly slap your hands on top of them, then get your fingers
underneath. They scratch unhappily at your skin, but they are only
the size of 50-cent pieces. It feels like a prickly manicure. Sometimes
you can get them to hang by their claws from the web of your thumb.

The first time Bun did this was in 2005, with his buddy Yancey
Orr, a waiter at Miya's who went on to get his Ph.D. in anthropol-
ogy at Yale and now teaches in Australia. They'd gone to the shore
because Bun wanted to use more local ingredients. But they had no

idea where to start. In Connecticut, Orr mused by e-mail, "no one really interacts with the environment at the level of caloric intake."

They tried oysters but worried about toxins in the filter feeders. They chewed seaweeds. Then they noticed the speckled brown crabs scuttling around the rocks. Bun, who grew up playing in Long Island Sound, didn't remember them from childhood. He discovered that they were Asian shore crabs, an invasive species that arrived in 1988, dumped out with the ballast from some cargo ship, and had already taken over the coastline from New Hampshire to New Jersey, like a marauding army of nanobots. "At that point," Bun says, "I was already working on evolving sushi into a cuisine centered around more planet-healthy ingredients. The invasive-species thing made perfect sense."

Bun and Orr had no idea what to do with the crabs. "We sautéed them, tried them soaked in red wine, boiled, raw, et cetera," Orr recalled. "Raw was a bit rough, as they crawled around in your mouth and didn't taste so great." Fried whole, however, they turned bright orange and ultracrispy, like Doritos with legs. The crabs have been a staple at Miya's ever since.

Bun is not your typical sushi chef. This 44-year-old son of New Haven has the smooth, rippled body of a porn star and a voice like Captain America. He grew up near Yale, where his Chinese father worked as a medical researcher. When he was nine, his parents divorced, his father moved away, and his Japanese mother opened Miya's, which was named for Bun's sister—though since he took over he has been threatening to change the name to Bun's After Dark and use the Underalls logo for his sign. He was the captain of his prep-school wrestling team, and he used to fight illegal mixed-martial-arts matches in a Waterbury, Connecticut, warehouse. Now he fights for food justice. On his bookshelves, you can find everything from *The Cornel West Reader* to *The Complete Idiot's Guide to Kickboxing*. During one of his previous foraging operations, he was arrested for trespassing while taking a leak in the woods.

A little lower down the dark beach, Joe Roman is pulling periwinkles off the rocks, tossing the little snails into another pail. A bespectacled, late-forties conservation biologist at the University of Vermont and the creator of a website called Eat the Invaders ("Fighting invasive species, one bite at a time!"), Roman tells us how *Littorina littorea*, a

European native, arrived in the Northeast in the 1860s and began eating salt marshes from Maine to New York. Our coasts are starker and less productive than they used to be, thanks to this file-tongued little mollusk, which has endangered numerous local species. In places you can find 700 periwinkles per square yard.

The Asian shore crab may wind up being even worse. It eats anything it can fit in its mouth, including native crabs and juvenile lobsters. "This is a totally different system now than just a few decades ago," Roman says. "Go to a place where the invaders are present and you see a battlefield." And the crab, which can lay up to 200,000 eggs per year, is expanding its forces in all directions.

Like their hundreds of fellow invasive species from Miami to Malibu, these two aggressors will continue to engulf the Republic. But not these particular troops. These will be dinner. If all goes according to plan, we will spend the next 24 hours apprehending the alien and the overabundant wherever they lurk. Then we will devour them.

The America you grew up in is history. It has been clogged by zebra mussels and snuffed by snakeheads. It has been swallowed by Burmese pythons and smothered by kudzu. It has been swarmed by crazy ants.

Forget the notion of stable ecological communities that have existed in harmony for thousands of years; what we have now is an endless war zone where invasive insurgents go from building to building, routing the locals. Simply strolling down Bun's driveway in the leafy Connecticut burbs the morning after our late-night crab-athon, Roman could point to all the slow-motion carnage. Dense mats of garlic mustard in the woods that drip chemicals into the soil to keep anything else from growing. "Invasive." Clots of burdock along the roadside. "Invasive." Dark ranks of knotweed infiltrating a stream bank. "Invasive."

Not all introduced species become invasive. Most newcomers move into town, settle down, and become part of the fabric of the place. Apple trees, for example, originally from Kazakhstan, have been model citizens since they arrived with colonists four centuries ago. But of the 7,000 or so introduced species that have made a new life in the United States, about 1,000 are trashing the place at a rate that puts most of our other concerns to shame. Worrying about the impact that climate change may have on a region's ecology while ignoring the work of invasive species is kind of like fretting over next year's crops while Vikings torch the harbor.

That's because, with little if any natural predators or diseases, an invasive species has few checks on its reproductive rates, and it quickly goes about outcompeting the locals, if not directly consuming them. The result: the collapse of a local species, followed by the collapse of the natives that depended on that species, followed by ecological death spiral.

Exhibit A: Asian carp, imported from China in the 1970s by fish farmers in the South who hoped that the carp, which feed on algae, would help keep their ponds clean. The carp soon escaped into the Mississippi River Basin and now fill the Midwest's rivers, where they sometimes comprise 90 percent of the biomass. These are the carp that weigh in at 50 pounds and jump ten feet out of the water when startled, whacking passing boaters upside the head like piscine two-by-fours. In 2014, the Army Corps of Engineers released its long-awaited master plan for keeping Asian carp out of the Great Lakes by severing all the arteries that connect the Mississippi River watershed to Lake Michigan. The price tag? Some $18.4 billion.

Exhibit B: the Burmese python, which first entered the Everglades in the 1980s or 1990s as escaped pets. Now as many as 150,000 of the snakes, which can grow to nearly 20 feet in length, inhabit Florida's river of grass, and they have eaten 87.5 percent of the bobcats, 98.9 percent of the possums, 99.3 percent of the raccoons, and all the rabbits and foxes, as well as untold birds and alligators. A highly publicized 2013 python hunt, involving more than 1,000 participants, managed to net only 68 of the elusive apex predators.

Exhibit C: the lionfish, which Carl Safina, founding president of the Blue Ocean Institute, calls "the perfect invasive storm." A native of the Indian Ocean that looks like it escaped from the cover of a Yes album, the lionfish is popular for aquariums. Dumped out of a few fish tanks into South Florida seas in the 1990s, it began showing up throughout the Caribbean in the 2000s. Bristling with poisonous spines, it has no local predators, and it can reproduce year-round, with the typical female producing one million eggs.

Most disastrous land invasion? Easy: *Sus scrofa*, the feral hog. The so-called pig bomb detonated in Texas in the 1980s after the Eurasian natives were stocked on game ranches, from which they quickly escaped and interbred with domestic pigs, but it has rippled out to 45 other states. Soon Alaska may be the only holdout. America is infested with at least five million wild hogs, half of them in Texas, which cause a good $1.5 billion in damages each year. Wild hogs uproot peanuts and other crops, destroy lawns, devour endangered species, spread diseases, and turn huge swaths of wetlands into eroding pigsties. They'll eat corn, sugarcane, wheat, vegetables, snakes, lizards, frogs, turtles, muskrats, deer, goats, lambs, calves, and even feral piglets. They reproduce three times a year and have no natural predators. Texas "harvests" more than 750,000 hogs per year, but the population is still doubling every five years.

You get the idea. A decade ago, researchers estimated the annual cost of invasive species in America at $120 billion, which is more than the U.S. spends to maintain its roads. And that includes only measurable items—such as crop losses, the $1 billion municipalities spend each year to scrub zebra mussels out of their water pipes, and so on. Ecological costs are harder to quantify but staggering: nearly half the species on the U.S. threatened and endangered species lists were put there by invaders. Then there are simple quality-of-life considerations. Imagine the South without fire ants. That's how it was until the 1930s, when the South American invader snuck into the port of Mobile, Alabama, on a cargo ship. Now they've been joined—in (where else?) Texas—by crazy ants, tiny invaders who swarm electronic components, wall sockets, and human skin by the millions.

Obviously, in a country that can't find an extra billion to buy new bridges, the government is not going to fund the war on invaders. (President Clinton established the National Invasive Species Council in 1999, but it still seems to spend most of its energy debating the definition of invasive species. Its 2013 meeting was canceled.) Market-driven approaches hold more promise: put the critters on a plate and let them bankroll their own demise. After all, we have chomped our way through mammoths, moas, dodos, and every oyster in New York Harbor, and we are closing in on the last tuna and swordfish. Why not channel that appetite in a more productive direction?

My first training in the way of the invasivore came a few months before I met Bun, when I sat in a Boston restaurant watching New

Hampshire chef Evan Mallett plate buttermilk-poached-dogfish salads. We were at the first Trash Fish Dinner, the start of a national series organized by Chefs Collaborative, a group of sustainability-minded chefs. The idea was to promote abundant fish that nobody eats, to take pressure off the familiar fare that's running out. A month earlier, draconian cuts in cod quotas had been announced, a development that was expected to put many New England fishermen out of business.

"They've been hammered so many times," Mallett told me. "I think we're looking at an extinct industry." Mallett is the chef and owner of the Black Trumpet Bistro in downtown Portsmouth. "I look out on a river that is the mouth of what both the natives and European settlers agreed was the prime fishing area," he said. "And now there's little there. It's incredibly depressing." So Mallett was pushing the spiny dogfish, a three-foot shark with a creepy Far Side grin that, while not technically invasive, has taken over the North Atlantic. When we overfished cod, dogfish rushed into the void. Trawlers fishing for cod now shred their nets on spiny dogfish instead. Unfortunately, the fish is virtually unsalable. ("Some sharks piss through their skin," Mallett explained to me. "Seriously.") But if gutted and bled immediately, he insisted, dogfish can be clean and delicious.

Which it was—not even a hint of pee. Mallett nodded. "We did a dogfish po'boy last summer. If we put it in front of someone and they ate it, they loved it. But trying to talk someone into ordering the dogfish po'boy was an exercise in futility."

Next to Mallett, Drew Hedlund, chef of the Fleet Landing Restaurant in Charleston, South Carolina, handed me a cup of lionfish ceviche with grapefruit, key lime juice, and candied citrus peel. "They're all over the reefs. It's alarming," he said. "And they keep expanding northward. You'd think these fish would be getting smaller as they leave the warm tropical waters, but it's the opposite. We seem to be getting much larger fish up north." Because they live amid delicate reefs, lionfish must be speared or netted by hand. Leading the charge is an organization called REEF (Reef Environmental Education Foundation), which holds lionfish derbies throughout Florida and the Bahamas. Last September, REEF broke its previous record, with 100 divers collecting 707 lionfish off Key Largo. Dozens of restaurants in the U.S., Mexico, and the Caribbean now serve lionfish.

Invasivorism is not a new idea. In 1997, Louisiana tried to solve its nutria problem by ringing the dinner bell on the South American marsh rodents, which have been called "mammalian lawn mowers" because of their ability to eat grasses down to bare mud. Many parts of Louisiana are infested with as many as 6,000 nutria per square mile. The state spent $2 million encouraging people to eat nutria, but the campaign fizzled. Studies found that nutria was embraced only by individuals who already favored muskrat.

But thanks to chefs, the invasivore movement has caught fire. Some of the worst invaders, like gypsy moths and Asian long-horned beetles, will not grace lunch counters anytime soon, yet where perniciousness meets deliciousness, there is hope.

The feral hog that plagues Texas, for example, is the same animal as the wild boar, the sacred *cinghiale* of Italian gastronomy. Now you can snack on local-boar chili in Houston or do a surf-and-turf of wild boar and invasive Asian tiger shrimp in Austin. In New Braunfels, Bubba's Bacon Station—a subsidiary of Ortiz Game Management and Hog Removal of Texas ("If you have large territorial hogs that are taking over your yard or destroying crops WE CAN HELP!")—buys or traps hogs, processes them under USDA inspection, and delivers them to the San Antonio Food Bank and other lucky clients. "They are an untapped, underused, available cuisine in ample supply in almost every county in Texas," says Bubba Ortiz.

Asian carp, which now fill some Midwestern rivers at the unbelievable density of 13 tons per mile, could feed half of Chicago. The drawback? Their soft flesh and countless bones disgust people. (Bun Lai likens carp anatomy to "a hairbrush smeared with peanut butter.") An effort to rebrand them as Kentucky tuna somehow failed to take off. Yet, at another Trash Fish Dinner, in Chicago last May, Paul Fehribach of the local Southern-cooking eatery Big Jones got raves for his crispy carp cakes. "Asian carp's got really sweet meat," he told me. "It reminds me so much of crab, but without the bottom-feeder funk, so I did it breaded and deep-fried in batter." Now he's working on carp fish sticks.

Yet the occasional trash-fish dinner is not going to change the status quo. It's a fine token, a way of getting people engaged, but what the world needs is trash-fish *diners*—joints slinging invaders and bycatch every night. Chefs willing to put their whole menu where their mouth is. What the world needs is Bun Lai.

Six years ago, Bun blew up his menu. He didn't want to feel bad anymore from putting foods like white rice and sugar in his body or anybody else's. And he didn't want to feel bad because he was serving the last bluefin on earth. He began to wonder if sushi could be used to heal bodies, communities, and oceans.

First, he swapped white rice for brown. "Then," he says, "I started taking ingredients away. First octopus, then sea urchin. I knew that would be easy. I wasn't killing it with sea urchin anyway. Then the big stuff started going. Unagi. That pissed people off. Then I did yellowtail. Then tuna in 2010. When I told my waiters I was going to remove tuna, they started hyperventilating. For them it can be really, really difficult to explain what we're trying to do."

In place of tuna, Bun offered sustainable options like the Water Pig Roll (applewood-smoked Connecticut mackerel, goat cheese, and cranberries) and the Kwanzaa Bonanzaa (a coconut-covered roll of fried Mississippi catfish, sweet potato, avocado, cream cheese, cantaloupe, burdock, and hot sauce). The sushi snobs savaged him online. ("This is not sushi. This is not sushi. This is not sushi.") Many walked out after perusing the menu. Many newcomers still walk out, but after a wobbly decade that saw Miya's flirt with bankruptcy, the restaurant has developed a loyal, even rabid, clientele who will follow Bun off any gastronomic cliff. They willingly made the leap into invasivorism. Five invasive species are now standard on his menu: the burdock in the Kwanzaa Bonanzaa roll; the seaweeds in the miso soup; the Asian shore crabs, fried and placed as if in mid-crawl on a pile of rolls and seaweeds meant to evoke the Connecticut shoreline; lionfish sashimi; and a notorious peanut-butter-and-jellyfish roll. ("Invasive cannonball jellyfish, trawled off the state of Georgia, is thin sliced and mixed with steamed invasive Australian rabbit and cucumber" and "seasoned with creamy roasted peanut butter.")

For special occasions, Bun goes further, breaking out the Japanese knotweed lemonade and the hog sashimi, first freezing it to five degrees for 20 days to kill any trichinosis worms. Last June, he held a special cicada dinner to celebrate the superabundance of the 17-year insects. He originally planned to hold it at Miya's. No, no, no, the health department said. So he moved it to his house and threw an open-invite party. About 50 people showed up, half of whom he didn't know. He served hundreds of cicadas, marinated in lime and chili, smoked, then crisped in a dehydrator. Reactions were mixed. "The outside was satisfyingly crispy," said one guest. "But as I bit into it, there was a pop/squish that was a little unexpected." Another: "It was weird flossing wings out of your teeth."

"They were a hit," Bun insists. "If I had a bunch, I'd be snacking on them right now. But if I had a basketful of cicadas and was standing outside Starbucks, I don't think I'd have gotten the same reception."

When the sushi snobs tell Bun this is not sushi, this is not sushi, this is not sushi, he tells them that sushi must evolve. It must again involve a covenant with nature. He tells them you need to use what nature gives you.

Which is how I find myself floating beneath a red buoy in Long Island Sound the afternoon after our crab hunt, sucking on a snorkel and wondering what else might be lurking in the warm, pea green water. I'd asked Bun and Roman, just how far can invasivorism go? Show me that you can eat well in Connecticut off the invasive and underutilized, and I'll believe that you can do it anywhere.

What nature is giving us at the moment is seaweed. Neon green wakame and creepy tendrils of something called dead man's fingers, both invasive as hell, cover the bottom of the buoy, which is pumping up and down in the swells, and I'm trying to rip them off with one hand while holding my breath and stuffing them into a sack tied around my other wrist without getting cold-cocked by the buoy on the downbeat. And I'm worrying that interacting with the environment at the level of caloric intake is, at best, a zero-sum game, but Bun assures me our cooler will soon be brimming with wild, nutrient-dense calories.

So I keep grabbing new breaths and diving back for more seaweed. Bun—who is wearing the longest flippers I've ever seen, comic-book flippers, really, instilling in me a deep sense of inferiority—has paddled over to a nearby rock in search of tunicates, which he has been threatening to serve me raw. Tunicates, also known as sea squirts, are gelatinous filter feeders that gum onto available surfaces by the thousands, smothering whatever is inside. Some are native to North

America, but this particular Japanese variety, known alternately as carpet tunicate and marine vomit, has single-handedly destroyed the Nova Scotia mussel industry and threatens to do the same for other shellfish growers throughout the Northeast. Bun would love to serve them, but uncharacteristically, he has decided not to pursue tunicate cuisine. "They look like uncircumcised penises, and when you bite them they squirt in your mouth."

"The tunicates were brutal," Roman agrees, mumbling something about ammonium.

The rope attaching the buoy to the bottom is caked with seaweeds and mussels—not invasive, but abundant to the point of nuisance, which in Bun's book counts—and the mussels are crusted in an orange slime of immature tunicates, so I suck some more air and follow the rope down, my mask pressed right up against it to see through the brown murk. Sure enough, they come off the rope easily, and soon my sack is filled with mussels and seaweeds.

Bun's sack is bigger than mine, of course, and Roman has also done well. We kick over to Bun's boat and offload our contents, and suddenly the cooler won't even close. The shore crabs from last night use the mussels as scaffolding to make a break for it, skulking around the boat, hiding in corners and waiting for a change in their fortunes.

A vision of invasive miso soup begins to dance in our heads as the evening sun cracks like an egg along the northwest horizon and we pilot the Bunboat up the sound. We have seaweeds, we have shellfish, we have seawater, we just so happen to have a giant wok and a propane tank, and we have nowhere to be. But we need clams.

We steal into a cove rimmed by a 20-foot wall of rock on one side and Connecticut McMansions on the other. We tie up to somebody else's mooring ball. At the bottom of the cove, Bun suspects, lurk quahogs (native but underutilized, at least by these Gatsbys).

"How will I know?" I ask.

"Just dive to the bottom and feel around."

"How deep is it?"

"Only one way to find out."

Right. Pale white faces peek out of upper-story windows and gardeners pause in mid-rake to watch the frogmen deploy. I fill my lungs with air and kick straight for Hades, my hands reached out in front, down, down into darkness.

Just about the time the vise is closing on my temples and I'm wondering if I have enough air for the return trip, my hands plunge into mud and almost instantly close on what feel like smooth, fist-sized rocks. I grab as many as I can and kick hard for the surface and explode into air, clutching handfuls of glossy black *Mercenaria mercenaria*. Then Bun shoots up with even bigger ones, and the quahog hunt is on. We are rooting in the mud like manatees, filling our sacks with clams and gasping for air in between. Eventually, I struggle back to the boat with a sack that feels as if it is full of bowling balls.

Half an hour later, we have commandeered an island of pink rock in the middle of the sound and chased the oystercatchers away. The burner under the wok is roaring like a jet engine, and shore crabs are dancing in dark sesame oil. Bun adds ginger, garlic, periwinkles, and dead man's fingers and cooks it down into a mushy green marine bruschetta. The other seaweeds, clams, and tunicate-crusted mussels go into a separate wok with a little seawater and miso paste. Soon the tunicates slide off the shells and dissolve into an orange bisque, and suddenly we have New Haven miso soup.

As the color fades from the sky and the day's heat radiates from the rock, we spoon out bowlfuls of soup swirling with green, brown, and red seaweeds, clacking with shells, and salted by the sea. There's also a fair amount of the bottom of Long Island Sound in the soup, grit and tunicate grinding between our molars, but hey, this is war.

And I now feel that it's a war we can win. Who could stop this Chinese-Japanese-American hero for our times, stirring a wok in his Hawaiian-print bathing suit and popping boiling crabs into his mouth? He and Roman have book projects in the works, online plans, speaking gigs, and I foresee a thousand invasivore clubs spreading across the land—not Miya's exactly, more like Bun's After Dark, an uprising of scrappy locals going all MMA on the invaders. Wherever the kingdom is threatened, we will be waiting with our chopsticks. For we are hungry. We are open-minded. And we are legion.

Learning How to Taste

By Daniella Martin

From Edible: An Adventure into the World of Eating Insects and the Last Great Hope to Save the Planet

⌇

Entomophagist is a fancy word for what Daniella Martin is: someone who eats insects. In this book, as well as her online cooking and travel show, Girl Meets Bug, she spreads the gospel of this ancient practice, the ultimate sustainable food source. Turns out she's not the only insectivore out there. . . .

There are nearly nineteen hundred recorded edible insect species on Earth and counting. How many different types of meat have you sampled in your lifetime? Most people never go beyond the standard dozen-plus basics of chicken, beef, pork, lamb, and maybe five to ten kinds of fish. Compared with the 500 varieties of insect eaten in Mexico alone, this is a fairly limited flavor palate—the "beginner box" of culinary Crayolas.

Insects represent the majority of the animal biomass on Earth. They have thousands of different habitats, and many species have evolved to eat a single type of plant. Considering all the different plants and ecosystems there are, and their corresponding insect populations, this opens up a kaleidoscope of flavors.

In general, insects tend to taste a bit nutty, especially when roasted. This comes from the natural fats they contain, combined with the crunchiness of their mineral-rich exoskeletons. Crickets, for instance, taste like nutty shrimp, whereas most larvae I've tried have a nutty mushroom flavor. My two favorites, wax moth caterpillars (a.k.a. wax worms) and bee larvae, taste like enoki-pine nut and bacon-chanterelle, respectively.

Recently, when I served this grub at the LA Natural History Museum's Bug Fair Cook-Off,* one kid on the judging panel said my "Alice in Wonderland" dish of sautéed wax worms and oyster mushrooms tasted like macaroni and cheese, while the rest agreed that my Bee-LT Sandwich tasted like it was made with real bacon.

The term "bug" has a specific taxonomic meaning, indicating an insect of the order Hemiptera, known as the "true bugs," and includes cicadas, aphids, plant hoppers, leafhoppers, shield bugs, and others. It is also widely used by non-entomologists as an umbrella term covering land arthropods in general, including arachnids like scorpions and spiders.

Having established that arachnids are included in our general discussion of entomophagy, their tastes should be included as well. In my experience, arachnids often taste like a light, earthy version of shellfish, crab, and lobster in particular. This makes sense since, from a biological standpoint, bugs and crustaceans are quite closely related. However, the air-breathing group of these invertebrates has one distinct advantage over its sea-steeped brethren: They aren't bottom-feeders. Scorpions, tarantulas, and other edible arachnids all catch their prey live, unlike crabs, which are just as happy to feast on detritus.

These examples are fairly tame and recognizable; most people can swallow the idea of nutty mushrooms and earthy shellfish. But there are also flavors in the bug world that can hardly be equated with anything familiar to most Westerners. The taste of giant water bug practically defies description; as one writer enthused after his first time eating them, "There is simply nothing in the annals of our culture to which I can direct your attention that would hint at the nature of [its] flavor."

When fresh, these aggressive beetles have a scent like a crisp green apple. Large enough to yield tiny fillets, they taste like anchovies soaked in banana-rose brine, with the consistency of a light, flaky fish. Dave Gracer likes to serve tiny filaments of their flesh atop cubes of watermelon, and even this minuscule amount of the bug is enough to infuse an entire mouthful. It's no wonder their extract is a common ingredient in Thai sauces.

---

* I lost to David George Gordon's delicious orthopteran stir-fry.

Conservative eaters are likely to prefer to stick to what they know, but if you're anything like me, you'll find this galaxy of mysterious new flavors simply too compelling to resist. Indeed, some of the world's top gastronauts have begun to explore it in earnest.

Noma is the much-buzzed-about restaurant in Copenhagen, Denmark, that beat out elBulli for *Restaurant* magazine's best restaurant in the world award in 2010 and has managed to hold on to the title for three years running. A tiny place on the waterfront edge of an old stone maritime warehouse, the restaurant's trappings are so subtle you'd miss it if you weren't really looking. Yet Noma turned down close to a million would-be diners in the last year alone. From its windows, the city skyline, with its slender church spires and geometric modern architecture, is silhouetted so beautifully in the pinkening sunset that famous head chef René Redzepi comes out to snap a quick photo, then ducks back in before becoming the subject of photos himself. Redzepi was recently named one of *Time* magazine's World's 100 Most Influential People.

Ten years ago, Copenhagen was virtually unknown as far as food went, a "culinary backwater," as Michael Booth called it in *Copenhagen Encounter*. In other words, no one went to Denmark for the food, unless they had a hankering for reindeer meat. Today people fly from all over the world to sample aspects of the fiercely home-proud food movement that has flourished here, known as the New Nordic Cuisine, largely established by Redzepi and his Noma cofounder, Claus Meyer.

Redzepi's perspective on the New Nordic Cuisine has extended its tentacles to gourmets around the world as chefs strive to imitate his style, for which intrepid diners pay $400 apiece to eat things like fried reindeer moss, hay ash, twigs, ants and seaweed. This may sound like the world's biggest rip-off, but the idea is that one is eating, well, ideas taken from nature, refined through art and tradition, and re-presented as nature on the plate.

"The flavors at Noma are intense. They're not for everyone," Daniel Giusti, the former chef of 1789 in Washington, DC, now a soldier in Redzepi's army, told the *Washington Post*. "There's an aura about this restaurant that I've never seen before. René can do anything he wants."

The New Nordic Cuisine is about the fusion of immediacy and history at once. It's about what is available locally, seasonally, and, generally, in abundance—the here and now of nutrient sources. It's also about the identity of a place, both naturally and culturally. In the Nordic region—which comprises Denmark, Finland, Iceland, Norway, Sweden, the Faroe Islands, Greenland, Svalbard, and Åland—food preservation techniques like fermenting and pickling have been popular for centuries, likely because of the percentage of the year spent in cold, dark winter. Food has to last, to warm, to nourish deeply—but also to inspire and invigorate during the long, lightless months. Ingredients can be extended but also intensified through the application of salt, yeasts, mold, and time.

This is all the easier to grasp now in the beginning of November, when it's already so cold I have to wear two jackets, gloves, and a thick hat at all times. I'm here in Copenhagen to visit Nordic Food Lab (NFL), the R&D branch of Noma.

Taking humble ingredients and elevating them to a lofty status is Redzepi's proven specialty. In early 2012, he posed the question: If he could serve bark, branches, weeds, and other dubiously edible ingredients at Noma, why couldn't he serve the humblest ingredient of all—insects?

He tasked NFL, the nonprofit institute he established and then dedicated to searching and stretching the boundaries of edibility, with discovering the answer. Since then, they've been experimenting with various species, trying to find the most delicious ways of presenting ingredients viewed as nonedible by the public.

Docked just across the cold black canal is NFL's floating houseboat of a home. Like Noma, it has an unassuming exterior—a small gray boat surrounded by bicycles. Much has been written about the relatively small expanse bracketed by Noma and NFL. But no one has written about their foray into edible insects.

I show up bright and early in the chilly rain. The boat looks cozy and inviting, with its squares of warm yellow glass gleaming against the gray; a clean, well-lighted place for cooks. I make it onto the boat's front porch, where I hover in front of the glass doors and wave.

A handful of edgily stylish, serious-looking men, each with his own air of focused intensity, ushers me inside. There's somber Michael Bom Frost, who splits his time between being director of NFL and director of studies for the Gastronomy and Health program at Copenhagen University. Next is animated Scotsman Benedict Reade, the new head of culinary research and development, followed by stoic, tattooed Lars Williams, Ben's predecessor and current R&D director at Noma, and keen-eyed Josh Evans, an intern from Yale Sustainable Food Project. These guys help dream up and then test some of the most innovative food ideas in the world. I peel off my wet layers in the warmth of the space, which is spare yet welcoming like many Danish interiors. The room is part designer kitchen, part laboratory, part casually elegant meeting space. Stacks of beakers and flasks coexist with pots and pans. Containers holding various colors and consistencies have labels like BEETS, BREAD YEAST 11/09 and SORREL, RED WINE, BARLEY MOLD 02/07. It looks like exactly what it is: a preternaturally hip foodie think tank.

Someone offers me coffee. I'd already decided to say yes to anything I'm offered here, and coffee's obviously a no-brainer. I am handed it black, in a lovely little handmade cup. No mention of cream or sugar is made—everyone's drinking theirs straight. I take a sip. It's fantastic. Later, I'll be very glad I had it—it revved my brain for the daylong conversation about food I was about to have with some of the world's foremost thinkers on the subject. NFL is a team of people passionate about exploring and expressing ideas, be it through food or words.

I ask them what they think of the idea that insects are the food of the future.

"Well, if any one thing becomes the food of the future, that's a very depressing future," says Ben Reade in his charming brogue. "We need diversity, and that's why we're interested in looking at insects—it's another walk of life that we can investigate. We have the whole phylogenetic tree that we can eat, so we have to look at all the different branches. I think it's really important to make sure people realize that insects are another ingredient that can be added to a repertoire, and not suddenly become *the* ingredient, when there is no *the* ingredient, is there? That's only an economist's way of looking at things. And if economists look at food too much, then things get dangerous."

"The same thing happened with soybeans, right?" adds researcher Josh Evans. "Soybeans have been used for hundreds of thousands of years in many cultures, and they're perfectly healthy if they're prepared the right way. But once they were touted as *the* ingredient that everyone will consume, that will save the world, that's when vast swathes of the Amazon were cut down."

"We see insects not as *the* food of the future but as an interesting addition to the foods we already have," says Michael Bom Frost, whose background is in sensory science (whatever *that* means). "To convince Europe to eat insects, it's not enough to fry them up or to extract the protein. I think we have to lower the barriers for first-time entomophagists. If you just hand someone a cricket, and say, 'Eat it!' I think there's a ninety-nine percent chance of rejection. But if you give them something that's really delicious, that's in a familiar setting, I think we can lower the outright rejection rate a lot. And I think that's really important because then we can start building on it."

Michael offers Singapore as an example, where they are using a water filtration system to treat and reuse the water from the sewers. If you think about it, they're drinking shit water, but the truth is it's perfectly safe to drink. On the one hand, there is disgust, but on the other, there is a societal need that must be addressed.

"We want to address this need with deliciousness as the vehicle for promoting insects, and not saying, 'Eat this because it's good for the environment,' or 'because it's healthy protein,' but 'because it tastes good,'" says Michael.

The term "deliciousness" is bandied about with great seriousness here at NFL, and we discuss how this mouth-first approach applies to eating insects—asking first, "How does it taste?" instead of "What is it?" Nothing edible should be considered off-limits just because of our prejudices about it.

"No *ideas* are inherently disgusting. That's food fascism," says Ben.

Michael, Josh, and I head out to the seashore to forage for periwinkle sea snails, shrimp, and "strand hoppers," which are essentially sand fleas. *Strand* is Danish for beach. We'll be fishing for aquatic invertebrates.

On the way over, I learn what it means to be a food sensory scientist. What Michael does is scientifically interpret taste tests, usually to help develop healthier products that still taste good. One of his most notable accomplishments was coming up with data suggesting that 0.5 percent fat in milk was the lowest amount necessary for consumers to feel satisfaction. Today, that category makes up 40 percent of milk sales in Denmark.

"It's about finding a sweet spot between health and good taste in a common food," says Michael with a twinkle in his eye. It's clear he is passionate about what he does.

The sparse, beautiful beach scene blows me away. The glassy waves of the Øresund Strait lap gently on the shore of the Amager Strand, an artificial island added by the city in 2005, which can be reached by metro. Wave-tangled, multicolored ribbons of seaweed line the sand, like the streamers of a wild, forgotten birthday party. It's almost winter, so there won't be any parties here today; it's about 40 degrees even in the intermittent sun. The only other people out here are a few locals walking their dogs.

Michael and Josh laughingly pull on their giant army-green waders, bought especially for the occasion. I ask how cold the water is, if people go swimming here in the summertime. I try to picture the empty beach full of people and noise, where now there's just wind and sand.

"People go swimming here all year round," says Josh. "Crazy Danes."

They gather up their nets: one giant, practically person-sized one for Michael, a smaller green one for Josh. They step into the waves and march out into the water, soon up to their hips in the chilly Øresund. The water is clear, so they can hone in on their tiny prey.

The ocean is a choppy slate-blue extension of the sky, through which billowy mountain ranges of cloud patterns pass. Denmark is big-sky country. The light changes every few minutes, and I snap madly away at the scene of the two epicurean fishermen/academics, caught between sea and sky as they collect ingredients from the blue expanse. A line of white wind turbines in the background completes the scene, as well as part of the context: Copenhagen aims to be the world's first carbon-neutral city by 2025. Crazy Danes, indeed.

"How is it out there?" I call. They've gone quite a ways out, insulated by the thick rubber and unimpeded by the smooth waves. They wave back, grinning.

Michael is the first to wade back in with his catch. He kneels down and shakes clumps of olive-green bladder wrack into a bucket. Sea snails, shrimp, and tiny, darting strand hoppers fall out.

Context, Michael and Josh say, is as important as the ingredients on the plate. Taste, woven with philosophy and shot through with science, seems to be the conversational culture of this team, members of which must be as steeped in this sort of rhetoric as their weeds are in fermenting brew.

"People eating food is the only way they get the full experience," Michael says.

"In the same way that there's no such thing as a painting without the context of the painting—even in the most modernistic of galleries, it's still a white wall," says Josh. "There's still a texture, there's still lighting, there's still a mood that's created. There's no such thing as a taste without a context."

The sea air bites at our cheeks, the wind flaps through our hair. The waves curl under, collapsing gently against the sand. Jellyfish nestled in masses of seaweed rock forward and back under the clear, undulating surface of the water. The clouds are piled high, slow as migrating herds across the wide blue sky. Josh runs down the beach and comes back with an armful of treasure: beach mustard. I grab a purple-flowered stalk and take a bite. It's just like a delicate broccoli, salted by the sea air.

Michael fishes out a nearly transparent, gangly shrimp from the bucket's brine. Like Lisa Simpson said, they aren't really that much different from grasshoppers.

"Noma currently serves a live shrimp on ice with a brown butter emulsion, and for that, people are like, *whoa*," says Josh. "It's still sort of at the frontier of what's seen as acceptable. Or even delicious."

"We can eat them alive and pretend we're at Noma," says Michael.

I find I have no qualms about putting the live shrimp in my mouth, especially in this context. I wasn't worried about hurting it—it would be crushed instantly between my teeth, as good a death as any it might encounter living in the wild. I recalled something Redzepi had said about these live shrimp: "The taste of these shrimp changes from day to day, depending on the conditions of the ocean. Eating them is really like tasting the ocean on that day."

Today the ocean tastes sweet, and tender, and fresh, with a subtle brightness that is hard to qualify. Maybe this is what the Japanese are on about, with their super-fresh food and live sushi.

Back at the lab, we boil up the sea snails we collected. Josh leads me on an appetizer journey around the kitchen. First I try the fermented grasshopper garum that tastes like fish sauce in its complexity and emphasizes the umami flavor of many insects. Then I taste the bee-larvae granola he's made for a breakfast event they're holding next week. It's crunchy and creamy and savory at once. Delicious.

The sea snails cook up quickly and are light, fresh, and chewy, like an extra-firm shrimp. As with all the other invertebrate morsels I've tried here, there certainly isn't anything off-putting about them. Quite the opposite, in fact. If you didn't know they were insects and snails, you'd never question them. Slap a fancy title on them, like they did with Chilean sea bass (a.k.a. Patagonian toothfish), put them on the menu at an upscale restaurant, and people would order them.

I leave before dinner at Noma (the restaurant books up months in advance), but the conversation during my day at NFL alone will keep me going for quite a while. Sometimes ideas are nourishment enough.

SEVEN BALD MEN AND A KUMQUAT TREE

By Amy Gentry

From Gastronomica

Austin Chronicle columnist Amy Gentry is plugged into
the creative life in Austin, whether it's her fiction
writing, her sketch comedy, her dance group, or her
blog (TheOeditrix.com). Profiling chef Rob Connoley,
she's interested not just in his self-taught technique
but in the astounding creative leaps he takes.

I have never seen a restaurant kitchen quite like this. The Kenmore
oven/stove combo with its electric range is the same make and
model as mine at home, but of an older vintage. Something that
looks like a thirty-year-old camping grill sits on the counter next to
the stove. Mason jars filled with rust-red hackberries, bumpy green
cholla fruit, and twigs with the leaves still attached litter the shelves
and countertops. On top of one sits a piece of spongy grayish-green
moss.

"What's that?" I ask. Rob Connoley, skinny and tall, with a shaven
head and lashless blue eyes that blink red in the smoky kitchen, picks
it up.

"Oh, just something I found in the woods. I'm going to take it to
Naava." That's Naava Konigsberg, local herbalist, whom Rob con-
sults for information about the various plants he forages, before taking them to the biology lab at Western New Mexico University for
further analysis. "I'll ask them, is it edible? Sustainable? Are there
toxic levels of pollutants?" He puts the moss back down. "Don't
worry, I also try it myself first. If I die, I won't serve it."

Rob keeps up the steady stream of chatter while he drops a squiggle of pale green watercress purée on four plates, tosses it with a bright saffron-yellow streak, and plants a white ball on one end that looks like fresh mozzarella (it is actually a curd made from sweet corn shoots). At the other end of the plate, trapezoidal hunks of acorn bread lean drunkenly against one another like the ruins of a small city. He plops a couple of elderflower boba—glistening, translucent balls resembling oversized golden whitefish caviar—onto a small heap of greens and moves to the next plate.

In December of 2012, Rob's restaurant, the Curious Kumquat, was named #39 in *Saveur Magazine*'s Top 100 destination restaurants. To understand how truly unlikely this ranking is, you should know that he has a PhD in sports psychology but no culinary degree and no restaurant experience at all outside of the one he opened in 2008; that he works almost completely alone, prepping, firing, and plating all the courses and washing his own dishes by hand at the end of the night; and that the Curious Kumquat is located in a mountain town with a population of 10,000 four hours from the closest commercial airport.

Despite all this, the restaurant regularly draws a crowd increasingly made up of food tourists from New York, Chicago, and LA. Between Mardi Gras and Valentine's Day, it's been a stressful week. "We served seventy tables for dinner last night," he says. "That's the biggest dinner we've ever done, and it's not even tourist season yet." He pauses and rubs his head. "I'm exhausted, and I still haven't done the courses for tomorrow night." Tomorrow, the restaurant is closed for one of the experimental tasting dinners Rob throws every few months. This time he's planning ten savory courses based around chocolate, presumably in honor of Valentine's Day. With forty reservations, the dinner is sold out.

"You mean you haven't prepped them?"

"I mean I haven't invented them."

Leah, the single server working the floor, pokes her head in to tell Rob that the five-top she just seated wants to be out in an hour. "They're watching the game."

"The *game*?" Rob says incredulously.

She nods. "And they want the tasting menu."

Rob shakes his head. "Seven courses in one hour, so they can watch the *game*," he says. "Unbelievable."

Although a server works the front of the house tonight, Rob still leaves the kitchen frequently to talk to the tables, which means he has to prep and fire and plate the courses with lightning speed. Just watching Rob buzz around the awkwardly laid-out kitchen makes me tired, not to mention activating long-dormant waitress neurons that make me feel like I should be grabbing a plate and running it out to table six, or at least refilling water glasses. Since I haven't had dinner yet, it also makes me hungry, which gives me the hiccups. Rob notices.

"Picture seven bald men," he recommends, opening the oven to check on a pan full of braised lamb acquired from the local 4H. "Tyler swears by it."

Tyler is Rob's husband. According to him, the hiccup cure works by engaging both sides of your brain: there are the images of the bald men themselves—and they have to be seven *different* bald men—and then there's the number seven, which is more difficult to picture than one through six. While your mind is working on the problem, you're not thinking about your body, and when you stop thinking about your body, it can let go and relax.

When I look at Bear Creek I see a bunch of leafless trees clumped around a stream about four feet wide at its widest points, rocks half-immersed in sludgy, algae-clogged water, and dead leaves curling thick on the forest floor. When Rob looks, he sees food.

The morning that I go foraging with him, the only acorns and hackberries are lying on the ground, and Rob won't touch them. "If the animals haven't eaten them by now, they're bad," he explains. It's mid-February, and although minuscule buds on the gray branches hint at an early spring, our 6:00 a.m. hike down the trail to Bear Creek Ranch, an abandoned piece of heavily forested property in the Gila Mountains, is a chilly one.

Rob points out an animal track here, a pile of dead, curled-up grape leaves there. "You can eat those," he says of the leaves. "I'm trying to figure out something to do with the dry ones. I have some rotting in a jar right now, to see how they taste." Decomposing leaves sound more like mulch than a meal to me, but later I will put one in my mouth and chew the papery, tasteless thing until *zing*, right at the end, I taste the sweet-sour tang of grape hiding in the pulped leaf.

"Just don't say 'fermenting,'" he continues. "Everyone is fermenting everything right now."

We trek down to the water, where floating clumps of tiny ear-shaped leaves form the only green patches in a sea of brown. "Watercress is my favorite," he says. "It's delicious, it grows year round, and it's abundant." He doesn't take from this batch, though; there's a better place upstream. "Here," Rob says, pointing at it. "The motherlode." A huge shoulder of rock blocks the stream, forming a little pool where the watercress leaves have taken over. They lie on the surface of the water in patchy, sun-dappled blankets, Monet-style.

Rob is not excited about putting his hands in the freezing cold water, so I offer to help. "You want to get your hands all the way under there, pull them up by the roots," he says. "I'll put them in water when I get back to the restaurant." I push up my sleeve and dip my hand into the icy water, wiggling my fingers down in the muck underneath a promising clump of green leaves, dredging up black, sodden roots, pine needles, and mud along with the handful of watercress. I've only pulled two or three clumps before he says, "Okay, that's enough for today," and we dump our handfuls in the plastic grocery bag he brought for his purpose. "No more than ten, fifteen percent at most. It's in my best interest to let this pool regenerate, so I can come back here."

That's all we get for the morning's hike—less than a pound of watercress. If Rob had more time this morning, we might head another mile upstream. But tonight is the tasting dinner, and Rob is nervous. He still hasn't planned all of the courses, and there's the bustling lunch crowd to prep for, the sandwiches and soups that help pay the bills. When he picked me up that morning, when it was still dark outside, he told me he hadn't slept a single hour since we parted ways the night before. He lay awake, staring at the ceiling.

"I tried picturing bald men. George Costanza, Daddy Warbucks, Lex Luthor. Me." He smiles. "It didn't help."

Rob got into the locavore movement in the late '90s, when it was picking up steam around a confluence of worries about the environmental effect of industrial farming, the global dominance of American fast food chains, and the amount of fossil fuel needed to haul food grown at one end of the world to consumers at the other. The principles behind local food are good: grow, sell, buy, and eat close to home.

That changed for Rob the day he bit into a local hothouse tomato that was as tasteless as anything he'd ever bought at a grocery store. "I was like, why are we even doing this? Is it more nutritional? Does it taste better?"

Others were coming to similar conclusions. By introducing non-native species to climates and conditions that are less than ideal, gardens and organic farms may produce food that is local in name only. Foraging, the practice of harvesting food from the wild, is a logical extension of the locavore movement—only take what *wants* to grow.

Critics of foraging point out that it can alter the natural environment, sometimes ravaging native plant populations beyond repair. Sensitive to these critiques, Rob set out to learn ethical foraging practices from Doug Simons, a Grant County local who claims to have foraged all of his food for seven years. Born in rural Colorado, Simons went on a spirit quest when he was seventeen, sitting out in the wilderness for three days without food or water, guided by a teacher of his from the Lakota tribe. In addition to being a wildcrafting and foraging expert, he refers to himself as a "plant communication specialist" and carries a little leather pouch of dried tobacco on his belt for making offerings to the "plant people."

Rob doesn't talk to the plant people, and has only tried Doug's more esoteric methods once, when searching for the perfect yucca plant. (It didn't work.) Still, he treats them with a healthy dose of respect.

"There are different plant-specific rules, seasonal rules. If it's a grove of cattails, I'll only take pollen from fifteen percent of the plants, and I do only one little flick from each plant." He demonstrates, squinting as if a cattail head were in front of him and miming a well-aimed flick. "You could get fifteen flicks from each plant, but I need them to pollinate and propagate." Additionally, he insists the plants be located as far as possible from known sources of toxic chemicals, including not just pesticides, but parking lots, roads, and run-off from roads.

He has been working on an ethical foraging manifesto. So far, it goes like this:

1. I will not forage if I can see a road, no matter the size.
2. I will not forage downhill from a road or within a mile of one, even if I can't see it.
3. I will harvest no more than fifteen percent, or whatever percentage is necessary to maintain the thriving and propagating of the plant.

When you take a look at the manifesto, the problem with foraging-focused restaurants becomes self-evident: how can a restaurant located close enough to the kind of wild land that yields abundant, pollutant-free ingredients charge enough to make the massive investment of time and energy involved in foraging worthwhile? Yet the fashion for foraging has created a slew of modish foraging restaurants in big cities. Rob grumbles that when a chef in a major metropolitan area (he won't name the restaurant) can boast about gathering dandelion greens from a vacant lot on the next block over, the fad has officially triumphed over the food's flavor and health value. "Who knows what chemicals are in those greens?" he says. "I wouldn't eat them. I certainly wouldn't serve them."

Rob is also skeptical of foraging chefs who glean off the edges of commercial or private property. Ultimately, problems similar to those he found in the locavore movement have begun to disillusion him with the foraging trend as well. "I'm no expert, but I know what's right and wrong. Stealing and serving polluted food is wrong," he says. "I'm not the foraging Nazi, but people need to think about this stuff."

Incidentally, there are no kumquat dishes on the menu. Kumquats are not native to southwest New Mexico.

Rob admits to having a touch of the "best little boy in the world" syndrome.

Tyler has it too, he says. Both men came out in their late twenties, having grown up just on the cusp of the generation of gay men who came out earlier, in their teens. "I think a lot of us funneled our energy into being overachievers. When you're not telling your family or friends, you do all this stuff to make up for that. And when you're in the closet, you don't have romantic relationships to worry about either, so all that energy just goes straight into your work."

Rob Pauley grew up on the north side of St. Louis—"not the good side"—in a liberal Catholic family, the child of a single mother and the youngest of two. Early on, he set himself the goal of getting into a Catholic college prep high school on the west side of town, and he made it. In high school, he started running fifty-mile "ultra-marathons." At 6 foot 4 and 170 pounds, he still has a distance runner's build; back then, he weighed 135. "I was so fragile, you could snap me in half," he says.

After an undergraduate career at Loyola University that included a little bit of everything—he started out double majoring in art and education, then moved to a marketing and business major with a focus in nonprofit management—he went on to get a PhD in sports psychology from Purdue, where he researched identity formation in college athletes. Describing their mentality, he shakes his head. "For them, first place is winning, and second place is losing," he says. (I am reminded of this when he speaks of obsessively checking the restaurant's online reviews first thing in the morning.)

When Rob graduated, he was offered a job running a gym in Colorado. He and his girlfriend of the time, an MA in health promotion at Purdue, wanted to move in together, and wound up getting married in order to placate her ultra-conservative family. Rob came out two years later, at the age of twenty-seven. "It was a really good marriage," he says. "We were best friends. I cooked and cleaned and did all the gay things."

Rob met Tyler Connor in the summer of 2000. Rob was freshly back from a hiking trip in Peru, visiting his family in Indianapolis with the intention of leaving for a long mission trip to South America in the fall. Tyler was a seminarian at Earlham School of Religion, where he wrote, for his thesis, a midrash about eunuchs in the Hebrew bible. They met at a church-sponsored movie night. "That night he told me he was planning to come out to the Catholic mission organization," says Tyler. "I thought to myself, there's no way he'd going on that trip. So I made sure that we hung out together as much as possible. It took him about two months to decide he couldn't go. And by then we'd fallen in love."

Since Rob had the more marketable degree, they agreed to move wherever he found a job, leaving Tyler to write full-time. Rob applied for a job in nonprofit management in Silver City, and was hired based on a phone interview. Faced with the prospect of moving to a town with a population of 10,000, located at the terminal point of a state highway three hours off I-10, Rob and Tyler spent exactly one weekend thinking it over. "On Monday we quit our jobs. And *then* we bought plane tickets to come out and look at the place."

We are having this conversation at a dinner party hosted by the foster parents of an eleven-year-old Rob and Tyler are hoping to adopt. The boy is bright and energetic and clearly adores both of them. Rob has been sitting across the room tending the kid's skinned knee—sheepishly, since he was the one who encouraged him to show off on his skateboard—but, hearing Tyler tell this part of the story, he looks our way. "We were crazy."

"We were crazy," Tyler agrees. But, having grown up in a missionary family in South Africa, he felt a strange affinity for the landscape right away, the combination of dry, red cliffs like Rhodesian sandstone covered with scraggly pines. Tyler Connor and Rob Pauley settled down, got married in the liberal United Church of Christ where Tyler is now pastor, and combined their names to "Connoley"—a naming convention Tyler says he was drawn to from the age of nine, before he had an inkling he was gay.

Tyler's missionary family was far more conservative than Rob's liberal Catholic one. His coming-out was accordingly more traumatic, and included having to play along with an "ex-gay" therapy to avoid getting kicked out of his Christian college. A deeply religious man, he struggled through many years of spiritual searching before returning to Christianity via one of the most liberal strands of American Protestantism (the United Church of Christ is unaffiliated with the Church of Christ).

Rob, by contrast, speaks of his closeted years with a peculiar gratitude. "I went to college in New Orleans. The drinking age was eighteen, and it was 1986 to 1990, the height of the HIV epidemic. If I had come out then, I know I would be dead now."

If it seems odd to credit such a choking restriction with saving one's life, keep in mind that Rob seems to flourish in an atmosphere of restrictions.

The Javalina isn't the only coffee shop in Silver City, but it may have the most interesting history. Located at the corner of Bullard and

Broadway, the two streets that constitute downtown Silver City, the Javalina's spacious rooms are filled with mismatched couches, dining room tables, potted plants, and jigsaw puzzles beneath high, white, tin-tiled ceilings. The walls here are hung, as they are everywhere in Silver City, with oil canvasses, including Southwestern landscapes, abstract moderns, and a trio of painted replicas of community theater posters. "This is an artist community," Tom Hester days drily.

Tom, a statistician from Washington, D.C., who retired here with his wife Consuelo, works in the archive annex at the Silver City Museum. He modestly deflects the title of "town historian," but it's hard to imagine anyone knowing more about the town than Tom. His eyes burn brightly under bushy eyebrows and wire-rimmed glasses, and he leans forward when he talks, a slow, nasal drawl emitting from beneath his mustache. Tom tells me that the Javalina was once a merchandise store owned by H. B. Ailman, who sold a profitable gold mine in Silver City, opened a bank that quickly went bust, and then met up with Edward Doheny in Arizona. The two later drilled the first oil well in Los Angeles. (A thinly veiled version of Doheny was memorably played by Daniel Day Lewis in *There Will Be Blood*.) Ailman also discovered the Gila Cliff Dwellings, eight-hundred-year-old structures built into natural caves halfway up a cliff face in the Gila National Forest. He stumbled across them while avoiding jury duty.

Tom has a theory about most things in Silver City, including the Curious Kumquat, where he and Consuelo are regular customers. "I say Rob's food is a sort of joke," he says. "Rob hates when I say that, but it's true. He deconstructs the food, and then he reconstructs it. And what you end up with is a pun—what you're eating is not what you're eating." I think of the mozzarella balls that are actually corn shoot panna cotta, the pomegranate boba that look like caviar. "*The Cook, the Thief, His Wife and Her Lover* is his favorite movie. You look at that movie, and you can figure out what he's doing in the kitchen." (Watching the film later, I am at a loss. I wonder who is being fed pages of his own books, and who is being cooked and eaten.)

Tom's theory about Silver City is oddly similar to his theory about the Kumquat: it's like a giant pun. Picture a copper mining nestled in the Gila Mountains just east of the continental divide. The northernmost city in Grant County, it's not on the way to anywhere, excepting the Gila National Forest, whose cliff dwellings and hot springs draw light tourism. Founded in 1870, Silver City looks like other small western cities, but unlike most, it was never a railroad town—more of a loading dock for ore. There wasn't so much as a switchback; trains had to back sixty miles into the station.

Speaking to outsiders, citizens of Silver City frequently cite this isolation as a reason why so many diverse populations can live alongside one another peacefully. Conservative Anglo-Protestant ranchers, Catholic Hispanic miners, liberal hippie retirees, gay artists, and spiritual seekers attracted to the Sufi retreat outside of town—they live and work side by side in the tiny town that dead-ends in the Gila Mountains. As Rob says, "It's so small and so isolated that people have to get along. If they don't like gay men, where are they going to eat?"

Where most see isolation from the outside world, however, Tom Hester sees forgotten money trails and political influence that have fueled internal conflicts since the town's inception. Tom has picked apart the town history, deconstructed it down to its basic units of old newspaper clips, correspondence, deeds, and ledgers. And when he reconstructs it again, it is not diversity that he sees, but divisions—lasting, bitter, and often silent. Mexican mineworkers may no longer be relegated to Chihuahua Hill, where running water and paved streets were scarce into the twentieth century, but there is still a stark racial divide between the historic downtown district, where the houses all have wind chimes and colorful pendants and hand-tiled walls, and the outskirts, where Hispanic miners and service workers form a second city marked by the presence of a Walmart and a strip of sagging motels with kitschy signs.

In the late 1940s, Silver City was the site of a famous mining strike, an incident that divided the town: striking Mexican miners and the Catholic church on one side, Anglo-Protestant miners and bosses on the other. The sheriff eventually buckled to pressure from New York investors to crack down on the labor unions, and a court order against the miners took them away from the picket lines. The miners' wives, however, took over the strike, and were eventually arrested and marched to the county jail in a public relations disaster, some with small children in tow. Director Herbert Biberman, one of the Hollywood Ten and an avowed Communist sympathizer, came to Silver City shortly afterward to film a barely fictionalized movie version of the strike. Biberman cast most of the parts with original participants, including union leader Juan Chacon as the character based on himself. Mexican actress Rosaura Revueltas, who played the female lead, was deported during the making of the film; it had to be finished with a body double. The film only screened once in New York in 1954, just long enough for Pauline Kael to hate it and Bosley Crowthers to like it, before it was locked away, the only film to be blacklisted in the U.S.

A few years ago there was a symposium on the film at the Silver City Museum. Aging white labor organizer Clinton Jencks (who played the character based on himself in the movie) gave a moving speech, which was recorded by the museum. Some of the Mexican women who had participated in the strike itself were at the symposium too, but their panel, held in soft-spoken Spanish, was not recorded. Meanwhile, Tyler informs me that a local storytelling project is getting nowhere with the Hispanic population, because those old enough to tell the stories aren't talking. "They know better," he says. "You don't tell those stories to white people. White people don't want to hear them."

As for the more recently arrived inhabitants of Silver City—the hippies, the artists, the retirees, the gays—they are an awkward fit with the town's most established residents, the low-income mine-workers and libertarian ranchers who do not appreciate efforts to protect the endangered wolf population, among other things.

It was the Fourth of July when I first discovered the Curious Kumquat. The bed-and-breakfast where I was staying was tricked out with red-white-and-blue ribbons. My friend and I were searching for a restaurant that would be open on the holiday, and the proprietor pressed a few flyers for local restaurants into our hands. One photocopied menu on the side table caught my eye—*venison, foraged greens*—and we asked about it.

She shrugged. "Oh, that's that new place." (At the time, the Kumquat had been in operation for five years.) "It's kind of strange." She pointed to another menu. "This is where the locals go. You know, that other restaurant isn't even open half the time. You have to call. No, I wouldn't go there."

It's the big night, the night that Rob has been stressing out about so much that he canceled lunch earlier that day—the second time in eight years.

At the Javalina, Tom Hester may have held court, but at the Curious Kumquat, his wife Consuelo reigns supreme, wrapped in a fur with a big sparkling butterfly brooch. I am given the seat of honor right across from her at the long table where many of Tyler and Rob's church friends are sitting. Throughout the meal, Consuelo gets special treatment; Rob brings her an extra bite of her favorite course, spoonfuls of experimental sauce that didn't make it into the dinner. She tells me that when she and Tom first started eating at the Kumquat, she used to play a guessing game, deciphering Rob's puns into their distinct flavors. She describes her first encounter with boba, the translucent balloons of flavor formed by hydrocolloids that look like large caviar. Consuelo put one in her mouth, thought and thought, and finally said, "It tastes like beets." From that day forward she has been his champion taster.

As courses begin coming to the table, Consuelo concentrates on the task at hand. She holds each bite in her mouth for a moment, chews and swallows it carefully, then methodically eradicates the sauce, using her fingers to clean the dish down to its original Ikea whiteness. Then she pronounces. The chocolate-dipped aloo gobi sitting in a puddle of scented butter is perfect. She adores the beet soup in a pint glass, although she can't taste the cacao smoke. She struggles a bit with the salmon-stuffed cocoa ravioli wreathed with strands of bitter moss in a pool of murky squid ink, then points out that if you eat the moss in the same bite with the salmon they balance nicely. I agree; furthermore, sipping on the malbec pairing brings out a nice smoky flavor in the moss. The chocolate tamale topped with crunchy bits of caramelized black garlic is universally adored.

Then comes the main course: the goat with a rub of cocoa powder, peanuts, and vanilla beans, garnished with a beautiful fuchsia fleurette of beet foam. The taste is delicious, wild and rich, but the texture is sinister. Several are complaining that it's too rare. The atmosphere grows tense as knives and forks make screeching noises on the plates, mingled with the sound of silver clinking to a resting position as, one by one, the more delicate constituents of the United

Church of Christ give up. When the server comes to the table, Consuelo draws herself up to her full height. "The goat did not go."

"Didn't go?"

"Tough. Inedible."

Tyler leans forward. "Sometimes with these local goats that's a problem," he says. There's a brief chuckle over the phrase "local goats," but it does not distract Consuelo from the matter at hand.

"Someone needs to tell Rob about *cabritos*," she says. "The young goats."

By now Rob himself has appeared in the doorway. "It *is* young! Like, four months."

"No, no, I'm talking about two months. Two or three weeks, even. *Cabrito*."

"This isn't Mexico," Rob says impatiently, and disappears to chitchat with the other room, which is filled with strangers and tourists.

Rob always talks to each table, even when the restaurant is packed, and he remembers most of their names. It makes every guest feel special; plus it helps him sell wine, which is where Rob's restaurant makes its money. (At $44 for the standard seven-course tasting dinner and a $5 discount for locals, he certainly isn't making it off the food.) In the kitchen yesterday, Rob boasted about his tableside manner, but a moment later admitted he desperately needs the positive feedback. "If they're not gushing when they leave, I haven't done my job," he says.

A few minutes later, Rob pokes his head back in and says, "By the way, the other room loves the goat." Consuelo rolls her eyes.

Near the end of the meal, everyone at the table has had a fair bit of wine and a lot of food, even the ones who skipped the goat. Rob appears every once in a while to sag, exhausted, against the doorframe, and then disappears into the other room to talk up the folks who are visiting from out of town.

Tom Hester, who is sitting on my right side, begins to reminisce about the parties Rob and Tyler used to throw before they opened up the restaurant. "Tell her about the cheese club," Tom calls across the table to Tyler, who is sitting near the end.

Years ago, when they owned a gourmet grocery store down the street in a space that is now the Yada Yada Yarn Store, Rob and Tyler had a cheese club. Tyler says they were getting drunk over dinner one night and lamenting the lack of good cheese in town. Tipsy, Rob decided they should start a club. "We could call it the Cut the Cheese Club," he suggested. "Our motto will be, 'We Have a Friend in Cheeses.'"

"That's when I knew it was going to happen," Tyler says. He reels off a list of parties Rob themed around such fanciful ideas—the Outhouse Open House, with its hinged toilet seat invitation, or the "hoedown," when they mailed out unshucked ears of corn with invitations tucked carefully inside the husks. Once Rob threw a birthday party for one of the town's oldest citizens, seemingly for the excuse of sculpting the man's likeness from a giant hunk of Velveeta cheese.

The first Cut the Cheese Club meeting took place in Tyler and Rob's modest, one-story house. "Half an hour before the party was supposed to begin, Rob all of a sudden looks at that carpet and grabs a little corner and pulls it up. He says, 'There's a beautiful wood floor under here.' And next thing I know, he's pulling up the carpet." Tyler sighs dramatically. "People are coming over for a party in twenty minutes, and Rob is literally pulling up the carpet."

"The floors were beautiful!" Rob protests. "Aside from some foam and some carpet tacks."

The Cut the Cheese Club became a huge success. Rob and Tyler would order the pricey cheeses, portion them, and label them. Members were supposed to keep the tags for the cheese they had eaten and pay at the door on the way out to offset the cost. The club grew and grew, quickly becoming the most popular party in town. It outgrew residences, and Rob and Tyler started renting venues. People passing through town would somehow hear about the cheese club parties and gate-crash. Soon enough, Consuelo interrupts indignantly, people weren't even paying—they would just float in, hoover up some cheese, and take off. Moreover, they were drinking the expensive bottles of wine that Rob and Tyler ordered and leaving bottles of cheap wine in their place, a blatant abuse of the BYOB rule. "We would end the night with a dozen bottles of 'two-buck Chuck,'" Tyler complains, miming pouring a bottle down the sink.

Eventually, there were hundreds of people showing up at each party. Rob began ominously invoking the "final clause" in his emails to the membership. ("Rob had actually written up bylaws for the Cut the Cheese Club," Tyler explains. "And the final clause stipulated that when it stopped being fun, the club would immediately be put to death.")

But the last straw was the infamous furniture store party. The club had outgrown the largest venues in town, and the furniture retailer was a venue of last resort. Perhaps putting 250 people and several gallons of red wine in a closed furniture store for an evening was not the best idea. Stained upholstery was just the beginning.

"We had ordered this particular wine to go with one of the cheeses," Tyler relates. "Rob was really excited about it. It was more than usually challenging."

"And *expensive*," Rob adds.

People who dropped in for the party went, as usual, for the free booze, ignoring the pairings and gobbling cheese at will. However, the wine proved too challenging for casual gate-crashers (and, it is just possible, for some of the regulars as well). Raucous, intoxicated guests began tipping their glasses of wine into the potted plants. In the morning, every plant in the store was dead, the furniture store owners enraged.

Nobody else in town wanted to host the cheese club after that. The final clause was invoked, and the Cut the Cheese Club was no more. It would seem that Rob had reached the limits of the town's patience for highbrow food culture—the haute ceiling, as it were.

Tyler puts it in a more positive light. "The cheese club showed us that there really was a core group in town who would turn out for this kind of thing," he said. Without the Cut the Cheese Club, Tyler explains, the Curious Kumquat would not exist.

He mused for a moment. "The thing is, Rob doesn't even really care about cheese, do you, Rob?"

Rob smiles. "Not really," he says.

FIXED MENU

By Kevin Pang

From Lucky Peach

Chicago Tribune features reporter Kevin Pang's usual
beat is the cheap-eats end of food. But in a freelance gig
for *Lucky Peach*, he ventured even farther, discovering
a cadre of accidental chefs who really make do with
nothing—or at any rate, whatever they can scrounge
within prison walls.

I type this sentence twenty minutes after eating leftover spaghetti
and clams for breakfast, a Hungry Man-sized portion at nine a.m.
It is an exertion of my free will to do so. It is within my civil right as
a dedicated grocery shopper and keeper of leftovers, imprinted in the
Charter of Man, that I am free to eat however much I want, of what
I want, when I want.

In prison, that right is stripped away. Craving pizza on a Saturday
night? Feel like washing it down with cold beer? It's not happening.
Your right is reduced to eating portion-fixed food dictated by a warden on a set schedule. If you're hungry after dinner, you'll go to bed
hungry.

The thought of losing this control sends me into a panic attack.

The town of Westville sits beneath the southern curve of Lake Michigan, an hour's drive from Chicago, past the belching steel plants of
Northwest Indiana. It is every small American town that ever existed, a patchwork of green and brown rectangles on Google Map's
satellite view. On the two January days I visited Westville Correctional Facility, the winter's second polar vortex was bearing down

on Middle America, plunging daytime wind chills to −25 degrees Fahrenheit. Westville's position south of Lake Michigan also makes the area prone to biblical lake-effect snowstorms. And so, against the howling white-out squall, the eighty-five-acre prison—occupying about one-eighth of Westville—appeared utterly *gulag*-ish.

The first thing you notice when walking into Westville, however, is that the staff is unflinchingly Midwestern. Their jocular disposition—beginning with your pat-down officer at the security checkpoint—is unnervingly pleasant. I remember a coroner I met years ago who had the most inappropriately morbid sense of humor—he mimed the suicide victim on the gurney blowing his brains out, complete with exploding hand gestures from his temple. It was, I realized, a coping mechanism to deal with the darkness he sees daily, one that might explain why the prison staff (at least in the presence of a reporter) seemed so sunny.

To enter the prison compound proper, you step through a mechanized door into a holding cell, and wait as that door closes before a second door slowly grinds its metallic gears open. When that second door clangs shut with a sound just like in the movies, you enter a world of around 3,300 inmates, each serving an average of four years for offenses from burglary and drug possession to arson and worse.

Their favorite pastime seems to be staring at you. An Asian reporter and Hispanic photographer are curios when every day's the same day: wake up at five a.m., don your beige prison garb, work your twenty-cents-an-hour job, sit around in the dorms until lights out at eleven p.m. So the inmates are eager to talk, if just to break up the monotony. And when you mention you're here to write about food in prisons, it's like ramming a car into a fire hydrant and watching the water gush skyward.

"Why don't you grab one and eat with us, bro? And you tell us what you think," says Shaun Kimbrough, who's wheelchair-bound and serving a five-year sentence for aggravated battery. "It's gonna hurt your stomach, but we're used to it."

The Westville cafeteria, or "chow hall," is where the state of Indiana spends $1.239 to feed each prisoner each meal, three times a day. They line up single file, shuffling forward until they reach a waist-height hole in the wall. Every five seconds, a hardened plastic tray of compartmentalized food slides into view and is quickly picked up.

The transaction between server and inmate is an anonymous relationship, a food glory hole.

Today is fish sandwich day at Westville, and conspiracy theories abound.

"They know y'all coming, that's why they served fish," Kimbrough says. Apparently fish is one of the better-tasting offerings the prisoners see, in the way that canker sores are the best kind of ulcers. "That's a top-notch tray right there. But that fish patty, it ain't meat. It's just breading."

The fish patty sits atop three slices of white bread—two to make a sandwich, and the extra slice presumably to meet the 2,500 to 2,800 daily calories as recommended by the American Correctional Association for adult males under fifty. There's also a corn muffin, steamed carrots and green beans, plus mac and cheese sloshing around in a puddle of bright orange water. Some trays hold elbow pasta, others have corkscrew. Beverage is a Styrofoam cup of powdered tropical punch.

The most coveted items on the tray are the salt and pepper packets. Every person I surveyed, without fail, used the word "bland" in describing chow hall food. Rather than prepare separate trays for inmates with high cholesterol or blood pressure, the kitchen serves low-sodium meals for the entire prison population. Even with the added salt, though, it tastes like a vague notion of lunch, with all the flavor and pleasure of food eaten one hour after dental surgery.

Says Thomas Powell, who's serving time for drug dealing: "You're salting something with no flavor to begin with. It's tasteless. It's horrible. It's repetitive day after day." Powell brings packets of powdered ramen soup seasoning to sprinkle over his food. He is not alone in his desire for flavor—up and down the rows of steel tabletops, inmates pull out bottles of hot sauce they bring from the dorms, dousing their breaded fish and three slices of white bread.

The next most frequently utilized food descriptor is "mush." Food texture is difficult to retain when most meals are prepared several days before service—cooked, then quickly refrigerated in an industry-standard practice called blast-chilling. Reheating it, workers in the production kitchen claim, turns everything into a one-note texture more suitable for nursing homes.

Two entrées exemplify mush: goulash and chop suey.

On days these dishes are served, many inmates will skip their meals altogether. Hearing them describe the dishes is like listening to grandpa recall war atrocities he witnessed: spoken with a heavy sigh, best left in the past.

On goulash: "Noodles in red sauce . . . his tray may have meat, mine may not . . . the noodles have been overcooked so much, it's compacted together so it's like mush. You try to pick up one noodle and eighteen go along for the ride."

Two inmates have a conversation explaining chop suey:

"It's a bunch of cabbage and water."

"That's it. It may have a few grains of rice."

" . . . And corn if you're lucky."

"See, in mine, I don't remember corn."

An inmate named James Rogers speaks more broadly about dining in incarceration: "I've been here for six years. It has never changed. You came here on a good day. If you came out when they served the other stuff, you'd be horrified. We have no choice but to eat it."

I ask Warren Christian, in Westville the last five years for robbery, how long it took him to adjust to prison food.

"Years. It took years. Some people never get accustomed to it."

What was the turning point?

"Finally accepting the situation you're in. That you're not going anywhere until they release you."

Food is also served three times daily to the inmates at Westville Control Unit, its maximum-security ward, aka "supermax." Two types of offenders get a ticket here: 1) Those whose behavior while incarcerated necessitates segregation from the general prison population, and 2) Shot-calling gang leaders and inmates who committed a heinous crime.

The prison isn't bragging when they call it supermax. To reach fresh air from lockup requires getting past nine gates of electrified or impenetrable steel doors. Regardless of the guards and a separation of bulletproof glass, supermax is a frightening place to be. The inmates know you're there. Suddenly everyone appears at their cell-door window, a dozen pairs of eyes laser-trained in your direction. They scream at you. Through the glass partitions, we hear muffled banshee wails demanding to know our business.

For the correctional officers who deal with these hardest of the already-hard, protocol is to err on the side of extreme caution. They're required to serve food in pairs while wearing body-armor vests. One officer's job is to lock and unlock the cuff door, the steel flap where food slides through, while the other delivers the tray through the slot. Even for murderers, food hygiene is imperative, so guards wear latex gloves and hairnets while serving.

Truth be told, most of the time the place is more boring than dangerous.

"Boring is good, it's just a nice easy day for everybody," says Sgt. Carrie Sipich, a ten-year veteran at Westville.

In Sipich's domain, rapists and killers are schoolchildren who get occasionally unruly, like when they throw trays or swallow razor blades. Nothing shocks her anymore. One time when an inmate inserted a plastic fork up his penis hole, her reaction was an exasperated, *"Really?"*

She says: "I need a vacation because I'm laughing at things that aren't funny."

Horror stories about prison food reach their unappetizing nadir in the form of one particular dish. Its official name on Aramark Correctional Services recipe card M5978 is "Disciplinary Loaf." Inmates know it as "Nutraloaf," a baked foodstuff with the express purpose of providing the required daily nutrients and calories, and nothing more. Flavor isn't an afterthought, it's discouraged.

Nutraloaf's awful reputation is built upon myth, which simultaneously serves as a deterrent for bad behavior. No one I talk to has ever been punished with Nutraloaf, but everyone knows someone who has. Nutraloaf is reserved for offenses such as taking part in a riot or assaulting prison staff. Violators get placed in segregation and served a nineteen-ounce brick of Nutraloaf twice daily, typically for three consecutive days or until, in the words of Indiana Department of Corrections spokesman Doug Garrison, it achieves its intent of "behavior modification." Sgt. Sipich says she's only seen it served to two offenders in her tenure.

Officially, Nutraloaf is a blend of shredded cabbage, grated carrots, dry pinto beans, mechanically separated poultry, dairy blend, soy oil, scrambled-egg mix, and twenty-four slices of bread. It's shaped into a loaf and baked at 375 degrees for fifty to seventy minutes.

But Jesse Miller, serving in Westville for armed robbery, says he cooked Nutraloaf when he worked in the kitchen at another prison. He claims the recipe is more slapdash: "Say a meal was pudding, meat, green beans, potatoes. They throw that all in a blender. They'll throw Kool-Aid powder in it too. They can't say, 'I didn't get my juice.' 'Yes you did, it's in the Nutraloaf.' Then they pour it in a pan like pancake batter. It looks like vomit. I tasted it. It had no taste. It was like eating a sponge."

I didn't get to try Nutraloaf, but Jeff Ruby, dining critic at *Chicago* magazine, wrote about sampling it shortly after the Cook County Illinois Department of Corrections began implementing the Aramark recipe in June 2010. This is how he described it: "a thick orange lump of spite with the density and taste of a dumbbell . . . the mushy, disturbingly uniform innards recalled the thick, pulpy aftermath of something you dissected in biology class: so intrinsically disagreeable that my throat nearly closed up reflexively."

Kelly Banaszak, a spokesperson for Aramark, says its recipes are developed by registered dieticians: "While nutrition plays a big role, variety, taste, eye appeal, among others are considered in creating healthy, satisfying meals every day."

Aramark is the largest provider of prison-food services in the country, serving one million meals a day in more than 500 correctional facilities. For governments, privatizing prison-food services is an easy cost saver. Aramark, which also provides food for schools and sporting venues, holds contracts with six state-prison systems. That includes the Indiana Department of Corrections, which saved $7 million in the first year it contracted with Aramark in 2005. This year, that cost breaks down to $3.717 per Indiana prisoner.

When food costs are regimented and calculated to the tenth of a cent, inmate satisfaction takes a backseat. At an Aramark-contracted Kentucky prison in 2009, dissatisfaction over food was a contributing factor to a riot in which six buildings were set on fire. At the state hearing, a correctional officer present at the riot said that food quality plays a role in prison safety: "If you're hungry, you're going to get ornery."

In the recorded history of inmates vs. prison food, inmates usually end up on the losing side. In 2009, state budget woes forced the Georgia Department of Corrections to eliminate Friday lunches. It had already cut lunch on weekends, compensating with larger portions during breakfast and dinner. In 2010, Cook County Jail in Chicago stopped delivering breakfasts to inmates at four thirty in the morning, opting instead to serve it in the chow hall. Sheriff Tom Dart said he expected inmates would choose sleep over breakfast, at a savings of $1 million a year.

I bring this up with John Schrader, Westville's public information officer. He strikes a balance of empathy with the inmates while batting down many of their conspiracy theories. One persistent rumor is that kitchen workers once discovered a food box that read: "For zoo use only." Another is that the kitchen will "stretch out" the meals by adding water. Untrue, Schrader says.

He says the reality lies somewhere in the middle. For example, once a month the prison organizes an outside-food day with a local restaurant, like the Westville Dairy Queen, where inmates can order burgers and Blizzards. (The restaurant gets a five-digit payday; Westville gets a cut of the sales.)

He agrees the food at the prison is bland and portion sizes are tight. But he also says inmates should have realistic expectations.

"Food cannot be used as a disciplinary measure. I can't say you're getting less food because you're acting out. Food is essential. It's a basic human right. But we're also not going to give you shrimp," Schrader says. "It's not the quality of what you can get out in the real world. But is it something that's bad? Absolutely not. If I really wanted to be healthy, I'd stop eating at home and start eating three meals a day here."

Charlie Smigelski, a registered dietician from Boston, disputes the notion that prison food is healthy. Smigelski briefly worked in the Suffolk County Massachusetts House of Corrections as a medical-care contractor. He seems particularly aggrieved speaking about his experience: "At my prison, vegetable is a joke. You might get seven or eight carrot coins at supper, some wimpy lettuce. No one is looking at quality. Calories are made up by sugar—heavily sugared peaches and pineapple. They're living on white rice, pasta, and four slices of bread. Commissary food is by and large abysmal as well. Prison is supposed to be about the loss of liberty, not loss of life."

This idea of prison food—mainly, "What is good enough?"—requires a fair bit of philosophical reconciling. Constitutional scholars have argued the extent to which prisoners' rights are afforded ever since the 13th amendment was adopted: "Neither slavery nor involuntary servitude, except as a punishment for crime whereof the party shall have been duly convicted, shall exist within the United States." These terms leave a lot of leeway for interpretation when it comes to deciding what's for dinner in lockup.

One argument is the inmates broke societal law and deserve to be here, thereby forfeiting their right to complain about the mushiness of food. Another is that taxpayers foot the bill, so if they don't like the watery goulash, well, tough shit. The counterargument is that the $3.717 spent on each prisoner covers not only food costs, but labor, paper towels, and cleanup supplies, plus equipment repairs. At that price, you cannot possibly provide sustenance resembling anything a free citizen would deign to call food.

But is being fed poorly inhumane? Should criminals be deprived of any pleasure from food? Isn't that counterproductive if the purpose of imprisonment is rehabilitation?

Prisoner advocacy organizations exist in every state, in the form of religious groups and the ACLU, but getting substantive legislative reform for prisoners' rights is perhaps the steepest of uphill battles. For one, making the voting public empathize with criminals is a hard sell.

"I think prisoners are the most dehumanized people in our society by far. There's no comparison," says Jean Casella, co-director and Editor-in-Chief of Solitary Watch, an organization that studies prison conditions, specifically solitary confinement. "What the public will tolerate in terms of how badly we treat prisoners is really bad."

In her reporting on inmates kept in segregation, Casella tells me one of the most common privileges to be revoked is access to commissary food. "I question the idea of food deprivation on top of losing your freedom. Within prisons, there's no judge or jury. It's prison officials deciding if you go to solitary and be deprived of sunlight and human contact. It's prison officials who put you on Nutraloaf. I think it's barbaric."

Jean Terranova is now director of food and health policy at Community Servings, a Massachusetts agency providing medically tailored meals to people with critical illnesses. When she was a criminal defense attorney, she remembers seeing clients go into prison and within a short period of time, start looking like a different person.

"They're not getting the proper nutrition, they become lethargic. You're creating a litany of physical and behavioral health problems by being short-sighted at the beginning and not seeing the huge costs in health care later."

A 2010 report from the American Medical Association warns: "The high concentration of long-term inmates, with their corresponding increase in health-care needs as they age, has contributed to concerns about the nutritional adequacy of their diets as a means of preventing and managing chronic disease." The report projects that by 2030, more than one-third of prisoners in the U.S. will be over the age of fifty.

"Food is such an important part of the lives of people who are confined. With so many restrictions on their daily lives, meal time is one of the very few activities prisoners have to look forward to," Terranova says. "If you give them good food, it could vastly improve the psychosocial dynamic of the place."

Whether or not you believe prisoners deserve decent meals, the fact remains that prison food is terrible, full stop. So in many cases, inmates take matters into their own hands. Every two weeks, prisoners with enough money (mostly through the generosity of outside family) can order snack foods from commissary. The type of food available is stuff you'd see in the nonperishable aisle at 7-Eleven: summer sausage, precooked rice, cheese, tuna pouches. Well-off inmates will use up every dollar of their $70 limit per order. Those without outside financial support have a tougher go—prison jobs only pay around $25 a month, and most of that is spent on soap, toothpaste, socks, and other necessities.

Antonio Bishop, in Westville for arson, puts it bluntly: "If you don't have commissary food, you'll *never* make it."

Goods bought through commissary are the currency of the underground prison market, where services are rendered in exchange for food, even if prison policy prohibits the practice.

"If you want someone to draw a portrait for your family, you pay them in commissary," says Zach Adams, serving for parole violation. "Maybe you have [postage] stamps and I don't. Or, you say, 'Make me a nice birthday card for my son, I'll give you some of my food.' I mean, you're not supposed to, but yeah, it's a black market."

Others tell me cigarettes and K2, a synthetic marijuana, are also traded for commissary food. The going rate for a prison tattoo is six soups, a meat log, and a few bags of chips—about $5 worth of food. (Prison tattoo ink can be made by microwaving bottled hair grease; the needle is fashioned from a piece of metal window screen.)

What's most remarkable to me is the culinary creativity the limited resources of prison yield. All Indiana Department of Corrections offenders in dorms have access to an ice maker, hot-water dispenser, and microwave. That's enough to concoct some wildly elaborate dishes out of commissary food. At one of Westville's sister prisons, inmates at Rockville Correctional Facility even published a fifty-three-page cookbook of commissary food recipes, from twice-baked potatoes to salmon soup.

I coaxed David Lawhorn into sharing his proprietary cookie cake recipe: "You take Oreo cookies, split them apart, and put the cream in a separate bowl. Take the cookies and crush it down. Then take Kool-Aid, not the sugar-free kind, put it with the crushed-up cookies, and add Pepsi to make a batter. Microwave it for seven minutes, and it turns out fluffy, like a cake you'd put in the window that costs $20. Take the Oreo cream and put that on top. I also sprinkle trail mix on mine."

Lazaro Valadez has earned some renown in dorm D-2 east for this dish: "Buy two bags of pork rinds, spicy Cajun mix, sweet corn, rice, and Kool-Aid tropical punch mix, not the sugar-free kind. You add a Cajun mix, corn, and pork rinds in a trash bag. Get Kool-Aid in a cup, mix it with a little bit of water until it's real thick, and pour it in the bag with the pork rinds. Mix all that up, and stick it in a microwave for six minutes. It comes out real gummy, and you layer that over rice. It's sweet and sour pork. It's not bad."

The most widely-traded commissary good is Maruchan-brand ramen noodles. Three bags cost $1. As food goes, it's a versatile product: its noodles can be used as a starch base and the soup packet as seasoning salt. I watch Kamil Shelton crush his "Texas Beef"-flavored ramen, boil the broken noodles inside its bag, squeeze out excess water, stuff with sausage, and form into a cylinder: prison burrito. "It's better than what they feed us in chow hall," he says.

There's no actual chicken in the prison chicken nugget recipe, but commissary connoisseurs still manage to re-create the dish as a placebo food. Two inmates named Jan Kosmulski and Troy Peoples explain:

Kosmulski: "Take ramen noodles, boil it down to literally mush. You ball it up, put a piece of cheese and beef sausage in the middle. Make sure it's tightly wound up. You cook it in the microwave for ten minutes until it's brown."

Peoples: "It's not actually a chicken nugget. It's the idea. It's only in your mind. If you ain't had a chicken nugget in a while, and it's in the shape of a chicken nugget, it'll remind you of a chicken nugget."

It's commissary day at dorm A-3, and four inmates gather in the microwave alcove. They've pooled their resources, each buying specific ingredients, and for the last two hours they have collaborated on a food project. Ingredients are organized with precision like mise en place at a fine restaurant.

The chef de cuisine is Mike McClellan, who's earned the reputation as the Thomas Keller of cellblock A-3. McClellan, a soft-spoken forty-four-year-old man sentenced through 2017 for stalking, says Westville is the therapeutic community he needs to turn his life around. Having earned his associate's and bachelor's degrees, he's now at work on his master's. McClellan says he has two passions in life: Jesus Christ and cooking.

Pastor Mike, as he's known, spearheads two recipes today: tortellini and chicken Florentine soup. I try a sip of the latter, made from pouch chicken, garlic powder, ramen soup mix, powdered coffee creamer, and dried Thai rice noodles. It tastes as you might expect— one step above emergency-packet soup reconstituted with hot water.

I offer: "That's pretty good."

Pastor Mike corrects me: "No, that's excellent."

With tortellini, his attention to detail is even more impressive. Pastor Mike takes pizza dough from a Chef Boyardee pizza kit and simmers it in water for three minutes in a microwave. He lays out the cooked squares of pasta. Pastor Mike creates the filling by dicing pepperoni and pepper jack cheese with the lid of a tin can. He hovers over his ingredients the way a molecular gastronomist hunches with tweezers.

He microwaves the filling with tomato pizza sauce and powdered creamer until it turns into a paste, which he encloses in dough and cooks once more in hot water. The finished product comes out as rustic crescents of dumpling, a nod to Pastor Mike's Italian heritage. For a moment the four cooks shed their prison wear and are dining at a fancy Italian restaurant. They eat like free men. Two hours toiling for a brief transportive respite from this forsaken place.

There's a secondary market for these kinds of prepared foods. Down the hall in dorm A-3, three inmates sit around a metal bench strewn with candy. Their setup is a complicated assembly line involving a microwave, plastic bowls, a container filled with ice water, popsicle sticks, and parchment paper. It looks like a home chemistry kit.

The three have spent the last few hours making lollipops at a pace of one every five minutes. They'll spend the next few hours making lollipops, until their candy stash runs out.

The head chef is John Hopkins, whose goatee and thick glasses makes him resemble Walter White circa Season 3 *Breaking Bad*. Seated next to him is Frederick Betts, Jr. who incredibly, is a dead ringer for Jesse Pinkman circa Season 4 *Breaking Bad*.

Hopkins learned the lollipop trade from a fellow inmate, and since that inmate's release, Hopkins has taken over as resident candy expert. He estimates he's cooked up six hundred-plus lollipops, and has mastered all the subtleties of the art.

He explains that different confectionaries have different melting points, depending on whether they are made of corn syrup or sugar. So they need to be cooked on a staggered schedule, with butterscotch discs going in the microwave first, followed by Jolly Ranchers, and Now And Laters last, which only need ten seconds to soften.

The mixture comes out of the microwave bubbling, which Hopkins immediately whips with a popsicle stick. At a precise moment, he dunks the bowl into an ice bath, which releases the hardening goo from its container. He wraps this with parchment paper and molds the lollipop by hand around the popsicle stick.

"Some guys, they make it flat and round, but it don't fit in the mouth that well," Hopkins says. "We make it into an egg shape. We say, 'customer friendly.'"

The base of the popsicle stick is marked with a letter. L is lemon drop. B is butterscotch. G is grape. I can already see these in a Brooklyn boutique, labeled PENAL SUCKERS and sold for $4 a pop.

I ask John: "What are you in Westville for?"

"Manufacturing meth."

Ron Edwards, 62, has worked within every aspect of the restaurant industry, from running the front-of-house at fine-dining establishments to owning his own place. Now, he teaches culinary arts to fourteen of the luckiest inmates at Westville.

Lucky, because students taste what they cook. When the alternative is goulash, chicken parmigiana is Christmas arriving twice a week.

Those accepted into the twelve-week cooking program are screened by case managers for past behavior and future potential, which is why Edwards has never had a problem giving inmates access to sharp implements. Completing the program has major incentives, too—graduates get three months knocked off their sentences. The waiting list for this class is around half a year.

We arrive for a luncheon cooked entirely by Edwards' students. Today's guests are a mostly female group who handle crisis management in the event a prison riot breaks out. The dining space is elegant in a way a mock restaurant at a high school home-economics program would be—adorned almost entirely in blue, decorated with portraits of inmates dressed in chef's whites.

A man with tattoos for sleeves brings out a starter course of shrimp cocktail. Shrimp cocktail! He does everything expected of a server at a white-tablecloth restaurant—walks through the dining room with erect posture, picks up silverware without a clank, and responds to your thank yous with, "You are very welcome." After the cocktail comes cream of broccoli soup and chef's salad with chopped ham. For the entrée: roast pork and gravy alongside mashed potatoes and "Hoosier beans," which are green beans with sautéed bacon and onions. Dessert is cheesecake with blackberries.

"Someone at the local newspaper recently asked for one of the inmates' recipes. It's the first time they're in the paper for something good, and not in the crime blotter," Edwards says. "The class is about teaching them the basic things about life. They don't have a lot of confidence. We try to instill that."

After the luncheon guests depart, the cooks and servers sit in the blue room to feast on their efforts. They eat their massive portions in silent preoccupation. If you remember that scene in *The Shawshank Redemption* where an exclusive group of inmates enjoy an ultra-rare treat of cold beers on the rooftop, you'll have a sense for the joy of these Westville men.

I ask them about what it means to lose the freedom to eat what they choose, and they begin to reminisce wistfully. Adam McDonald brings up his grandmother, who made him appreciate food at age ten when she taught him to cook steaks and grilled cheese sandwiches. He worked at several fast-food chains before getting sent to Westville for burglary. When he's released in six months, McDonald says he'd like to cook in a fine-dining restaurant.

"In a prison system, there are times you look around and you don't feel like anything," McDonald says. "To eat off of glass dishes and metal forks instead of plastic bowls and spoons . . . I've been in a better mood since I started this class."

While serving a thirteen-year sentence for cocaine possession, Jauston Huerta became a published author—writing a children's book called *Micheliana & the Monster Treats*. It's about a dragon that attacks a village, and the young princess who hatches a plan to feed the dragon to stop its rampage.

Huerta says, "Next to my family, food is a definite component that's a constant reminder my freedom has been taken. Because I have to eat something I don't want to eat. It causes you to really appreciate your freedom and what you left behind out there."

A kitchen worker walks by with a platter filled with shrimp cocktail.

Huerta's eyes follow. "That's the point. That's the point."

Says McDonald: " . . . to feel human again."

LAST MEALS

By Brent Cunningham

From Lapham's Quarterly

⟨⟨&⟩⟩

Journalist Brent Cunningham, who is deputy editor of
the *Columbia Journalism Review*, keeps us honest with
his determination to buck the trends, to tell the stories
that *aren't* being told—in this case, on Death Row.

I n January 1985, Pizza Hut aired a commercial in South Carolina
that featured a condemned prisoner ordering delivery for his last
meal. Two weeks earlier, the state had carried out its first execution
in twenty-two years, electrocuting a man named Joseph Carl Shaw.
Shaw's last-meal request had been pizza, although not from Pizza
Hut. Complaints came quickly; the spot was pulled, and a company
official claimed the ad was never intended to run in South Carolina.

It's not hard to understand why Pizza Hut's creative team thought
the ad was a good idea. The last meal offers an irresistible blend
of food, death, and crime that drives a commercial and voyeuris-
tic cottage industry. Studiofeast, an invitation-only supper club in
New York City, hosts an annual event based on the best responses
to the question, "You're about to die, what's your last meal?" There
are books and magazine articles and art projects that address, among
other things, what celebrity chefs—like Mario Batali and Marcus
Samuelsson—would have for their last meals, or what the famous and
the infamous ate before dying. Newspapers reported that Saddam
Hussein was offered but refused chicken, while *Esquire* published
an article about the terminally ill François Mitterrand, the former
French president, who had Marennes oysters, foie gras, and, the *pièce*

de résistance, two ortolan songbirds. The bird is thought to represent the French soul and, because it's protected, is illegal to consume.

While the number of yearly executions in the United States has generally declined since a high of ninety-eight in 1999, the website Dead Man Eating tracked and commented on last-meal requests of death-row inmates across the country during the first decade of the new millennium. One of the site's last posts, in January 2010, was the request of Bobby Wayne Woods, who was executed in Texas for raping and killing an eleven-year-old girl: "Two chicken-fried steaks, two fried chicken breasts, three fried pork chops, two hamburgers with lettuce, tomato, onion, and salad dressing, four slices of bread, half a pound of fried potatoes with onion, half a pound of onion rings with ketchup, half a pan of chocolate cake with icing, and two pitchers of milk."

There are also efforts to leverage the pop-culture spectacle of last meals to protest the death penalty. An Oregon artist has vowed to paint images of fifty last-meal requests of U.S. inmates on ceramic plates every year until the death penalty is outlawed. Amnesty International launched an anti–capital punishment campaign this past February that featured depictions of the last meals of prisoners who were later exonerated of their crimes.

No matter your stance on capital punishment, eating and dying are universal and densely symbolic human processes. Death eludes the living, and we are drawn to anything that offers the possibility of glimpsing the undiscovered country. If, as the French epicure Anthelme Brillat-Savarin suggested, we are what we eat, then a final meal would seem to be the ultimate self-expression. There is added titillation when that expression comes from the likes of Timothy McVeigh (two pints of mint-chocolate-chip ice cream) or Ted Bundy (who declined a special meal and was served steak, eggs, hash browns, toast, milk, coffee, juice, butter, and jelly). And when this combination of factors is set against America's already fraught relationship with food, supersized or slow, and with weight and weight loss, it's almost surprising that Pizza Hut didn't have a winner on its hands.

The idea of a meal before an execution is compassionate or perverse, depending on your perspective, but it contains an inherently curious paradox: marking the end of a life with the stuff that sustains it seems at once laden with meaning and beside the point. As Barry Lee Fairchild, who was executed by the state of Arkansas in 1995, said in regard to his last meal, "It's just like putting gas in a car that don't have no motor."

On January 14, 1772, in Frankfurt am Main, Susanna Margarethe Brandt prepared for her execution—she had killed her infant daughter—by sitting down to a sprawling feast with six local officials and judges. The ritual was known as the Hangman's Meal. On the menu that day were "three pounds of fried sausages, ten pounds of beef, six pounds of baked carp, twelve pounds of larded roast veal, soup, cabbage, bread, a sweet, and eight and a half measures of 1748 wine." Had she committed the crime in neighboring Bavaria, Brandt likely would have preceded the meal with a morning drink in her cell with the man who would later decapitate her with a sword. This shared aperitif was called St. John's Blessing, after John the Baptist, who is said to have forgiven those who were about to behead him.

Brandt, who was twenty-five years old and is supposed to have inspired Johann Wolfgang von Goethe's character Gretchen in *Faust*, reportedly managed nothing more than a glass of water. Her companions in the repast fared little better.

The origins of the last-meal ritual aren't settled. Although the earliest record of the death penalty is the Sumerian Code of Ur-Nammu in the twenty-second century BC, some scholars suggest the last meal may have begun in ancient Greece, and in Rome gladiators were fed a sumptuous last meal, the *coena libera*, the night before their date in the Colosseum. In eighteenth-century London, favored or better-off prisoners were allowed a party with food and drink and outside guests on the night before they were hanged. The next day, as the prisoner traveled the three miles from Newgate Prison to the gallows at Tyburn Fair, the procession would stop at a pub for the condemned's customary "great bowl of ale to drink at their pleasure, as their last refreshment in life." (England's noble or high-born criminals, such as Anne Boleyn and the earl of Essex, were beheaded elsewhere, often at the Tower of London; Walter Raleigh reportedly took a last smoke from his tobacco pipe before he lost his head in Old Palace Yard at Westminster.) In the New World, the Aztecs feasted some of those who were tapped for ritual sacrifice, as part of a pre-execution deification ceremony that could last up to a year. Typically, these were warriors captured on the battlefield, and in some cases, after they were killed, their captor was given much of the body for use in *tlacatlolli*, a special stew of corn and human flesh that was served at a banquet with the captor's family.

Today, most countries that use the death penalty as part of their criminal-justice systems offer some sort of last meal. Along with the United States, Japan and South Korea are the only industrialized democracies among the fifty-eight countries in the world that employ capital punishment, and in Japan, the condemned don't know when they will be executed until the day arrives. In the 2005 documentary *Last Supper*, by the Swedish artists Mats Bigert and Lars Bergström, Sakae Menda, who spent thirty four years on death row in Japan, said inmates may request whatever they want; if no request is made, prison officials provide "cakes, cigarettes, and drink." Duma Kumalo, who spent three years awaiting death in South Africa, told the filmmakers that he was served a whole deboned chicken and given seven rand—about six dollars—to purchase whatever else he wanted. "What we bought before execution, it was not things that we wanted to eat," said Kumalo, who was spared for reasons he does not explain, just hours before he was to be killed. "Those were the things which we were going to leave behind with those who would remain. Because people were starving."

In America, where the death rows—like the prisons generally—are largely filled with men from the lower rungs of the socio-economic ladder, last-meal requests are dominated by the country's mass-market comfort foods: fries, soda, fried chicken, pie. Sprinkled in this mix is a lot of what social scientists call "status foods"—steak, lobster, shrimp—the kinds of foods that in popular culture conjure up the image of affluence. Every once in a while, though, a request harkens back to what, in the Judeo-Christian West, is the original last meal—the Last Supper, when Jesus Christ, foreseeing his death on the cross, dined one final time with his disciples. Jonathan Wayne Nobles, who was executed in Texas in 1998 for stabbing to death two young women, requested the Eucharist sacrament. Nobles had converted to Catholicism while incarcerated, becoming a lay member of the clergy, and made what was by all accounts a sincere and extended show of remorse while strapped to the gurney. He sang "Silent Night" as the chemicals were released into his veins.

The musician Steve Earle, whom Nobles asked to be among his witnesses at the execution, wrote of the experience in *Tikkun* magazine, "I do know that Jonathan Nobles changed profoundly while he was in prison. I know that the lives of other people with whom he came in contact changed as well, including mine. Our criminal justice system isn't known for rehabilitation. I'm not sure that, as a society, we are even interested in that concept anymore. The problem is that most people who go to prison get out one day and walk among us. Given as many people as we lock up, we better learn to rehabilitate someone. I believe Jon might have been able to teach us how. Now we'll never know."

As of June of this year, governing bodies in the U.S. and its colonial predecessors had executed some 15,825 men and women since the first permanent European settlements were established. The majority of them, it seems, did not get a special last meal; the Newgate Prison parties didn't make the crossing with William Bradford and John Carver aboard the *Mayflower*. There is no record of a last meal for George Kendall, believed to be the first Englishman executed in the New World, who was accused of spying for Spain and shot in Jamestown in 1608. (The nature of criminal justice around that time was such that Kendall would also have been shot—or hanged, beheaded, or burned at the stake—for stealing grapes.)

Scott Christianson, who has written extensively on the history of American prison culture, believes the standardized last meal probably emerged around the end of the nineteenth century or the beginning of the twentieth, with the rise of a modern administrative state. Messy and raucous public executions fell out of favor with the more refined sensibilities of the upper and middle classes, and ideas of man's ability for moral improvement fueled opposition to the death penalty. Rehabilitation, rather than simply deterrence and retribution, became an important aim of criminal sanction. At the same time, though, there was still a strong fear of social disorder; the assertive state governments were eager to find better ways to keep the peace in a fledgling nation whose cities were growing, industrializing, and diversifying.

The answer, or so it seemed, was to replace the more communal sanctions of the colonial and early republic era—fines, banishment, floggings, labor—with long-term incarceration in state-run penitentiaries. Criminals would be isolated from society and purged of their deviant impulses. Executions, which had long been believed to have a scared-straight effect on the public, were now thought to inspire the very violence they were meant to deter. They moved to yards inside the prisons, where the witnesses were only a select few, usually prominent officials and merchants.

In addition to efficiency and decorum, Christianson writes, another "new aspect of this choreographed ritual of death entailed the release of detailed reports to the public that described," among other things, "precisely what the condemned had requested as his or her last meal." This gave the impression of a humane and dispassionate custodial government authority, but it also—intentionally or not—tapped into a bit of the old public fascination with executions, when a family might hop in the wagon, ride to the town square with a picnic basket in tow, and watch someone be "launched into eternity."

The press, Christianson says, "ate it up." This was the dawning of the penny press, when steam-driven printing presses spurred the development of a mass media in America. As executions vanished inside penitentiaries, newspapers discovered that the public was still eager for accounts of the proceedings. In 1835, for instance, readers of New York's *Sun* and *Herald* newspapers learned that Manual Fernandez, among the first men at Bellevue Prison to be privately executed, enjoyed cigars and brandy on his last day, compliments of the warden.

Nearly two hundred years later, America is in the grips of a revolution in communication technology even more pervasive than the penny press. The death penalty was resurrected in 1976, after a ten-year-long, nationwide moratorium, and public interest in last meals was rekindled along with the debate over capital punishment. But, initially due to the rapidly merging news and entertainment industries, and eventually to the Internet, the debate was amplified and widened. In 1992, presidential candidate and Arkansas governor Bill Clinton was excoriated over his refusal to stop the execution in his state of Rickey Ray Rector, a man so mentally impaired that he asked to have the slice of pecan pie he had requested as part of his last meal saved so that he could eat it later—and that morbid fact became the story's enduring detail. Before long, state corrections departments began posting last-meal requests on their websites. Texas, which was the first to do so, shut down its last-meals page in 2003, after it received complaints about the unseemly nature of the content.

The last meal as a cultural phenomenon grew even as capital punishment faded from public view, and in less than two centuries the country has gone from grisly public hangings, in which the prisoner was sometimes unintentionally decapitated or left to suffocate, to lethal injection, the most common form of execution in America today, in which death is "administered." The condemned are often sedated before execution. They are generally not allowed to listen to music, lest it induce an emotional reaction. Last words are sometimes delivered in writing, rather than spoken; if they are spoken, it might be to prison personnel rather than the witnesses. The detachment is so complete that when scholar Robert Johnson, for his 1998 book *Death Work*, asked an execution-team officer what his job was, the officer replied: "the right leg."

The public disappearance of state-sanctioned killing mirrors the broader segregation of death in an increasingly death-shy society. Dying, which had traditionally happened at home, surrounded by family and friends, began migrating into hospitals in the late nineteenth century, which is where most people die today.

Rituals like the Hangman's Meal and the Aztec sacrificial feasts were anything but detached. They were concerned with the spirituality of death—forgiveness, salvation, appeasing the gods, marking the transition from living to dead. Although prisoners may still pray with clergy, the execution process has been drained of its spiritual and emotional content. The last meal is an oddly symbolic and life-affirming ritual in the vigorously dehumanized environment of death row. In that sense, it's hard to see the modern last meal in America as actually being about anything.

The last meal, though, is in some ways just an extreme example of the intimate relationship between food and death that is a part of end-of-life customs in nearly all societies. Christianity, after all, tethers the very idea of death to a culinary transgression: Eve and that damned apple. The ancient Egyptians painted images of food on the walls of tombs, so that if the deceased's ancestors ever failed in their duty to make offerings, his soul would still be nourished and comforted. Native Americans observed a variety of ceremonies involving food when a member of a tribe died. The northeastern Hurons, for example, held a farewell feast to help them die bravely: the dying man was dressed in a burial robe, shared special foods with his family and friends, gave a speech, and led everyone in song.

Buddhists make food offerings to appease what the Japanese call *gaki*, or "hungry ghosts," lest they return to haunt the living. Food is integral to Mexico's Day of the Dead—which descended from Aztec festivals—when it is believed that departed souls return to earth. Graves are cleaned and repainted, and offerings of special foods—tamales and moles, sweet *pan de muerto*, skulls concocted of sugar (historically made of amaranth seeds), and liquor—are left for the dead to entice them to visit. And in America, food is brought to the family of the deceased after a funeral for comfort and convenience.

The Chinese, especially, use food to nourish and protect the dead—ancient Chinese even buried their dead with miniature models of stoves so they could prepare meals eternally—but they also, in return, hope to secure the dead's blessings of prosperity, good health, and fertility upon the surviving family members.

When someone dies, one of the first tasks for the family is to help the deceased break from the community—to physically leave it—and begin the transformation from corpse to ancestor. Food is central to this process, sometimes as enticement and at other times as prod. In her book *The Cult of the Dead in a Chinese Village*, Emily Ahern describes how in one funerary ritual, a small bowl of cooked rice and a cooked chicken head are dumped on the ground. A dog is shown the food, and once the dog gets the chicken head in its mouth, it is "beaten with a long, whiplike plant until he dashes away in a frenzy . . . The dog represents the dead man, the chicken head the property" that belongs to his family. The idea is to chase away the dead man and make clear that "he has enjoyed his share of the property, so he should not come back and bother the living."

What unites these customs is an emphasis on the needs of the living, not just the dead; so too with last meals before an execution. When Susanna Margarethe Brandt sat down to the Hangman's Meal, she signaled that she was cooperating in her own death—that she forgave those who judged her and was reconciled to her fate. Whether she actually made those concessions or not is beside the point; the officials who rendered and carried out her sentence could fall asleep that night with a clear conscience.

With the American public now excluded from the execution process, much of the larger societal meaning of capital punishment, and last meals, has been lost. The community is no longer involved. In colonial America, executions were opportunities to reinforce publicly the Calvinist belief in the innate depravity of man, and also provided a little entertainment. People thronged to see how someone facing the final mystery of life behaved. On October 20, 1790, a crowd of thousands watched thirty-two-year-old Joseph Mountain, convicted of rape, be hanged on the green in New Haven, Connecticut. Would he confess and repent, as authorities hoped, or would he die "game," denouncing the sentence?

Over the latter half of the twentieth century, with the notion of deterrence unproven and the promise of rehabilitation mostly forgotten, retribution and general incapacitation became the primary goals of the American criminal-justice system. This was in part due to the changing political climate. The neoconservative movement rose from the ashes of Barry Goldwater's defeat in the presidential election of 1964, tapping into public concerns about the rising crime rate, a growing disaffection for social-welfare programs, and the unrest evident in the opposition to the Vietnam War as well as urban race riots. In response came the Rockefeller drug laws in New York, which launched over thirty years of tough-on-crime policies, and Ronald Reagan's warning of the corrosive effects of the "welfare queen" who cheats the system. "Individual responsibility" became the defining doctrine for everything from America's economic life to its crime-fighting strategies.

In 2007 the U.S. Supreme Court effectively upheld the retributive theory of capital punishment, and the idea of individual responsibility, when it ruled that a mentally ill prisoner could not be executed if he lacked a rational understanding of *why* the state was killing him, even if he was aware of the facts of the state's case. As Justice Anthony Kennedy wrote for the court, "It might be said that capital punishment is imposed because it has the potential to make the offender recognize at last the gravity of his crime and to allow the community as a whole . . . to affirm its own judgment that the culpability of the prisoner is so serious that the ultimate penalty must be sought and imposed."

In other words, the public's need for retribution requires criminals that are somehow irredeemable monsters who still know right from wrong and freely chose to do horrible things; they are certainly not the profoundly disabled or the unfortunate byproducts of societal or familial breakdowns. But the image of the morally culpable public enemy is difficult to sustain in a criminal-justice system that strips away the prisoner's individuality and free will, reducing him to something seemingly less than human. It's hard for people to experience a satisfying sense of retribution when the state is, in effect, exterminating something aberrant and abstract, much as a surgeon removes a malignant tumor.

In the nineteenth century, when the American government was ending public executions, officials struggled with a similar dilemma. Historian Louis P. Masur explains how, without the official moralizing sermons that had accompanied public hangings, people "were free to construct their own interpretations rather than receive only an official one." There was concern that executions carried out in private could foster doubts that justice was being done—that the prisoner was in fact guilty and that the proceedings had been fair. In short, whether the convict was indeed an irredeemable monster. In an effort to reclaim control of the narrative of capital punishment, the authorities saw the benefit of the new mass-circulation newspapers to feed the public information about executions. The press accounts made it seem that the public still had some sort of informal oversight of the killing done in its name.

Daniel LaChance, an assistant professor of history at Emory University, has argued that the rituals of a last meal—and of allowing last words—have persisted in this otherwise emotionally denuded process precisely because they restore enough of the condemned's humanity to satisfy the public's desire for the punishment to fit the crime, thereby helping to ensure continued support for the death penalty. As LaChance puts it, "The state, through the media, reinforces a retributive understanding of the individual as an agent who has acted freely in the world, unfettered by circumstance or social condition.

And yet, through myriad other procedures designed to objectify, pac-ify, and manipulate the offender, the state signals its ability to maintain order and satisfy our retributive urges safely and humanely." A win-win. The state, after all, has to distinguish the violence of its punishment from the violence it is punishing, and by allowing a last meal and a final statement, a level of dignity and compassion are extended to the condemned that he didn't show his victims. The fact that the taxpayers are picking up the tab for these sometimes gluttonous requests only bolsters the public's righteous indignation.

The final turn of the screw is that prisoners often don't get what they ask for. It is the request, and not what is ultimately served—let alone what's actually consumed, which is often little or nothing—that is released to the press and broadcast to the public. Most states have restrictions on what can be served and how much of it, a monetary limit, for instance, or based on what's in the prison pantry on a given day.

So that filet mignon and lobster tail? It's likely to end up being chopped meat and fish sticks, according to Brian Price, an inmate who cooked final meals for other prisoners in Texas for over a decade before he was paroled in 2003 (and subsequently wrote a book about the experience called *Meals to Die For*). The 2001 book *Last Suppers: Famous Final Meals from Death Row*, includes this teaser: "How's this for a last meal: twenty-four tacos, two cheeseburgers, two whole onions, five jalapeño peppers, six enchiladas, six tostadas, one quart of milk, and one chocolate milkshake? That's what David Castillo, convicted murderer, packed in the night before Texas shot him up with a lethal injection."

What Castillo, who was executed in 1998 for stabbing a liquor-store clerk to death, actually got for his last meal was four hard-shell tacos, six enchiladas, two tostadas, two onions, five jalapeños, one quart of milk, and a chocolate milkshake. A hefty spread, but not quite the jaw-dropper he ordered.

And so it came to pass in Texas in 2011 that the state stopped offering special last meals, after Lawrence Russell Brewer ordered two chicken-fried steaks, one pound of barbecued meat, a triple-patty bacon cheeseburger, a meat-lover's pizza, three fajitas, an omelet, a bowl of okra, one pint of Blue Bell Ice Cream, some peanut-butter fudge with crushed peanuts, and three root beers—and ended up not eating anything. This prompted an outraged state senator to threaten to outlaw the last meal if the department of corrections didn't end the practice.

For his crackdown on taxpayer-funded excess, the senator surely earned hearty handshakes from his tough-on-crime constituents. But it is somehow fitting that the sham of the last meal, in Texas at least, which has executed hundreds more people over the last thirty years than any other state, was allowed to fade into history with its bundle of contradictions intact, buried by the calculated denunciation of a politician seizing on a way to stroke his base. Now in the Lone Star State, the men and women killed by the government get whatever is on the prison menu that day. Justice will be served.

Recipe Index

Permissions Acknowledgements

Grateful acknowledgement is made to all those who gave permission for written material to appear in this book. Every effort has been made to trace and contact copyright holders. If an error or omission is brought to our notice, we will be pleased to remedy the situation in subsequent editions of this book. For further information, please contact the publisher.

Rayner, Jay. "Age of Innocence." Copyright © 2014 by Jay Rayner Limited. This article, first published in *Saveur*, September 2013, draws on material in *A Greedy Man in a Hungry World* (HarperCollins Publishers, 2013). Used by permission of the author.

Krader, Kate. "Are Big Flavors Destroying the American Palate?" Article originally appeared in the May 2014 issue of *Food & Wine* magazine.

Gravois, John. "A Toast Story." Copyright © 2014 by *Pacific Standard*. Used by permission of the publisher.

Estabrook, Barry. "Five Things I Will Not Eat." Copyright © 2013 by Barry Estabrook. Originally published by CivilEats.com. Used by permission of the author.

Sax, David. "Baconomics 101." From *The Tastemakers: Why We're Crazy for Cupcakes but Fed Up with Fondue*. Copyright © 2014 by PublicAffairs, a member of the Perseus Books Group. Used by permission of the publisher.

Torres, JT. "The Right to Eat." Copyright © 2014 by JT Torres. Originally published by *Alimentum*, April 2014. Used by permission of the author.

Birdsall, John. "America, Your Food Is So Gay." Copyright © 2013 by John Birdsall. Originally published by *Lucky Peach*, June 2013. Used by permission of the author.

Edge, John T. "Debts of Pleasure." Copyright © 2013 by John T.

ABOUT THE EDITOR

Holly Hughes is a writer, the former executive editor of Fodor's Travel Publications, and author of *Frommer's 500 Places for Food and Wine Lovers*.

Submissions for Best Food Writing 2015

Submissions and nominations for *Best Food Writing 2015* should be forwarded no later than May 15, 2015, to Holly Hughes at *Best Food Writing 2015*, c/o Da Capo Press, 44 Farnsworth Street, Boston MA 02210, or emailed to best.food@perseusbooks.com. We regret that, due to volume, we cannot acknowledge receipt of all submissions.